Economic Analysis of Law in European Legal Scholarship

Volume 17

The purpose of the book series "Economic Analysis of Law in European Legal Scholarship" is to publish high quality volumes in the growing field of law and economics research in Europe, from a comprehensive theoretical and practical vantage point. In particular, the series will place great emphasis on foundational and theoretical aspects of economic analysis of law and on interdisciplinary approaches in European Legal Scholarship. Following Nobel laureate Ronald Coase's famous essay "The Problem of Social Cost" (1960) fifty years ago law and economics has become the lingua franca of American jurisprudence. In recent decades, law and economics has also gained widespread popularity in Europe and its influence on Legal Scholarship is growing significantly.

Therefore, the economic analysis of law in European Legal Scholarship academic book series illustrates how law and economics is developing in Europe and what opportunities and problems – both in general and in specific legal fields – are associated with this approach within the legal traditions of European countries. Rather than further exploring economic analysis as such, the main focus of this series lies on the implementation of economic methods in legislation and legal adjudication from a European perspective. It takes into account the particular challenges the European legal systems face. Volumes will address law and economics research in Europe from a critical and comparative viewpoint. The studies in this series are strong and bold narratives of the development of economic analysis of law in European Legal Scholarship. Some are suitable for a very broad readership.

Contributions in this series primarily come from scholars in Europe. The purpose is to provide the next generation of European lawyers with the models and skills needed to understand and improve the economic analysis of law in their own legal field. The series includes monographs focusing on specific topics as well as collections of essays covering specific themes.

Klaus Mathis · Avishalom Tor

Editors

Law and Economics of Justice

Efficiency, Reciprocity, Meritocracy

 Springer

Editors
Klaus Mathis
Faculty of Law
University of Lucerne
Lucerne, Switzerland

Avishalom Tor
School of Law
University of Notre Dame
Notre Dame, IN, USA

ISSN 2512-1294   ISSN 2512-1308 (electronic)
Economic Analysis of Law in European Legal Scholarship
ISBN 978-3-031-56821-3   ISBN 978-3-031-56822-0 (eBook)
https://doi.org/10.1007/978-3-031-56822-0

This Springer imprint is published by the registered company Springer Nature Switzerland AG
The registered company address is: Gewerbestrasse 11, 6330 Cham, Switzerland

Paper in this product is recyclable.

Preface

This edited volume «Law and Economics of Justice: Efficiency, Reciprocity, Meritocracy» is a collection of papers which were due to be presented at the annual Law and Economics Conference in Lucerne on the 17th and 18th March 2023, co-organised by the University of Lucerne, Institute for Economy and Regulation and the Notre Dame Research Program on Law and Market Behavior (ND LAMB).

This conference aimed to examine the methodological and philosophical foundations of law and economics in general and in particular efficiency, reciprocity, and meritocracy and their relation to law and justice from an interdisciplinary perspective. The thematic scope of this volume spans both the theoretical foundations and specific practical applications in an international and comparative context.

We take this opportunity to thank all those who have contributed to the successful completion of this volume. In particular, we are grateful to Lea Röthlin, BLaw, Philipp Gisler, BLaw, Sarah Bisang, and Simon Schmid for their diligent proofreading. Special thanks go to the Swiss nation go to the Swiss national Science Foundation (SNSF), the Research Commission (FoKo) of the University of Lucerne and the Hofstetter Foundation for supporting the conference. Finally, we also thank Anja Trautmann at Springer Publishers for overseeing the publishing process.

Lucerne, Switzerland   Klaus Mathis
Notre Dame, IN, USA   Avishalom Tor
December 2023

Contents

Contributors

Michael K. Addo Professor of Law, University of Notre Dame Law School, London, UK

Ido Baum Haim Striks School of Law, Rishon LeZion, Israel

Marius Daniel Baumann Center for Ethics and Philosophy in Practice, Ludwig-Maximilians-Universität Munich, Munich, Germany

Jarosław Bełdowski Warsaw School of Economics, Warsaw, Poland

Patrick M. Corrigan Notre Dame Law School, Notre Dame, IN, USA

Łukasz Dąbroś Warsaw School of Economics, Warsaw, Poland

Malte Dold Pomona College, Claremont, US

Fabrizio Esposito NOVA School of Law and CEDIS, Universidade Nova de Lisboa, Lisbon, Portugal

Eran Fish Max Planck Institute for the Study of Crime, Security and Law, Freiburg I. Br., Germany

Steven M. Garcia Graduate School of Management, University of California, UC Davis, US

Andrew Gewecke Pomona College, Claremont, US

Zsófia Hajnal Corvinus University of Budapest, Budapest, Hungary

Behrang Kianzad Department of Business Law, Lund University, Lund, Sweden

Régis Lanneau Institut de Préparation À L'Administration Générale, Université Paris Nanterre, Paris, France

Salil K. Mehra Beasley School of Law, Temple University, Philadelphia, US

Dario Picecchi Universities of Lucerne and Fribourg, Lucerne and Fribourg, Switzerland

Joaquín Reyes Universidad San Sebastián, Santiago, Chile

Avishalom Tor Law School, University of Notre Dame, Notre Dame, US

Kalpana Tyagi Maastricht University, Maastricht, The Netherlands

Rolf H. Weber University of Zurich, Zurich, Switzerland

Part I
Markets, Market Failure and Distributive Justice

Chapter 1
The Malleability of Inequality Trade-Offs

Avishalom Tor and Steven M. Garcia

Abstract Debates about economic inequality permeate public discourse around the globe, and researchers devote much attention to studying its causes, consequences, and more. While the psychological study of inequality is still in its relatively early stages, this chapter considers the role of inequality in distributive decisions from a social comparison perspective. This perspective is particularly apposite, since the subject matter of social comparisons—that is, people's relative outcomes or positions—is what defines inequality. The social comparison approach to inequality suggests that factors that influence decision-makers' social comparison concerns are also likely to affect their decisions when inequality is at stake. After making the theoretical case for the role of the situational factors of social comparison in decisions that implicate inequality, we illustrate it through extant findings on social categorisation as well as exploratory evidence of the effect of another situational factor—the number of recipients of an unequal distribution. With respect to both factors, we identify the impact of social comparison by studying the weight decision-makers give to equality in resource allocations that require trade-offs between equality and competing distributive considerations (e.g., efficiency). Importantly, the findings we discuss indicate that decision-makers' equality preferences are malleable and depend in part on situational factors that can bear little normative relevance for those important trade-offs between inequality and other distributive considerations.

A. Tor (✉)
Law School, University of Notre Dame, Notre Dame, US
e-mail: ator@nd.edu

S. M. Garcia
Graduate School of Management, University of California, UC Davis, US

© The Author(s), under exclusive license to Springer Nature Switzerland AG 2024
K. Mathis and A. Tor (eds.), *Law and Economics of Justice*, Economic Analysis of Law in European Legal Scholarship 17, https://doi.org/10.1007/978-3-031-56822-0_1

1.1 Introduction

Concerns about economic inequality permeate public discourse around the globe.[1] People care about inequality for a variety of reasons. Some worry that inequality brings about negative consequences for individuals and societies,[2] while others argue that it is unfair,[3] or even immoral.[4] Irrespective of the many debates surrounding inequality, however, it is important to recognise that, unlike many other concerning social phenomena, such as inadequate health care, low-quality education, or poverty, inequality is defined solely with reference to individuals' relative positions rather than to their absolute outcomes.[5] For this reason, both the incidence of inequality and its consequences are inextricably linked to people's subjective perceptions. Individuals must perceive inequality to care about it or to be directly affected by its presence.[6]

The psychological study of inequality is still in its early stages, notwithstanding its rapid recent growth. We contribute to this developing literature by examining the role of inequality in allocation decisions from a social comparison perspective. Social comparison theory posits that individuals compare themselves to others as a means for fulfilling the basic need for self-evaluation,[7] and studies have found that individuals dislike some upward comparisons—that is, situations in which they compare unfavourably to others—such as when some are allocated fewer resources than others.[8] The social comparison perspective is thus highly relevant to the study of inequality because the subject matter of social comparisons—that is, people's relative outcomes or positions—is also what defines inequality. Indeed, much research in psychology, neuroscience, and economics further supports the notion that people dislike social comparisons that entail disadvantageous inequality.[9]

The social comparison approach to inequality also offers a wealth of evidence regarding the factors that influence social comparison concerns and thereby can affect decision-making when inequality is at stake. Specifically, a substantial body of research documents the role of situational factors on social comparison.[10] These situational factors, such as social categorisation or rankings, are features of the decision

---

[1] Tor And Garcia (2023).

[2] Piketty (2014).

[3] Saez (2017).

[4] E.g., Frankfurt (2015); Niebuhr (2013); Sen (1995).

[5] This observation differs from the question of whether economic inequality is best *measured* by objective or subjective metrics as discussed, for instance, by Sen (1997).

[6] e.g., Hauser and Norton (2017): 21–25; Wienk et al. (2022); Willis et al. (2022).

[7] Festinger (1954).

[8] Id.; Johnson, (2012).

[9] Lambert et al. (2003); Jukka and Uusitalo (2010); Tor and Garcia (2023); Tricomi et al. (2010); Walster et al. (1978).

[10] Garcia et al. (2013); Garcia et al. (2020); Garcia and Tor (2023).

environment that tend to affect similarly situated individuals, variously enhancing or dampening social comparison concerns.[11]

Some of our previous work has demonstrated the effect of the situational factor of social categorisation on decision-making when inequality is at stake. In addition, we offer some exploratory evidence of the role of another such factor—the number of individuals (N) affected by the unequal outcomes of a decision. With respect to both of these factors, we identify the impact of social comparison by studying how decision-makers tasked with allocating resources trade off equality against competing considerations, such as efficiency or equity.

To this end, Part 2 offers a brief overview of the psychological literature on distributive decision-making, with a focus on the competing considerations that shape allocations, Part 3 clarifies the close relationship between social comparison and inequality, and Part 4 details the growing evidence for the impact of the situational factors of social comparison on decisions that implicate inequality. Part 5 concludes.

1.2 Equality and Competing Considerations in Distributive Decision-Making

Beginning in the 1960s, the distributive justice literature has identified many competing considerations that guide distributive decision-making.[12] Further analysis indicated, however, that these various norms primarily reflect the three overarching principles of equality, equity, or need.[13] Early arguments in favour of equality in particular as a distributive principle were based on normative considerations, such as the importance of treating people equally or of recognising the equal value of every individual.[14] At the same time, researchers started developing more concrete psychological accounts of decision-makers equality preferences when allocating resources. Schwinger argued, for instance, that equal allocations are appealing because they are easily explained and predicted.[15] This account was crystallised by Messick and colleagues, who suggested that equality serves as a social decision heuristic for allocators,[16] noting that "the idea of dividing equally is a salient, defensible, simple, and effective (in that it does the job) rule…. A short-cut that is often used without regard to other questions of deservingness or… goals…".[17] The heuristic view thus draws on both normative and practical considerations to explain the attractiveness of equality as an allocation rule.

---

[11] Garcia et al. (2006); Garcia and Tor (2007); Garcia et al. (2005).

[12] Deutsch (1975); Deutsch (1985); Yaari and Bar-Hillel (1984).

[13] Cook and Hegtvedt (1983); Deutsch (1975); Deutsch (1985); Mannix et al. (1995).

[14] Deustch (1985).

[15] Schwinger (1980).

[16] Messick (1993); Messick (1995).

[17] Messick and Schell (1992, p. 313).

Despite its advantages as a distributive principle, however, equality often stands in tension with other principles, such as equity or efficiency. Equity—the principle of rewarding people in proportion to their contributions or merit—is an attractive allocation principle because it follows individuals' expectations of proportionality between inputs and outputs in social relationships.[18] Some early scholarship has even asserted equity's dominance as the fundamental principle that underlies all other distributive considerations.[19] Yet, whenever recipients provide differing inputs (e.g., effort or productivity) or possess different degrees of merit (such as ability or performance on a relevant task) allocators cannot fully satisfy both equality and equity principles and must therefore either choose one over the other or arrive at an allocation that reflects some trade-off or compromise between these competing principles.

Unsurprisingly, therefore, research shows that preferences for equality versus equity in allocation decisions depend on factors such as the goal of the social interaction within which the allocation is made or the nature of the relationship among the recipients.[20] For instance, equity tends to dominate allocations in economic settings, when productivity is a primary goal, while equality takes centre stage when allocators aim to foster enjoyable or harmonious relations or a sense of solidarity.[21] Additionally, allocators who anticipate future interaction among the recipients may wish to avoid the social strain imposed by equity-based allocations,[22] or allocators may face recipients whose efforts and contributions are more interdependent than independent.[23] Finally, in line with its role as a decision heuristic, the relative advantage of equality as a distributive principle also increases in situations that render equity-based allocations more complex and therefore difficult to implement and explain.[24]

Although the literature devoted greater attention to equality-efficiency trade-offs, scholars have also examined allocators' preferences for equality versus efficiency—in the sense of maximising the allocation's overall benefits.[25] Efficiency is another appealing distributive principle since it maximises the benefits to society, or at least to a given group of recipients, from the available resources.[26] More recent research has identified some factors that specifically affect equality-efficiency trade-offs. For instance, the great majority of participants in Mitchel et al.'s studies accepted greater inequality when the economic outcomes of all recipients were improved, but not when only the aggregate outcomes of the group were improved.[27] In another set of studies, Matania and Yaniv found that participants gave greater weight to efficiency versus

---

[18] Adams (1965).

[19] Mikula (1980); Schwinger (1980); Walster et al. (1978).

[20] Sampson (1975).

[21] Lerner (1975); Lerner et al. (1976).

[22] Bagarozzi (1982); Mannix et al. (1995); Prentice and Crosby (1987).

[23] Meindl (1989).

[24] Debusschere and van Avermaet (1984); Harris and Joyce (1980).

[25] Baron (1993); Baron and Pfeffer (1994); Mitchel et al. (1993).

[26] e.g., Deutsch (1975); Reiter (1989).

[27] Mitchel et al. (1993).

equality when allocating less basic or less essential resources than when distributing more basic or more essential ones.[28]

1.3 Equality and Social Comparison

While the diverse findings described in Part 2 demonstrate the range of factors that can influence the weight of equality vis a vis competing considerations in allocation decisions, our present analysis focuses on the impact of the fundamental psychological process of social comparison on such decisions. Our focus on social comparison here is natural, since distributive justice concerns "the comparative allocation of goods and bads to people."[29] More generally, scholars recognise a "widely accepted social scientific dictum that when people judge how fairly they are treated they take into account the manner in which others are treated,"[30] which means that comparison information is central to individuals' assessments of distributive decisions.[31]

On its part, social comparison research offers a robust account of individuals' equality concerns. Social comparison theory posits that people satisfy their basic need for self-evaluation by comparing their outcomes to the outcomes obtained by others.[32] Individuals often dislike upward comparisons—that is, circumstances in which they compare unfavourably to others[33]—such as when some recipients are allocated fewer resources than others. Several decision-making and social psychological studies have linked social comparison with individuals' willingness to tolerate inequality as well.[34] Furthermore, several additional research streams in psychology, neuroscience, and economics further support the notion that people dislike social comparisons that entail disadvantageous inequality.[35]

Despite the close association between social comparison and inequality concerns, however, most studies of allocations to date have not sought directly to manipulate social comparison to test its effects on the manifestation of equality concerns in distributive decisions. One scholar noted that "[a]lthough few dispute the underlying role of ... social comparisons in assessments of justice, little research explicitly studies these processes".[36] One rare study that did focus on the role of social comparisons in allocations (albeit from the recipients' perspective rather than the of allocators) found that when reward levels were held constant while participants'

---

[28] Matania and Yaniv (2007).

[29] Furby (1986).

[30] Greenberg et al. (2007).

[31] Hegtvedt (2006).

[32] Festinger (1954).

[33] Id.; Johnson (2012)

[34] Bazerman et al. (1992); Blount and Bazerman (1996); Loewenstein et al. (1989); Messick and McClintock (1968); Messick and Sentis (1979).

[35] *E.g.*, Lambert et al. (2003); Jukka and Uusitalo (2010); Tricomi et al. (2010); Walster et al. (1978).

[36] Hegtvedt (2006, p. 58).

social comparisons and their comparisons with reward expectations were orthogonally varied, only social comparisons affected the perceived fairness of the allocations. Social comparisons also explained more of the variance in participants' outcome satisfaction than did their comparisons with reward expectations.[37]

In addition, a large field study by Pfeffer and Langton suggests social comparison plays an important role in shaping allocators' equality-equity tradeoffs in organisational wage decisions but did not directly manipulate social comparison.[38] Pfeffer and Langton collected data from over 60,000 faculty respondents in 1,805 academic departments belonging to 303 colleges and universities, to examine factors that might be associated with the degree of inequality in employee reward allocations. They found that wage inequality was reduced in departments in which more contact and information facilitated social comparison among faculty, implying that organisational decision-makers accounted for social comparison concerns in their faculty wage allocations.[39]

All in all, therefore, even though the literature has recognised the close connection between social comparison and inequality, focused empirical study of this intersection has been rather limited.

1.4 Situational Factors and Inequality Concerns

Our social comparison-based approach to the study of distributive decisions that implicate inequality turns on the situational factors of social comparison. These situational factors are features of the decision environment that affect the extent to which individuals engage in social comparison, both generally and in distributive decision-making in particular.[40] As we recently noted, "the list of situational factors identified by the literature continues to grow."[41] There is already substantial evidence for the role of a number of these factors in shaping social comparison concerns, including decision-makers' proximity to a comparison standard and ranking effects,[42] their social categorisation, the number of comparison targets,[43] and more.

Importantly, the evidence showing that the presence of such situational factors facilitates social comparisons suggests that these factors are also likely to increase concerns for inequality in distributive decisions, in which case allocators will tend to give greater weight to equality vis a vis competing distributive principles. This dynamic is illustrated by Pfeffer and Langton's finding that wage dispersion was associated with the presence of situational factors—such as department size, the nature of

---

[37] Austin et al. (1980).

[38] Pfeffer and Langton (1988).

[39] Id.

[40] Garcia et al. (2013); Hegtvedt (2006).

[41] Garcia and Tor (2023).

[42] Garcia et al. (2006); Garcia and Tor (2007).

[43] Garcia et al. (2013).

faculty research, social interactions among faculty, or the public availability of salary data—that increased interpersonal contact and information exchange.[44] Apparently, these factors not only facilitated social comparisons among faculty recipients but also led allocators to lower wage dispersion in recognition of the heightened social comparison concerns of the recipients.

More recent work further shows how the direct manipulation of some situational factors of social comparison—specifically the two factors of social category fault lines and the number of comparison targets—can shape allocators' equality trade-offs. In the case of social categories, individuals associate themselves with many types of groups—from demographic ones (e.g., based on gender, race, religion, or country) through self-selected groups (e.g., college, company, or private association), to arbitrary groups (like handedness or pogo-stick jumping ability)—that the literature collectively denotes "social categories" or "social category groups."[45] Unsurprisingly, the social identity literature found that competition between groups from different social categories, namely inter-category competition (e.g., Americans versus French), tends to involve greater social comparison concerns and increased competitive behavior compared to competition between two groups that share a social category, or intra-category competition (e.g., Americans versus Americans).[46]

In a similar vein, studies show that distributive decisions that affect individual recipients across social category fault lines raise greater social comparison concerns than similar allocations that are made within one social category. In one study, Garcia, Tor, Bazerman, and Miller compared decision-makers' choices between two task payoff structures, one of which offered an equal but lower $1 payoff to all recipients while the other offered a higher but unequal payoff of $2 to half of the recipients and $5 to the other half (i.e., a more efficient but unequal allocation). Participants strongly preferred the more efficient but unequal payoff structure in the control condition, but significantly fewer participants exhibited the same choice when the unequal payoffs were made to recipients of different social categories (women versus men).[47]

The authors also found this pattern in another study that compared equality-efficiency trade-offs between the provision of accommodations of lower but equal quality and accommodations of higher but unequal quality to students on a university-sponsored trip. Decision-makers showed a significantly greater preference for equality versus efficiency when distributing accommodation between two groups of students from different institutions than when making a similar allocation between groups of students from the same institution.[48]

Additional research by Garcia, Bazerman, Kopelmen, Tor, and Miller further showed that a manipulation of social category fault lines is capable of shaping both equality-efficiency trade-offs and equality-equity trade-offs.[49] In one study, for

[44] Pfeffer and Langton (1988).

[45] McGarty (1999).

[46] Hogg (2000); Turner et al. (1979).

[47] Garcia et al. (2005).

[48] Id.

[49] Garcia et al. (2010).

example, these authors found that decision-makers favoured unequal but more efficient payoffs among experimental participants but the reverse preference was manifested for a comparable allocation that entailed inequality across gender categories (male versus female participants).[50]

Another study illustrated this pattern for distributive decisions that pitted both efficiency and equity against equality. In this case, the unequal payoffs were based on the (hypothetical) performance of college interns at a major U.S. bank. The study highlighted the equitable principle of paying more to those who performed better, in addition to offering higher aggregate payments in the unequal payoff condition. Results showed that participants, once again, favoured the efficient and equitable but unequal allocation when the distribution was not made to interns of different academic institutions. Yet the participants exhibited the opposite preference, favouring equality over the two other competing principles, when facing a similar trade-off across this social category fault line (of different institutional affiliations).[51]

Much like the situational factor of social category fault lines, the number of comparison targets can influence the intensity of social comparison and the behaviours associated with it. Findings on the N-Effect, for instance, demonstrate that the intensity of competition increases as the number of competitors decreases (even when controlling for expected value), and that social comparison concerns play a role in this phenomenon.[52] To illustrate, participants in one experiment were asked to complete an easy quiz as fast as they could without compromising accuracy, after they were informed that the top-performing 10% among them would get a cash price and assigned to a competition pool of either 10 competitors (small-N competition) or 100 competitors (large-N competition). Results showed that participants completed the easy quiz significantly faster in the small-N competition than in the large-N competition. Additional studies found that social comparison concerns also decrease with N and that social comparison mediates the effects of N on competitiveness.[53]

In addition to this experimental evidence, studies suggested that merely being among a few versus many competitors can affect one's competitive motivation and performance. A panel analysis of scores from the Scholastic Aptitude Test., a college entrance exam, found that as the number of test-takers at a given testing venue increased, the average scores of the test-takers tended to decrease, even after controlling for various demographic factors.[54] More recent evidence is beginning to reveal other competitive implications of the N-Effect, including how applicants are more likely to fake or misrepresent themselves in employment interviews when among few versus many competing applicants[55] and how employee promotion contests can

---

[50] Id.

[51] Id.

[52] Garcia and Tor (2009); Tor and Garcia (2010).

[53] Id.

[54] Id.

[55] Ho et al. (2019).

increase employee effort when held at the division level—with fewer competing employees—rather than at the firm level.[56]

Where distributive decisions are involved, we anticipate that the number of social comparison targets—in this context, the number of allocation recipients—will exert a similar influence. In other words, as in the case of the situational factor of social category fault lines, we expect that decision-makers faced with trade-offs that pit equality against other distributive principles will favour the former more strongly when allocating to a smaller number of recipients than when allocating to a larger group.

Although this prediction is yet to be systematically studied, two exploratory studies we recently conducted support it, suggesting this is a fruitful venue for further exploration. Both exploratory studies looked at equality-efficiency trade-offs in hypothetical scenarios presented to participants on Amazon Mechanical Turk. In the first study, depending on the experimental condition, decision-makers made allocations among either 8 or 40 other participants, in each case making a series of choices between an equal but less efficient (lower-paying) distribution and an unequal but more efficient one.

In the second study, participants were asked to decide how to distribute a donation to an organisation directed at improving child education in an African village, having been informed that the organisation focuses on particularly poor areas and identifies children who will benefit most from donations. All decision-makers were told that the money could provide a larger educational benefit to a smaller number of children or a smaller educational benefit to a larger number of children. However, one group of participants made the decision concerning a smaller number of children while another group made it for a larger group of children (5 versus 30).

The results of both exploratory studies supported the prediction that the situational factor of the number of allocation recipients affects the weight decision-makers give to equality in the face of competing considerations. Whether the distributive decision at hand concerned monetary payoffs to experimental participants or educational benefits to African children in need, decision-makers tended to give equality consideration greater weight when faced with a smaller number than when faced with a larger number of recipients. Thus, although these results are tentative and do not yet demonstrate the role of social comparison concerns in equality trade-offs, they align with our theoretical expectations based on the broader literature on the effects of situational factors.

1.5 Conclusion

The social comparison perspective on inequality is informative and deserving of further study. The subject matter of social comparisons—that is, people's relative outcomes or positions—is what defines inequality. Moreover, the social comparison

---

[56] Fang et al. (2020).

approach to inequality suggests that factors that influence decision-makers' social comparison concerns are also likely to affect their decisions when inequality is at stake. In particular, the situational factors of social comparisons can shape decisions that implicate inequality, as illustrated by extant research on the role of social category fault lines. Our recent exploratory studies further indicate the likely role of another situational factor of social comparison, that of the number of allocation recipients. Importantly, the findings we discuss in this chapter imply that decision-makers' equality preferences are malleable and depend in part on situational factors that can bear little normative relevance for those important trade-offs between inequality and other distributive considerations.

Acknowledgements The research underlying this chapter has benefited from the generous support of Notre Dame Law School and the helpful comments of participants at the Lucerne conference on "Law and Economics of Justice: Efficiency, Reciprocity, Meritocracy." Sam Haward provided excellent research assistance.

Bibliography

Adams JS (1965) Inequity in social exchange. Adv Exp Soc Psychol 2:267, et seqq.

Austin W et al. (1980) Internal standards revisited: effects of social comparisons and expectancies on judgments of fairness and satisfaction. J Exp Soc Psychol 16:426, et seqq.

Bagarozzi DA (1982) The effects of cohesiveness on distributive justice. J Psychol Interdisc Appl 110:267, et seqq.

Baron JN and Pfeffer J (1994) The social psychology of organizations and inequality. Soc Psych Vol. 57 pp. 190 et seqq.

Baron J (1993) Heuristics and biases in equity judgments: a utilitarian approach. In: BA Mellers, J Baron (eds) Psychological perspectives on justice: theory and applications. Cambridge, p 109

Bazerman MH et al. (1992) Reversals of preference in allocation decisions: judging an alternative versus choosing among alternatives. Admin Sci 37(2):220, et seqq.

Blount S, Bazerman MH (1996) The inconsistent evaluation of absolute versus comparative payoffs in labor supply and bargaining. J Econ Behav 30:227, et seqq.

Cook KS and Hegtvedt KA (1983) Distributive justice, equity, and equality. Ann Rev Socio 9:217, et seqq.

Debusschere M, van Avermaet E (1984) Compromising between equity and effects of situational ambiguity and computational complexity. Euro J Soc Psych 14(3):323, et seqq.

Deutsch M (1975) Equity, equality, and need: what determines which value will be used as the basis of distributive justice? J Soc Issues 31:137, et seqq.

Deutsch M (1985) Distributive justice: a social psychological perspective. New Haven

Fang D et al. (2020) Turning up the heat: the discouraging effect of competition in contests. J Pol Econ 128:1940, et seqq.

Festinger L (1954) A theory of social comparison processes. Hum Rels 7:117, et seqq.

Frankfurt HG (2015) On inequality

Furby L (1986) Psychology and justice. In: RL Cohen (ed) Justice: views from the social sciences. New York

Garcia SM et al (2010) The price of equality: suboptimal resource allocations across social categories. Bus Ethics Q 20:75

Garcia SM, Miller DT (2007) Social categories and group preference disputes: the aversion to winner-take-all solutions. Grp Processes Intergroup Rels 10(4):581, et seqq.

Garcia SM, Tor A (2007) Rankings, standards and competition: task vs scale comparisons. Org Behav Hum Decision Processes 102:95, et seqq.

Garcia SM, Tor A (2009) The N-effect: more competitors, less competition. Psych Sci 20:871, et seqq.

Garcia SM, Tor A (2023) Social comparison and competition: general frameworks, focused models, and emerging phenomena. In: SM Garcia, A Tor, AS Elliott (eds) Oxford handbook on the psychology of competition. Oxford

Garcia SM et al (2020) Social comparison before, during and after the competition. In: J Suls, R Collins, L Wheeler (eds) Social comparison, judgment and behavior. Oxford

Garcia SM et al. (2005) Profit maximization versus disadvantageous inequality: the impact of self-categorization. J Behav Decision Making 18:187, et seqq.

Garcia SM et al. (2006) Ranks and rivals: a theory of competition. Personality Soc Psych Bull 32:970, et seqq.

Garcia SM et al. (2013) The psychology of competition: a social comparison perspective. Perspectives on Psych Sci 8:634, et seqq.

Greenberg et al (2007) Social comparison processes in organizations. Org Behav Hum Decision Processes 102:22, et seqq.

Harris R, Joyce M (1980) What's fair? It depends on how you ask the question. J Personality Soc Psych 38:165, et seqq.

Hauser OP, Norton MI (2017) (Mis)perceptions of inequality. Curr Opin Psych 18:21, et seqq.

Hegtvedt, KA (2006) Justice frameworks. In: PJ Burke (ed) Contemporary social psychological theories. Stanford

Ho JL et al (2019) The influence of competition on motivation to fake in employment interviews. J Personnel Psych 18(2):95, et seqq.

Hogg MA (2000) Social identity and social comparison. In: J Suls and L Wheeler (eds) Handbook of social comparison: theory and research. New York

Johnson C (2012) Behavioral responses to threatening social comparisons: from dastardly deeds to rising above. Soc Psych Compass 6:515, et seqq.

Jukka P, Uusitalo R (2010) A 'leaky bucket' in the real world: estimating inequality aversion using survey data. Economica 77:60

Lambert PJ et al (2003) Inequality aversion and the natural rate of subjective inequality. J Pub Econ 87:1061, et seqq.

Lerner MJ (1975) The justice motive in social behavior: introduction. J Soc Issues 31:1, et seqq.

Lerner MJ et al (1976) Deserving and the emergence of forms of justice. Adv Exp Soc Psych 9:133, et seqq.

Loewenstein et al. (1989) Social utility and decision making in interpersonal contexts. J Personality Soc Psych 57:426, et seqq.

Mannix et al (1995) Equity, equality or need? The effects of organizational culture on the allocation of benefits and burdens. Org Behav and Hum Decision Processes 63:276, et seqq.

Matania E and Yaniv I (2007) Resource priority, fairness, and equality-efficiency compromises. Soc Just Rsch Vol. 20(4) pp. 497 et seqq.

McGarty C (1999) Categorization in social psychology. Thousand Oaks

Meindl JR (1989) Managing to be fair, an exploration of values, motives, and leadership. Admin Sci 34:252, et seqq.

Messick DM, McClintock CG (1968) Motivational bases of choice in experimental games. J Exp Soc Psych 4:1, et seqq.

Messick, DM, Schell, T (1992) Evidence for an equality heuristic in social decision making. Acta Psychologica 80:311, et seqq.

Messick DM, Sentis KP (1979) Fairness and preference. J Exp Soc Psych 15:418, et seqq.

Messick DM (1993) Equality as a decision heuristic. In: BA Mellers and J Baron (eds) Psychological perspectives on justice: Theory and applications. Cambridge

Messick DM (1995) Equality, fairness, and social conflict. Soc Just Rsch 8:153, et seqq.

Mikula J (1980) On the role of justice in allocation decisions. In J Mikula (ed) Justice and social interaction: experimental and theoretical contributions from psychological research. Göttingen

Mitchel et al (1993) Judgments of social justice: Compromises between equality and efficiency. J Personality Soc Psych 65(4):629, et seqq.

Niebuhr R (2013) Moral man and immoral society: a study in ethics and politics. Louisville

Pfeffer J, Langton N (1988) Wage inequality and the organization of work: the case of academic departments. Admin Sci 33:588, et seqq.

Piketty T (2014) Capital in the twenty-first century

Prentice DA, Crosby F (1987) The importance of context for assessing deservedness. In: JC Masters, WP Smith (eds) Social comparison, social justice, and relative deprivation. Mahwah

Reiter S (1989) Efficient allocation. In: J Eatwell, M Milgates, P Newman (eds) Allocation, information and markets. London

Saez E (2017) Income and wealth inequality: Evidence and policy implications. Contemporary Econ Policy Vol. 35(1) pp. 7 et seqq.

Sampson EE (1975) On justice and equality. J Soc Issues 91:45, et seqq.

Schwinger T (1980) Just allocation of goods: decisions among three principles. In: J Mikula (ed) Justice and social interaction: experimental and theoretical contributions from psychological research. Göttingen

Sen A (1995) Inequality reexamined. Oxford

Sen A (1997) On economic inequality. Oxford

Tor A, Garcia SM (2010) The N-effect: beyond probability judgments. Psych Sci 21:748, et seqq.

Tor A, Garcia SM (2023) The neuroscience of social comparison and competition. Cogn Affect Behav Neurosci 23:920, et seqq.

Tricomi E et al (2010) Neural evidence for inequality-averse social preferences. Nature 463:1089, et seqq.

Turner JC et al (1979) Social comparison and group interest in ingroup favouritism. Euro J Soc Psych 9:187, et seqq.

Walster E et al (1978) Equity theory and research. Boston

Wienk M et al (2022) The social psychology of economic inequality, redistribution, and subjective well-being. Euro Rev Soc Psych 33(1):45, et seqq.

Willis GB et al (2022) The psychosocial effects of economic inequality depend on its perception. Nature Revs Psych 1(5):301

Yaari M, Bar-Hillel M (1984) On dividing justly. Soc Choice Welfare 1:1, et seqq.

Chapter 2
Overcoming the Antagonism Between Efficiency and Distributive Justice

Rolf H. Weber

Abstract Efficiency is a key objective of the Law & Economics movement that potentially is in an antagonistic relation to the more socially oriented distributive justice. But a closer look at the manifold roles of law and the legitimacy functions shows that measures exist for tempering the antagonism. In particular, justice failures must be avoided or overcome. Possible remedies are the standardisation of distributive justice principles through international guidelines and special regulatory "innovations" (such as the "regulatory impact analysis" and the "regulatory lookback"). The newest developments go in the direction of tensions mitigation.

2.1 Introduction and Notions

For decades, efficiency and distributive justice have been seen as different policy objectives; usually, potential contradictory developments are discussed. However, such kind of antagonism must be overcome.

(i) *Efficiency* is generally described (in market-oriented and political discussions) as means for improvement of productivity and efficacy based on a competitive pricing mechanism of markets[1]; as elements of comparison, two sequential points of time are used to show the positive developments. Efficiency can be realised for example by rationalising processes if the advantages prevail over the disadvantages for a majority of the concerned persons. In the Law & Economics (L&E) theory increased efficiency usually means an improvement of the economic performance without regard to the income distribution (so-called Kaldor-Hicks-Efficiency).[2]

---

[1] Williamson (1985), passim.

[2] For further details see Fletcher (1996), pp. 158 et seq.

R. H. Weber (✉)
University of Zurich, Zurich, Switzerland
e-mail: rolf.weber@ius.uzh.ch

Efficiency has always been an important element characterising the mentioned L&E approach. Over time, however, objections against efficiency as a "pure" normative objective increased (for example in the context of a comparison of measures and aims[3]), i.e. in the meantime it is widely accepted that values other than efficiency should also be considered. Indeed, efficiency can equally serve as an instrument for the achievement of other societal goals.[4]

(ii) According to Aristotle (Nicomachean Ethics), general *justice* comprises all positive virtues; Aristotle distinguishes two main forms of particular justice, namely the distributive and the commutative justice[5]:
  • Distributive justice attempts at realising an equal (and fair) allocation of—broadly understood—State-driven goods and services; in principle, however, distributive justice does not exclude an unequal allocation of services if an equal rule is applied.
  • Commutative justice requires a balance of the goods' allocation in private contexts without regard to the position of the concerned person (exchange justice) or reparation in case of a damage occurrence (corrective justice).

Over the centuries, philosophers and legal theorists further developed the understanding of distributive justice, mainly in the context of the so-called utilitarianism. According to Jeremy Bentham[6] and similarly to John Stuart Mill,[7] this philosophical concept considers distributive justice as given in case of any action that increases the overall welfare in society whereas any action that decreases welfare is bad.[8]

The understanding of justice by the eminent US scholar John Rawls encompasses three relevant key components, namely.

(i) a commitment to individual rights and liberties,
(ii) the prioritisation of these rights, liberties, and opportunities, as well as
(iii) the assurance that all citizens have the basic goods necessary to use these freedoms.[9]

In addition, Rawls developed a theory about justice as fairness that is based on three basic ideas, namely.[10]

(i) the equality of people in rights and liberties,
(ii) the equality of opportunities for all, and
(iii) an arrangement of economic inequalities focused on benefit maximisation for those who are least advantaged.

---

[3] Dworkin (1980), p. 204.
[4] Mathis (2019), p. 237.
[5] Aristotle (1985), Ch. V/6, 1130b–1131a.
[6] Bentham (1789), passim.
[7] Mill (1863), pp. 8 et seqq.
[8] For a general overview see Miller (2002), pp. 17 et seqq.
[9] Rawls (1999a), p. 14.
[10] Rawls (1999b), pp. 266 et seq.

The subsequent deliberations are based on the outlined broad understanding of distributive justice that encompasses the socially fair and just distribution of available resources.[11]

2.2 Relations Between Efficiency and Distributive Justice

The (partly antagonistic) relations between the efficiency paradigm and the distributive justice concept require a certain alignment for policy purposes. As mentioned, a deviation from distributive justice is possible as long as an equal rule is applied. However, a static perspective would not be justified, distributive justice must be understood as a dynamic process, i.e. institutions have to establish a framework allowing that appropriate processes to be realised to implement the materially just principles.[12]

According to Klaus Mathis, efficiency and distributive justice can stand in three different relations to each other, namely.[13]

- the goal harmony (the two goals pursue the same objectives),
- the goal neutrality (the two goals can be achieved in parallel), and
- the goal conflict (the two goals follow different patterns).

The antagonistic conflict situation does lead to a concave transformation curve; consequently, more efficiency is often associated with less justice, and vice-versa; the concave line shows that a growing concentration on one of the two goals increasingly sacrifices the other goal.[14] But two aspects merit special attention[15]: (i) From an empirical perspective, what actual trade-off can be observed in a society between just income distribution and the efficiency of the economy? (ii) From a normative perspective, how can the problem of value competition between efficiency and distributive justice be resolved, or what mixture of efficiency and justice does a society want to achieve? In addition, notwithstanding the exact slope of the curve, the positive correlations should also be identified in order to avoid strong tensions.[16]

The realisation of the distributive justice principle can cause certain efficiency losses, for example[17]:

- A redistribution of goods and services in the interest of distributive justice is usually tied to administrative costs and binds resources which could be productively used otherwise.

---

[11] See also Miller (2002), pp. 143 et seqq.

[12] Rawls (2001), pp. 34 et seq.

[13] Mathis (2019), p. 230.

[14] Mathis (2019), p. 237.

[15] See also Mathis (2019), p. 242.

[16] For example see Mathis (2019), p. 243.

[17] Okun (1975), pp. 91 et seqq.

- A redistribution of goods and services might have a negative impact on those persons that take advantage of the reallocation since the attractiveness of investing their own efforts and assets might diminish over time.
- A redistribution of goods and services could have a negative effect on investments and savings.

In addition, the following aspect merits attention: Notwithstanding possible efficiency losses, a procedural separation between efficiency and justice does not appear to constitute a justified approach, particularly not a distinction between private law instruments (efficiency) and public law instruments (justice).[18] The relations between the manifold stakeholders are so complex that individual and social impact factors need to be considered in a long-term perspective, i.e. a unilateral approach does not sufficiently mirror the needs of civil society.

Moreover, markets need to be embedded into a larger scheme of social cooperation. Thereby, equality should play a more important role. According to Amartya Sen, equality can be seen as a generic feature of virtually every normative social theory or theory of justice. The question is what social goods the theory demands to be equalised and for what goods the theory will tolerate distributive inequality.[19] In assessing the potential tensions, the respective balancing of interests test should be based on technology-neutral premises.

The failure to achieve some morally desirable forms of equality might cause negative impacts on civil society. In this context, the concept of justice failure has been developed by looking at the imminent boundaries of the welfare States' activities by triggering adequate movements towards equality consistent with efficiency.[20] Apart from business ethics, social and distributive justice need to address the following questions: What steps should be taken in order to achieve more egalitarian and just outcomes? Does the failure of justice-procuring institutions change the ethical demands of efficiency-procuring institutions like corporations?[21]

2.3 Distributive Justice and Its Potential Failures

2.3.1 Role of Law

The law must strive at establishing a neutral and objective system of socially acceptable norms that apply to all members of civil society equally. In principle, law is a structural system that contains information issued by the regulator and addressed to the concerned part of society.[22] The substance of law is condensed into normative

---

[18] For further details see Weber (2023), p. 376.

[19] Sen (1996), p. 395.

[20] See hereinafter ch. 2.3.

[21] Singer (2018), p. 106.

[22] For a general overview see Weber RH (2017), pp. 253 et seqq.

rules containing behavioural rules that have a guiding or even coercive effect; since law usually expresses normative expectations, it can be said that information transported by law is a special type of data delivery that requests the actual addressee to take note of its substantive contents.[23]

The functions of law crystallise in a system of rules and institutions that underpin civil society, facilitate orderly interaction, and resolve conflicts and disputes arising despite the rules. Law can be created through different processes, for example by the imposition of legal rules by governing bodies, by the evolution of self-regulatory mechanisms or by negotiations among the concerned norm addressees ("social contract").[24] The legal system is not a predetermined construct; moreover, it is embedded in other socially relevant systems. A "meaningful law" in an open system is composed of norms that are perceived as legally binding; as a result, the law should be able to govern behaviour appropriately and allow people in a community to determine the limits of what can and cannot be done in their collective interests.[25] Or more concretely, the law tries to address privately-induced failures by restricting private transactions that have a deleterious effect on social welfare.[26]

Law enjoys relative autonomy, i.e. the legal norms differ from the "rules" and "guidelines" set by other social sciences (for example moral or ethical commitments), and the word relative indicates that exchanges between the law and other social spheres take place in both directions. As a consequence, law should remain flexible in order to be adaptable to changing circumstances.[27]

2.3.2 Function of Legitimacy

Legitimacy corresponds to the justification of authority in the sense that the governed people do have the impression that their own values are represented in the decision-making context. Legitimacy corresponds to the "right to rule"; this interpretation can be traced back to a translation of the Latin word "legitimus" as meaning "lawful, according to law".[28]

Legitimacy can also be perceived as a factual, sociological phenomenon. By analysing the general reasons why State authority is factually accepted, Max Weber distinguished three ideal types of governance, namely (i) the rational or legal, (ii) the traditional and (iii) the charismatic authority.[29] Legitimacy may further be understood in a wider sense, encompassing an ethical-philosophical dimension, which heaves legitimacy above positive law. A similar differentiation has been adopted by

---

[23] See for example Black (2001), pp. 103 et seqq.

[24] Weber RH (2021), p. 13.

[25] Weber RH (2021), p. 14.

[26] Singer (2018), p. 102.

[27] Weber RH (2021), pp. 14 et seq.

[28] Weber RH (2009), p. 109.

[29] Weber M (1976), pp. 122 et seqq.

scholars distinguishing between "normative theories" on legitimacy, which set out general criteria for evaluating the right rule, and "empirical theories", which focus on belief systems of those subject to government.[30] Consequently, legitimacy can either be justified by formal ideas as rule of law rationale (legality) or by substantial value rationality based on morality and justice.[31]

The legitimacy of policy-making decisions may be enhanced by procedural aspects within the different governing entities. This comprehension of legitimacy goes back to Niklas Luhmann, who argued that legitimation can be realised by adequate procedures.[32] This approach is complemented by a result-oriented type of legitimacy, i.e. a substantive conception that looks at the outcome of the legitimising processes. However, the result-oriented legitimacy is rather difficult to operationalise; therefore, Jürgen Habermas tried to link the procedural aspects with specific notions of contents to the "discourse principle" assuming that just those norms can claim validity that receive the approval of all potentially affected people.[33] These normative considerations are the foundation for the following discussions of justice failures.

2.3.3 Justice Failures

2.3.3.1 Notion and Types of Justice Failures

The term "justice failure" is usually defined as failure to achieve some morally desirable form of equality, without regard to efficiency criteria. Justice failures causing a lack of more egalitarian and just outcomes are often reflected in the institutional maldistribution of resources and incomes.[34] Obviously, the nature and the extent of material inequalities that should be tolerated in civil society are subject to debates.

According to Roberto Unger, political and social processes must be created that can serve as an impartial device for summing up the wills of individuals about the proper role of the State.[35] The liberal idea of a normative framework attempts at establishing a fair and just environment. The avoidance of justice failures can help to reconstruct the existence of particular practices and policies while also explaining what business ethics demands within this context.

Academics distinguish between three different classes of justice failures, namely (i) political justice failures, referring to the failure to secure a government sufficiently democratic or independent of economic and social interests, (ii) social justice failures, referring to an insufficiently equal enforcement of rights and opportunities, and (iii) distributive justice failures, referring to the failure to secure an appropriate

---

[30] Clark (2005), pp. 18 et seq.

[31] Weber RH (2009), p. 110.

[32] Luhmann (1975), pp. 9 et seqq.

[33] Habermas (1992), p. 161; see also Weber RH (2009), p. 111.

[34] Singer (2018), p. 107 and p. 112.

[35] Unger (1983), p. 607.

distribution of wealth.[36] For each appearance of justice failure, different issues need to be discussed; hereinafter, the focus is laid on distributive justice failures.

2.3.3.2   Characteristics of Justice Failures

As mentioned, the term "distributive" refers to the institutional maldistribution of resources and income. The other types of justice failures also concern maldistribution, however, in the "distributive" form the number of relevant factors is broader and encompasses market architectures that produce undue material inequality, normative frameworks giving undue advantages to certain parties over others and ineffective/inadequate/non-existent welfare measures incapable of redistributing appropriate resources.[37] Therefore, the distinction between distributive justice failures from other justice failures makes sense even if they do often not operate in isolation.

A second reason to distinguish the distributive justice failures is based on the assumption that the understanding of justice could be particularly controversial, even if it is generally acknowledged that some appreciation of what justifies private enterprises must be given.[38] In comparison with political and social justice, usually, less agreement is given in respect of distributive elements, for example on what kinds of material inequalities can be tolerated in a liberal society.[39] Distributive justice is a particularly difficult weighing factor in connection with social inequalities; therefore, it appears to be possible to disagree about the nature and extent of distributive justice failures (and what ought to be done about it), but still agree about other classes and kinds of justice failures.[40] Examples are the potential evasion of taxes or the non-compliance with collective bargaining processes in the labour market field that would allow allocating a greater share of wealth to employees.[41]

The newest research has also produced neurocomputational evidence that conflicting prosocial motives influence distributive justice; behavioural factors can lead to the situation that distribution decisions are guided by three distinct motives, namely inequality aversion, harm aversion, and rank reversal aversion, which interact with each other and deter individuals from pursuing equality.[42] In addition, businesses should not merely follow the laws intended to promote social equality, but the spirit of the laws; often the spirit is going towards an approach of actively combatting inequality. In particular, distributive justice failures are to be avoided; therefore, respect for the law must not be done based on a pure cost–benefit analysis.[43]

---

[36] Singer (2018), p. 108.

[37] Singer (2018), p. 112.

[38] Heath (2004), p. 73.

[39] Singer (2018), p. 112.

[40] Singer (2018), p. 112; a detailed analysis of inequality elements is given by Stigler (2015), pp. 57 et seqq.

[41] Singer (2018), p. 113.

[42] See Li et al. (2022), passim.

[43] Singer (2018), p. 103 and p. 112.

2.3.3.3 Newly Emerging Justice Failures

During the last ten years, new emanations of distributive justice failures emerged around the globe, particularly expressed in the form of social inequality and environmental challenges.

(i) *Social inequality:* When a State organises taxation in a way that allows for equal chances, distributive justice will increase. In particular, Thomas Piketty is focusing on the taxation of capital income to combat inequality by hindering the accumulation of wealth at a faster pace than the growth of the overall economy.[44] Traditional thinking postulates a trade-off arguing that more equality could only be achieved at the expense of the overall economic performance. However, the extreme inequality between rich and poor countries on the one hand and the increasing welfare gap also within States of the developed world, on the other hand, has led to the acknowledgement that greater equality and improved economic performance are no longer rival goals.[45] Justice and solidarity can even be seen "as the wellsprings of rights".[46]

(ii) *Environmental challenges:* Already more than 50 years ago, the Club of Rome described the limits to growth.[47] In 1997, the "Kyoto Protocol" was adopted as masterpiece for the goal of climate protection. As a consequence, distributive justice should no longer be analysed without the environmental perspective. In any decision-making context of distributive justice, the causes and origins of distributive injustice also are important starting points.

Therefore, distributive justice must contain elements of environmental or ecological justice. This emanation of justice can develop a multi-faceted and integrated notion of justice that can apply to human relations in respect of environmental risks in civil societies.[48] Environmental or ecologic justice is an essential part of distributive justice since it has become indisputable that resources are limited, that climate change firstly often affects the poorest countries and that secondary detrimental effects like hunger and migration will affect all populations around the globe.

2.4 Remedies for Distributive Justice Failures

Potential remedies for distributive justice failures have been developed for some years.

---

[44] Piketty (2014) passim; see also Miller (2002), pp. 145, 146 and 149.

[45] See also Stiglitz (2012), pp. 122 et seqq.; for a critical assessment of the Stiglitz approach being more based on experience than on econometric data see Girgis (2013), pp. 3 et seqq.

[46] See Mahlmann (2023), p. 310.

[47] Club of Rome (1972), pp. 45 et seqq.

[48] Schlosberg (2007), ch. 5 and 6.

2.4.1 Right Measures for Efficiency Evaluation

By using potentially misleading metrics, politics often focuses on suboptimal parameters. Meanwhile, there is a growing consensus that the GDP does not constitute the best measure of the overall economic performance since these figures do not reflect sustainability issues or homogenous living standards.[49] Because distributive justice should also care about health, environment, security, and fairness, relevant aspects of social welfare might need a higher prioritisation.[50] Measures in this respect could be investments in education, improvement of workers' rights and establishment of effective transfer policies. Distributive justice in form of greater equality might be particularly important for States with low natural resources that depend more on human brains than on optimised productivity.[51]

Obviously, the application of optimal economic parameters is of utmost importance for the assessment of efficiency and of distributive justice failures. However, this contribution mainly addresses regulatory issues hereinafter.

2.4.2 Standardisation of Principles Through International Guidelines

Standardisation can build an efficient tool for the realisation of distributive justice principles. Many advantages exist or can at least be achieved if participants of a market segment are using harmonised standards based on a common understanding for the development of goods or in the context of services. Even though often invisible, standards are of importance for raising the levels of product quality, efficiency, interchangeability, and sustainability by providing a framework for the assessment of their conformity.[52]

Being instrumental in facilitating trades, standards make things work. Once the majority of a particular market segment's goods or services are in line with the standards set, a state of market-wide standardisation can evolve.[53] Standards for goods and services also work as strategic tools for businesses that thereby reduce their costs by minimising errors and faulty/unsuccessful developments. Obviously, the quality of the standards must reflect the needs of an appropriate distributive justice understanding.[54]

During the last decade, the number of international guidelines attempting at the realisation of distributive justice has increased. In the course of the negotiations of

---

[49] See Stiglitz (2015), pp. 57 et seqq.

[50] See above Ch. 2.3.3.

[51] Stiglitz (2015), passim.

[52] Weber RH (2021), p. 9.

[53] Senn (2011), p. 173.

[54] Weber RH (2021), p. 9.

such international guidelines, the controversies about the conceptions of distributive justice have at least been channelled into some specific directions.[55]

The main examples of internationally accepted guidelines in the context of distributive justice are the UN Sustainable Development Goals (SDG)[56] and the OECD Guidelines for Multinational Enterprises[57] (being in revision) incl. the specific Due Diligence Guidance for Responsible Business Conduct (RBC)[58] containing concrete behavioural rules of conduct that are designed to also contribute to better lives, i.e. to distributive justice.[59]

2.4.3 Regulatory Innovations

2.4.3.1 Concept of "Regulatory Impact Analysis"

The acknowledgement that "control mechanisms" could be necessary to overcome justice failures is not completely new; the possible antagonism of efficiency and distributive justice can be balanced in form of a regulatory impact analysis.[60] This form of assessment has been proposed by the OECD already in 1995. In Switzerland, the approach of the regulatory impact analysis is known since the year 2000, however, the actual implementation of such an assessment does often not go very deep. Instruments introduced by the legislator and their efficacy can be assessed under several relevant aspects[61]:

- Necessity and possibility of State actions;
- Impacts of these actions on different societal groups;
- Impacts of these actions on the whole economy;
- Potential alternative regulations;
- Suitability and expediency of the instruments for enforcement.

A regulatory impact analysis should encompass a cost–benefit-analysis that in most cases automatically includes efficiency aspects. The key aspects concern the prospective analysis of possible effects of normative regulations and legal instruments.

---

[55] To the particularities of the network infrastructure see Weber RH (2021), pp. 11 et seq.

[56] https://www.undp.org/sustainable-development-goals?utm_source=EN&utm_medium=GSR&utm_content=US_UNDP_PaidSearch_Brand_English&utm_campaign=CENTRAL&c_src=CENTRAL&c_src2=GSR&gclid=EAIaIQobChMIqcj08qu_-wIVqIKDBx1djAZSEAAYASAAEgI33fD_BwE.

[57] https://www.oecd.org/corporate/mne/.

[58] http://mneguidelines.oecd.org/OECD-Due-Diligence-Guidance-for-Responsible-Business-Conduct.pdf.

[59] For a detailed analysis see Kaufmann (2018), pp. 29 et seqq.

[60] For Switzerland see https://www.seco.admin.ch/seco/de/home/wirtschaftslage---wirtschaftspolitik/wirtschaftspolitik/regulierung/regulierungsfolgenabschaetzung.html.

[61] Mathis (2019), p. 250; Zwahlen (2010), p. 35.

The consideration of a cost-/benefit analysis in the context of a regulatory impact analysis is a consequence of the L&E-movement. Quantitative and economically valued elements are often based on supposed scenarios, however, the discussion of potential consequences of economic effects optimises the legislative processes.[62]

Nevertheless, some weaknesses cannot be overlooked: Security and satisfaction of civil society are difficult to address and to include in the assessments. In particular, in the United States, authors express doubts that detailed case studies lead to convincing results since precise, reliable and quantifiable assessments remain unfeasible, and the respective efforts are seen as "guesstimated".[63]

2.4.3.2 Concept of "Regulatory Lookback"

In the United States, less in Europe, the concept of the "regulatory lookback" is increasingly discussed. Since future-oriented analyzes are subject to errors and misunderstandings, because unexpected circumstances can hardly be foreseen, a past-oriented assessment of regulatory quality can also give guidelines for the design of the regulatory environment and legal instruments.[64]

Concretising the concept of the regulatory lookback can be done in different manners: Cochrane proposes agencies to state the goals of regulations, to state measures to be achieved, to state the market failure theory underlying regulation, to state the cause and effect channels and to conduct a quantitative analysis; leaving all this in the open for public review and review by larger public bodies could be a good start and may nip some genuinely bad regulation.[65] The instrument might depend on the given circumstances.

Such an approach appears to be particularly worthwhile in the context of fast-developing technologies. Many States have introduced so-called sandbox regulations or experimental rules which are assessed and reviewed in regular intervals based on the gained practical experiences.[66]

Switzerland has not yet thoroughly addressed such an approach in its legislative activities. Systematic reviews of implemented regulations are missing. In addition, the introduction of so-called "sunset provisions" has so far been restricted, i.e. introduced regulations do not have a time-wise life span.[67]

---

[62] Weber RH (2023), pp. 378 et seqq. with further references.

[63] See Coates IV (2015), p. 882.

[64] Sunstein (2014), passim.

[65] Cochrane (2014), p. 102.

[66] Weber RH (2023), pp. 380 et seq. with further references.

[67] Weber RH (2023), p. 381.

2.5 Outlook

The L&E movement was quite substantially efficiency-driven. More than twenty years ago, Klaus Mathis was one of the first academics to raise the question of whether efficiency should be pursued "instead of justice".[68] Since then, the debate on the relationship (or the antagonism) between efficiency and distributive justice as policy objectives are going on. The yearly L&E conferences organised by Klaus Mathis substantially contribute to the academic exchanges. Their tenth anniversary is a good moment to make an intermediate stop and analyse the current situation.

A look into the crystal ball of the real world shows the increasing importance of the issues of social inequality and sustainability as potential distributive justice failures. These issues, taken seriously, show that a "pure" L&E efficiency approach does not correspond to the given societal needs. Standardised principles of international guidelines and regulatory innovations (such as the regulatory impact assessment and the regulatory lookback) help to temper the previous tensions between efficiency and distributive justice. Therefore, the good news for the anniversary may consist in the desirable insight that the "original" antagonism has been largely overcome.

Bibliography

Bentham J (1789) An introduction to the principles of morals and legislation, London
Black J (2001) Decentring regulation: understanding the role of regulation and self-regulation in a 'post-regulatory' world. Curr Leg Probl 54:103–146
Clark I (2005), Legitimacy in international society, New York
Club of Rome (1972) The limits to growth. A report for the club of Rome's project on the predicament of Mankind, Washington
Coates JC IV (2015) Cost-benefit analysis of financial regulation: case studies and implications. Yale L J 124:882–1011
Cochrane JH (2014) Challenges for cost-benefit analysis of regulation. J Leg Stud 43:63–105
Dworking RM (1980) Is wealth a value? J Leg Stud 9:191–226
Fletcher GP (1996) The basic concepts of legal thoughts, New York et al.
Girgis C (2013) Joseph Stiglitz: the price of inequality. A critical assessment, November 27, https://www.academia.edu/543365/Joseph_Stiglitz_The_Price_of_Inequality
Habermas J (1992) Faktizität und Geltung. Beiträge zur Diskurstheorie des Rechts und des demokratischen Rechtsstaats, Frankfurt a.M
Heath J (2004) A market failure approach to business ethics. Stud Econ Eth Phil 9:69–89
Kaufmann C (2018) OECD MNE Guidelines quo vadis? Making responsible business conduct work for better lives. In: OECD (ed.), OECD Guidelines for Multinational Enterprises: a Glass Half Full, Paris, 29–36
Li Y, Hu J, Ruff CC, Zhou X (2022) Neurocomputational evidence that conflicting prosocial motives guide distributive justice, PNAS, November 29, https://doi.org/10.1073/pnas.2209078119
Luhmann N (1975) Legitimation durch Verfahren, 2nd ed. Darmstadt/Neuwied
Mahlmann M (2023) Mind and rights, Cambridge
Mathis K, Shannon D (2009) Efficiency instead of justice? Searching for the philosophical foundations of the economic analysis of law, Berlin (Translation of Mathis [3rd ed. 2009])

---

[68] Mathis & Shannon (2009) and Mathis (2019).

Mathis K (2019) Effizienz statt Gerechtigkeit? Auf der Suche nach den philosophischen Grundlagen der Ökonomischen Analyse des Rechts, 4th ed. Berlin

Mill JS (1863) Utiliarianism, London

Miller D (2002) Social justice, Oxford (reprint of 1976 version)

Okun AM (1975) Equality and efficiency—the big tradeoff, Washington D.C.

Piketty T (2014) Capital in the 21st century, Cambridge MA/London

Rawls J (1999b) A theory of justice. Revised Edition, Cambridge MA

Rawls J (1999a) The law of peoples, Cambridge MA

Rawls J (2001) Justice as fairness. A restatement, Cambridge MA/London

Schlosberg D (2007), Defining environmental justice: theories, movements, and nature, Oxford

Sen A (1996) On the status of equality. Political Theory 24:394–400

Senn M (2011) Non-state regulatory regimes. Understanding institutional transformation, Heidelberg

Singer A (2018) Justice as failure: efficiency and equality in business ethics. J Bus Ethics 149:97–115

Stiglitz JE (2012) The price of inequality: how today's divided society endangers our future, London/New York

Stiglitz JE (2015) Rewriting the rules of the American economy. An agenda for growth and shared prosperity, New York

Sunstein C (2014) The regulatory lookback. Boston Univ L Rev 94:579–602

Unger RM (1983) The critical legal studies movement. Harv L Rev 96:561–675

Weber M (1975) Wirtschaft und Gesellschaft, Grundriss der verstehenden Soziologie, 5th ed. Tübingen

Weber RH (2009) Shaping internet governance: regulatory challenges, Zurich

Weber RH (2017) The role of law in constituting financial markets. J Int Banking Law Regulation 32:253–260

Weber RH (2021) Internet governance at the point of no return, Zurich

Weber RH (2023) Law is code—Effizienz and Gerechtigkeit beim Einsatz neuer Technologien im Recht. In: Nobel P, Baumann AG-C, Aliverti E (eds) Law and Economics in all seinen Facetten, Festschrift zu Ehren von Klaus Mathis, Berlin 2023, 367–385

Williamson O (1985) The economic institutions of capitalism, New York

Zwahlen SA (2010) Kosten-/Nutzenanalyse mit Regulatory Scorecards, am Beispiel der Finanzmarktregulation, Bern/Stuttgart/Wien

Chapter 3
Just Prices, Market (In)Efficiency and Wealth (In)Equality

Joaquín Reyes

Abstract This chapter analyses the normative appeal of a conception of the just price based on the value of market efficiency (the 'Efficiency Conception'). The chapter suggests that the Efficiency Conception is a normatively attractive conception of the just price only under conditions of wealth equality and discusses two common objections to the feasibility of a price system committed to wealth equality.

3.1 Introduction[1]

The concept of the just price is a normative concept. A normative concept is a concept that identifies a value which is shareable among participants of a social practice. However, although normative concepts are shareable among practitioners, there can be differences in their criteria for the application of that concept. As Ronald Dworkin puts it,

> people participate in social practices in which they treat certain concepts as identifying a value or disvalue but disagree about how that value should be characterized or identified. The concept of justice and other moral concepts work in that way for us.[2]

If the concept of justice is a normative concept, then, *mutatis mutandis*, the concept of the *just* price is also a normative concept. The concept of the just price identifies a value—justice—which is shareable despite different criteria of application of the concept. Dworkin famously referred to the different criteria of application of a concept as "conceptions".[3] To claim that there are alternative criteria of application

---

[1] This chapter reproduces some of the arguments in Reyes (2023). The author acknowledges the financial support provided by Agencia Nacional de Investigación y Desarrollo (ANID) through FONDECYT de Iniciación N° 11240813.

[2] Dworkin (2011), p. 160.

[3] Dworkin (1977), p. 167; See also Dworkin (1986), p. 70; (2006), pp. 10–11, (2011) pp. 158–170.

J. Reyes (✉)
Universidad San Sebastián, Santiago, Chile
e-mail: joaquin.reyes@uss.cl

© The Author(s), under exclusive license to Springer Nature Switzerland AG 2024
K. Mathis and A. Tor (eds.), *Law and Economics of Justice*, Economic Analysis of Law
in European Legal Scholarship 17, https://doi.org/10.1007/978-3-031-56822-0_3

of the *concept* of the just price is to claim that there are alternative *conceptions* of the just price.

Alternative conceptions of the just price arise from disagreements about the *grounds* of price justification. The grounds of price justification are the values that underlie each conception and serve as the justificatory reasons that allow us to identify a given price as the *just* price of a certain good. Thus, for instance, if a given price manifests the value of autonomy, and autonomy is a ground for price justification, then, according to an autonomy-based conception of the just price, that price would be normatively justified: it is the *just* price to pay for that good according to that conception.

In what follows, I would like to review one particular conception of the just price according to which the just price is nothing but the *market price, i.e.,* the price fixed by supply and demand. This conception of the just price is arguably the most popular way of thinking about just prices since the development of the doctrine of the just price by medieval jurists. Indeed, for medieval jurists to claim that the just price was the market price was "so obviously correct as to be almost a truism."[4]

I have argued elsewhere against taking market prices—i.e., prices fixed exclusively by supply and demand—as a normative standard of fair pricing because they lack normative pull: they are the result of a series of prices that do not have any necessary connection to justice.[5] I have illustrated this point with the following example borrowed, with slight modifications, from Walsh and Lynch:

> *Housing Prices.* I buy a house in Lucerne under extortionate circumstances and pay double the ongoing market price. Those extortionate circumstances that forced me to pay that price replicate all over Lucerne for 6 months. By the end of the period, the market price for my house is equivalent to the price I paid for it.[6]

In *Housing Prices*, the new market price is the final result of an extended series of unjust prices. But if the price I paid for my house under extortionate circumstances was unjust, then it must be the case that all prices that led to the new market price paid under the same circumstances were also unjust. But if market prices are just, then the new market price ought to be just regardless of being an aggregate of unjust prices. We can call the idea that a just market price would consist of an aggregate of unjust individual prices the *Just Market Price Paradox*.

The *Just Market Price Paradox* illustrates the counterintuitive results of the idea of taking market prices as just prices. However, in this chapter I would like to explore one attempt to dispel the paradox, namely, that what accounts for this normative failure is that the new market price in *Housing Prices* is the result of an aggregate of *inefficient* prices. In other words, I would like to consider the possibility that the value of *efficiency* can serve as a ground for price justification and, therefore, as a way out of *the Just Market Price Paradox*. I call the view according to which efficiency serves as a just-making feature of prices the 'Efficiency Conception' of the just price.

---

[4] Langholm (1979), p. 580, (1998), p. 85.

[5] Reyes (2021).

[6] Walsh and Lynch (2008), p. 135.

This chapter proceeds as follows. Section 3.2 ('The Efficiency Conception of the Just Price) expands on the Efficiency Conception, along with some of the critiques that have been put forward in the literature to the ideal of market efficiency. Here I suggest that the Efficiency Conception is a normatively attractive conception of the just price only under conditions of wealth equality. Section 3.3 ("The Feasibility of a Just Price System) discusses this claim further by analysing two objections to the feasibility of a price system committed to wealth equality.

3.2   The Efficiency Conception of the Just Price

There are at least two ways to understand the Efficiency Conception, depending on whether one takes an *economic* or a *contract-law* (bilateral) perspective of efficiency. The economic perspective of efficiency focuses on the efficiency of the price of a certain commodity in the market and not within the context of a bilateral exchange, whereas the contract law perspective of efficiency focuses on the price of a given commodity within the context of a bilateral exchange. The economic understanding of efficiency is based on the allocative properties of market prices (which translate into welfare advantages), as well as on the epistemic benefits of the price mechanism as a system of decentralised decision-making. General equilibrium theorists tend to emphasise the welfare advantages of market prices rather than their epistemic benefits. These welfare advantages of the market are explained by the so-called 'Two Fundamental Welfare Theorems' in welfare economics, according to which (i) an economy under general competitive equilibrium leads to a Pareto-efficient allocation of resources, and (ii) any Pareto-efficient allocation of resources is attainable by general competitive equilibrium, given the price mechanism leading to redistribution.[7] By contrast, critics of general equilibrium tend to emphasise the epistemic advantages of market prices rather than their welfare benefits.[8]

From an economic perspective, the market price manifests the value of efficiency because it is both *allocatively* Pareto-efficient (it allocates scarce resources to their best employment more efficiently than any alternative) and *epistemically* efficient (it conveys information about the relative scarcity of a commodity more efficiently than any alternative). An allocation of resources is said to be Pareto-efficient or Pareto-optimal when it is impossible to reallocate resources in order to make at least one individual better off without making at least one individual worse off. Thus, a Pareto-improvement is possible whenever an individual can be made better off without making anyone worse off.

Allocative and epistemic efficiency are two different features of market prices, but they are inextricably linked: a price that tracks relative scarcity conveys information that is necessary to direct goods and labour to their best employment.[9] By contrast,

---

[7] The canonical statement of these theorems is given by Arrow (1951), pp. 90–97.

[8] Hayek (1945), p. 35; (1948), (2002), p. 9.

[9] Heath (2018), p. 27.

a price does not manifest the value of efficiency—and it would be, therefore, an unjust price, according to this view—when it does not reflect relative scarcity and, therefore, creates an inefficient allocation of scarce resources. Eric Posner and Glen Weyl have recently defended a version of this idea, arguing that a radical expansion of fully competitive markets and the liberation of the price mechanism from traditional institutional limits would lead to more efficient outcomes, which would in turn lead to a more just society.[10]

The contract law or bilateral view of efficiency is different. From a contract law perspective, a price is efficient when it is the result of an efficient allocation of contractual risks and burdens. The allocation of contractual risks and burdens is efficient, in turn, when contractual risks and burdens are borne by the party who can bear them at least cost. James Gordley explains it thus:

> Risks and burdens should be placed on the party who can bear them at least cost. The price then should be adjusted to compensate him for bearing them. As we have seen, the contract will be unfair if the party who can bear a risk at least cost succeeds in shifting it to the other party since the party shifting the risk would prefer to bear it himself if he had to compensate the other party fairly.[11]

The price in a contract is justified, therefore, when it adequately—i.e., efficiently and, therefore, depending on the exact formulation of the Efficiency Conception, justly or potentially justly—compensates for the risks and burdens borne by each party in a contract.[12] The need for compensation after allocation is a consequence of choosing Kaldor-Hicks efficiency rather than Pareto-efficiency as the normative criterion for efficiency. Unlike a Pareto-improvement, a Kaldor-Hicks improvement is compatible with making individuals worse off, provided those that are made better off could *hypothetically* compensate those that are made worse off. Most economic analyses of law have now switched from Pareto-efficiency to Kaldor-Hicks efficiency because, among other things, Pareto optimality is impractical: most policy decisions tend to make at least one individual worse off. In contrast, Kaldor-Hicks improvements are compatible with individuals being made worse off provided that compensation is at least hypothetically feasible (compensation could in fact not happen and that would still count as a Kaldor-Hicks improvement). While every Pareto improvement is also a Kaldor-Hicks improvement, not every Kaldor-Hicks improvement counts as a Pareto improvement.

The contract-law perspective of efficiency focuses on the bilateral relationship between the parties, and it draws its normative appeal from the idea that there should be equality between what each contracting party gives, including the corresponding risks and burdens she bears, and what each party receives. In other words, it draws its

---

[10] Posner and Weyl (2018); For another defence of efficiency as a justification for the price mechanism, see Heath (2018).

[11] Gordley (2001), p. 323.

[12] For a concise but clear analysis of both efficiency criteria, with a focus on the economic analysis of law, see Mathis (2009), pp. 31–50.

normative appeal from the idea of preserving equality between things exchanged—i.e., from commutative justice.[13] Therefore, a proper analysis of a conception of the just price based on a contract-law perspective of efficiency would have to consider its connection to commutative justice. This relationship has its own problems, and I have discussed some of the issues associated with the value of commutative justice elsewhere.[14] For the present purposes, and for the sake of clarity, in what follows I shall refer to efficiency understood only from an economic perspective, and not from a contract-law perspective.

The Efficiency Conception is an attractive conception of the just price—in other words, market prices can be deemed *pro tanto* just if they are efficient—only if it is feasible to disentangle the unfair distributive outcomes of the price system from its epistemic benefits—or so I shall argue in this chapter. More precisely, I shall argue that the EC is normatively attractive only if (i) the negative distributive effects produced by market prices can be either eliminated or reduced to a minimum and (ii) their ability to track relative scarcity can be disaggregated from background injustices in wealth distribution. As it will become clear later, I think condition (ii) is one of the main problems with some proposals of market fairness, such as Posner and Weyl's proposal of "radical markets."[15] Thus, unless a massive redistribution of wealth precedes the radical political and economic reforms that the authors propose, then individuals or companies with massive amounts of wealth could buy whatever they want, leaving those with less behind. I do not think that a massive redistribution of wealth is necessarily incompatible with the proposal of radical markets, but the authors of the book are conspicuously silent about wealth redistribution.[16]

I shall say more about this later on, but first let me explain how the economic view of efficiency could be thought of as serving a justificatory function for market prices. I have explained the 'Just Market Prices Paradox' with the example of *Housing Prices* to motivate the view that ongoing market prices have no normative pull. Now, one possible reply to that view of market prices would be to claim that a market price which is the product of extortionate circumstances fails to track the relative scarcity of a good, and, therefore, is economically inefficient. Prices fetched under extortionate circumstances would be inefficient prices because they reflect non-scarcity-related facts such as background inequalities among market participants. If this is the case, then *Housing Prices* would fail to establish that market prices cannot provide an adequate normative standard of fair pricing. It would only establish that *inefficient* market prices fail to provide such a normative standard.

The Efficiency Conception claims that, under non-extortionate circumstances, market prices are efficient because they are the result of an efficient system of resource allocation. A system of decentralised decision-making such as the market has clear epistemic advantages over a system of centralised planning.[17] In a decentralised

---

[13] Gordley (1981), (2001), (2022).

[14] Reyes (2021), (2023).

[15] Posner and Weil (2018).

[16] As noted by Pistor (2019), pp. 230–231.

[17] On this, see Mises (1932); Hayek (1945); Steele (1992).

system, prices are *epistemically efficient*: they can communicate information about the relative scarcity of a product faster and more accurately than any other alternative. Epistemic efficiency, in turn, contributes to achieving *allocative efficiency*, which helps to reduce the inevitable mismatch between production and consumption in society, i.e., between *goods-that-need-to-be-produced*, on the one hand, and *goods-that-people-would-like-to-consume*, on the other, as well as between supply and demand of labour, i.e., between *work-that-needs-to-be-done* and *work-that-people-would-like-to-do*.[18] When market prices reflect relative scarcity, they help in producing this match "more ruthlessly than any other system, largely because of the 'hard budget' constraint that firms face, which serves as a check on sentimentality."[19] It is the ability to direct goods and labour to their best employment which makes market prices that reflect relative scarcity efficient and hence just (or at least what makes market prices satisfy a necessary condition to be just).

The Efficiency Conception concedes that market prices are aggregate prices, that the market price in *Housing Prices* reflects the point at which supply and demand intersect at a given time, that the price paid under extortionate circumstances is unjust, and that the new market price in *Housing Prices* should also be deemed unjust. However, it denies that market prices lack any normative pull by introducing a distinction between efficient and inefficient market prices. Prices that manifest the value of efficiency would be, therefore, just (or at least, they would satisfy a typical condition for prices to be just).

There are different ways to challenge the Efficiency Conception. Some writers have focused on the inadequacy of the whole conceptual apparatus of mainstream economics, including the concepts of relative scarcity, demand, preferences, etc. all of which are essential to make sense of the economic idea of efficiency. This kind of critique is very popular among heterodox approaches to economic theory. Thus, for instance, Frederich S. Lee has claimed that

> The objects of study of mainstream economics, such as preferences-utility, marginal products, demand curves, rationality, relative scarcity, and homogeneous agents, are ill-defined, have no real world existence, and, where relevant, are non-quantifiable and non-measurable.[20]

Others have stressed the lack of normative appeal of economic criteria for efficiency. For instance, some critics of Pareto-efficiency, such as Amartya Sen and Philip Pettit, have highlighted the fact that economic efficiency is insensitive to individual traits of character. This makes it the case that certain allocative results that are Pareto-efficient are nonetheless morally unacceptable. Consider, for instance, the Pareto-efficient allocation of two apples between two individuals, Greedy and Nice, where Greedy always prefers to have more than anyone else, and Nice always prefers others to have more than what she has. According to the Pareto criterion,

---

[18] Heath (2018), p. 30.

[19] Ibid.

[20] Lee (2018), pp. 1–2.

giving two apples to Greedy and zero to Nice would be a Pareto-efficient allocation of the apples.[21]

Other scholars have criticised the account of practical reason and well-being presupposed by the Pareto criterion. For instance, Alasdair MacIntyre has argued that the economic understanding of efficiency stops at the level of preference satisfaction, leaving little room for a critical evaluation of the reasons underlying one's own preferences and desires:

> To maximize utility was on an earlier utilitarian view to maximize pleasure and to minimize pain. More recently the thought has been that to maximize utility is to maximize preference satisfaction. Neither formulation pays regard to the fact that what we are each of us pleased or pained by and what we each of us prefer depend in key part upon our prior moral formation, upon how far we are just, courageous and temperate, and therefore disposed to act rightly. How we conceive utility thus depends on our prior formation and commitments, so that it cannot provide a standard independent of them. To propose utility maximization as such as the measure of right action must therefore be a mistake. What, then, are we in fact doing when we make decisions on the basis of cost-benefit analyses as we often do? The answer is that we are always working with some highly determinate and contestable conception of what is to count as a cost and what as a benefit in this or that type of case and with some prior determination of whose costs and whose benefits are to be counted, whose costs and whose benefits ignored. It is evaluations already made or presupposed that allow us to find application for the notion of utility in our decision making. The notion of utility maximization as a freestanding notion that by itself provides guidance for action is a philosophical fiction.[22]

While I am sympathetic to some of these critiques of economic efficiency, for the present purposes, however, I would like to put forward a critique of a different sort. I would like to put into question the alleged epistemic and allocative benefits of ongoing market prices. Regarding the epistemic benefits of market prices, I deny that market prices efficiently reflect relative scarcity—or, at least, that they *only* reflect relative scarcity. I would like to suggest that what market prices actually do is *to present themselves* as exclusively reflecting relative scarcity. In reality, however, they also reflect non-scarcity-related factors. This fact has a direct impact on the ability of the price mechanism to allocate resources according to their best employment, thus also undercutting the allocative effects of the market. Moreover, I argue that even if prices did reflect relative scarcity, allocating resources on the basis of such prices, when the underlying distribution of resources is unequal, is *unfair* to those with less background wealth.

The argument relies on the fact that background wealth inequality has a direct effect on each discrete price that leads to the market price. This is because background wealth has a direct effect on the reservation prices of both buyers and sellers. When there is inequality in the distribution of resources, justifying market prices on the grounds of efficiency simply naturalises those inegalitarian patterns of wealth distribution. If this is true, then those with more background wealth—the 'rich'— can effectively impose their prices on those with less—the 'poor'. This makes the Efficiency Conception normatively unattractive unless it is preceded by a massive

---

[21] Sen (1982), pp. 54–73; Pettit (2001).

[22] MacIntyre (2016), p. 77. See also ibid. pp. 183–189.

redistribution of wealth. In sum: (1) I *deny* that ongoing market prices are epistemically and allocatively efficient, and, even if they were, (2) I claim that manifesting the value of efficiency is not enough to consider a price just when the background conditions of exchange reproduce inegalitarian patterns of wealth distribution. Or, to put it in positive terms, I argue that the Efficiency Conception is normatively attractive only if and only when background conditions of wealth equality obtain.

Let me start with the epistemic benefits of market prices. The Efficiency Conception rests on an empirical claim about the normal functioning of the price system, namely, that prices typically convey information about the relative scarcity of a given commodity unless impeded by some extraordinary circumstances. However, empirical evidence about the actual functioning of the price system does not seem to support such a claim. As recent empirical research suggests, market prices are typically unable to disentangle information about scarcity-related factors from non-scarcity-related ones—or, to put it somewhat differently: relative scarcity is determined by non-scarcity-related factors. Studies in behavioural economics have shown that ongoing market prices track all kinds of non-scarcity-related information, including cognitive biases of buyers and sellers such as loss aversion (the tendency to prefer avoiding losses to acquiring equivalent gains) and the 'endowment effect' (the tendency to place a higher value on a good that one owns than on an identical good that one does not own).[23] In fact, These cognitive biases and other findings led Daniel Kahneman and Amos Tversky to develop their alternative to the classical 'expected utility' theory of rational choice: the so-called "prospect theory" of choice, which earned Daniel Kahneman the Nobel Memorial Prize in Economics in 2002.[24]

Moreover, anthropological studies on market exchanges among different types of groups also support this claim, noting that market prices are best understood as "cyphers for a complex entanglement of actors, relations, ideologies, things, and environments."[25] Since the epistemic benefits of market prices depend on their ability to track relative scarcity, the fact that information about relative scarcity is inseparable from non-scarcity-related factors poses a real problem for the Efficiency Conception.

Despite their inability to track exclusively scarcity-related factors, prices are nonetheless *perceived* by market agents as communicating information about the relative scarcity of market goods and nothing else. Market prices are perceived by market agents as bits of typically reliable information about supply and demand of market goods, but not as bits of reliable information about non-scarcity related factors such as, for instance, the working conditions under which goods are produced.[26] This effectively conceals from view the background conditions of exchange, including any underlying injustices in the chain of production and distribution.

A real-life example might help to bring out this point: In 2014, British Primark customers found stitched messages sewn into the clothes they had bought: 'Forced

---

[23] Kahneman, Knetsch & Thaler (1990), p. 1325.

[24] On the prospect theory of choice, see Kahneman, Slovic & Tversky (1982); Kahnemann and Tversky (2000); Gilovich, Griffin an d Kahnemann (2002).

[25] Luetchford and Orlando (2019), p. 2.

[26] Herzog (2020).

to work exhausting hours', 'Degrading sweatshop conditions' etc.[27] Although these messages were apparently a hoax carried out within the UK; they brought to light the fact that not only do we typically ignore the working conditions under which many of these products are produced when we are buying them, but also that we don't even think about those conditions when we're buying these goods when the price does not seem 'suspicious', that is, when the price that we are offered corresponds to what we think the ongoing market price for that kind of good is. As market agents, we usually operate under epistemic conditions that *exclude* paying attention to the spheres of production and distribution, and, therefore, to the fact that many products we buy are produced under degrading conditions that, in non-market contexts, most of us would characterise as unjust or even extremely unjust. Under typical market conditions, therefore, the epistemic benefits of market prices are not as salient as the Efficiency Conception considers them to be. Since the market price is a price that both *reflects* and *conceals* the background conditions of exchange, the Efficiency Conception facilitates the naturalisation of underlying injustices in the chain of production and distribution. Under unjust background conditions of exchange, to reflect the relative scarcity of a given good is simply to efficiently reflect and conceal injustice.

Readers familiar with Marx's theory of exploitation may be reminded of Marx's claim that in order to understand the sale of and purchase of labour power as a commodity we should leave the sphere of circulation of goods—the market—and focus instead on the sphere of production: "Here we shall see, not only how capital produces, but how capital is itself produced."[28] While I agree with the idea of not taking the market in isolation and looking into the whole process of production of commodities, I am not convinced by Marx's almost exclusive focus on the private ownership of capital. Indeed, *pace* Marx, Paul Samuelson proved that it does not matter from the perspective of wealth distribution whether capital hires labour or labour hires capital. An economic model in which propertyless producers rent the means of production from capitalists yields the same distributive results as a model in which workers rent their labour to capitalists.[29]

Now, if prices are not epistemically efficient, then their allocative benefits are also put into question, for this would mean that resources are not allocated to their best employment, but to the employment that is more consistent with the combination of information about scarcity-related and non-scarcity-related factors that prices do, in fact, communicate.

---

[27] Susanna Rustin, 'This Cry for Help on a Primark Label Can't Be Ignored | Susanna Rustin' *The Guardian* (25 June 2014) <https://www.theguardian.com/commentisfree/2014/jun/25/primark-label-swansea-textile-industry-rana-plaza> accessed 27 February 2023; 'Primark Claims "cry for Help Labels" Are a Hoax Carried out in the UK' (*The Independent*, 28 June 2014) <http://www.independent.co.uk/news/uk/home-news/primark-claims-cry-for-help-lab els-are-a-hoax-carried-out-in-the-uk-following-investigation-9569990.html> accessed 27 February 2023.

[28] Marx (1890), pp. 279–280.

[29] Samuelson (1957), p. 47. See also Roemer (1988), pp. 90–107, (1994), p. 37; Burczak (2006), pp. 105–107.

The efficiency theorist may insist on the claim that market prices *always* reflect relative scarcity by relying on a definitional point: that relative scarcity conceptually depends on supply and demand. The argument would be that, since by definition market prices are those that track supply and demand, market prices *always* track relative scarcity. If they do not, then they are not market prices.[30] But this is simply to concede that market prices are not efficient in any normatively meaningful sense.

Now, let us suppose that some ideal circumstances exist in which prices are indeed epistemically efficient, such as those imagined by Eric Posner and E. Weyl in their book *Radical Markets*.[31] Posner and Weyl propose to eliminate private property rights and replace them with contingent (temporal) use rights, and that each person records the value of her assets in a public register which will be the basis for a wealth tax. If people increase the value of their assets, then they would have to pay more taxes, but if they undervalue them, then they expose their assets to being acquired by others who can make unilateral offers for those assets, unilateral offers that would effectively remove those assets from one's resource pool: if one refuses to sell, that would count as theft (unlike our current legal arrangements, in the world imagined by the authors *price trumps consent*: unilateral offers are binding even without one's consent). Suppose further that not only such institutional arrangements are feasible, but that prices that stem from such arrangements indeed manifest the value of efficiency. Would that be enough to consider them just?

To answer this question, we would have to look at the allocative effects of market prices, that is, at their alleged ability to direct goods and labour to their best employment. If it is true that epistemic efficiency leads to allocative efficiency, then we would have a strong reason to consider efficient prices as just, or at least as justice apt, in the sense that such prices would be necessary for a just allocation of resources in society.

I think there is something to say for the claim that, although ongoing market prices do not manifest the value of efficiency, they would be at least *pro tanto* just if they actually did. However, there is one worry that efficiency advocates should be aware of, namely, that the allocative effects of efficient market prices seem to systematically benefit those with more background wealth. If this is the case, then institutional arrangements leading to efficient prices would not cease to be questionable from the standpoint of justice. In other words, if allocative efficiency naturalises and reinforces inegalitarian patterns of wealth distribution in society then the fact that prices manifest the value of efficiency does not seem to be enough reason to consider them even *pro tanto* just.

To see this, let me focus on a factor that market prices are bound to reflect, even in institutional arrangements such as those imagined by Posner and Weyl: concentration of *wealth*. 'Wealth' is not used here as accountants and economists use it. By wealth, I mean to include both stock and flow, i.e., the accountant's concept of wealth (stock) plus income (flow). Concentration of wealth is necessarily reflected on market prices because background wealth has a direct impact on the reservation prices of both

---

[30] Cf Collingwood (1926), pp. 175–176; Heath (2018), pp. 27–28.

[31] Posner and Weyl (2018).

buyers and sellers—the highest price the buyer is able to offer and the lowest price the seller is able to receive. The upshot of wealth inequality for market prices, therefore, is that those with more background wealth have more *power* to set prices than those with less background wealth. Indeed, as Adam Smith noted, wealth *is* power, and concentration of wealth is therefore concentration of power—power to impose one's will on those who cannot afford to do otherwise:

> Wealth, as Mr. Hobbes says, is power. (…) The power which that possession immediately and directly conveys to him, is the power of purchasing; a certain command over (…) the produce of other men's labour, which it enables him to purchase or command. The exchangeable power of everything must always be precisely equal to the extent of this power which it conveys to its owner.[32]

If background wealth has an impact on reservation prices, then the price system works in such a way that those who have more background wealth ('the rich' for short) are at liberty to impose their will—their willed *prices*—on those who have less ('the poor' for short) without the poor being able to do much about it. It is an aggregation of these prices—the prices imposed on the poor by the rich—what constitutes the market price of a given commodity. As Posner and Weyl remind us, the market operates as an auction writ large: it allocates resources in such a way that the person who can offer *more* money for a certain commodity can have it, even if the other person wants it or needs it more.[33] This 'auction-writ-large' character of the market mechanism is widely acknowledged.[34] It is, in fact, at the centre of Dworkin's argument for resource egalitarianism: a large part of Dworkin's argument relies on a thought experiment involving survivors of a shipwreck on an uninhabited island, where they distribute all their resources equally using a mechanism similar to that of a competitive market.[35] Now, if the background distribution of wealth makes it the case that some people can habitually offer more money for goods than the rest, then those people effectively possess control—decentralised control, but control nonetheless—over the allocation of resources in society, and usually more and better goods will be allocated to those in control, and less and worse goods to everyone else. If this is true, then to claim that market prices are just because they are efficient (or at least that this is a necessary condition for the justification of prices) simply covers under a shroud of legitimacy the fact that ongoing market prices systematically benefit the rich. Thus, the kind of allocative efficiency that market prices possess would seem to be normatively unattractive in a society with inegalitarian patterns of wealth distribution. Market-price allocation under conditions of background inequality of wealth would systematically advantage those with more background wealth and disadvantage those with less.

In sum, the alleged epistemic and allocative properties of market prices do not seem to translate into benefits under inegalitarian patterns of wealth distribution.

---

[32] Smith (1976), p. 48.

[33] Posner and Weyl (2018).

[34] Cf Steiner (1984).

[35] Dworkin (2000); For a critique of the way Dworkin understands the auction mechanism, see Heath (2004).

If efficient market prices track background wealth inequality through each party's reservation prices, then market price efficiency is normatively unappealing under conditions of background inequality of wealth. This means that efficiency is *conditionally valuable*: it is valuable or normatively attractive *only if equality of wealth obtains*. However, if a massive redistribution of wealth in society is a necessary condition for efficiency to be valuable, then the Efficiency Conception would be correct only if a particular version of the just price—one according to which a price is just only if the price system is compatible with equality of wealth—is also correct. But is a price system committed to wealth equality even possible? Is it not the case that the very existence of a price system promotes inequality between those who participate in it? To these and other related questions I now turn.

3.3 The Feasibility of a Just Price System

There are two distinct but mutually supportive arguments for the alleged unfeasibility of the application of a price system committed to wealth equality.[36] The first argument concerns the very nature of the price system—that is, the very function prices are supposed to fulfil within a society. According to this argument, a price system committed to keeping equality of wealth could not communicate information about the relative scarcity of goods and would be, therefore, unable to work properly as price systems. Call this the *Epistemic Objection*. The second argument concerns the price system's incentive structure—that is, the incentives it gives to market agents for acting upon the information given by a well-functioning price system. According to this objection, an egalitarian price system would be severely inefficient due to the lack of economic incentives to work: without the promise of a wage differential, people would simply not work as hard as under an inegalitarian price system. I call this the *Incentives Objection*. I shall deal with these objections separately in what follows.

3.3.1 The Epistemic Objection

The *Epistemic Objection* focuses on the epistemic function of market prices. As noted above, one of the main functions of prices in a well-functioning price system is to communicate information about the relative scarcity of a given good. According to the objection, it would be impossible to fulfil this epistemic function without allowing for wealth inequalities among market participants. To understand the real force of the objection, one must be reminded that this function of market prices holds true not only for consumption goods, but also for wages—the price of labour. Now suppose that we design a price system committed to wealth equality and we equalise wages so

---

[36] *Cf* Carens (1981), pp. 12–17, 23–93.

that everyone earns the same as everyone else. In such a case, the resulting equalised wages would no longer reflect the relative scarcity of each kind of labour: regardless of their levels of supply and demand, the price for different kinds of labour would always be identical. This lack of information regarding the relative scarcity of each kind of labour would be bound to create significant inefficiencies in the system. We would have no information about how to allocate resources in a way that maximises economic output: producers would not be able to know what kind of resources are needed, nor how much labour would be necessary to produce them. The inefficiencies in production would, in turn, create inefficiencies in resource allocation: demand for consumption would not match the goods supplied by production. Economic chaos in the name of equality would quickly ensue.

The epistemic deficits of a price system that does not track relative scarcity were forcefully stressed by Hayek:

> If [people] are to be able to judge what they ought to do, they must be given some readily intelligible yardstick by which to measure the social importance of the different occupations. Even with the best will in the world it would be impossible for anyone intelligently to choose between various alternatives if the advantages they offered him stood in no relation to their usefulness to society. To know whether as the result of a change a man ought to leave a trade and an environment which he has come to like, and exchange it for another, it is necessary that the changed relative value of these occupations to society should find expression in the remunerations they offer.[37]

Given these considerations, it seems clear that a system in which wages are equalised by *fiat* would be unfeasible. An egalitarian price system would be, by definition, insensitive to changes in supply and demand, and, consequently, it would be so severely inefficient that one might wonder if there would be any reason at all for having a price system in the first place.

I believe the best reply to this objection is simply to concede the point. If a price system does not track relative scarcity, then indeed one of the main reasons for having a price system disappears. Note, however, that this does not entail that a price system is not feasible within a society with egalitarian institutional arrangements. It only entails that a price system in which prices are equalised *by fiat* or otherwise fixed without taking relative scarcity into account is unfeasible. But this is not the only way to design a price system that preserves wealth equality (more on this later on). The only conclusion that follows from this, therefore, is that any price system, egalitarian or otherwise, must be able to track relative scarcity, and that a feasible egalitarian price system cannot afford the luxury of equalising prices *by fiat*. An egalitarian price system must reflect differences in the relative scarcity of different goods, and these differences must be reflected in different price rates and different wage rates or else we would lack information that is necessary to have an efficient system. If prices do not track relative scarcity—or, as Hayek puts it, if they do not "measure the social importance of the different occupations"[38]—then the price system cannot be said

---

[37] Hayek (1944), p. 129.

[38] Ibid.

to be functioning properly. This holds true also for inegalitarian or otherwise unjust price systems.

Before proceeding to analyse the second (and, in my view, much more pressing) objection against an egalitarian price system, I would like to note that conceding the motivating thought behind the Epistemic Objection, as I have, does not entail conceding a somewhat pervasive use of the *Epistemic Objection* in political discourse which tends to blow the force of the objection out of proportion in order to oppose any form of state intervention—and therefore, any sort of institutional reform—in the ongoing price system (Hayek's *Road to Serfdom* is probably the clearest expression of such a blown-out-of-proportion political use). Indeed, one can safely discard the political use of the argument if one takes into account that it is not the case that existing price systems track relative scarcity, or, at least, that relative scarcity is not the *only* thing that prices are tracking within such systems. As I stressed throughout the previous section, our current market prices typically track wealth inequality and other power imbalances along with relative scarcity in a way that makes it difficult to separate these factors from each other. Thus, if anything, an egalitarian price system would have a *pro tanto* epistemic advantage compared to our current price system, for it would not track inequalities of wealth. Thus, the political argument can be turned on its head: for market prices to fulfil their epistemic function, radical change is required. The political use of the argument (no change to the current price system) is inconsistent with its motivating premise (the epistemic benefits of market prices).

3.3.2   The Incentives Objection

Let me now turn to the *Incentives Objection*. This second argument against the feasibility of an egalitarian price system focuses on the incentives that the market system is supposed to provide to individuals to act upon the information given by market prices. According to this argument, even if prices were to track relative scarcity and were not, therefore, equalised by *fiat*, an egalitarian price system would fail to provide incentives for labour and production, leading to a society with less available resources to distribute among citizens. To see the force of the argument, let me modify the situation imagined for the *Epistemic Objection* and now suppose that different wage rates are indeed permitted, that prices and wage rates reflect the relative scarcity of goods and labour, but that there is a tax system in place which is used to equalise income available for individual consumption. In our imagined scenario, while pre-tax income would depend on the wage rates earned by each individual, those different individual earnings would be distributed equally among every member of society afterwards. Thus, pre-tax income would be indeed different for each individual, but post-tax income (the actual income available for individual consumption) would be equal for all. Prices in this system would be able to manifest both the value of efficiency (because they track relative scarcity and therefore communicate information to allocate resources to their best employment) and distributive justice (because they would secure or at least not impinge upon wealth equality).

The problem with this system—and this is the important point of the *Incentives Objection*—would be that the elimination of post-tax wage differentials would have also eliminated the incentive to work, and more efficient production of wealth with it. This creates a problem for an egalitarian price system, for the epistemic benefits of market prices would only be achieved at the expense of allowing post-tax wage differentials and, therefore, inequality of wealth.

The relationship between equality and incentives has been extensively discussed in the literature, usually against the background of Rawls' political philosophy and his defence of the difference principle—namely, that inequalities are justified when they benefit the worse off. However, the idea that inequalities are justified when they benefit the worse off is not exclusive to Rawls' difference principle. It also figures prominently in authors with very few egalitarian credentials such as Hayek.[39]

Why are economic incentives thought to be incompatible with wealth equality? Because they are, by definition, incentives to receive a larger share of resources, upsetting therefore the ideal of equal distribution of wealth to which an egalitarian society aims at. Therefore, the incentives structure embedded within the price system would not conform to the normative ideal of distributive egalitarianism. The price system—even an egalitarian price system—would be, therefore, inherently at odds with wealth equality.

We can state the challenge against the feasibility of an egalitarian price system as a dilemma: either prices are equalised by fiat, in which case the price system would be so severely inefficient that there is no reason for having it in the first place, or they are not, in which case the price system itself would promote inequality of outcome. In both cases, an egalitarian price system would be unfeasible.

I believe there is a solution to the *Incentives Objection*—and, therefore, to the previously mentioned dilemma.[40] However, before expanding on my own answer to the problem, let me review some other lines of reply one could take.

The first line of reply can be called the *Marxist Reply*. The *Marxist Reply* is pretty straightforward: it consists in eliminating the inequalities created by economic incentives embedded in price mechanisms by eliminating the price mechanism altogether. Any other solution—including advocating for a mechanism of *just* prices—would reproduce and perpetuate structural injustice. Needless to say, I am using the term 'Marxist' only to denote those who affirm the elimination of the price system as the only solution to the *Incentives Objection*. I would not want to deny the possibility of some idiosyncratic 'Marxist' theory of the just price built upon different grounds (such as, for instance, some account of Marx's labour-theory of value as the benchmark for just value).

To the Marxist (in the restricted sense described above), advocating for an egalitarian price system and for just prices is merely a conservative half measure. In his address entitled *Wages, Price, and Profit* (1865) Marx explicitly warned against what he perceived as the danger of conservative reformism embedded within the demand of the working class for fair wages:

---

[39] See Hayek (1990), pp. 39–48.

[40] Cf Reyes (2023).

[The working class] ought not to forget that they are fighting with effects, but not with the causes of those effects; that they are retarding the downward movement, but not changing its direction; that they are applying palliatives, not curing the malady. They ought, therefore, not to be exclusively absorbed in these unavoidable guerrilla fights incessantly springing up from the never-ceasing encroachments of capital or changes in the market. (...) Instead of the *conservative* motto, "*A fair day's wage for a fair day's work*" they ought to inscribe on their banner the *revolutionary* watchword, "*Abolition of the wages system!*"[41]

The *Marxist Reply* brings to the fore the possibility that the search for a just price entails an unstable and normatively unattractive compromise between distributive justice and efficiency. The underlying idea behind this rejection of a system of just prices is that, normatively speaking, whenever we are forced to choose between market efficiency and distributive justice, we should always choose the latter. According to the *Marxist Reply*, the dilemma between distributive egalitarianism and efficiency is, in fact, inescapable.

The *Marxist Reply* to the *Incentives Objection* is fundamentally flawed, and this for two reasons. First, because, contrary to the Marxist suggestion, wealth equality would be impossible to achieve without the price mechanism. In a society where people value different things for different reasons, not only economic coordination, but economic equality itself depends upon a shared metric of value. Market prices provide this shared metric. Without market prices and the commensuration of value they make possible, wealth equality would be utterly unintelligible.[42]

Secondly, the *Marxist Reply* fails to take the *Epistemic Objection* seriously enough. In effect, it downplays the importance of the epistemic benefits of markets for coordination. There is now widespread consensus among economic scholars that Ludwig von Mises' argument about the inefficiency of what he calls 'socialism'— more precisely, about the inefficient resource allocation that necessarily follows from the epistemic failures of a system in which the factors of production have no market prices—was indeed correct, and that the outcome of the 1920s-1940s debate over what in economic theory is called the 'economic calculation problem'— the problem for central planners of calculating prices without information given by market prices of the factors of production—suggests that centralised planning cannot provide market agents with enough information to allocate resources to their best use.[43] The failure of the economic socialist experiments of Cuba, China, the Soviet Union and the Eastern Bloc—and, we might add, the failure of price control policies in Venezuela—seems to have brought some empirical confirmation to this claim.

The failure of the *Marxist Reply* highlights the fact that while justice may be, as Rawls famously claimed, "the first virtue of social institutions",[44] it is certainly not the *sole* virtue of social institutions, nor is it a one-dimensional virtue. Prices can be unjust for reasons other than because they manifest distributive injustice. Indeed, certain failures to respect the efficient allocation of resources can also constitute

---

[41] Marx (1968), pp. 225–226; For an insightful comment on this passage, and on Marxism's attitude towards social reform, see Cohen (2000), pp. 71–72, 58–78.

[42] Cf Dagan (2020), p. xvi; Dworkin (1981), p. 283.

[43] Mises (1932); On the economic calculation problem, see generally Steele (1992).

[44] Rawls (1971), p. 3.

injustices. Moreover, it might be *unjust* to realise perfect distributive justice at the expense of efficiency. Achieving equality without benefitting anyone might fulfil the requirements of wealth equality, but depressing everyone's condition would hardly be considered a just societal arrangement, even if motivated by principles of justice and wealth equality. Therefore, a just price system—that is, a system that generates just prices—must be sensitive to considerations that are not directly related to distributive justice and display virtues other than distributive justice such as, for instance, efficiency, as well as circumstances of fact that may affect the effective realisation of the principle. Justice alone ought not to dictate policy.[45]

A second line of reply to the *Incentives Objection,* which might be called the *Trade-Off Reply,* suggests itself from these remarks. Like the *Marxist Reply,* the *Trade-Off Reply* also bites the bullet: efficiency and distributive egalitarianism are indeed incompatible. Unlike the *Marxist Reply,* however, the *Trade-off Reply* claims that a trade-off between efficiency and distributive justice is a better solution than simply eliminating the price mechanism. This line of reply concedes that an efficient price mechanism will always produce inegalitarian outcomes and claims that the solution to the incentives problem is a matter of policy: we must decide whether we are willing to endorse a system of market prices that allocates resources to their best employment at the expense of a more egalitarian distribution of resources, or whether we are willing to sacrifice efficiency in order to get economic outcomes that maximise distributive justice. For most economists, the former option is normally preferable to the latter. Due to their advantageous effects on society, the decision not to forego potential increases in welfare despite their inegalitarian effects is one that, for efficiency-minded theorists, recommends itself.[46]

I have no objections to this line of reply as a matter of policy. In effect, policymaking, and the design of rules regulating the price system, almost inevitably leads to trade-offs between equality and efficiency. However, just price theory is not *only*—and not even primarily—a matter of policy or of institutional design. It is fundamentally about the analytical and normative implications of justice when applied to prices and the price system, and there are indeed a few conceptual and normative points that one must bear in mind before accepting the trade-off solution as definitive or as the only sensible reply.

Indeed, trade-offs are only necessary when circumstances make it the case that one must choose efficiency at the expense of distributive justice or vice versa, i.e., when there is no better option available. But there is, in principle, a better option available, namely, one in which economic incentives are not necessary for incentivising the well-off, i.e., one in which the well-off in society work as hard *without* asking for extra economic motivation. This would be the case, for instance, in a society in which labour is conceived as the satisfaction of one's duty towards society and where this duty alone—or some other similar virtuous motivation, such as, for instance, solidarity among fellow citizens or a different virtue that could track a deep concern for the wellbeing of others, conjoined with an equally deep commitment to material

---

[45] For a similar point, see Cohen (2008), pp. 302–307.

[46] Heath (2018).

equality as a condition to seeing each other as equals—provides sufficient motivation to work even in the absence of further economic incentives.[47] Thus, the need for a trade-off only makes sense under one critical assumption, namely, that those in society who are benefitted from the ongoing distribution of resources are not willing to work as hard without economic incentives and, therefore, are unwilling to renounce their wage differentials. This is, in fact, the insight at the heart of G. A. Cohen's critique of Rawls' difference principle.[48]

To be sure, it may be the case that, as a matter of fact, the well-off simply *will not work as hard* without economic incentives, and in that sense, this is a fact that needs to be dealt with by policymakers when establishing incentives to work. Indeed, it would be bad policy *not* to take it into account. But the normative point that I would like to highlight is that this fact is not a necessary condition that follows from the very nature of the price system. The lack of an *ethos* of commitment to equality of wealth is simply a contingent fact of our current world. Moreover, it is the very behaviour of well-off people which makes this fact true, for it is certainly *possible* for them to work as hard as they currently do without economic incentives, and without, therefore, generating inequalities. Whatever its merits, the point is that a price system focused on giving incentives to the well-off to work harder simply because they are not willing to work as hard without the promise of wage differentials cannot be said to be *equally just* as one in which the well-off do not require such incentives. Jan Narveson has nicely illustrated the normative concern behind the incentives argument for economic inequality with an imaginary dialogue between two people—Well-off and Worse-off—which I take the liberty to reproduce in full:

> Well-off: "Look here, fellow citizen, I'll work hard and make both you and me better off, provided I get a bigger share than you."
>
> Worse-off: "Well, that's rather good; but I thought you were agreeing that justice requires equality?"
>
> Well-off: "Yes, but that's only a benchmark, you see. To do still better, both of us, you understand, may require differential incentive payments to people like me."
>
> Worse-off: "Oh. Well, what makes them necessary?"
>
> Well-off: "What makes them necessary is that I won't work as hard if I don't get more than you."
>
> Worse-off: "Well, why not?"
>
> Well-off: "I dunno… I guess that's just the way I'm built."
>
> Worse-off: "Meaning, you don't really care all that much about justice, eh?"
>
> Well-off: "Er, no, I guess not."[49]

This brings me to a second point: assuming that people will be motivated by economic incentives is not always the best option as a matter of policy. The assumption that wage differentials will incentivise the well-off to work more is usually made

---

[47] The case for the feasibility of a scheme in which equality and efficiency are satisfied has been made, among others, by Carens (1981), (1986); Wilkinson (2000); White (2003); Cohen (2008).

[48] Cohen (2008), pp. 27–86.

[49] Narveson (1978), p. 281; Quoted with approval in Cohen (2008), p. 27.

on the basis that institutional design must assume the perspective of a self-interested individual. In effect, according to a very respectable line of political philosophers, economists, and jurists, including, among many others, authors such as Machiavelli, Mandeville, Hume, Smith, Bentham, John Stuart Mill, Francis Y. Edgeworth, Oliver Wendel Holmes Jr., and (with some qualifications) Hayek, the institutional design must assume that *everyone* is self-interested.[50] According to this view, the purpose of institutional design is, as Bowles puts it, "harnessing knaves",[51] i.e., making self-interest work for the public good. On this view, to assume that people will not be willing to work as hard without getting some economic reward out of it would always be good policy advice when designing the incentive structure of a price system.

While the assumption of universal self-interest can indeed be a sensible assumption to make in certain cases, it can quickly become problematic when conjoined with one further assumption, namely, that economic incentives and moral considerations are, as economists put it, *additively separable*—that is, that the effects of variations in one do not depend on variations on the other.[52] By making this assumption, policy-makers can easily overlook the relevant synergies between economic motivation and ethical considerations. Empirical research has shown that additive separability does not always obtain, and this is for two main reasons. First, there are cases in which economic incentives often do not work as well as intrinsic motivation. But also, and more importantly for our present purposes, because sometimes the mere presence of economic incentives makes people act more self-interestedly than in their absence. When this happens, the assumption of self-interest typically becomes a self-fulfilling promise.

A theory of the just price can accommodate the fact that it is not necessary, and it might even be counterproductive, to always assume self-interest as a matter of policy, and that it is possible to conceive a society in which citizens sufficiently motivated by equality would not need economic incentives or the promise of a higher income in order to work as hard as they do under current institutional arrangements. The upshot of this view for the price system is that price-related institutional arrangements with a different incentive structure—one that does not rely so heavily on the assumption of self-interest—could help shape individual motivation towards a more egalitarian ethos. If that situation, however unlikely, indeed obtains, then in such a world we would not require any trade-offs between efficiency and justice. In such a world, the epistemic benefits of market prices would not clash with equality. If citizens were motivated by the virtue of justice, a just price system would indeed be potentially feasible.

---

[50] Cf Bowles (2016), pp. 9–39.

[51] Ibid. p. 16.

[52] For this paragraph, see Bowles (2016) *passim*, but especially pp. 21–25.

Bibliography

Arrow K (1951) An extension of the basic theorems of classical welfare economics. In: Neyman J (ed) Proceedings of the second berkeley symposium on mathematical statistics and probability, University of California, Oakland

Bowles S (2016) The moral economy: why good incentives are no substitutes for good citizens, New Haven

Burczak T (2006) Socialism after Hayek, Ann Arbor

Carens J (1981) Equality, moral incentives, and the market: an essay in utopian politico-economic theory, Chicago

Carens J (1986) Rights and duties in an egalitarian society. Political Theory 14:31, et seqq.

Cohen GA (2000) If you're an Egalitarian, How Come You're So Rich?, Cambridge

Cohen GA (2008) Rescuing justice and equality, Cambridge

Collingwood RG (1926) Economics as a philosophical science. Int J Ethics 36:162, et seqq.

Dagan H (2020) The law of the market. Law Contemp Problems 83(2):i–xviii

Dworkin R (1977) Taking rights seriously, London

Dworkin R (1981) What is equality? Part 2: equality of resources. Philos Public Affairs 10:283, et seqq.

Dworkin R (1986) Law's empire, London

Dworkin R (2000) Sovereign virtue: the theory and practice of equality, Cambridge

Dworkin R (2006) Justice in robes, Cambridge

Dworkin R (2011) Justice for hedgehogs, Cambridge

Gilovich T, Griffin D, Kahneman D (eds) (2002) Heuristics and biases: the psychology of intuitive judgment, Cambridge

Gordley J, Jiang H (2020) Contract as voluntary commutative justice. Michigan State Law Rev 725–801

Gordley J (1981) Equality in exchange. California Law Rev 69:1587, et seqq.

Gordley J (2001) Contract law in the Aristotelian tradition. In: Benson P (ed) The theory of contract law: new essays

Hayek F (1945) The use of knowledge in society. Am Econ Rev 35:519–530

Hayek F (2002) Competition as a discovery procedure. Quarterly J Austrian Econ 5(3):9–23

Hayek F (1944) The road to Serfdom, London

Hayek F (1948) The meaning of competition. In: Individualism and economic order, pp. 92–106

Hayek F (1990) The constitution of liberty, London

Heath J (2018) On the very idea of a just wage. Erasmus J Philos Econ 11(2):1–33

Heath J (2004), Dworkin's auction, politics. Philos Econ 3:313, et seqq.

Herzog L (2020) The epistemic division of labour in markets: knowledge, global trade and the preconditions of morally responsible agency. Econ Philos 36(2):266–286

Kahneman D, Knetsch J L & Thaler R H (1990) Experimental Tests of the Endowment Effect and the Coase Theorem, Journal of Political Economy, Vol. 98, pp. 1325 et seqq.

Kahneman D, Slovic P, Tversky A (eds.) (1982) Judgment under uncertainty: heuristics and biases, Cambridge

Kahneman D, Tversky A (eds) (2000) Choices, values, and frame, Cambridge

Langholm O (1979) Price and value in the aristotelian tradition: a study in scholastic economic sources, New York

Langholm O (1998) The legacy of scholasticism in economic thought: antecedents of choice and power, Cambridge

Lee FS (2018) Microeconomic theory: a heterodox approach. London

Luetchford P, Orlando G (eds) (2019) The politics and ethics of the just price: ethnographies of market exchange, Bingley

MacIntyre A (2016) Ethics in the conflicts of modernity: an essay on desire, practical reasoning, and narrative, Cambridge

Marx K (1890) Capital: a critique of political economy 1(4)

Marx K (1968) 'Wages, Price and Profit', In Marx and Engels: selected works in one volume, London, pp. 185–226

Mathis K (2009) Efficiency instead of justice? Searching for the Philosophical Foundations of the Economic Analysis of Law, London

Mises L (1932), Socialism: an economic and sociological analysis, vol 2, Indianapolis

Narveson J (1978) Rawls on equal distribution of wealth. Philosophia 7:281, et seqq.

Pettit P (2001) The virtual reality of homo economicus. In: Mäki U(ed) The economic worldview: studies in the ontology of economics, Cambridge, pp. 75–97

Pistor K (2019) The code of capital: how the law creates wealth and inequality, Oakland

Posner E, Weyl EG (2018) Radical markets: uprooting capitalism and democracy for a just society, Princeton

Rawls J (1971) A theory of justice, revised edition, Cambridge

Reyes J (2021) Beyond commutative justice: contract law, justice, and just prices, Latin American. Leg Stud 7:363–390

Reyes J (2023) Just price theory: a reassessment, London

Roemer J (1988) Free to Lose: an introduction to Marxist economic philosophy, Harvard

Roemer J (1994) Egalitarian perspectives: essays in philosophical economics, Cambridge

Samuelson P (1957) Wages and interest: a modern dissection of marxian economic models. Am Econ Rev 47:884, et seqq.

Sen A (1982) Choice. Welfare and Measurement, Chicago

Smith A (1976) An inquiry into the nature and causes of the wealth of nations, vol 1, Indianapolis

Steele DR (1992) From Marx to Mises: post-capitalist society and the challenge of economic calculation, Chicago

Steiner H (1984) A liberal theory of exploitation. Ethics 94 :225, et seqq.

Walsh A, Lynch T (2008) The morality of money: an exploration in analytic philosophy, London

White S (2003) The civic minimum: on the rights and obligations of economic citizenship, Oxford

Wilkinson TM (2000) Freedom, efficiency, and equality, London

Chapter 4
The Institutional Turn in Corporate Governance Towards Addressing Corporate Externalities and Public Goods

Patrick M. Corrigan

Abstract Traditionally, the academic literature on corporate law and governance has cabined problems of externalities—unpriced economic effects on nonconsenting third parties—to other legal domains, such as tort law and employment law. However, the most critical private-ordering mechanisms of corporate governance, including executive compensation and takeover discipline, depend critically on market prices, which may be incomplete if externalities are present. The central argument of this chapter is that many corporate social responsibility efforts and ESG investments are in fact best understood as private-ordering responses to the information and incentive problems arising from corporate externality problems. Because externalities are ordinarily unpriced in market transactions, social enterprises that consider externalities in their decision-making face unique institutional challenges: information costs, coordination costs, and other transaction costs. Legal, institutional, and private-ordering developments are already advancing to meet these challenges. The chapter argues that an area ripe for future research is institutional and legal design that minimises information, transaction, and agency costs for coalitions of stockholders with similar preferences that seek to coordinate corporate production around non-financial objectives.

4.1 Introduction

Corporate law theorists have long dismissed the idea that externalities are a matter of concern for corporation law from an internal perspective. The general normative position is that externality problems are not a proper concern for corporation law

P. M. Corrigan (✉)
Notre Dame Law School, Notre Dame, IN, USA
e-mail: pcorrig3@nd.edu

© The Author(s), under exclusive license to Springer Nature Switzerland AG 2024
K. Mathis and A. Tor (eds.), *Law and Economics of Justice*, Economic Analysis of Law
in European Legal Scholarship 17, https://doi.org/10.1007/978-3-031-56822-0_4

because they are better addressed by other bodies of law, like tort law or environmental law.[1]

The marginalisation of externalities typically gets imported from public matters in the study of corporate *law* into private-ordering matters in the study of corporate *governance*. Having bracketed externalities as a theoretical matter, the standard model of corporate governance is primarily motivated by concerns about the misalignment of incentives between corporate managers and stockholders.[2] The application of insights from the theory of externalities and public goods to corporate governance as a matter of private ordering has, thus, gone underdeveloped.

Private ordering as embodied by corporate governance cannot escape externality problems. The mechanisms of corporate governance—including the two most critical mechanisms of executive compensation and takeover discipline—function almost exclusively through the mechanism of market prices. If market prices are incomplete because externality effects are unpriced, then the mechanisms of corporate governance will also be incomplete with respect to externality and public goods problems.

Nevertheless, stockholders and managers of corporations have recently elevated concerns about corporate environmental sustainability and corporate social responsibility to the fore of current debates about corporate governance. I use the term "corporate social responsibility" to refer to a range of costly commitments and objectives that directly advance the interests of individuals that are not stockholders of the corporation (such efforts may indirectly advance the interests of stockholders). Considerations about the role of firms in contributing to global climate change are perhaps the most significant catalyst of the recent corporate social responsibility debate, but the debate also encompasses a broader array of other considerations, including labour rights, human rights, and community impact. Discussions about the importance of corporate social responsibility have emerged not only from corporate managers but also from investors, large and small.

This book chapter develops two arguments. The first argument is that at least some corporate social responsibility efforts and ESG investments are best understood as private-ordering responses to the information and incentive problems that arise due to externality and public goods problems in the wake of globalisation, mass production, and technological trends. Put another way, the current framing of the academic debate on corporate purpose as primarily about concern for corporate stakeholders is, in at least some cases, less descriptively accurate than a framing as primarily a concern about unpriced or mispriced economic effects. The second argument is that market participants who wish to address externalities and public goods in their coordinated corporate activity must utilise institutional and mechanism design to curb market failures around externalities and public goods. Put simply, if we do not expect markets to solve externality and public goods problems on their own, we also should not expect corporate production subject to market forces to address these issues any better in the absence of institutions and mechanisms specifically designed to address

---

[1] Armour et al. (2017), p. 23.

[2] Jensen (2001), p. 305.

externality problems. These institutional designs, which require costly trade-offs, are well known in the academic literature on externalities, and public goods, but have so far been under-appreciated in the literature on corporate governance.[3] A research agenda is discussed that examines some of the key information and incentive frictions that social enterprises must overcome in order to internalise externalities and produce public goods.

4.2 Concerns About Externalities and Mispricing Explain Certain Corporate Social Responsibility and ESG Activities

The dominant view on corporate purpose among legal scholars is that corporations should be managed to increase the long-term financial value of the firm, measured by profits or share price, for the financial benefit of stockholders.[4] This rule is not written down in statutes, but some courts have interpreted a director's duty of loyalty to require a profit-maximising orientation towards the corporate purpose under certain circumstances.[5] The stockholder wealth maximisation position has various justifications, but the primary one is that corporate orientation towards profit-maximisation also maximises welfare.[6] By maximising their own well-being, agents coordinating their economic activity through corporations also maximise societal well-being. Other arguments support this claim. Since stockholders are the beneficiaries of the firm's residual value, it is argued that stockholder control minimises information, monitoring, and other transaction costs.[7] Moreover, it is argued that managerial orientation towards an easily ascertainable metric like corporate profits provides the most efficient means for holding managers accountable for misuse of corporate resources.[8]

A leading alternative view to the stockholder wealth maximisation paradigm is stakeholderism.[9] The term "stakeholders" usually refers to any individuals that have an interest in corporate activity other than stockholders. This term usually encompasses workers, creditors, suppliers, customers, and the members of the community in which the corporations operate. The strong form of the stakeholderism paradigm posits that corporate directors and managers can and ought to manage the firm to benefit all corporate stakeholders, not just stockholders.

---

[3] *See generally* Ostrom (1990).

[4] Rock (2021a, b), p. 371.

[5] Revlon, Inc. v. MacAndrews & Forbes Holdings, Inc., 506 A.2d 173 (Del. 1986). *See also* eBay Domestic Holdings, Inc. v. Newmark, 16 A.3d 1, 34 (Del. Ch. 2010); Dodge v. Ford Motor Co., 204 Mich. 459, 170 N.W. 668 (Mich. 1919).

[6] Jensen (2001), p. 302.

[7] Hansmann (1988), pp. 273 et seqq.

[8] Bainbridge (2023), p. 138.

[9] *See generally,* Freeman (1984); Blair and Stout (1999); Blair (2012).

The debate on stakeholderism has largely focused on whether directors and officers inappropriately privilege classes of corporate patrons ahead of stockholders when they take a stakeholderist perspective. A central challenge, it is argued, is that stakeholderism offers no way to "keep score."[10] The debate is framed as a question about how the surplus value created by corporate activity should be distributed. A related framing is that stakeholderism is an attempt to address "political dysfunction."[11] A leading criticism of stakeholderism is that it constitutes an undesirable diversion of corporate surplus from stockholders to other corporate stakeholders. The leading version of this critique is that corporate managers use corporate social responsibility and ESG as pretexts for explaining poor economic performance and for avoiding accountability from stockholders. Another version of the critique is that it unfairly deprives stockholders of their rights and privileges to decide which social causes to advance. It is best to distribute corporate surplus to the stockholders, who can then decide whether to provide charity to workers, the community, or the environment. It is also often said that corporation law provides substantive voting and economic rights to stockholders as a class, and it is inappropriate for managers to privilege other classes of corporate patrons that do not have such rights under corporate law.

In this chapter, I assume that stockholders, directors, and managers organise corporations to advance the interests—financial or otherwise—of stockholders. However, as will become clear, the interests of at least some stockholders may include addressing the information and incentive problems that arise when some of the costs and benefits of the corporation's activities go unpriced in markets. Without taking sides on the efficiency, optimality, or desirability of corporate objectives, I merely assume here that at least some stockholders desire to coordinate their economic activity through a corporate vehicle in a way that accounts for externality and public good problems. These concerns might emerge from a private or social welfare perspective, depending on the framework of the relevant corporate decision-makers.

The chapter, thus, advances an overlooked explanation for certain corporate social responsibility and ESG efforts, one that is complementary to stockholder primacy theories: private-ordering responses to the information and incentive problems arising from corporate externalities. As a private-ordering mechanism, corporate social responsibility is motivated by an operational or normative concern that the markets in which corporations operate are failing to price in certain sources of value or certain risks. Operational concerns about externalities and public goods are motivated by a desire to overcome information and incentive problems to accumulate more profits for the corporation. Normative concerns about externalities are motivated by stockholder commitments to take responsibility for the social costs of corporate activities or to pursue business in line with a mission or a set of values.

Below, I create a typology of four types of social enterprises in light of externality theory and I survey their core characteristics. Before turning to the typology, I briefly

---

[10] Jensen (2001), p. 298, Bainbridge (2023), p. 135.

[11] Rock (2021a), p. 367.

describe why the theory of externalities introduces important market failures that may be of proper concern to stockholders and corporate managers.

In externality theory, an externality is generally defined as an economic effect on a third party that is unpriced in market exchanges.[12] A classic example is a factory that emits particulate matter in the course of production that makes individuals in the community ill. The harm to the third-party community members from the economic activity of the factory is not fully priced into market transactions and the third parties that bear the externality costs are not compensated (assuming tort litigation is costly or imperfect).

Where externalities are present, they create information and incentives problems that lead to market failures.[13] By market failures, I mean that the market produces an outcome that does not maximise aggregate welfare. Markets for externalities are missing because no one has the information or incentives to complete the markets for the unpriced costs or benefits. Because markets fail to price negative externalities like pollution, markets overproduce goods or services that produce negative externalities. Because markets fail to price positive externalities, like certain public transportation systems, these goods or services are underproduced.

The Coase theorem provides a reason to believe that market participants will be able to internalise externalities and produce the optimal amount of public benefits through private ordering under certain conditions when property rights are well defined and when transaction costs are low.[14] Fishermen can pay the firm to stop dumping toxic waste into the water. Community members can raise money to pay for public transportation. And so on. The result of this bargaining process is that equilibrium will reflect the efficient amount of production.

However, there are good reasons to believe that the many corporate externality problems will not be resolved by the type of bilateral bargaining described by the Coase theorem. It was a lot easier to exhaust value-maximising bargains in commerce when everyone got their milk from the neighbourhood cow and bought their carriages from the town blacksmith. Today, milk may be shipped from overseas, and cars are assembled using parts made across the entire world. Production is globalised and specialised. Collective action problems, hold-up problems, the absence or ambiguity of property rights, and other conditions make modern Coasian bargains over corporate activity extremely complex and costly, particularly after the globalisation wave of recent decades. Moreover, bargaining attempts around global commons externalities, like climate change, are particularly intractable.

Given the foregoing, externalities have been traditionally cited as a first-order justification for government regulation.[15] When the market does not price externality costs, there are profitable gains from trade that are not realised and there is room for a social planner to improve on outcomes generated by the market.

---

[12] Cornes and Sandler (1986).

[13] Id.

[14] Coase (1960).

[15] Cornes and Sandler (1986).

The logic of externality theory applies to corporate production when transaction costs are sufficiently high so that Coasian bargains are unlikely to resolve externality problems. Corporations, like individual agents, produce positive and negative externalities in the course of their economic activities. If externalities are generally expected to generate market failures, there is no reason to believe that coordinated corporate economic activity will avoid this outcome. Therefore, there might be room for externality-minded stockholders to improve their own welfare or social welfare relative to outcomes generated by the market.

The globalisation of capital and production complicates the traditional argument that private actors should disregard externality problems and instead rely on public regulation of externalities. Globalisation of production and economic activities enables forum-shopping by producers and may incentivise a race-to-the-bottom for externality regulation among jurisdictions, weakening the ability of any one jurisdiction to optimally regulate externalities.

Moreover, consideration of externalities complicates the traditional rationale for stockholder wealth maximisation. Recall that the traditional justification is that a corporate objective that seeks to maximise stockholder wealth is efficient in the sense that it maximises welfare. However, this conclusion must be qualified if corporate activities produce negative externalities. If the uncompensated costs on society outweigh the efficiency gains from corporate profit-seeking activities, then a pure profit-seeking objective would not be efficient from a social perspective. In such a case, the socially optimal corporate activities would depend heavily on the magnitude of externalities and the transaction costs that hinder efficient private ordering in light of externalities.

I now turn to the typology of unpriced or mispriced costs that may be relevant to stockholders and corporate governance decision-makers that care about externalities. At least four types have relevance: unpriced intangible value or risks for firms; unpriced inter-firm externalities; unpriced social harm; and unpriced normative commitments to a mission. By using the term unpriced, I mean that certain economic effects are not priced in market transactions, including in transactions for the corporation's stock. The four categories are not mutually exclusive; stockholders and managers may be motivated by pricing concerns in more than one category. Moreover, stockholders and managers in the same corporation may have conflicting preferences or may even advance concerns about externalities as a pretext for advancing other motivations, like self-enrichment. Some of the information and incentive problems created by conflicting preferences and information frictions are discussed in Sect. 4.3.

Mispricing of intangible assets and risks in the short term is the first—and perhaps the most significant—category of pricing issues that motivate corporate social responsibility and ESG efforts. For purposes of the analysis, I reserve a discussion of this issue for last. The problems of mispricing intangible assets, I argue, share a similar structure as a public goods problem. However, the other three categories of pricing considerations relate more directly to externalities and public goods, and I discuss them first.

The second pricing category that is relevant to corporate governance is inter-firm externalities.[16] The starting point for this paradigm is that many stockholders are diversified investors with financial interests in the entire market. If one firm in a diversified portfolio imposes a negative externality on another firm, then the universal owner will bear the costs of the negative externality.

Consider an owner of two companies, a mining company and a manufacturing company. As part of its production processes, the mining company produces a toxic sludge by-product and a risk that the sludge might slide down the mountain and destroy a factory at the bottom of the hill. The owner of the mine might be incentivised to underinvest in safely securing and disposing of the toxic sludge. The mine will incur all of the costs of securing the sludge. However, if tort litigation is imperfect, or if the mine receives a subsidy from limited liability, the owner of the mine will not bear all the costs if the sludge destroys the factory. The factory owner will bear those costs. Now consider the case where the same individual owns both the mine and the factory. Now the same owner will bear all the costs of both safely securing the sludge and destruction of the factory. The universal owner should want the mine to incur costs to safely store its sludge as long as those costs did not exceed the expected benefits of avoiding damage to the factory. In that case, the universal owner will have incentives to invest in the optimal amount of safety precautions for the sludge, thereby eliminating inefficient inter-firm externalities.

It is sometimes overlooked that universal owners also prefer individual firms to create public goods that positively affect portfolio value for the exact same reasons that they prefer to internalise externalities at a portfolio level. Consider investments in human capital. Individual firms bear all the costs of training the workers, but they will only acquire a small amount of the benefit of the investment in human capital if the worker quits and moves to a different firm. Each firm, therefore, has incentives to push down the amount of training and development that they invest in a worker because of the risk that the worker will quit and transfer. Thus, firms have insufficient incentives to produce the optimal amount of human capital (from the perspective of a diversified stockholder) and the market is likely to deliver a socially sub-optimal amount of employee training and knowledge. However, the universal owner will still enjoy the benefits of the increased human capital at the worker's new firm. From the universal owner's perspective, the human capital asset is merely transferred from one portfolio company to another. Thus, universal owners have incentives to encourage production of public goods that is efficient at the portfolio level rather than at the firm level.

The famous 2019 letter to stockholders from Larry Fink, Chief Executive Officer of the asset manager Blackrock, on corporate purpose and the importance of sustainability may be interpreted as advancing the portfolio maximisation approach.[17] There is no more significant universal owner than the largest asset managers like Blackrock, Vanguard, and State Street. These entities manage funds that have exposure to most

---

[16] Condon (2020), Hansen and Lott (1996).

[17] Larry Fink, 2019 Letter to CEOs: Purpose and Profit, https://www.blackrock.com/corporate/investor-relations/2019-larry-fink-ceo-letter.

major corporations in the world. These owners maximise their financial payoffs if their portfolio companies efficiently manage inter-firm externalities.

A third type of unpriced costs that are relevant to corporate governance in at least some cases are negative externalities that impose uncompensated costs on third parties. These costs are relevant to corporate governance if corporate stockholders have normative commitments to avoid social costs or otherwise have preferences to internalise negative externalities. If stockholders care about, for example, keeping the oceans clean, presumably they would prefer corporations to incur at least some level of costs to avoid polluting the oceans in connection with corporate production.

The seminal work of Professors Hart and Zingales considers stockholders who feel responsible for the social costs of firm activities.[18] They model these stockholders as incorporating social costs into their decisions about corporate governance and policies. The stockholders they consider are the type of people who will incur a cost to pick up their own litter in the park, but they will not incur a cost to go into the park on a weekend and pick up other people's litter. The idea that stockholders only place value on something when they feel responsible for it is non-standard in the economics literature, where preferences are considered to be more stable. Hart and Zingales defend this assumption by pointing to the classic distinction in moral philosophy between acts of omission and commission. This distinction is also embodied in the structure of criminal law. It is considered graver to affirmatively commit a crime or an unethical action rather than merely to stand by and prevent the same wrong from occurring.

Corporations that choose to adhere to the United Nations Guiding Principles on Business and Human Rights are likely to incorporate some form of concern about the negative externalities caused by human rights violations made related to their own activities or those of their suppliers.[19] Similarly, the asset managers directing more than $100 trillion in assets who have signed onto the Principles of Responsible Investment pledge, which focuses on ESG issues broadly, may be expressing concern about taking responsibility for internalising negative corporate externalities.[20]

There is ample evidence that at least some stockholders do feel responsible for negative externalities and that they prefer for corporations to internalise at least some negative externalities. Recent studies have provided survey or experimental evidence suggesting that large majorities of investors have a substantial willingness to pay for sustainable investments and are willing to sacrifice monetary gains to promote social causes,[21] and they are willing to place lower valuations on firms with negative

---

[18] Hart and Zingales (2017).

[19] United Nations Human Rights Office of the High Commissioner (2021), Guiding Principles on Business and Human Rights, https://www.ohchr.org/sites/default/files/documents/publications/gui dingprinciplesbusinesshr_en.pdf.

[20] Principles for Responsible Investment, https://www.unpri.org/about-us/what-are-the-principles-for-responsible-investment.

[21] Scott Hirst et al., How Much Do Investors Care About Social Responsibility? ECGI Law Working Paper No. 674/2023 (Jan. 2023), p. 4.

social externalities[22] or boycott those firms entirely.[23] Some large stockholders are explicit about their normative commitments to advancing social purposes through their business enterprises. For example, Bill Ackman of Pershing Square Capital has claimed that advocating for ESG policies in his portfolio companies is an extension of his philanthropic enterprises.[24]

Unpriced public goods are the final type of unpriced economic effect that may be relevant for corporate governance. Stockholders may be motivated by normative or religious commitments to serving the common good or otherwise creating a benefit enjoyed by third parties rather than the corporation itself.

Many firms with stockholders motivated by religious concerns fit into the category of caring about unpriced public goods. For example, Chick-fil-A foregoes millions of dollars in revenues by closing its stores on Sundays, but, presumably, the relevant corporate decision-makers believe that there is some important non-financial benefit to doing so. Hobby Lobby famously resisted providing its employees insurance that covered birth control, even if this decision might have made Hobby Lobby less competitive in the labour market.[25] This decision was presumably consistent with the relevant corporate decision-maker's understanding of Hobby Lobby's corporate commitment to "operat[e] the company in a manner consistent with Biblical principles."[26]

Indeed, many firms express a mission to serve some public good. In some cases, these firms are primarily owned by a not-for-profit trust or foundation. Bosch, a German manufacturer and technology provider, espouses a corporate purpose of "mak[ing] the community a better place."[27] To effectuate this mission, a non-profit foundation that engages in exclusively charitable purposes owns 94 per cent of Bosch's stock.[28] A not-for-profit foundation that supports scientific research through grants and charitable contributions has voting control and owns 30 per cent of the capital of Carlsberg, the Danish beer company.[29] Patagonia is another for-profit company that is owned and controlled by two non-profits. The holder of voting stock, the Patagonia Purpose Trust, was designed to "ensure that there is never a deviation from the intent of the founder and to facilitate what the company continues to do best: demonstrate as a for-profit business that capitalism can work for the planet."[30]

---

[22] Jean-Francois Bonnefon, Augustin Landier, Parinitha Sastry and David Thesmar, Do Investors Care about Corporate Externalities? Experimental Evidence (Working Paper, TSE, MIT and HEC, 2019), p. 5.

[23] Oliver Hart, David Thesmar, and Luigi Zingales, Private Sanctions (ECGI Finance Working Paper No. 866/2023, 2023), pp. 2 et seq.

[24] Pershing Square Holdings, Pershing Square Holdings, Ltd. 2020 Annual Report, 12–14 (2020).

[25] Burwell v. Hobby Lobby Stores, Inc., 573 U.S. 682 (2014).

[26] Id.

[27] Bosch, Bosch Builds Community, https://www.bosch.us/our-company/social-responsibility/

[28] The Bosch Constitution, https://www.bosch-stiftung.de/en/bosch-constitution.

[29] Carlsberg Group Frequently Asked Questions, Shares and Bonds https://www.carlsberggroup.com/investor-relations/investor-home/faq/#Governance.

[30] Patagonia Works, Patagonia's Next Chapter: Earth Is Now Our Only Stockholder, https://www.patagoniaworks.com/press/2022/9/14/patagonias-next-chapter-earth-is-now-our-only-stockholder.

The holder of nonvoting stock, the Holdfast Collective Trust, is required to use every dollar it receives in distributions to "protect nature and biodiversity, support thriving communities, and fight the environmental crisis."[31] Patagonia has estimated that it would distribute $100 million every year to the Holdfast Collective Trust.[32]

I now return to a discussion of the significance of the mispricing of intangible assets for corporate governance. The idea that stock markets systematically under-price ESG investments in the short term is perhaps the most widely accepted view about the benefits of corporate social responsibility. According to this view, paying greater attention to stakeholders increases profits for stockholders and firm value in the long run.[33] Environmental and social issues are sources of risk or value in the same way that, say, litigation factors and brand reputation are risk factors and value factors. Firms with managers that account for these ESG factors and that embrace a clear corporate purpose and certain corporate social responsibility commitments are posited to be higher-performing financial firms. Under this approach, corporate social responsibility is not pursued as a mechanism to benefit stakeholders, but as a mechanism for increasing firm profits and long-term firm value. As Alex Edmans puts it, "ESG is both extremely important and nothing special."[34] By delivering value to customers, suppliers, and other stakeholders, the firm is rewarded financially in the long run.

Many corporate managers have recently touted the importance of corporate social responsibility efforts for the long-term value of their firms. The Business Roundtable's recent, controversial statement on the purpose of a corporation may be interpreted as expressing concern for the mispricing of intangible assets and risks.[35] While the statement was thick with the language of supporting stakeholders, the statement claimed that it was in service of "the future success of our companies…".[36]

Even more prominently, some large investors have also advanced this enlight-ened stockholder position. The recent stockholder letters from Larry Fink discussed above may also fit this category.[37] Larry Fink's 2022 letter to stockholders clar-ified that "[w]e focus on sustainability not because we're environmentalists, but because we are capitalists and fiduciaries to our clients."[38] Other examples abound. For example, Elliot Management, an activist hedge fund, advocated in connection with a profit-seeking campaign against a company called Evergy that Evergy should make a strong push into sustainability which would drive stockholder value "and

---

[31] Id.

[32] Id.

[33] *See generally* Edmans (2020).

[34] Edmans (2023), p. 3.

[35] Business Roundtable, Statement on the Purpose of a Corporation, https://system.businessroun dtable.org/app/uploads/sites/5/2023/02/WSJ_BRT_POC_Ad.pdf.

[36] Id.

[37] Larry Fink, 2019 Letter to CEOs: Purpose and Profit, https://www.blackrock.com/corporate/inv estor-relations/2019-larry-fink-ceo-letter.

[38] Larry Fink, 2019 Letter to CEOs: The Power of Capitalism, https://www.blackrock.com/corpor ate/investor-relations/2019-larry-fink-ceo-letter.

provide tangible benefits to all of Evergy's key stakeholders, including customers, employees, regulators, and the broader communities its utilities serve."[39]

The mechanisms for both the sources of ESG value and risk and for investor mispricing are not well-established in the academic literature and are worthy of future research. One widely posited mechanism is that a company's brand or reputation creates goodwill that induces favourable treatment from firm patrons. For example, workers who believe in the social mission of a company may be motivated to work harder or to accept a below-market wage. Put another way, the non-financial values of patrons induce them to pay or contribute to the firm in ways that increase firm value. Raising wages for workers above-market wages may introduce an accounting cost in the short term, but it might create an intangible benefit for the corporation by reducing shirking, improving morale, or reducing quits and turnover costs. A reputation for good working conditions, in turn, may attract more talented job applicants. As another example, consumers who object to the environmental externalities created by a corporation's production may boycott the corporation's products and services.

The mechanisms for why sources of ESG value and risks may be mispriced by investors in the short term are also not well-developed and are also worthy of future study. Absent this assumption, firms could just disclose the value of their intangible assets and there would be no disagreement over the value of intangibles because the value would get capitalised into the stock price. One explanation given for this mispricing is that it is difficult for companies to credibly report the value of their intangible assets. Evidence potentially supporting this assumption includes a study showing that the list of the "100 Best Companies to Work for in America" are associated with significantly abnormal returns over their peers over a 28-year period.[40] There are also concerns that accounting rules provide limited information to investors in valuing intangible assets. While investments in tangible assets are capitalised and depreciated, investments in intangible assets, like human capital, are expensed immediately even though they may pay out over a long term and may improve long-term labour employment overall.[41] Moreover, many of the sources of value or risk underlying ESG-related intangible assets reflect unpriced psychological concerns like fairness[42]; trust[43]; social outrage[44]; fair working conditions[45]; and so forth.

The externality perspective offered here provides a related explanation for the difficulty to price intangible assets: many intangible assets share the incentive and

---

[39] Nikitha Sattiraju, "Elliott Puts More Stress on ESG", The Deal (Sept. 28, 2020), available at https://www.thedeal.com/activism/elliott-puts-more-stress-on-esg/.

[40] Edmans (2011), p. 621.

[41] Baruch Lev, Intangibles (working paper, 2018), p. 3.

[42] Akerlof and Yellen (1990), p. 255.

[43] Shleifer & Summers (1988).

[44] Oliver Hart, David Thesmar, & Luigi Zingales, Private Sanctions (ECGI Finance Working Paper No. 866/2023, 2023), pp. 2 et seq.

[45] Edmans (2012).

information properties of externalities. Like public goods, intangible assets have some degree of non-rivalry in use and some degree of limited excludability.[46] First, consider a brand, like Mickey Mouse. The brand is non-rivalrous in the sense that any individual could put the image of Mickey Mouse on coffee mugs, t-shirts, or in a movie. However, Disney can earn profits from the brand because it is able to exclude others from using the brand. Exclusion is accomplished through the exercise of Disney's intellectual property rights to Mickey Mouse.

However, other intangible assets are not excludable, or have limited excludability. When intangible assets are both non-rivalrous and have limited excludability, they create similar incentives and information problems as classic public goods do. Consider, for example, intangible capital in the form of investments in training and knowledge of the workforce. This intangible asset is non-rivalrous in the sense that it can be deployed to multiple production processes and work streams across a firm or different firms. The intangible asset is non-excludable in the sense that the employees generally have the right to quit their job and bring their human capital to a different firm. Given this non-excludability issue, it should not be surprising that there are informational difficulties in valuing intangible assets and in credibly communicating the facts underlying valuation analyses of intangible assets.

4.3   Institutional Challenges Raised by Externality and Public Good Considerations

To date, much of the conversation has been focused on the question of whom should govern the corporation. Stockholders or stakeholders? This chapter suggests that the core focus of the corporate social responsibility and ESG research, policy, and regulatory agenda should instead be: when stockholders prefer to account for unpriced externalities for whatever reason, how should corporate governance and institutional mechanisms be ordered to elicit information about externalities and align incentives to coordinate corporate activity accounting for externalities?

Some legal scholars have characterised the task of advancing profits and purpose simultaneously as an impossible one.[47] True, there are severe information and incentive problems that arise when non-financial objectives are pursued. But this fatalistic statement is too simplistic. The theory of externalities, public goods, and club goods advises that the feasibility of this objective and its costs depend crucially on institution and mechanism design.

Generally, it can be said that social enterprises must incur increased transaction costs to account for externalities in their production activities. In classic general equilibrium theory, an externality is a "missing market."[48] By accounting for externalities, the core task of corporate managers is to identify these missing markets and

---

[46] Crouzet et al. (2022), p. 30.

[47] Bainbridge (2023), pp. 141 et seqq.; Jensen (2001), pp. 310 et seqq.

[48] Arrow (1969).

to make new markets where they are missing. Of course, making markets is costly. It involves information costs and coordination costs. Thus, one way to think of social enterprises is as entrepreneurs that are making markets in negative externalities and public goods.

The core challenge for social enterprises engaged in corporate social responsibility is how to acquire information about economic activity outside the pricing mechanism and how to incentivize managers to optimally respond to such unpriced economic activity.[49] The field of corporate governance is ripe for a research agenda focusing on institutional design that minimises the information and other transaction costs for coalitions of stockholders that seek to coordinate economic activity around non-financial objectives.

Externality theory points to four categories of implementation challenges.

The first challenge relates to information costs about unpriced effects and intangible sources of risk and value. Prices are ordinarily a low-cost source of information about costs and value in economic exchanges, but this information is not provided by markets for externalities and public goods. Externalities, by definition, are economic effects outside the pricing mechanism. Corporations must incur costs to gather information about these costs. For example, the members of a community who have to breathe polluted air emitted by a factory will have good information about the costs that pollution imposes on them, but the managers of the firm will have relatively little information about these costs. Corporate managers may have to survey residents or hire consultants and scientific experts to obtain information about negative externalities. Obtaining good information about the existence and magnitude of firm externalities is the first operational challenge highlighted by externality theory.

The second challenge is coordination costs. Professor Hansmann has argued that stockholders emerged as the "owners" and decision-makers in most corporations because it is efficient for the providers of capital to have this role.[50] In theory, other firm patrons (suppliers, customers, workers, etc.) could be the owners and decision-makers, but it is more costly for these patrons relative to managers to acquire information, monitor managers, and resolve decision-making disputes among stockholders. It is most efficient for these other patrons to have fixed claims on the firm while providers of capital have residual claims. According to Professor Hansmann, the relative cost-savings by coordinating around firm value rather than non-financial objectives is one factor that helps to explain why providers of capital beat out other firm patrons in long-run equilibrium as "owners" of and decision-makers for corporations that it's more costly for these other patrons to resolve disputes amongst themselves and to coordinate decisions.

From this efficiency perspective, it is no coincidence that many of the firms with the most notable commitment to social responsibility are family- or foundation-owned. It is costly for many different stockholders to coordinate around non-financial objectives. Stockholders may have conflicting preferences over social issues. Some

---

[49] For a leading account of governance arrangements that address externality and public goods problems outside of the corporate context, see Ostrom (1990).

[50] Hansmann (1988), pp. 273 et seq.

stockholders may place significant value on environmental issues while others will place more value on efforts to restrict gun violence. Other stockholders will prioritise religious issues. Stockholders will have varying preferences around precisely how much profit they are willing to forego in order to advance social agendas. The decision costs created by intra-stockholder conflicts around preferences are exacerbated by the information uncertainty discussed above about the magnitude and nature of the social costs of firm activities and uncertainty about the social preferences of various stakeholders that affect the firm's reputational capital. Just as limiting membership to a country club can aid in the production of a communal golf course, limiting the association of stockholders is one possible solution in the corporate context. Close corporations, "club" corporations, and other associational mechanisms are potential mechanisms worthy of further study.

The third challenge involves constraining managerial agency costs. When corporate managers have two masters—stockholders and stakeholders—it may be more difficult and costly to monitor corporate managers and align their incentives to advance the dual corporate purposes. When a manager is evaluated based on share price alone, it is relatively easier to evaluate the manager's performance. If the share price goes up (down), it's a rough proxy for good (bad) performance. However, evaluation is relatively more complex when stockholders have to evaluate managers based on share price performance and non-financial objectives. The same information problems that make it difficult to address externality and public goods problems in the first place make it difficult for stockholders to monitor managers who are tasked with addressing these problems. Moreover, opportunistic managers may shirk their duties and blame poor performance on the diversion of resources to address externality problems.

Many legal scholars place decisive weight on this accountability problem, citing it as a reason to support a sole corporate objective of maximising the financial payoffs for stockholders. However, managerial accountability is not the end of the matter even under standard principal-agent models. Some level of agency costs is considered to be constrained efficient. Stockholders only incur monitoring costs up until the point that the benefits of monitoring exceed the costs. Similarly, if managers can use their discretion to improve social welfare by addressing externality or public goods problems, stockholders that place weight on social welfare should still pursue these objectives up to the point where the managerial agency costs exceed the benefits.

The final challenge revealed by the theory of public goods is the challenge of making intangible assets excludable. One of the reasons that markets underproduce public goods is that they are non-excludable or partially excludable. If a firm could exclude others from enjoying the benefits, then the conditions leading to underproduction would disappear. Consider again the underproduction of human capital when employers fear that employees will leave shortly after receiving costly training. Where employers do not have a property right over the public good they produce—such as in the case of human capital—substitutes for excludability might be attempted, including efforts to make employees more satisfied with their job by providing benefits or paying workers an above-market "efficiency" wage.[51]

The excludability problem is the real reason why corporate greenwashing is so pernicious. Companies may invest in corporate social responsibility as a brand strategy in order to build goodwill with customers. However, unlike the Mickey Mouse brand, corporations cannot exclude other firms from adopting the social responsibility brand. For example, numerous coffee companies advertise responsible sourcing of coffee. However, if other firms can costlessly profit from a socially responsible brand through greenwashing, it reduces the returns to investment in "real" social responsibility and pushes down social responsibility investment ex ante.

4.4 Evidence of the Turn to Institutionalising Externality and Public Goods and Its Implications

The practice of marginalising externality considerations in corporate governance is changing. Corporate externalities and the production of public goods are assuming increased importance in legal and privately-ordered institutional frameworks.

This Section surveys arguments and evidence that the institutional turn in corporate law and governance towards addressing the externality and public goods problems has already begun. This section is descriptive. It identifies trends and posits an explanation. It does not take sides on the desirability or optimality of such trends. Indeed, the information problems underlying externality and public goods problems make evaluation extremely difficult. Many of these trends are incipient, imperfect, costly, and susceptible to window-dressing and greenwashing. Whether these trends solidify and expand will depend in part on the ability of institutional and market mechanisms to overcome the severe information frictions and incentive problems created by externality and public goods issues.

One marker of the turn to institutionalisation of concerns about externalities and public goods is simply the reinvigorated and expanded debate over corporate purpose. In 2001, Professors Hansmann and Kraakman famously wrote in their article The End of History for Corporate Law that "[t]here is no longer any serious competitor to the view that corporate law should principally strive to increase long-term stockholder value."[52] Since that time, however, the debate has been far from settled. Corporate purpose is now the hot topic for corporate law scholars and investor conferences around the world.[53] Even as there is scepticism about the role of non-financial activities among corporations, prominent legal scholars are now debating institutional questions such as what is the best organisational form for a purpose-driven business.[54]

---

[51] Shapiro and Stiglitz (1984).

[52] Hansmann and Kraakman (2001), p. 439.

[53] See, e.g., Hart and Zingales (2022); Bainbridge (2023); Bebchuk and Tallarita (2020); Rock (2021a); Rock (2021b).

[54] Rock (2021b) p. 28; Brakman Reiser (2013).

One of the most significant recent legal developments in this area is the establishment of public benefit corporation statutes.[55] Public benefit corporations remove the discomfort that directors of a corporation might have that using corporate resources to internalise negative corporate externalities or to produce corporate public goods might be a violation of their fiduciary duties. Under a stockholder wealth maximisation interpretation of the duty of loyalty, a director might feel uncomfortable with, say, voluntarily installing costly pollution filters on factories. Benefit corporation statutes make it clear that benefit corporation directors may consider the interests of stakeholders that are not stockholders when making corporate decisions.[56]

While more limited, the U.S. Department of Labor's recent final rule would have a similar effect on pension trustees as public benefit corporation statutes have on directors; it removes ambiguity about the ability of plan fiduciaries to consider mispriced or unpriced effects on third parties when such considerations are relevant risk-return factors or otherwise related to the provision of benefits under the relevant pension plan. The rule is another instance of the institutionalisation of externality concerns.[57]

Moreover, there is evidence that entrepreneurs and investors are privately ordering their affairs and choosing institutional frameworks to address the information and incentive problems created by externalities. Recent research shows that public benefit corporations are receiving investments from typical sources of venture capital at significant rates.[58] At least 19 public benefit corporations have undertaken initial public offerings in recent years. Social enterprises of other entity types have also flourished in recent years.[59] Professor Eldar has found that social enterprises perform a "measurement" and "information-gathering" function on commercial features about their patrons, in line with the concerns that externality and public goods problems face severe information asymmetries.[60] And firms are increasingly linking executive compensation to ESG metrics.[61]

Another sign of the institutionalisation of externalities and public goods in privately-ordered corporate governance is the rise of investment funds that utilise ESG factors in their investment decisions. ESG funds provide investors with an institutional mechanism for sorting into ESG-focused investments. One study finds that these funds offer their investors increased ESG exposure and vote differently than non-ESG funds, without sacrificing returns.[62]

The pressure by institutional investors for companies to voluntarily disclose information about their carbon emissions and the SEC's recent proposal to require public

---

[55] *See generally* Fisch and Davidoff Solomon (2021).

[56] *See generally* Winston (2018).

[57] Employee Benefits Security Administration, Department of Labor, Prudence and Loyalty in Selecting Plan Investments and Exercising Stockholder Rights, 87 Fed. Reg. 73,822 (2023).

[58] Michael B. Dorff et al. (2021), p. 147.

[59] Eldar (2020).

[60] Eldar (2017).

[61] See e.g., Bebchuk L, Tallarita R (2022), The Perils and Questionable Promise of ESG-Based Compensation (working paper).

[62] Curtis et al. (2021), p. 393.

companies to disclose certain information about their carbon emissions is another example of the turn towards institutionalisation of externalities. Professor Coffee has described this pressure from institutional investors as an institutional shift to portfolio-wide decision-making, consistent with an increased focus on inter-firm externalities.[63] The SEC's proposal for mandatory disclosure is controversial and it has many problems on multiple facets. As a theoretical matter, the strongest defence of the proposed rule is rooted in externality theory. Global climate change is a risk factor for many public companies. To the extent that externalities from carbon emissions are unpriced, market prices produce relatively little information about the costs of carbon emissions. Mandatory disclosure may help mitigate this information problem, consistent with the traditional justification for mandatory disclosure requirements where markets underproduce information that generates positive externalities.[64]

4.5 Implications of the Externality Perspective for Corporate Governance

What does this externality perspective on corporate purpose imply for the law of corporate purpose? Should corporation law permit, or even encourage, corporations to address externality and public goods decisions? Should corporate governance address these issues? I do not discuss all dimensions of these questions in this chapter. However, the beginning of a discussion can be made based on the externality perspective set forth below. In what follows, I assume that corporation law provides the requisite flexibility, at least through public benefit corporation statutes or corporate constituency statutes. I do not take sides on whether all these considerations generally apply in ordinary corporation law statutes in all jurisdictions.

Most significantly, the externality perspective suggests that corporate social responsibility is less about the concerns raised by critics of stakeholderism—arbitrary distributional decisions by managers—and more about ordinary business judgement. Managerial efforts to address externalities require pricing, valuation, and operational decisions, which are exactly the core decisions that are delegated to managers and stockholder directors through the power-conferring rules of corporation law. Under long-standing doctrines, courts should not second-guess these decisions as long as they are made in an informed, unconflicted, and good-faith manner. Courts and commentators that second-guess market participants risk getting evaluations of business judgments wrong, just as courts and commentators always risk getting it wrong when they second-guess valuation or other routine business decisions.

Some theorists may argue that the problems of managerial agency costs are so severe that corporate law ought to use robust fiduciary duty rules to rein in managerial efforts to address externalities and public goods. However, this one-size-fits-all rule

---

[63] Coffee (2021).

[64] Coffee (1984), p. 722.

clashes with the notion that private ordering is the most efficient way to organise business activity, particularly in the presence of the types of information and incentive problems created by externalities.

True, corporate fiduciaries will sometimes have to use their discretion to balance the costs and benefits of diverting corporate resources to various corporate stakeholders. But concerns about the ability of corporate directors and officers to evaluate trade-offs and make decisions about the types of information and incentive problems raised by externalities are overstated.[65] The reason is because important constraints on managerial attention to externalities and public goods outside of fiduciary duty doctrines apply.

First, there are direct governance limitations. Corporate directors and managers are bound by the law and any restrictions in the corporation's governing documents. Stockholders that do not approve of corporate social responsibility efforts can undertake the necessary corporate governance procedures to amend the governing documents to limit managerial attention to externalities and public goods.

Second, managerial agency costs are constrained by the stockholder franchise and the legal requirement of annual director elections. If managers are inefficiently diverting resources to corporate social responsibility, investors can always vote out the management. In Delaware, powerful doctrines prevent insiders from improperly interfering with the exercise of the stockholder franchise.[66] In cases where the stockholder franchise protection is weak, such as when there is a controlling stockholder, investors receive protection at the time they make their investment decision through securities laws. The securities laws require firms undertaking public offerings of their securities to disclose their governance arrangements, conflicts of interest, and any limitations on or statements about the corporate purpose or activities. Accordingly, public investors should be fully informed about any limitations on the risks of investing in a corporation with a controlling stockholder or other governance restrictions. While oppression of minority stockholders remains an evergreen concern, the need to protect stockholders against misunderstandings about corporate purpose is less persuasive in an age of large institutional investors. Director elections implement corporate governance much more effectively than lawsuits involving allegations of fiduciary duty breaches, and for good reason.

Third, managers face personal and professional constraints that incentivize them to avoid diverting excessive value towards externalities and public goods. Managers know that they will be fired and replaced if the performance of the corporation does not please stockholders. Moreover, in many cases, directors and officers internalize their legal duty to act in an informed manner and in a good faith belief that they are advancing the best interests of the corporation.

Overall, the externality perspective suggests that many corporate responsibility initiatives are market-based or institutional-based efforts to create constrained efficient responses to information frictions and incentive problems or efforts to take

---

[65] Gold and Miller (2018).

[66] *Blasius Indus., Inc. v. Atlas Corp.*, 564 A.2d 651 (Del. Ch. 1988).

responsibility for the corporation's production activities. This is not a blanket statement that all ESG investments are good ones. Strong information frictions make it difficult to assess whether any particular company is successfully addressing externality issues optimally. Instead, it's a statement that certain investments in ESG are best explained as second-best attempts to coordinate economic activity outside the price mechanism with the aim of overcoming information frictions and better aligning incentives for the benefit of the corporations and their stockholders. Delegating to managers the ability to address unpriced externalities and public goods involves the same types of risks to stockholders that they face when they delegate business and operational decisions to managers. In the daily course of business operations, managers have to evaluate value and risk, make trade-offs, and make decisions amidst information uncertainty. These are exactly the types of decisions managers make when they address externality and public goods issues.

Others have argued that externalities should be kept out of corporate governance because they are better addressed by governments. One problem with this view is the race to the bottom for externality regulation enabled by globalisation of supply chains and business problems. But there is a deeper problem with relying on outsourcing externality solutions to governments—investors and market participants have heterogeneous beliefs about the optimal regulation of externalities. Professor Edward Rock has suggested that the argument for cabining externalities and social problems to non-corporate bodies of law is not as strong if there is political dysfunction.[67] While generally persuasive, the argument as made is too general because it overlooks important private-ordering implications. For any given profile of political regulation of externalities and social problems, there will always be investors and market participants who prefer a different regulatory profile. In my view, the state should not, for example, prohibit Chick-Fil-A from closing its stores on Sundays even though such a nationwide ban would never make it through the democratic process into law. The relevant trade-offs ought to be made by individuals privately ordering their affairs, not by statehouses. The externality and public good perspectives argue that corporation law ought to permit them to operate through limited liability entities to carry out business in a way that accords with their normative commitments and their decisions about financial and non-financial value. The challenging part for institution and mechanism design involves figuring out how to coordinate economic activity around objectives outside of the pricing mechanism.

Acknowledgements The research underlying this chapter benefited greatly from the support of Notre Dame Law School and the helpful comments of participants at the Lucerne Conference on Law and Economics and the Brigham Young University Winter Deals Conference. Silvio Pantoja provided excellent research assistance.

---

[67] Rock (2021b).

Bibliography

Akerlof GA, Yellen J (1990) The fair wage-effort hypothesis and unemployment. Quart J Econ 105(2):255–283

Armour J, Enriques L, Hansmann H, Kraakman R (2017) What is corporate law? In: Kraakman R, Armour J, Davies P, Enriques L, Hansmann H, Hertig G, Hopt K, Kanda H, Pargendler M, Ringe WG, Rock E (eds) The anatomy of corporate law, 3d ed, Oxford, 1-28

Arrow KJ (1969) The organization of economic activity: issues pertinent to the choice of market versus non market allocation. In: Congress of the United States, The analysis and evaluation of public expenditures: the PPB system 47

Bainbridge S (2023) The profit motive, Cambridge

Bebchuk LA, Tallarita R (2020) The illusory promise of stakeholder governance. Cornell Law Rev 106:91–178

Blair M, Stout L (1999) A team production theory of corporate law. Univ Virginia Law Rev 85(2):247–328

Blair, M (2012) The stockholder value myth, Oakland

Coase RH (1960) The problem of social cost. J Law Econ 3:1–44

Coffee JC Jr (1984) Market failure and the economic case for a mandatory disclosure system. Virginia Law Rev 70:717–753

Coffee JC Jr (2021) The future of disclosure: ESG, common ownership, and systematic risk, Columbia. Business Law Rev 2:602–650

Condon M (2020) Externalities and the common owner. Univ Washington Law Rev 95(1):1–81

Cornes R, Sandler T (1996) The theory of externalities, public goods and club goods, Cambridge, 2d ed

Crouzet N, Eberly JC, Eisfeldt AL, Papanikoulaou D (2022) The economics of intangible capital. J Econ Perspect 36(3):29–52

Curtis Q, Fisch J, Robertson A (2021) Do ESG funds deliver on their promises? Mich Law Rev 120:393–450

Dorff MB, Hicks J, Solomon SD (2021) The future or fancy? An empirical study of public benefit corporations. Harvard Bus Law Rev 11(13):113–158

Edmans A (2011) Does the stock market fully value intangibles? employee satisfaction and equity prices. J Financ Econ 101:621–640

Edmans A (2012) The link between job satisfaction and firm value, with implications for corporate social responsibility. Acad Manag Perspect 26:1–19

Edmans A (2023) The end of ESG. Financ Manage 52(1):3–17

Edmans A (2020) Grow the pie, Cambridge

Eldar O (2017) The role of social enterprise and hybrid organizations. Columbia Bus Law Rev 2017(1):92–193

Eldar O (2020) Designing business to pursue social goals. Univ Virginia Law Rev 106(4):937–1005

Fisch J, Davidoff Solomon S (2021) The "Value" of a public benefit corporation, in: Pollman E, Thompson RB (eds) research handbook on corporate purpose and personhood, Northhampton, 68–90

Freeman RE (1984) Strategic management: a stakeholder approach, Cambridge

Gold AS, Miller PB (2018) Fiduciary duties in social enterprise, in: Means B, Yockey JW (eds) The Cambridge handbook of social enterprise law, Cambrigde, 321–340

Hansen RG, Lott JR Jr (1996) Externalities and corporate objectives in a world with diversified stockholders/consumers. J Financ Quant Anal 31(1):43–68

Hansmann H (1998) Ownership of the firm journal of law. Econ Organ 4(2):267–304

Hansmann H, Kraakman R (2001) The end of history for corporate law. Georgetown Law J 89:439–468

Hart O, Zingales L (2017) Companies should maximize stockholder welfare not market value. J Law Financ Account 2:247–274

Hart O, Zingales L (2022) The new corporate governance university of Chicago. Bus Law Rev 1:195–216

Heeb F, Kolbel J, Paetzold F, Zeisberger S (2022) Do investors care about impact? Rev Financ Stud 1–51.

Jensen MC (2010) Value maximization, stakeholder theory, and the corporate objective function. Eur Financ Manag 7(3):297–317

Miller P (2021) Corporate personality, purpose, and liability, in: Pollman E, Thompson RB (eds) research handbook on corporate purpose and personhood, Northhampton, 222–239

Ostrom E (1990) Governing the commons: the evolution of institutions for collective action. Cambridge University Press

Reiser DB (2013) Theorizing forms for social enterprise. Emory Law J 62:681–739

Rock E (2021a) For whom is the corporation managed in 2020? The debate over corporate purpose. Bus Lawyer 76:363–395

Rock E (2021b) Research handbook on corporate purpose and personhood. In: Pollman E, Thompson RB (ed) Research handbook on corporate purpose and personhood, Northhampton, 27–46

Shapiro C, Stiglitz JE (1984) Equilibrium unemployment as a worker discipline device. Am Econ Rev 74(3):433–444

Shleifer A, Summers LH (1988) Breach of trust in hostile takeovers, in: Auerbach AJ (ed) corporate takeovers: causes and consequences, Chicago, 33–56

Winston E (2018) Benefit corporations and the separation of benefits and control. Cardozo L Rev 39:1783–1841

Chapter 5
Justice Without Markets?

Salil K. Mehra

Abstract In a series of legal fields, from constitutional law to contracts to competition law, the market mechanism has provided a claimed neutral baseline against which to measure justice. Rights and remedies have been benchmarked against what "the market" would have provided the parties. That neutrality was always something of a legal fiction—economics has long understood that in some contexts, the market mechanism does not deliver a single, stable equilibrium. However, that did not stop the law from fixating on the cases where market mechanisms do deliver a single, stable equilibrium as a baseline proposition from which to measure rights and remedies. The rhetorical strength of the law's adoption of a purported neutral market baseline bolstered classical liberals, Chicago School adherents, and others who favoured the translation of market ordering into the positive legal framework.

5.1 Introduction

In a series of legal fields, from constitutional law to contracts to competition law, the market mechanism has provided a claimed neutral baseline against which to measure justice. Rights and remedies have been benchmarked against what "the market" would have provided the parties. That neutrality was always something of a legal fiction—economics has long understood that in some contexts, the market mechanism does not deliver a single, stable equilibrium. However, that did not stop the law from fixating on the cases where market mechanisms do deliver a single, stable equilibrium as a baseline proposition from which to measure rights and remedies. The rhetorical strength of the law's adoption of a purported neutral market baseline bolstered classical liberals, Chicago School adherents, and others who favoured the translation of market ordering into the positive legal framework.

However, "*the* market"—in the sense of one market for all—is increasingly an illusion. Sure, brick-and-mortar stores, online marketplaces such as Amazon and eBay, and smartphone apps that serve us basics like food, shelter and transportation

S. K. Mehra (✉)
Beasley School of Law, Temple University, Philadelphia, US
e-mail: s.mehra@temple.edu

© The Author(s), under exclusive license to Springer Nature Switzerland AG 2024
K. Mathis and A. Tor (eds.), *Law and Economics of Justice*, Economic Analysis of Law
in European Legal Scholarship 17, https://doi.org/10.1007/978-3-031-56822-0_5

all create an image of transparent and frictionless market-based choices serving consumers.[1] But today, the market mechanism increasingly diverges from the ideal of an open market with low barriers to participation by newcomers. Instead, markets now often operate via siloed algorithms processing massive data troves to automate price-setting and target selected groups—or even individual consumers—for offers.[2] A key challenge for law going forward will be how to assign rights and measure remedies without a simple neutral market baseline.

In particular, the perception that markets can provide a simple neutral baseline has underpinned how the courts administer law to provide parties justice. The development of mainstream economics and the rise of liberalism promoted a widespread acceptance of a central role of this market baseline.[3] However, a longer historical view shows how the acceptance of justice requires widespread acceptance of the market baseline as neutral. Consider the concept of the "just price" rooted in the work of Thomas Aquinas and Albertus Magnus and developed in the canon law centuries before even the antecedents of today's mainstream economics such as Adam Smith.[4] Market order, classical economics and liberalism overcame competition from doctrines such as the just price by providing a neutral baseline that typically provided a uniform price for goods and services in a standard, observable way that could be compared to the laws of the natural and physical world.[5]

The fixation on market neutrality and determinism was always something of a legal fiction—economics has long understood that in some contexts, the market mechanism does not deliver a single, stable equilibrium.[6] Indeed, some would argue that "[s]ingle equilibria are rare in anything more complicated than the toy models used in an introductory microeconomics course."[7] One of the most famous examples of multiple equilibria is George Akerlof's "market for lemons," in which perfect information about used-car quality would lead to a high-level (in terms of price and quantity) equilibrium, but asymmetric information about whether a particular used-car is a low-quality lemon would lead to a low-level equilibrium—a context that should be well-understood by law, given the relevance of warranties to addressing the

---

[1] See generally Evans and Schmalensee (2016), p 51 (arguing, despite title of book, that "[a]lthough the turbocharged platforms [including Uber] are more powerful than earlier ones, they follow the same economic principles as their older siblings").

[2] See, e.g., Federal Trade Commision (2014).

[3] In the U.S. context, Lochner v. New York, 198 U.S. 45 (1905) has been pointed to as exemplifying the adoption of this view. See Sunstein (1987), p. 874 (arguing that by the time of that decision, "[m]arket ordering under the common law was understood to be a part of nature rather than a legal construct, and it formed the baseline from which to measure" whether government intervention affecting the "existing distribution of wealth and entitlements" was permissible).

[4] See de Roover (1958), pp. 423–25 (describing how the concept of the "just price," often fixed by law or determined by common custom, competed with market pricing in the sixteenth century).

[5] See Bork (1978), p. 3 (adopting the characterization of a "crisis" in antitrust and advocating a paradigm shift, in a conscious echo of Kuhn (1962) and how it portrayed crises in physics and chemistry).

[6] See Allingham (1989) (describing situations that will not have unique equilibria).

[7] Woods and Kandel (2002), p. 3.

market failure Akerlof described.[8] However, that did not stop the law from fixating on the cases where market mechanisms do deliver a single, stable equilibrium with uniform prices as a baseline proposition from which to measure rights and remedies. Perhaps this is understandable: a judge would find it difficult to state to a winning litigant that, in the counterfactual world in which they were wrong, there would be multiple possible equilibria leading to different measures of damages, and the judge will simply pick one.

Judges could avoid this dilemma by pointing to a unique solution mirroring the uniform prices seen in traditional markets. But uniform prices in traditional markets are being supplanted—an alternative to the traditional market is rising: the algorithmic matching platform. Of course, matchmaking mechanisms have been used in place of markets in the past, particularly where important non-economic values were at stake or where market allocation was considered repugnant.[9] Think, for example, of the role of nonmarket alternatives in terms of placing babies for adoption or organs for transplant.[10] In the past, the additional cost of using a nonmarket alternative could only be justified in such unusual scenarios where the traditional market mechanism was deemed repugnant—the spectre of auctioning babies to the highest bidder repelled people enough to incur significant costs in building a largely nonmarket system. But increased data collection and processing power has reduced nonmarket alternatives' cost disadvantage and allowed them to expand into other relatively lower-stakes areas, particularly where there are non-price, non-quantity considerations—consider Airbnb (host/guest reputation) and Uber (driver/passenger reputation) versus respective traditional alternatives such as hotels and taxis that did not assess such qualitative concerns to the same degree.[11]

Crucially, algorithmic matching by siloed platforms often does not produce a single, uniform observable price. Instead, a consumer can become "a market of one," receiving targeted, individualised offers at prices that differ from those offered to their counterparts. This Chapter argues that as this indeterminacy and individualization of results and the role of top-down design becomes more widely appreciated, the image of a single, efficient market-driven result will become more contestable. In a series of areas, the increasing doubts about a neutral market baseline will lead to questions about whether justice is being done. Certainly, the move from largely single-price, open markets to a more siloed and targeted form of algorithmic competition will raise questions of fairness and justice in markets for goods and services. But the effects of this transition will likely be broader. The legitimation of "marketplaces for ideas" and "politics as markets" as doing justice will also be impacted. The use of the tools of algorithmic competition to increasingly segment and target individual consumers

---

[8] Akerlof (1970).

[9] See, e.g., Krawiec (2009), p. 4 (describing several examples of repugnant markets, including potential market for human babies); Roth (2008), p. 52 (observing that "[r]epugnance can be a real constraint on markets" and describing matching programs for in-kind kidney exchange and gastroenterologist training placement as palatable alternatives).

[10] See generally Roth (2016).

[11] For an argument that there may be a downside to this type of growth, see Calo (2016).

and citizens will undermine the claim to universalism and equality that markets have enjoyed; as a result, the concept of a neutral market baseline will have reduced power to mark outcomes as "just." Whether this is good, in stripping away the undue power of "the market" as a rhetorical baseline, or bad, by leaving legal results increasingly unpredictable, will depend on how society handles these challenges.

5.2 Justice, Markets and Aggregation Versus Individuation

consumer surplus –

Consumers' surplus is a measure of consumer welfare and is defined as the excess of *social* valuation of a product over the price actually paid. It is measured by the area of a triangle below a demand curve and above the observed price.[12]

consumer welfare –

Consumer welfare refers to the *individual* benefits derived from the consumption of goods and services. In theory, *individual* welfare is defined by an *individual's* own assessment of his/her satisfaction, given prices and income. *Exact measurement of consumer welfare, therefore, requires information about individual preferences.*[13]

We have entered a new era of algorithmic competition, in which mass data collection, enhanced connectivity and powerful computer processing make possible the targeting of individual consumers to degrees and in ways that were not previously possible. For example, arrive in a new country, and your smartphone may betray your location to advertisers who, without direct human intervention, may suddenly notify you of offers on cell phone minutes or rideshares. Sure, a few decades ago they may have done so via airport billboards, but there are important differences now, not least of which is the ability to target you based on individualised information.

At the heart of the new algorithmic competition paradigm is the disaggregation of a uniform market price. Certainly, the phenomenon of price discrimination has been well-known among economists for a long time. As the economist Jules Dupuit observed over 150 years ago, the railway companies of his time made more revenue by charging differently for first-, second- and third-class carriages, but faced a key problem: How to get passengers to voluntarily separate themselves by the willingness to pay. He posited that a railway company might do such things as operate roofless third-class carriages exposed to wind and rain to "hit[…] the poor, not because it wants to hurt them, but to frighten the rich" away from considering cheaper, third-class travel.[14]

Algorithmic competition makes the task of separation and segmentation of consumers that Dupuit identified potentially much less arduous for producers. Increasingly, a producing firm can use computer power to sift through troves of data on the behaviour of individual consumers to identify various characteristics

---

[12] OECD (2008) (emphasis added).

[13] OECD (2008) (emphasis added).

[14] Beard and Ekelund Jr (1991), pp. 1156–58.

about them, including consumers' willingness to pay. Certainly, there are positives to this development. If we consider the airport example a couple of paragraphs above, there was some waste of advertising expenditure in the past when billboards advertised taxis or ridesharing, since many passengers, such as those returning to their hometown, might not have needed them. Moreover, sellers and advertisers can observe consumer behaviour after the consumer sees an online ad, and then adjust their ad spending; such observational data was tougher to come by before algorithmic competition and targeted ads. As John Wanamaker, the founder of a large U.S. department store chain said of offline, brick-and-mortar ads in an earlier era: "I know half the money I spend on advertising is wasted, but can never find out which half."[15] The tools of algorithmic competition increasingly make it possible for John Wanamaker's successors to know which half of ad spending they are wasting, and to cut that spending back.

Over the past few decades, competition law worldwide has claimed to have become focused on consumer welfare as its guiding principle. As the definition at the start of this section points out, consumer welfare is about the *individual* benefit a consumer receives. But, in fact, competition law has used consumer *surplus* as a proxy for consumer *welfare*, even though consumer surplus aggregates the benefits to consumers, putting aside their individuality. Consumer surplus as a measure of consumer welfare has long had a powerful advantage: It was the only practicable proxy, and so the natural starting point for a standard.

Aggregation made sense as an administratively easier way to deal with consumers in open, largely single-priced markets. If all consumers were treated the same, from the perspective of rough justice, it made sense to aggregate them. But we live in an era in which highly granular data about individual consumers' choices are available to producer firms for purchase. Indeed, data about the choices consumers make is no longer limited to the revealed preference of price and quantity purchased—increasingly we even have data about the choices consumers *did not* make—something previously unimaginable.

The increasing ability to target individual consumers raises questions about the law's use of a neutral market baseline to avoid hard questions of justice and just prices. These questions come up routinely in calculating remedies, in such varied contexts as competition law, consumer fraud, contracts, and torts. But without a generalised price available to all, as in a traditional open marketplace, can law's neutral market baseline still answer disquieting questions about justice and just prices? The fragmentation of markets by individual targeting may make it increasingly difficult for the law to convince individual citizens that justice is being done for them.

---

[15] Mayer (1958), p. 259.

5.3 Justice After the "Marketplace of Ideas" Closes

The phrase "marketplace of ideas" first appeared in a 1953 U.S. Supreme Court opinion by Justice William O. Douglas.[16] The concept of different ideas competing like varied goods hawked by rival sellers in a marketplace is no doubt older than the mid-twentieth century. But it has taken on a new urgency in our era of algorithmically-curated social media feeds.

A generation ago, the rise of the Internet led to concerns about whether the tendency of people to listen and speak only to the like-minded and filter out others was compatible with the healthy operation of a republican form of government.[17] But during the first years of this century, this concern could be answered with an appeal to the logic of markets and consumer choice—to the extent that citizens "clicked" on the webpage of a news source or online community that shared their beliefs, that was their decision in the marketplace of ideas.

This rationalization of the "filter bubble" via consumer choice has crumbled.[18] As people delegated more of their online choices to what, for example, Google served them, it became clear that they were not so much actively choosing information from a particular viewpoint as entering Google's own filter bubble. If anything, this problem has been accentuated by the rise of social media over the past decade.

Perhaps nothing encapsulates the concern about the decline of the "marketplace of ideas" and the rise of "algorithmically-curated" feeds in recent years than the story of Twitter. Before its takeover by Elon Musk, and even before it banned then-President Donald Trump, it had become integral, perhaps too much so, to public debate in the U.S. Critics worried that journalists had become too reliant on Twitter, making it a de facto gatekeeper of the news agenda and allowable public opinion.[19]

Prior to its acquisition by Musk, American conservatives raised concerns that Twitter was actively suppressing their expression. However, they had relatively little access to any relevant evidence. After all, Twitter was a private company, and the process by which its algorithms chose "tweets" to promote was proprietary. Despite its private existence, Twitter has had a powerful impact on the public sphere, most prominently via the platform it provided Trump in the run-up to the 2016 election.[20]

After Musk acquired Twitter, a series of disclosures of internal communications have made it clear that there were active decisions to suppress some viewpoints and highlight others.[21] Because of the anti-conservative trends in these decisions, these disclosures have fed an uncharacteristic desire among American conservatives to regulate Twitter and other private companies, based on the rationale that they function

---

[16] United States v. Rumely, 345 U.S. 41, 56 (1953).

[17] Sunstein (2001).

[18] Pariser (2011).

[19] Ingram (2018).

[20] Barbaro (2015) (describing, more than a year before the 2016 presidential election, how Trump "ha[d] mastered Twitter in a way no candidate for president ever has").

[21] Peters (2022).

as gateways to political discourse.[22] While it is unclear yet whether these moves will succeed, they underline the decline of the "marketplace of ideas" concept—whether due to tipping points, network effects, or other causes, the belief that counter speech on a different private platform can suffice to air opposing viewpoints seems to have waned. The image of an open marketplace in which all may bring their ideas much as they might bring goods for sale seems to have become obsolete; the combination of the Internet and algorithmically curated feeds seems to have convinced observers that targeting readers or viewers individually via a dominant platform is now the sole realistic avenue for political speech.

This will create a significant problem: What balance of prioritised speech will do justice? Much as an open, single-priced market for goods obviates questions of what is a "just" price, faith in the concept of a marketplace of ideas required not much more than content-neutral access to that marketplace. If we replace our belief in a marketplace of ideas with one that sees political discourse guided by the algorithmically-curated feeds dispensed to individual users by monopolists or oligopolists, regulation may need to more invasively scrutinise and dictate the content of those feeds. Content-based regulation opens up a host of thorny questions, not least of which, who will do the regulation—notably the Biden Administration's attempt to create a "Disinformation Governance Board" was put on hold after only three weeks.[23] It remains to be seen whether that is a stable, tenable outcome, or instead, the opening of a new conflict.

5.4   Justice, and Politics as Markets?

Looking at the politics in pluralist, liberal democratic systems through the framework of markets has a long pedigree.[24] Indeed, leading U.S. constitutional law scholars have often deploy the metaphor of "politics as markets"—extending the market metaphor from such fields as securities law and corporate governance to that of politics and its public law background.[25] The market paradigm helps to justify the outcomes, political arrangements, and legal framework by grounding it in the notion of bottom-up choice, substituting voters for consumers.

The market analogy for politics was imperfect even before the development of technologies that gave rise to algorithmic competition. As long ago as 1969, U.S. Supreme Court Justice John Harlan II foresaw that in the then near future:

> A computer may grind out district lines which can totally frustrate the popular will on an overwhelming number of critical issues. The legislature must do more than satisfy one man

---

[22] Serwer (2022).

[23] Lorenz (2022).

[24] Lindblom (1977).

[25] Issacharoff and Pildes (1998).

one vote; it must create a structure which will in fact as well as theory be responsive to the sentiments of the community.[26]

That future has long since come to pass. Starting roughly in the 1990s, access to modern computer power plus highly granular statistics about the voting patterns of residents at the block-by-block level made possible extreme partisan gerrymanders—that is, the strategic design of geographic voting districts to ensure that a particular political party will retain that legislative seat.[27] While voters still choose at the ballot box, those voters have been pre-selected by politicians during the decennial redistricting process.

The problem of partisan gerrymandering has drawn significant attention from the Supreme Court and its observers over the past two decades.[28] Moreover, it can undercut the market metaphor and the legitimacy it provides to the political process. If voters no longer have the same degree of power to choose politicians as they have had to choose goods and services, they may lose trust in the political system and the politicians who run it.

However, there is another side to the political system that also deserves attention, particularly in light of the tools of algorithmic competition. Politicians, once elected, provide benefits to their constituents, generally paid for out of tax revenue. Though a variety of benefits, such as public education, social security and health care, may be provided universally or via neutral screening tests, that outcome is not inevitable; indeed, before the mid-twentieth century rise of the U.S. federal administrative state, some public benefits were parcelled out at an individual level via urban political machines that had an almost feudal quality in terms of rewarding loyalty and punishing dissent.[29]

5.4.1 Political Gerrymandering of Benefits with Postal Codes?

Starting roughly with the onset of the COVID-19 pandemic, U.S. politicians, particularly at the state and municipal level, have begun to use geographic districts to target various public benefits, including priority for COVID vaccinations and admission to top public high schools.[30] In particular, politicians with access to highly detailed data about their voters and residents have seized upon using ZIP codes—the U.S.'s version

---

[26] Wells v. Rockefeller, 394 U.S. 542, 551 (1969) (Harlan, J. dissenting).

[27] Barnes (1989).

[28] See, e.g., Issacharoff (2002), p. 600 (stating that partisan gerrymandering reduces politicians "accountability to shifting voter preferences"); Levinson and Sachs (2015), pp. 416–18 (arguing that gerrymandering can shift and determine political outcomes).

[29] Erie (1988).

[30] Milkman (2022) (reporting results of a vaccine lottery administered by the City of Philadelphia for selected ZIP codes); Sargent v. Sch. Dist. of Phila., 2022 U.S. Dist. LEXIS 140262 (E.D. Pa. 2022) (challenging ZIP code-based allocation of public high school admission).

of postal codes—to parcel out public benefits. Arguably, ZIP codes have no special relevance in and of themselves. They are the product of a mid-twentieth century "across-the-board, interlocking effort" by the U.S. postal service to improve mail service.[31] In 1962, the Advisory Board of the Post Office Department recommended the development of a nationwide address coding system, as a way to manage the increased volume without adding employees.[32] After considering several potential programs, the Department announced on November 28, 1962[33] that the ZIP (Zoning Improvement Plan) code would launch on July 1, 1963.[34] By consolidating regional, city and state information into a five-digit code, the new system would eliminate the need for clerks to memorise the names and locations of Post Offices, thus addressing labour cost concerns.[35] Further, by reducing steps in the sorting process, the ZIP code was intended to increase delivery speed and reduce incorrect deliveries.[36]

The ZIP code was an essential component of two key strategies within the Post Office Department's Nationwide Improved Mail Service program (NIMS).[37] First, the ZIP code was part of a larger plan to automate mail sorting. The Postmaster General stated in the 1963 Annual Report that the ZIP Code's "ultimate fruition [would] not be realised until the optical scanner, [then] under development, [was] operational."[38] Second, the ZIP Code further increased efficiency by fostering public cooperation in the mail-handling process. Bulk mailers would be able to sort and

---

[31] United States Post Office (1963), p. 7 ("Major new elements of this across-the board, interlocking effort to provide Nationwide Improved Mail Service (NIMS) were launched in fiscal 1963 to accelerate the collection and delivery of business mail (ABCD) and to reduce the number of steps in mail-handling procedures through the use of ZIP Code numbers.").

[32] POSTAL SERVICE HISTORY, *supra* note 1, at 56 ("To cope with rising mail volumes, the Department needed to sort and distribute mail more efficiently. Adding more and more employees to sort ever-increasing volumes of mail was not an option. Costs aside, there was nowhere to put them, as many large postal facilities were already cramped."); *see also id.* at 7-8 ("ZIP Code was designed to help the Department efficiently handle the rapidly mounting mail volume without a correspondingly large increase in manpower—to contain costs and forestall the day higher postage rates might become necessary."); *Graph Presentation of the ZIP Code System, supra* note 8, at 60 ("Because of the fantastic rate of growth in this country, it is absolutely essential that we devise improved methods of processing mail.").

[33] See Hahn (1962) (presentation slides that accompanied November 1962 announcement of the ZIP code by Postmaster General Day); see also Day (1962).

[34] United States Post Office (1963), p. 7; POSTAL SERVICE HISTORY, *supra* note 1, at 56.
    POSTAL SERVICE HISTORY, *supra* note 1, at 57.
    United States Post Office (1963), p. 8.

[35] POSTAL SERVICE HISTORY, *supra* note 1, at 57.

[36] United States Post Office (1963), p. 8.

[37] See United States Post Office (1963), p. at 7 ("Major new elements of this across-the-board, interlocking effort to provide Nationwide Improved Mail Service (NIMS) were launched in fiscal year 1963 to accelerate the collection and delivery of business mail (ABCD) and to reduce the number of steps in mail-handling procedures through the use of ZIP Code numbers.").

[38] Id.

bundle their own mailings by ZIP Code and dispatch them directly to mail distri-bution centres, "thus bypassing as many as six handling steps between deposit and delivery."[39]

That said, the ZIP continued to develop, with the transition to a nine-digit ZIP code recommended by a five-member task force investigating ways to reduce Postal Service costs.[40] The move from five to nine digits increased the number of ZIP codes from forty thousand to twenty-one million[41] and facilitated a significant expansion of machine-automated mail sorting.[42] This increased automation was intended to reduce mail processing costs and "contribute to postage rate stability."[43] The additional digits allow mail to be directed to a specific mail carrier rather than to the delivery office where it would need to be manually sorted.[44] Optical character reading (OCR) equipment reads the nine-digit code, translates it into a bar code, and then prints that code onto the envelope.[45] Using the printed barcodes, automated barcode sorters then sort the envelopes all the way to the carrier level.[46]

The sixth and seventh digits ZIP code digits correspond to a "sector", which may be as large as a geographic area or as small as a single block, apartment building, or office building.[47] It is important to note that sectors are not uniform in their geographic area, and commercial sectors are much smaller than residential sectors.[48] The eighth and ninth digits correspond to a segment within a sector.[49] Segments designate a delivery point, and like sectors, segments vary substantially in their geographic scope. They can be as large as a street or as small as a cluster of mailboxes.[50]

---

[39] Id. at 8.

[40] Karp (1986).

[41] Karp (1986).

[42] STATUS REPORT TO THE CONGRESS, *supra* note 31, at 64.

[43] Id.; see also Hirsch (1982), p. 26 (reporting on comments of Postmaster General William F. Bolger at the National Postal Forum).

[44] Id.; see also OFFICE OF TECHNOLOGY ASSESSMENT, *supra* note 33, at 2 ("Use of ZIP + 4 allows USPS to sort letters down to the city block, building, or post office box, whereas the 5-digit ZIP code permits sorting only to the level of a smaller post office zone or a geographical area within a larger post office zone.").

[45] OFFICE OF TECHNOLOGY ASSESSMENT, *supra* note 33, at 2.

[46] Id.

[47] STATUS REPORT TO THE CONGRESS, *supra* note 31, at 53; *see also* POSTAL **Service** HISTORY, *supra* note 1, at 68 ("The sixth and seventh digits denoted a delivery sector: several blocks, a group of streets, a group of Post Office boxes, several office buildings, a single high-rise office building, a large apartment building, or a small geographic area.").

[48] STATUS REPORT TO THE CONGRESS, *supra* note 31, at 53.

[49] Id. at 52–53 (detailed explanation and depiction of the ZIP + 4 geographic scheme).

[50] Id. at 54 ("A segment—the last two digits of the add-on code—can be one side of a street between intersections; both sides of a street, including cul-de-sacs; a company or building; a floor or group of floors within a building; a cluster of mailboxes; sections of post office boxes; or any other designated delivery point.").

5.4.2 Public Benefit Targeting and the Risk of Algorithmic Competition

In some cases, politicians may have resorted to using ZIP codes to target public benefits with good intentions, for example, by prioritising residents of a ZIP code with high levels of COVID-19 infection for vaccination. But as the discussion above suggested, ZIP codes were created for a very different purpose than public benefit targeting, and whether they serve the latter purpose well remains to be seen. Moreover, the most granular form of the ZIP code, the 9-digit version, allows for the identification of very small numbers of voters or residents contained within the corresponding geographic sector.

The acceptance of ZIP-code or similar forms of benefit targeting could lead to negative consequences. Much like partisan gerrymandering, they can help to break the bond between benefits to citizens and citizens' power via their voting preferences—politicians could choose only to distribute benefits preferentially to sufficient identifiable voters to gain re-election, reducing politics' sensitivity of benefits to other voters' choices. While politicians may have wanted to do this in the past, in practice it would have been difficult to identify voters and parcel benefits so finely. However, recent technological advances, including the tools of algorithmic competition, may make this type of "price discrimination" on the public benefit side more feasible.

Consider the possibility of politicians or a government that employs the tools of algorithmic competition, either in-house or by hiring a consultant. Drawing on aggregated data from residents' smartphones and other connected devices, political actors may use computing power to glean whose re-election-clinching support may be won most cost-effectively by providing those voters—and possibly not others—public benefits. Of course, we may expect pushback in the form of arguments about horizontal fairness. That said, such arguments may face an uphill battle where existing norms of equal protection do not hinge on geographic district-based arguments. Additionally, uncovering this kind of differential treatment may be difficult given the well-known "black box" problem inherent to some algorithmic processes.[51] In sum, the marriage of ZIP code or other benefit targeting with the tools of algorithmic competition raises concerns that bear watching.

5.5 Conclusion

The phenomena described above, involving the disaggregation of markets for goods and services, the marketplace of ideas, and political markets, may progress. If they do, it is possible that consumers and citizens may react negatively. Certainly, this was a potential Arthur Pigou foresaw a century ago in the context of price discrimination: "Since a hostile public opinion might lead to legislative intervention, [the seller's]

---

[51] Pasquale (2016).

choice must not be such as to outrage the popular sense of justice."[52] As the techniques of algorithmic competition develop the potential for, effectively, fine-tuning price discrimination down to the individual level, the law's role should be to channel potential outrage into useful responses.

References

Abbott A (2018) Antitrust and the winner-take-all-economy, Legal Memorandum 224:1–12, https://www.heritage.org/government-regulation/report/antitrust-and-the-winner-take-all-economy

Akerlof GA (1970) The market for 'lemons': quality uncertainty and the market mechanism, Quarterly J of Econ 84(3):488–500

Alexis A (2017) Hipster antitrust' comes under senate spotlight, Bloomberg Law, https://www.bna.com/hipster-antitrust-comes-n73014473208/

Allingham M (1989) Uniqueness of equilibrium. In: Eatwell J, Milgate M, Newman P (eds), General equilibrium: the new Palgrave, New York, pp. 324–327

Averitt NW, Lande RH (2007) Using the 'consumer choice' approach to antitrust law, Antitrust LJ 74:175–264

Azar J, Schmalz MC, Tecu I (2018) Anticompetitive effects of common ownership, J Fin 73(4):1513–1565

Barbaro M (2015) Pithy, mean and powerful: how Donald Trump mastered twitter for 2016, NY Times, https://www.nytimes.com/2015/10/06/us/politics/donald-trump-twitter-use-campaign-2016.html

Barnes JA (1989) Drawing the lines, Natl J 21:787–797

Beard TR, Ekelund RB Jr (1991) Quality choice and price discrimination: a note on Dupuit's conjecture, Southern Econ J 57:1155–1163

Bork R (1978) The antitrust paradox, New York

Calo R (2016) Privacy and markets: a love story, L Rev 91:649–690

Channick R (2016) Airlines doing better, But Passnegers are More Unhappy, Chicago Tribune, https://www.chicagotribune.com/business/ct-airline-performance-0405-biz-20160404-story.html

Cohen P, Hahn R, Hall J, Levitt S, Metcalfe R (2016) Using big data to estimate consumer surplus: the case of uber, NBER Working Paper No. 22627, http://www.nber.org/papers/w22627.

Crane D (2007) Antitrust modesty, Cambridge

Data Brokers: A Call for Transparency and Accountability (2014) Federal Trade Commission, https://www.ftc.gov/system/files/documents/reports/data-brokers-call-transparency-accountability-report-federal-trade-commission-may-2014/140527databrokerreport.pdf

Day JE (1962) Announcement of inauguration by PMG Day, November 1962, in: Bentley Hahn H (ed) Personal Papers, Postal Files, 1953–1983 (HBHPP-001–022), John F. Kennedy Presidential Library and Museum, Boston, http://www.jfklibrary.org/Asset-Viewer/Archives/HBHPP-001-022.aspx

Dayen D (2017) This Budding Movement Wants to Smash Monopolies, The Nation, https://www.thenation.com/article/archive/this-budding-movement-wants-to-smash-monopolies/

de Roover R (1958) The concept of the just price: theory and economic policy, J Econ Hist 18:418–434

Edlin A, Haw R (2013) Cartels by another name: should licensed occupations face antitrust scrutiny?, U Penn L Rev 162:1093–1164

Elhauge E (2016) Horizontal shareholding, Harv L Rev 129:1267–1317

---

[52] Pigou (1924), p. 250.

Erie S (1988) Rainbow's end: Irish–Americans and the dilemmas of urban machine politics, 1840–1985

Evans DS, Schmalensee R (2016) Matchmakers: the new economics of multisided platforms, Harv Bus Rev Press

First H, Waller SW (2013) Antitrust's democracy deficit, Fordham L Rev 81:2543–2574

Ginsburg D H, Klovers K (2018) Common sense about common ownership, Concurrences Rev No. 2

Hahn HB (1962) ZIP Code marketing and publications: presentation slides, in: Bentley Hahn H (ed) Personal Papers, Postal Files, 1953–1983 (HBHPP-001–028), Archives of the John F Kennedy Presidential Library and Museum, Boston, http://www.jfklibrary.org/Asset-Viewer/Archives/HBHPP-001-028.aspx

Hirsch P (1982) ZIP+4 to Sharply reduce Bulk Mailer's costs, Computerworld, https://books.google.com/books?id=dpKltAUoYAAC&lpg=PA26&dq=four%20digit%20ZIP%20code%20bolger%201983&pg=PA26#v=onepage&q=four%20digit%20ZIP%20code%20bolger%201983&f=false

Hovenkamp H (2009) United States competition policy in crisis 1890–1955, Minnesota L Rev 94:311–367

Hovenkamp H (2017) Appraising merger efficiencies, George Mason L Rev 24:703–741

Hovenkamp H (2018) Whatever did happen to the antitrust movement?, L Rev 93:583–637

Hovenkamp H (2016) Federal antitrust policy, St. Paul

Hyman D, Kovacic W (2013) Institutional design, agency life cycle, and the goals of competition law, Fordham L Rev 81:2163–2174

Ingram M (2018) Do journalists pay too much attention to Twitter?, Colum J Rev, https://www.cjr.org/the_media_today/journalists-on-twitter-study.php

Issacharoff S (2002) Gerrymandering and political cartels, Harv L Rev 116:593–648

Issacharoff S, Pildes RH (1998) Politics as markets: partisan lockups of the democratic process, Stan. L Rev 50:643–717

Jacobs M, Devlin A (2010) Antitrust error, William and Mary L Rev 52:75–132

Kaplow L (2012) On the choice of welfare standards in competition law, in: Zimmer D (ed), Goals of competition law, Cheltenham, pp. 3–26

Karp J (1986) Nine-Digit ZIP code: winning number or technological Turkey, Wash Post, https://www.washingtonpost.com/archive/politics/1986/07/15/nine-digit-zip-code-winning-number-or-technological-turkey/d90fd9dc-0ff1-4b13-ad1a-da803c13f7bc/

Khan L (2017) Amazon's antitrust paradox, Yale L J 126:710–805

Khan L (forthcoming) The separation of platforms and commerce, Columbia L Rev 119

Koenig B (2019) FTC's Wilson sees pluses of 'total welfare' antitrust standard, Law360, https://www.law360.com/articles/1129690/ftc-s-wilson-sees-pluses-of-total-welfare-antitrust-standard

Krawiec K (2009) Show Me the money: making markets in forbidden exchange, Law and Contemp Probs 72:1–14

Kuhn T (1962) The structure of scientific revolutions, Chicago

Lande RH (1983) Wealth transfers as the original and primary concern of antitrust: the efficiency interpretation, Hastings LJ 34:65–151

Levinson D, Sachs BI (2015) Political entrenchment and public law, Yale LJ 125:400–482

Lindblom CE (1977) Politics and markets: the world's political economic systems, New York

Lorenz T (2022) How the Biden administration let right-wing attacks derail its disinformation efforts, Wash Post, https://www.washingtonpost.com/technology/2022/05/18/disinformation-board-dhs-nina-jankowicz/

Lynn BC (2010) Cornered: the new monopoly capitalism and the economics of destruction, John Wiley and Sons, Hoboken

Mayer M (1958) Madison Avenue U.S.A., Los Angeles

Mellor W, Carpenter DM II (2016) Bottleneckers: gaming the government for power and private profit, New York

Milkman KL et al (2022) A citywide experiment testing the impact of geographically targeted, high-pay-off vaccine lotteries, Nature Hum Behav 6:1515–1524

Miller A (2014) What do we worry about when we worry about price discrimination?, J Tech L 19:41–104

Odlyzko AM (2003) Privacy economics, and price discrimination on the internet, in: Sadeh N (ed) ICEC2003: fifth international conference on electronic commerce, Pittsburgh, pp. 355–366

OECD (2008) OECD Glossary of statistical terms, OECD Publishing, Paris https://doi.org/10.1787/9789264055087-en

Orbach B (2013) How antitrust lost its goal, Fordham L Rev 81:2253–2277

Pariser E (2011) The filter bubble: how the new personalized web is changing what we read and how we think, New York

Pasquale F (2016) The black box society: the secret algorithms that control money and information, Cambridge

Peters J (2022) The finale of the great internet grievance wars is here, Slate, https://slate.com/technology/2022/12/elon-musk-twitter-files-bari-weiss-matt-taibbi-shadowbanning.html

Pigou AC (1924) The economics of welfare, London

Posner E, Weyl G, Naidu S (2018) Antitrust remedies for labor market power, Harv L Rev 132:536–601

Roth A (2008) Repugnance as a constraint on markets, J Econ Persp 21:37–58

Roth A (2016) Who gets what—and why: the new economics of matchmaking and market design, New York

Schnurman M (2018) How much harm is too much? The U.S. and AT&T Spar over Time Warner Merger, Dallas News, https://www.dallasnews.com/business/att/2018/03/09/much-harm-much-us-att-spar-time-warner-merger

Serwer A (2022) Why conservatives invented a 'right to post', The Atlantic,https://www.theatlantic.com/ideas/archive/2022/12/legal-right-to-post-free-speech-social-media/672406/

Slesnick DT (2018) Consumer surplus, in: Vernengo M, Caldentey EP, Rosser Jr BJ (eds) The new Palgrave dictionary of economics, 2nd edn., London, https://doi.org/10.1057/978-1-349-95121-5_626-2

Stevens M (2017) Chicago airport security officers to shed 'Police' Label After United Airlines Dragging Episode, NY Times, https://www.nytimes.com/2017/07/12/us/united-chicago-airport-security.html

Stigler GJ (1971) The theory of economic regulation, Bell J Econ and Mgmt Sci 2:3–21

Sunstein CR (1987) Lochner's Legacy, Colum L Rev 87:873–919

Sunstein CR (2002) Republic.com, Princeton

Tepper J, Hearn D (2019) The myth of capitalism: monopolies and the death of competition, Hoboken

Tepper J (2019) Why regulators went soft on monopolies, The Am Conservative, https://www.theamericanconservative.com/articles/why-the-regulators-went-soft-on-monopolies/

Tor A (2019) Justifying competition law in the face of consumers' bounded rationality, in: Mathis K, Tor A (eds) New developments in competition law and economics, Switzerland, pp. 3–26

Trump Antitrust Policy After One Year (2018) The heritage foundation, https://www.heritage.org/crime-and-justice/event/trump-antitrust-policy-after-one-year

United Mileage Plus (Pre-Merger), Flyertalk Forums, https://www.flyertalk.com/forum/united-mileage-plus-pre-merger-504/

United States Post Office (1963) Improving post office operations and services, in: Annual report of the postmaster general, US Govt, Washington, pp. 7–26, https://babel.hathitrust.org/cgi/pt?id=mdp.39015079861178&view=1up&seq=669&skin=2021&q1=1963

Williamson O (1968) Economics as an antitrust defense: the welfare tradeoffs, Am Econ Rev 58:18–36

Wittgenstein L (1958) Philosophical investigations, Oxford

Woods H, Kandel AV (2002) Market transformation and multiple equilibria, in: Proceedings of the American council for an energy-efficient economy, https://www.aceee.org/files/proceedings/2002/data/papers/SS02_Panel6_Paper26.pdf

Wright JD, Ginsburg D (2013) The goals of antitrust: welfare Trumps choice, Fordham L Rev 81:2405–2423

Wright JD, Klick J, Rybnicek JM, Dorsey E (2019) Requiem for a paradox: the dubious rise and inevitable fall of hipster antitrust, Az St LJ 51:293–369

Wu T (2018) The curse of bigness: antitrust in the new gilded age, New York

Part II
Efficiency

Chapter 6
Beyond Justice Versus Efficiency: Reconciling Law and Economics Approaches to Fairness

Behrang Kianzad

Abstract Recent years have seen the dominance of neoclassical, marginalist and welfarist schools of Competition Law and Economics being challenged more vigorously than ever [See two major collecting works in: Fennell and McAdams (2013) and Cappelen and Tungodden (2019)]. Although the core assumptions of the neoclassical school regarding overt reliance on rationality and efficiency ever since the inception of the school have been target of much criticism [Flynn (December 1988), pp. 713–43 and Dworkin (1980), pp. 191–226], the latest decades of both research and real life developments have reinvigorated the criticim [An indication is the title of the latest Global Competition Forum, themed "Time for a Reset?", see here: http://www.oecd.org/competition/globalforum/GFC-2020-agenda-en.pdf, accessed 2020-12-07]. Nowhere is the influence of neoclassical and marginalist economic approaches, in turn underscored by Legal Realism and Legal Positivist approaches, more prevalent, than laws governing economic activities, chief among them antitrust law and policy. The famous "Antitrust Revolution" in the late 70s by the likes of Robert Bork (1978) and Richard Posner (2014) still today dominates mainstream law and economics of not only US Antitrust law, but also of European [Bartalevich (2016), pp. 267–83] and global competition law [Stiglitz (2017)]. Leaving behind decades long (and one would say, centuries long) fairness-related approaches to law and economics [Watkins (1922)] (which in this article will be dubbed Kantian although the core philosophy predates Kant by eons), we now also note insights in bounded rationality [Piron and Fernandez (1995)], which further underscore the previous theoretical and philosophical approaches. Using the legal prohibition against "unfair pricing" as an optimal proxy [See e.g. Treaty on the Functioning of the European Union Article 102a, prohibiting unfair pricing imposed by a dominant undertaking capable of affecting trade between member states or in substantial part of the Union; See also Kianzad and Minssen (2018), pp. 133–48], the present article juxtaposes the neoclassical and marginalist approaches to this area of political economy, by way of using Kantian ethics and Kantian legal philosophy to demonstrate the inaptness of the so-called mainstream Law and Economics approaches to

B. Kianzad (✉)
Department of Business Law, Lund University, Lund, Sweden
e-mail: behrang.kianzad@har.lu.se

the matter "fairness in law and economics". A return to Kantian philosophy of law [White (2019), pp. 53–76] and a balanced approach between law and economics disciplines, more so regarding laws governing economic activity, is forwarded, making the case that whether one is Kantian or Utilitarian in the normative will invariably affect the substantive positive legal and economic analysis. This fact is independent of the claims to "rationality", "objectivity" or "humanity" and "divinity" made by either approach. Following the introduction framing the "paradox" regarding the return of Kantian, fairness-based approaches to law and economics, the second section depicts the Posnerian attack on Kant construed alongside Wealth Maximisation as an optimal goal of law and economics. The third section describes the supposed division between fairness and welfare, or efficiency, as an optimal goal of law and economics. The fourth section in turn constructs the Kantian comeback. The fifth section concludes.

6.1 Introduction—Neoclassical Economics and Positivist Law Against Kantian Ethics

As described by Holler and Leroch "According to conventional wisdom, "everybody knows what is just, nobody knows what is efficient." Obviously, this "everybody" here does not refer to economists. Economists know about efficiency. Yet, economists have problems with getting hold of justice."[1]

The bulk of the Neoclassical and Welfarist criticism against fairness considerations in legal and economic policy is grounded on the assertion that such considerations take their cue and are grounded in artificially erected and highly subjective social norms, while reliance on "objective" notions such as rationality and efficiency would be a more coherent and "rational" manner of applying laws and economic policies. For many decades, both law and economic disciplines have strived for "objectivity", "rationality" and "scientificity", thus creating strict borders between "moral" and "legal" / "economic".[2]

The focus on scarcity of resources, law and demand and supply, the optimal allocation through the market, human agent rationality, efficiency and wealth maximization further underpins the notion of Homo Oeconomicus[3] where rational agents seek to maximize their utility. Wealth maximization as the most optimal "objective" of law and policy to be pursued according to its proponents in this context does not denote strictly monetary terms, but rather "the summation of all the valued objects, both tangible and intangible, in society, weighted by the prices they would command were they to be traded in markets."[4]

Consequently, nowhere are the normative tensions between Law and Economics disciplines as prevalent as regarding the prevention of undue wealth transfer and

---

[1] Holler and Leroch (2010).

[2] Sery (2017).

[3] Mathis (2009), pp. 7 et seqq.

[4] Posner (2003), p. 252, cited in Mestmäcker (2007), p. 11.

profiteering, where the Chicagoan Economic Analysis of Law with its singular focus on "efficiency", "total welfare" and "wealth maximisation" faces off with a near universal legal prohibition against unfair, excessive pricing and its twin concept, price gouging.

Nevertheless, the recent tide of excessive pricing cases in the EU, after the concept's untimely death being proclaimed by a chorus of "mainstream" law and economics in the past decades, is a testament to the vitality of the notion of "fairness" when approaching political economy in general, and "unfair pricing" and undue profiteering, in particular. This "renaissance" can only be understood by recourse to Kantian Legal Philosophy as the meta-norm behind the legal prohibition, why attempts to analyse and understand the prohibition via neoclassical and marginalist approaches translate to an intellectual dead-end.

The legal system relies on abstract notions such as 'fairness' and 'reasonableness' more often than not (FRAND[5] being another example in an IP setting). Even though the concepts are in and of themselves prone to subjective interpretation, the Kantian experimental thought-scheme discussed above aids the legal system in arriving at a more 'objective' and 'a priori' point in regard to these abstract notions. Ontological subjectivity can still produce epistemological objectivity, or else all studies of social sciences and observer dependent fields would be impossible to organise in a rational, objective and practical fashion.

This process is not always a conscious, philosophical exercise in the minds of judges and lawyers, many of whom might not even be aware of the Kantian tradition influencing their reasoning, but even where it is tacit, the influence is observable.[6] But when undertaking a teleological interpretation, the argument can be made that this is ipso facto a Kantian exercise, whether conscious or unconscious.

Using prohibition as a proxy, the argument is made that the Kelsenian approach to law, as well as the Posnerian approach to economics, stand against an understanding of law and political economy in the tradition of Aristotle, Kant and even Adam Smith. The ratio legis of the prohibition against "unfair pricing" in European law has little to do with "hipster antitrust",[7] if one by this labelling understands a radical use of competition law in regards to re-distribution. The ratio legis is evident from the human bias towards fairness in pricing and transactions.[8]

As it will be demonstrated, both the positivist legal approach, as well as the neoclassical/marginalist economic approach, stand in opposition to the Kantian Legal Philosophy, here defined as postulating that the ultimate function of laws, even laws covering economic activity, is to bring about justice and fairness by way of rational experience.[9]

What the soul and goal of the law, including competition law, ought to be thus reverts to the perennial question of how a unified theory of law would be construed

---

[5] Hovenkamp (2020).

[6] Some parts of this section on Kantian legal-philosophy is an excerpt from Kianzad (2020).

[7] Wright et al. (2018).

[8] Eyster, Madarasz, and Michaillat (2020).

[9] Kant (1797), trans. Hastie (1887, 2010).

regarding substance, rule of law, procedure, authority, validity and universality, to name a few determining elements of such a unified legal theory.

The present section will begin by depicting the general contours of legal, philosophical and economic approaches to the matter of justice and fairness, read against what is defined as Kantian Legal Philosophy, denoted as demanding that laws have their ultimate object to bring about justice and fairness.

6.1.1 Legal-Philosophical approaches to Justice and Fairness

Attempts at formulating such a unifying legal theory have been rather abundant throughout (European) legal history, ranging from Aristotle to Aquinas to Grotius and Pufendorf to modern thinkers such as Radbruch,[10] Raz,[11] Kelsen,[12] Ross,[13] Hart,[14] Rawls,[15] Dworkin[16] et alia. To offer a full account of the intricacies of these thinkers´ diverging and converging ideas is outside the scope of the present article.

Generally speaking, the inter-connection between law, morality and religion defined the nature of legal questions and inquiries on fairness and justice during a considerable time-period, where the normative authority of the law was sought in some divine or imperatorial power.[17]

The question of what constitutes fairness and justice, its conditions and conditionality, and its volition and volatility, has been a defining character of the legal, philosophical, and ethical debates since time immemorial. According to various Natural Law schools, fairness and justice are the departing notion, and final outcome, of the legal discipline, having its roots in religious texts via imperial decrees and later, the first legal texts and treaties. Other schools, such as legal realists and legal positivists, rather emphasise procedural fairness and the process of codification as the main element of the legal discipline.[18]

Justice, as per one of the foundational documents of Western legal discipline, Codex Juris Civilis, was defined as "Justice is the set and constant purpose which gives to every man his due".[19] This maxim seems to incorporate both of the Aristotelian notions of justice as conduct in agreement with authoritative law on social

---

[10] Radbruch (1978).

[11] Raz (1990), pp. 331–39.

[12] Kelsen (2009, originally printed 1934).

[13] Ross (2019a, b, originally printed 1959).

[14] Hart (2012, originally printed 1960).

[15] Rawls (1999, originally printed 1971).

[16] Dworkin (1977).

[17] Ross (2019a, b).

[18] Kelsen (2009, originally printed 1934).

[19] Institutiones of Justinian (i. 1. 1), "justitia est constans et perpetua voluntas jus suum cuique tribuens.", https://www.gutenberg.org/files/5983/5983-h/5983-h.htm#link2H_4_0002, accessed 2021–02-01; The maxim has also been translated as "justice is the constant and perpetual will to

and moral conduct, on the one hand; and justice as moral virtue regarding one´s moral disposition, on the other hand. In this sense, as per Aristotle:

> Justice in the sense of Equality has to do with external and commensurable things; it is concerned with the proportionate ratio of commensurable goods. Thus, a "just" wage is a wage proportionate to the type and amount of labour invested; it is one which is neither too great nor too little (disproportionate), but midway between the two extremes. Similarly, a just law is the ideal mean between the two extremes of defect and excess.[20]

The codified versions of the Roman Empire (Corpus Juris Civilis)[21] and of the Catholic Church (Canon Law)[22] bridged between the ancient and pre-modern times in Europe and where the latter is still in a continuum, the former has exercised considerable authority over the formation and codification of Modern European Law.[23] Thus the law in that period could never be wrong, unjust, or inefficient, as it would deny the divine or imperatorial authority.

This "natural law" tradition was partly overturned through Enlightenment, combining Utilitarian and social contract theory in the tradition of Hobbes, Locke and Rousseau. The human society and rationality were now front and centre, and law was seen not as a creation by God, but by humans, through consensus. Furthermore, Locke in his assault on Platonism rejected "...inner consciousness and innate ideas altogether, and imposed a strict empiricism."[24]

The universality of justice, and its decoupling from the relativity of the "will of people", is indeed an enduring concept, in the words of Alexis de Tocqueville "A general law - which bears the name of Justice - has been made and sanctioned, not only by a majority of this or that people, but by a majority of mankind."[25]

The division of the Justice and Fairness concept along the lines of reciprocity, equality and conformity to social and moral norms or laws has thus dominated much of the Western discourse on Justice and Fairness. As such, concepts such as consequentialism, deontology and virtue ethics have subsequently been developed. Consequentialists put the emphasis on maximisation of beneficial outcomes, aligning the theory with utilitarianism, focusing on both individual and societal maximisation of "utility", counting Jeremy Bentham among others as an important figure.

Deontological discourse ("deon" from the Greek word for duty and "logos" regarding science) denotes the diametrical opposition of utilitarianism, in that the

---

render to each one his right"; Edward Westmarck, "The origin and development of the moral ideas", https://www.gutenberg.org/files/52106/52106-h/52106-h.htm#v1page141, accessed 2021–02-01.

[20] Chroust and Osborn (1942); Aristotle, trans. Ross (1999).

[21] Compiled between 529 and 534 AD by the order of the Justinian I, in three parts (Digesta, Codex, Institutiones).

[22] The law of the Catholic Church, comprised of ius antiquum, the ius novum, the ius novissimum and the Codex Iuris Canonici, see Code of Canon Law, http://www.vatican.va/archive/cod-iuris-canonici/cic_index_en.html, accessed 2020–10-10.

[23] Mousourakis (2015).

[24] The History of Economic Thought, "The Utilitarians", http://www.hetwebsite.net/het/schools/utilitarian.htm, accessed 2020–10–10.

[25] Tocqueville, Chapter XV: Unlimited Power of Majority, And Its Consequences -Part II (1835), translation by Reeve (2002), p. 287.

discourse put the emphasis on the moral value and volition inherent in actions, and not, the outcome and consequences. The outcome, even if not beneficial from a strictly utilitarian viewpoint, is secondary to the moral good inherent in the action.

The Natural Law approach to universal and eternal values regarding good and evil hence was replaced with a subjective, Utilitarian view of such values alongside hedonistic ethics on pain aversion and pleasure seeking. Morality was defined as the maximization of the "good", where this would be defined individually and subjectively.

The emergence of the legal-positivist and "pure theory of law" in the Kelsenian[26] tradition sought further to detach the legal discipline from other disciplines, methodologies, values and norms, and thus organize the law within its own internal normative system with some meta-legal basic norms, accessible to judges and practitioners by way of a strict methodological approach.

Legal Realism, on the other hand, emerging in the latter part of twentieth century refuted this approach, and elevated the institutional and individual factors relevant to how law is made, interpreted and applied. This amounted to an engagement with other social sciences such as psychology, political science, sociology and economics, emphasizing both the "internal" and "external" elements of legal statutes and legal discipline.

Later in twentieth century, Neo-deontological, Natural-rights schools inspired by Dworkin[27] and Rawls[28], as well as other schools such as Critical Legal Studies[29], Law and Economics[30] and Economic Analysis of Law[31] were developed.

The aim of the above condensed exposé over some 2000 years of various ways of thinking about the law, the legal discipline, its objects and subjects, internal and external elements, what law "is" and what law "ought" to be—is to illustrate the difference, and importance, of normative meta-values and meta-discourses informing the doctrinal analysis and application. It is important to note that the legal history invariably coincides with and parallels the philosophical history of thinking about morality, rights and wrongs, and ethics at large.

It is argued that one such approach to the legal science, dubbed positivist (in the tradition of Alf Ross, Hans Kelsen and more recently, Shavell and Kaplow et alia.) contrasts with a Kantian legal philosophy, defined as an approach where justice is the main defining characteristic of what constitutes a law.

Alf Ross famously chided that "Justice is a whore to be bought by anybody", referring to the subjective and lucid properties of justice and fairness, why the legal science should be decoupled from "morality", making the validity of the laws not conditioned toward what "just" end results they could bring by, but how the laws

---

[26] Kelsen (2009, originally printed 1934).

[27] Dworkin (1977).

[28] Rawls (1985).

[29] Unger (1983).

[30] Marciano and Ramello (2014), p. 8.

[31] Posner (1986).

were enacted and a just legal procedure, legal certainty, equality before the laws and so on.

6.1.2 Economic Approaches to Justice and Fairness

Turning over to the economic science and its relationship with the matter of "justice and fairness", ever since the "marginalist revolution" by Marshall, Jevons et alia some 100 years ago, all the way to the so-called Chicago School championed by the likes of Robert Bork, Richard Posner et alia, advocating a neat divorce between "economics" and "ethics", it can be argued that such neoclassical approach translates to an inherent conflict with the originating roots of political economy of both Aristotle and Adam Smith, a professor of moral philosophy.[32]

This critique has in turn been formulated by the likes of Marc Blaug, Uskali Mäki, Richard Dworkin and the entirety of behavioural and experimental schools, which have empirically demonstrated the hollowness of some of the core "presumptions" of the utility, rationality and efficiency-oriented schools of economics.

The rationality and utility arguments are countered by the ground-breaking research done by behavioural scientists in the past decades,[33] demonstrating concepts such as bounded rationality, loss aversion and the human bias towards fairness in transactions,[34] which could and should not be ignored in the context of "unfair pricing". As noted by Hausman and McPherson on the general divide between ethics and economics:

> There is nothing suspect or intolerant about believing that some answers to moral questions are better than others and that rational argument can help one to judge which answers are better. These beliefs are implicit in individual moral judgments and in policy making, and it is hard to deny them without denying that there is any such thing as morality.[35]

There is indeed ample evidence pointing to the fact that human beings do care about fairness and justice, as a matter of hardwired biology—and not only as a function of differentiated cultural or social norms, although the latter naturally plays a significant role. We now know that individuals sometimes attach a higher value to generalized notions of fairness than their own "utility"; and they care about fairness and justice as normative, ex-ante metrics, and not only as distributional or corrective ex-post matters, nor as pure manifestations of altruism.[36]

This position could also be described as the divide between Fairness and Efficiency in neoclassical, marginalist and welfarist economists which have come to dominate much of not only the economic realm, but also the legal realm, most prominent in legal areas such as antitrust law or other laws governing market activity.

---

[32] Smith (1861), pp. 389–538.

[33] Sunstein, Thaler, and Jolls (1998).

[34] Malc et al. (2016), pp. 3693–97.

[35] Hausman and McPherson (2006), pp. 3–11.

[36] Fehr and Schmidt (2006), pp. 615–91.

The main argument in the present article is that the focus on "wealth maximization" as well as "efficiency" is more often than not at odds with other legal values such as "fairness" and "justice", even more so when approached from a Kantian perspective.

The classic tension between neoclassical economics with its singular focus on efficiency and "total welfare" can be seen to stand in bright contrast with the legal discipline's focus on the administration of fairness and justice.[37] A contrast that post financial crisis of 2008/9 as well as the recent COVID-19 crisis seem to call for an updated approach to what role economics, and what kind of economics at that, should play in e.g. competition law analysis.

One could use the problem of excessive pricing of essential goods during a crisis as a proxy to frame the above, where the neoclassical approach by recourse to self-correcting markets or supply–demand offers little of intellectual value.[38]

6.1.3 Kantian Legal Philosophy and Fairness in Law and Economics

A Kantian approach to the philosophy of jurisprudence[39] further informs the interpretation alongside *"malum in se"* as regards the nature of laws and legal discipline.

If notions and preferences relating to fairness are only treated as externalities by "mainstream" economics, this approach stands in direct conflict with the core ratio legis of a statute such as Article 102a TFEU, which by its wording as well as its legal history prohibits the "unfairness" element of pricing behaviour.

It can be argued that this "Kantian" interpretation of the ratio legis behind excessive pricing prohibition in European competition law is reflected in the wording in United Brands,[40] where "unfair pricing" per Article 102a TFEU were defined as prices having "no reasonable relation to the economic value of the product."[41]

The excess in turn could be determined objectively if it would be possible to calculate it through a comparison between the selling price of the product and its cost of production, which would disclose the "profit margin". Finally, the question

---

[37] Nance and von Platz (2018), pp. 250–68.

[38] Kianzad (2022).

[39] Kant (1797).

[40] Judgment of the Court of 14 February 1978 in Case 27/76, United Brands Company and United Brands Continentaal BV v Commission of the European Communities, ECLI:EU:C:1978:22; See paras 250–253 regarding the test for excessive pricing.

[41] In turn defined in Case 26–75, General Motors Continental NV v Commission of the European Communities, ECLI:EU:C:1975:150, para 12.

to be determined would consist in answering the question if the disclosed difference is "either unfair in itself or when compared with competing products".[42]

In light of the above, the assertion is made that there is indeed an upper bound to be found in regard to "unfair, excessive pricing" in European competition law, which is construed alongside equality and equity in exchange per the Aristotelian and Just Price tradition informing the ratio legis of the prohibition, but also its ratio oeconomica.

The present article asserts the roots of the prohibition of excessive and unfair pricing in European competition law to display clear elements of Natural Law and Kantian legal philosophy, in part relying on Roman Legal Norms of contract, tort, liability and related matters, although the Just Price is more scholastic than Roman in its nature.

Thus, one looking for the roots of the "unfair pricing" is best advised to search for the roots of the prohibition in the Justum Pretium[43] (Just Price) and Scholastic writings, but also in the Kantian legal philosophy.

As opposed to some of what is described as "mainstream" economic schools on the subject, and some (erroneous) legal-historical claims[44] in regard to the origin of the prohibition in European competition law, the legal discipline has castigated excessive, exploitative pricing since many centuries as **malum in se**, an inherent evil in and of itself, where it is the object and not only effect that is of interest, due to the "unfairness" the undue profiteering is perceived to entail.

The reason for this per se illegality approach is made clearer through behavioural economics research on the subject and insights into bounded rationality as well as context-specific preferences regarding fairness.[45]

A Kantian point of departure, borrowed from White, might serve well to frame the analytical conceptualisation of fair pricing in contrast with "profit maximisation" in relation to firm behaviour, as explained by White:

> Principled behaviour can also be seen in producers or firms who incorporate ethical considerations into their decision-making. Under the standard assumption of profit maximization, the firm engages in ethical behaviour—such as corporate philanthropy, environmental initiatives, or political action - only if it is the best use of resources to increase profits. Such "strategic" ethical behaviour is rightfully criticized as insincere from a moral point of view (leading to terms such as "greenwashing" and "pink washing"), and shifts credit to the firm's customers and business partners, whose ethical preferences drive the firm's "ethics" in the same way that consumer preferences drive product design. This does not mean, however, that a firm cannot behave sincerely according to Kantian motives of acting for the sake of duty. Firms can commit to a certain code of behaviour[46]

---

[42] Judgment of the Court of 14 February 1978 in Case 27/76, United Brands Company and United Brands Continentaal BV v Commission of the European Communities, ECLI:EU:C:1978:22; See paras 250–253 regarding the test for excessive pricing.

[43] Isaacs' (1920).

[44] Werden (2021), pp. 682–713.

[45] Korobokin and Ulen (2000), pp. 1051–1144.

[46] White (2019), p. 64.

As laws ultimately do have a normative as well as disciplinary function, the prohibition against unfair pricing can be contrasted to what normative weight and definition, if any, is given in economic schools of thought to how "fairness" affects the concomitant positive law and economic analysis and theory of harm. But also the legal analysis normative approach to the matter of fairness and justice affects the analysis.

It is important to recall that an understanding of fairness and justice along "reciprocity", "proportionality" and "equity", also targeting economics, dates back to the days of Aristotle,[47] Christian,[48] Jewish[49] and Islamic[50] writings on the topic of "unfair" and "inequitable" transactions, such as the concept of usury[51] and Just Price.[52] Such thinking has informed the legal prohibition since time immemorial.

Fairness, as it is argued in the present article relying on a vast body of research in modern economics and political economy at large, is not only able to function as an economic concept, but acts also as noted by Adam Smith as "what holds the whole edifice together",[53] thus building the basis of the "political" in political economy.

The claim that "fairness is not an economic concept"[54] does simply not stand "serious scrutiny",[55] as it is a matter of choice and values inherent in rejecting fairness as being an incalculable externality,[56] to be dealt with in other disciplines. Indeed, an immense body of economics has concerned itself with different nuances of fairness and equity.[57]

As demonstrated by behavioural and experimental research, both firms and consumers take fairness considerations seriously regarding pricing.[58] We have also now ample evidence that humans are hard-wired towards fairness in transactions.[59]

This further testaments to the universal character of the concept and social preferences, that evolved during the human evolution. This view of fairness, as being both universal as well as evolutionary, is in line with the reasoning of Darwin, Smith, Kant, Rawls, Binmore et alia, and further demonstrated by neuro-economic and neuro-psychological research.[60]

---

[47] Miller (2011).

[48] See Mark 4:24, Matthew 7:2 and Luke 6:38; See also: Koehn and Wilbratte (2012), pp. 501–26.

[49] Kleinman (1987); Makovi (2016).

[50] Bashar (1997), pp. 29–52.

[51] Christian writings include among others Leviticus 19:9, Ezekiel 18:13, Deuteronomy 23:19, Leviticus 25:37 and Proverbs 28:8, to name a few.

[52] Von Nell-Breuning (1950), pp. 111–22.

[53] Smith (1767), p. 148.

[54] Jenny (2018), pp. 5–70.

[55] Lianos (2020), pp. 3–86.

[56] Ulen (2015).

[57] Fennell and McAdams (2013).

[58] Rotemberg (2011), pp. 952–81; Kahneman, Knetsch and Thaler (2000), pp. 317–34; Herz and Taubinsky (2018), pp. 316–52.

[59] McAuliffe et al. (2017).

[60] Cappelen et al. (2014), pp. 15, 368–72.

The next section will depict the Posnerian attack on justice- and fairness-based approaches to law and economics, where Richard Posner in turn forwarded wealth maximisation as the most rational, most objective and most "common sense" approach to the disciplines, thereby chastising the Kantian approach as being subjective, unscientific and prone to be captured by populism.

6.2 Posner and Wealth Maximisation as an Argument Against Kantian Ethics

As noted by Mestmäcker in criticism of Posner´s (Economic Analysis of Law) approach to the legal discipline: "Kant's theory is incompatible with Posner's and Holmes' interpretation of contracts as an acquisition of an option to break it."[61]

Indeed, in the reading of Posner of Kant, Kant is not a Kantian. This is also the main challenge with the Posnerian positing of wealth maximisation as an ethical value, even more so in the context of European competition law.[62] It is imperative to note that Posner wrote and analysed common law, an entirely different legal tradition than the European continental legal tradition, which relies on manifestly different roots.[63]

Evidently, there is a manifest tension between certain strands of economics and legal science, where the legal science by tradition and the letter of the law in its Kantian and Rawlsian versions focuses on the administration of fairness and justice, and not on maximizing efficiency, while the law in the Kelsenian more is pre-occupied with procedural fairness and legal certainty.[64]

The issue of wealth maximisation, framed as a normative value, has generated considerable debate between the law and economics disciplines, and, when framed as profit maximisation, is an essential theme of the present inquiry on "unfair pricing" as per the United Brands test. Most of the writings on the theme do not engage fully with the normative departing points underlining the arguments made against unfair pricing enforcement, where monopolistic profits even are cited as something inherently good, or at least, not an evil per se.[65]

One of the main proponents of economic analysis of law, Richard Posner, did indeed attempt at framing wealth maximisation as a value, which led to responses by Dworkin, Kronman et alia.; a debate which still today is highly relevant, even more so when attempting at defining ratio legis of competition law in general, and prohibition of undue profiteering, in particular.

---

[61] Mestmäcker (2007), p. 51.

[62] Posner (1980); Posner (1979b); Posner (1979a), p. 281.

[63] Spector (2004), p. 22.

[64] Ulen (2015).

[65] For a summary of neoclassical, marginalist and welfarist arguments, see: Jenny (2018).

Notably, and most relevant for the present work, Posner sought[66] to re-connect the principle of Pareto Optimality and personal autonomy to Kantian ethics, although, as will be demonstrated, this was an equally unsuccessful as misguided attempt. Kantian ethics, and most importantly, Kantian philosophy of law, run counter to the Posnerian ditto. This section will outline the Posner argument, before turning to the criticism and rebuttal by Dworkin,[67] Kronman[68] and Mestmäcker.[69]

Posner framed wealth maximisation as the best approximation of justice, combining both Utilitarian as well as Kantian approaches, though not having any of the weaknesses of both schools. Posner forwarded wealth maximisation as an:

> Ethically attractive objective to guide common law adjudication, rather than social choice generally... wealth maximization, especially in the common law setting, derives support from the principle of consent that can also be regarded as underlying the otherwise quite different approach of Pareto ethics... the political counterpart of consent-consensus-explains the role of wealth maximization in shaping the common law... it is also possible to locate Pareto ethics in a different philosophical tradition from the utilitarian, in the tradition, broadly Kantian, which attaches a value over and above the utilitarian to individual autonomy. One ethical criterion of change that is highly congenial to the Kantian emphasis on autonomy is consent. And consent is the operational basis of the concept of Pareto superiority.[70]

Furthermore, in relation to his understanding of Kant, Posner noted:

> Suppose we consider consent an ethically attractive basis for permitting changes in the allocation of resources, on Kantian grounds unrelated to the fact that a consensual transaction is likely to increase the happiness at least of the immediate parties to it"[71]

To re-capitulate regarding Pareto and Kaldor-Hicks efficiency mentioned by Posner "A change from one distribution of goods to another is said to be "Pareto superior" when at least one person is made better off relative to that person's preferences, and no one is made worse off (everyone else is indifferent between the situation before and after the change). Similarly, a move is "Pareto inferior" when at least one person is made worse off (relative to that person's preferences), and no one is made better off.

A "Pareto optimal" situation is one where no one can be made better off without at least one person being made worse off. Under Kaldor–Hicks efficiency, a move is Kaldor–Hicks superior if those who have benefited by some change could compensate those left worse off in a way that, after the (hypothetical) compensation, those worse off would now be at least indifferent, and those made better off would still be left better off. (Again, it is important to remember that this is hypothetical compensation; if those better off had actually compensated those made worse off to the level of at least being indifferent, the result would be a Pareto superior move.

---

[66] Posner (1980).

[67] Dworkin (1980).

[68] Kronman (1980), pp. 227–42.

[69] Mestmäcker (2007).

[70] Posner (1980).

[71] Posner (1980).

The argument is that a Kaldor–Hicks superior situation is one that is in some sense equivalent to the Pareto superior situation, and thus to be treated as an improvement over the status quo. At the same time, it is clear that Kaldor–Hicks analysis does require a willingness to trade off some people's gains against other people's losses.[72]

However, regarding the Kaldor-Hicks test, as noted by Kronman, there is no set guarantees that compensation will occur, and if this is the case, the principle runs counter to the Kantian approach, since the moral principle would have been violated, and thus "for a Kantian, the Kaldor-Hicks has no significance".[73] Posner further pre-supposed voluntary exchange as one foundational criterion, nevertheless, as explained by Kronman:

> Voluntary agreements have a special claim to recognition since the limit the actions of those who are parties to them in the only way that is consistent with their autonomy as persons. This idea is a familiar and important one and lies at the heart of contrarian tradition from Hobbes to Rawls.[74]

As noted by Kronman, while Posner seeks to frame wealth maximisation as manifestly different than "efficiency" regarding the design of legal rules, they are indeed the one and same, since the voluntary transfers that Posner uses as illustrations also satisfy the Pareto principle and it could be argued that it is this which gives them their appeal. This would in turn mean that wealth maximization and efficiency for Posner are different names for the same thing, although Posner denied that these two principles are equivalent.[75]

Posner sought to frame wealth maximisation as rather "uncontroversial" as opposed to maximising utility, since in his view, economic approaches in general, and wealth maximization in particular, would offer the highest value to voluntary market transactions (again, in his view, as such transactions, almost by definition, make all parties to the transaction better off). Contrary, in circumstances where voluntary transactions would not be possible or feasible, the welfare-maximising approach to law and policy would determine what choices people would have made, which could be dubbed "hypothetical consent".[76]

The choice of the Pareto principle is the Posnerian rejection of unchecked Utilitarianism, which does not accord any value to whose happiness has been increased and along what routes, thus building the moral element of Posnerian theory, where wealth maximisation would act as a check on increasing utility.

Posner further applied the theory to accident law, approached via negligence and liability routes, a matter which leads the present analysis stray and has been addressed by others in other settings. Starting with the framing the positing of wealth maximisation as a value as opposed to egalitarian and equitable outcomes, Dworkin in his response noted:

---

[72] Bix (2017).

[73] Kronman (1980).

[74] Kronman (1980).

[75] Kronman (1980).

[76] Bix (2017).

Wealth maximization, as defined, is achieved when goods and other resources are in the hands of those who value them most, and someone values a good more only if he is both willing and able to pay more in money (or in the equivalent of money) to have it. An individual maximizes his own wealth when he increases the value of the resources he owns; whenever he is able, for example, to purchase something he values for any sum less than the most he would be willing to pay for it[77]

As noted by Kronman in his response to Posner regarding positing of wealth as a normative value, thus lacking the drawbacks of Utilitarian as well as Kantian (in Posner's definition Pareto Superiority) approaches, wealth maximization would not offer a "happy compromise" between utilitarianism and Pareto superiority, a compromise which somehow retains the best and eliminates the worst features of these other two principles.[78] As Kronman explains, regarding Posner's approach to wealth maximisation:

Wealth maximization is not utilitarianism limited by a respect for rights: if it is a species of utilitarianism at all, wealth maximization is utilitarianism constrained by a respect for something which is neither rights nor utility, something of uncertain and, as Ronald Dworkin has shown, dubious value.[79]

Many years have passed since the debate between Posner, Kronman and Dworkin, and even Posner today seems to have accepted some of the critiques, although some scholars continue to argue that wealth maximization, or some other form of efficiency, is a worthy objective, "they concede that it is merely one objective among many, and it may need to be traded off against fairness and justice and other objectives."[80]

Regarding the "Kantian" claim by Posner, as evident already by the rather brief account of Kantian moral-philosophy in this chapter, and as also noted by Dworkin "Posner…defines "Kantian" so as to describe a political theory that rejects "any form of consequentialism. Kant is not, on this definition, a Kantian."[81] The manifestly misguided reading of Kant by Posner was also addressed by Mestmäcker, noting:

Even though, according to Kant, all duties (obligations) as such are part of ethics, it does not follow that the rules ("Gesetzgebung") that result are ethical. The example of contracts is a case in point. In the words of Kant: "Ethics commands that I perform a contractual obligation even though the other party cannot enforce my performance: the rule (pacta sunt servanda), however, and the corresponding duty are part of the law.[82]

There are however many instances in real life, and in jurisprudence, where a strict Kantian approach will not be workable, as opposing interests where one party suffers a harm to its interest must be accepted, if there can be an overall, societal gain to be realised.

This would mean introducing some elements of Utilitarianism, and the Pareto Principle, to soften the strict Kantian approach. However, relaxing the Kantian

---

[77] Dworkin (1980).

[78] Kronman (1980).

[79] Kronman (1980); referrering to Dworkin (1980).

[80] Williams referring to Posner, Economic Analysis of Law.

[81] Dworkin (1980).

[82] Mestmäcker (2007).

approach, and its philosophy of what laws ought to be, is not akin to abandoning the core Kantian principles.

As such, even if a Kantian would accept the Pareto principle as an appropriate expression of the so-called individual autonomy against the intervention by the Sovereign, but would be troubled about the principle's practicality, there would be an opportunity to "relax its demanding requirements by expanding the notion of actual compensations. He will not have a reason of any kind, however, to soften the Pareto Principle by adopting wealth maximization as his guiding norm."[83] As also noted by Brain Bix:

> Wealth maximization's analyses in terms of ability to pay create well-known paradoxical outcomes: for example, it seems that one would increase social wealth by giving the prized possessions of a poor person to her rich neighbour, even if the possessions meant everything to the poor person and almost nothing to the rich neighbour, simply because the rich person was able and willing to pay more to own those possessions than the poor person would be able to pay.[84]

Finally, as aptly summarized by Eli Salzberger, if one expands economic models to include the possibility of preference changes resulting from, among others, legal rules, and takes those preference changes into account in any overall normative assessment, the justification for the use of wealth maximization criterion weakens considerably.[85]

6.3 Fairness Versus Welfare Argument Against Kantian Ethics

Having dealt with the matter of wealth maximisation as a contrarian argument against a Kantian approach to law and economics, some of the most notable proponents of the supposedly possible "trade-off" between Fairness and Welfare, include welfare economists Steven Shavell and Louis Kaplow. The famous assertion by Shavell and Kaplow asserts that "any non-welfarist policy violates the Pareto-principle."[86]

This claim is only relevant if one adheres to and accepts the basic criterion set up by the Pareto principle, ignoring the fact that a Kantian, rights-based legal system does and cannot adhere to this core principle, but to principles of justice and fairness, in and of itself as the legitimizing basis of "whole edifice", as formulated already by Adam Smith.

This is not merely a philosophical note, but relevant in the positive analysis, a point seized upon by Glick and Lozada "economic efficiency is not about justice, but

---

[83] Kronman (1980).

[84] Bix (2017).

[85] Salzberger (2007), p. 29.

[86] Kaplow and Shavell (2003), pp. 331–62.

the law presumably is. Accordingly, Law and Economics' obsession with efficiency, whether real or contrived, has little place in the law."[87]

Nevertheless, neoclassical and libertarian economists have more often than not rejected any other "value" to be reckoned with beyond "efficiency", with some casting equitable concerns with fairness and justice in economics "a naive and basically infantile anthropomorphism."[88]

It is important to distinguish this "normative" argument from the "positive" argument against e.g. price gouging laws examined briefly in the previous section, as the latter targets the actual, empirical realities, or rather, it aims to do so.

In the words of Jenny "...the complementary concept of "fairness" is again a concept alien to economic analysis"[89] but this statement is only true given a narrow definition of "economics", as one could also argue that economics might indeed contain a conceptual basis for fairness,[90] as the law on its part indeed has shown to be able to accommodate economic reasoning.

The sheer number of economic papers on fairness in pricing and transactions as well as Nobel prizes awarded to economists in one way or another addressing fairness-related issues also speaks for itself. Offering a contrary view, in the words of 2001 Nobel Laureate in Economics Joseph Stiglitz "This fallacious idea is that you can separate equity from efficiency. It´s sometimes referred to as the Second Welfare Theorem. We now know that those two issues can´t be neatly separated in that way."[91]

This "fallacious idea" of creating a strict dichotomy between total welfare and consumer welfare as regards the normative goals of intellectual property rights and competition law respectively needs indeed to be revisited and re-evaluated, as it affects both the holistic as well as the specific analysis of what these laws ought to be. On that normative note, as observed by Calabresi:

> Of Bentham, Mill said that he approached all ideas as a stranger and if they did not fit his test (the test of utility), he dismissed them as vague generalities. Mill then went on to say that what Bentham didn't realize was that "these generalities contained the whole unanalysed experience of the human race.[92]

The aforementioned evidence from behavioural and neuro-economics invariably demonstrate innate human morality and fairness preferences in transactions, and not, a sense of "utility maximisation" or proneness to "efficiency".[93]

The matter is not so much that the economic analysis of law prefers "efficiency", which has no empirical, neural underpinning, but rather the normative failure of

---

[87] Glick and Lozada (2021), p. 91.; Although they use the term "Law and Economics", they are more commenting on the Chicagoan Economic Analysis of Law in the tradition of Aaron Director and Richard Posner than the tradition of Guido Calabresi.

[88] Johnson (1973), p. 54; cited in Okun (1975), p. 5.

[89] Jenny (2018), pp. 56–57.

[90] Kahneman et al. (1986a, b), p. 285.

[91] Stiglitz (2019), pp. 16–17.

[92] Calabresi (2019).

[93] Koenigs et al. (2007); Berns et al. (2012); Cappelen et al. (2014); Greene et al. (2004).

claims that "efficiency" is an optimal, even the optimal, goal to be pursued by legal rules.[94]

The efficiency-paradigm in neoclassical law and economics, whether construed alongside Pareto, Kaldor-Hicks or Consumer Surplus,[95] are all in inherent conflict with the legal discipline framing of e.g., excessive and unfair pricing, oftentimes alongside a winner-loser stratum.[96] This is a matter acknowledged by Calabresi, but ignored by Posner.

This focus on justice further underpins legal authority in the first place, if one subscribes to the Kantian and Rawlsian notions of legal and moral philosophy. Economic Analysis of Law in some of its most classical approaches by Bork, Posner, Kaplow and Shavell thus entail a near-insuperable conflict with the ratio legis of European competition law, but also with Common law.[97]

The assertions and the Economic Analysis of Law approach by Posner[98] as well as the welfarist approach by e.g. Shavell and Kaplow demonstrate this fundamental conflict. The inevitability of Fairness considerations in law if viewed in its interconnection with a democratic order is also noted by Screpanti and Zamagni, noting:

> But economic democracy and political democracy cannot diverge too much and for too long, otherwise the very foundations of the market system would be dangerously affected. Which is tantamount to saying that keeping the allocative objective and the redistributive objective separate does not meet the criteria either of efficiency or of equity[99]

The "value-free" and "objective" approach of an efficiency-oriented cost and benefit analysis is anything but "value-free" and "objective", and furthermore, as noted by Ernst-Joachim Mestmäcker:

> Cost-benefit analysis is end-neutral. It can be applied to any given purpose. Constitutions, statutes and precedents, however, are as a rule not end-neutral. The question then is how to accommodate the normative implications of economic analysis with diverse non-economic legal purposes.[100]

The claim that fairness is not an economic concept seems refuted by the very essence of political economy, where the main element of rent theory was the inequitable effect it produced, as developed by David Ricardo, John Stuart Mill, Henry George et alia. As noted by Ken Binmore on the matter:

---

[94] Salzberger (2013).

[95] Pareto Efficiency, or Pareto Optimality, concerns a situation where at least someone is made better off, an improvement without making someone else worse off. However, since this criterion might be difficult to achieve in reality, Kaldor-Hicks Efficiency in turn categorizes a situation where the benefits exceed the costs of improvements and those who have benefited somehow compensate those who have been made worse off.

[96] Driesen and Malloy (2017); Veljanovski (1981); Dworkin (1980).

[97] Glick and Lozada (2021).

[98] Posner (1980); Kaplow and Shavell (2003), pp. 331–62; Kaplow and Shavell (2001), pp. 961–1388; Posner (1979b).

[99] Screpanti and Zamagni (2005).

[100] Mestmäcker (2007), p. 13.

But efficiency isn't the only issue. Fairness also matters. Libertarian economists evade this issue in various ways. The most blatant is the attempt to define the fairness issue out of existence by saying that any efficient outcome is "socially optimal". That is to say, society can never be made better off by moving from one efficient outcome to another. Underpinning this claim is the unsound dogma that interpersonal comparisons of utility are intrinsically meaningless.[101]

Recognizing the concept and collective preferences in regard to fairness is nevertheless only the first step in complementing the theories of harm and models used, as the fairness-concept need to be integrated as well. As noted by Schwartz "The difficult question is not whether non-economic considerations are a proper, indeed conventional, component of the antitrust calculus, but how to take them into account."[102]

By mounting a powerful attack on the philosophical foundations of Posnerian position and contrasting it to Hayek´s views but also drawing on Kant and Nietzsche, Mestmäcker seeks to re-connect the core function of the law (and law and economics) with legal and moral philosophy which is and ought to be the DNA of the laws - although supplemented by sound economic analysis of laws where applicable. As noted by Mark Blaug on the matter of efficiency versus fairness:

This notion of a neat divorce of efficiency from equity, of an objective value-free definition of efficiency, has haunted economics from its outset but it is, of course, a will-o'-the-wisp: there is in fact a different efficiency outcome for every different distribution of income, and vice versa. Efficiency is necessarily a value-laden term and welfare economics is necessarily normative, that is, a matter of good or bad and not true or false.[103]

As Kaplow and Shavell also partly concede, theirs is just another moral theory, albeit lacking all aspects of morality, defined in Kantian, Aristotelian terms or otherwise:

In several different respects, the approach of welfare economics involves value judgments. First, value judgments underlie the assumptions that social welfare depends on individuals' well-being, that this dependence is positive, and that factors unrelated to individuals' well-being are irrelevant. In other words, to adopt welfare economics is to adopt the moral position that one should be concerned, positively and exclusively, with individuals' well-being.[104]

The trade-off envisioned by Kaldor-Hicks efficiency, with the winners in theory being able to compensate the losers, is a non-starter already in the normative, let alone its impractical, practical application. As noted by Kronman:

...someone committed to the Kantian idea of individual autonomy would rightly feel that his moral principle had been violated, and it would not make any difference, from his point of view, that compensation could potentially be made even though it was not. For a Kantian, the Kaldor-Hicks test has no significance.[105]

---

[101] Binmore (2005), p. 189.

[102] Schwartz (1979).

[103] Blaug (2001), p. 47.

[104] Kaplow and Shavell (2001), p. 986.

[105] Kronman (1980).

Fairness becomes relevant in these contexts simply because the core analytical structure of neoclassical and welfarist theories of harm do not neatly encompass the law and economics of the pharmaceutical sector with in-elastic demand, payer-insensitivity, legal barriers to entry, the public duty to provide affordable health-care and faulty presumption related to the impact of supra-competitive profits on innovation and risk-taking.

The Pareto-principle forwarding "welfare" in turn defined as the individual´s utility is further conditioned on two limbs - the first centred on the truthfulness of the assumption, i.e. individuals care most about their own utility; and secondly how "welfare" is defined beyond "utility".

As it has been demonstrated by Fleurbaey, Tungodden and Chang: "Kaplow and Shavell...base their crucial assumption on an "observation" that welfarism and the Pareto indifference condition are equivalent. This claim is surprising because it is well known among social choice theorists that no Pareto condition by itself entails welfarism."[106]

The argument that some policies grounded on fairness tend to make everyone worse off is only truthful and relevant if one agrees with the assumption of what being worse off means, on both individual and societal level—The focus being on individual well-being, and social welfare defined as the sum of the individual wellbeing, leads to a circular reasoning in regard to why legal rules do not emphasize the individual well-being as the sole object of the laws.

Kaplow and Shavell reduce collective and societal fairness considerations to a matter of individual taste, stating "...individuals have a taste for a notion of fairness, just as they may have a taste for art, nature, or fine wine."[107] The problematic nature of such a claim is rather self-evident, since most human beings can do without art, fine wine or hikes in wonderous natural surroundings, but few would survive without a just and fair society based on inalienable rights regardless of physical power, gender, material wealth and so on.

Although there is a myriad of individual, subjective "tastes" regarding fine wine, art and hikes in the nature, we have substantial empirical, historical and normative findings pointing to an innate, universal and "objective" sense of fairness in human beings.[108] This might in certain situations lead to everyone being "worse off" if defined per efficiency-route, but is not in and of itself an argument against framing fairness as the core underlying rationale in regard to codified laws.

To accept the assertion by Shavell and Kaplow would be akin to granting slavery a free pass if it would fit the "individual tastes", where abolishing slavery would violate the cherished Pareto principle, since it most definitely would make the slave-owners worse off. As stated by Amartya Sen "A state in which some people are starving and suffering from acute deprivation while others are tasting the good life can still be Pareto optimal."[109]

---

[106] Fleurbaey et al. (2003), pp. 1382–85.

[107] Kaplow and Shavell (2001), p. 982.

[108] Hsu, Anen, and Quartz (2008), pp. 1092–95.

[109] Sen (1984), p. 95.

6.4 The Kantian Requiem—Against Wealth Maximisation and Efficiency in Law and Economics

The famous Kidney-problem illustrates the tension between fairness and efficiency approaches regarding the present theme of excessive pharmaceutical pricing perfectly. The not-so hypothetical case concerns "fair" division and allocation of an indivisible good,[110] such as a kidney, between two patients suffering from kidney failure. Patient A will survive 25 years with a kidney-transplant, whereas patient B will survive 20 years. One option would be to approach the matter from a strictly "efficiency" perspective, awarding the kidney to Patient A since there would most the most utilitarian and efficient outcome.

The second option would be to use a lottery, including or excluding strengths of the claims. The third, and the most "fair" option held by some, would be to destroy the kidney altogether, respecting the sanctity of life and right to health of both patients as any other allocation would overrule the fairness-paradigm.[111] This is many times the dilemma facing health and reimbursement systems, having a limited budget, and thus having to prioritise between different patient groups, and in so doing availing themselves a host of different metrics, economic Cost-effectiveness being only one.

The errand of this article is not to solve this puzzle or reconcile law and economics, or fairness with efficiency, once and for all. Rather the aim is to indicate the relevancy of fairness considerations as a matter of black letter law, legislative history and sound economics related to certain goods[112] where fairness in the Kantian sense must be defined as equitable exchange on a competitive market when concerning laws governing economic activity.

Relative, subjective and abstract as the concept of fairness might present itself, the entirety of human history and experience is filled with in-depth inquiries on the matter of fairness and justice, alongside philosophical, legal, economic, psychological and even neurological studies in search of what constitutes fair and unfair, respectively.

The concept of fairness and the conceptual understanding of it has rarely been fixed in spatiotemporal terms, nor has it been a fully arbitrary and random process, owning to the fact that despite the manifest subjective character of the concept, there are both universal conceptual approaches as well as neurological and anthropological evidence for an innate human bias towards fairness, in various forms.[113]

If this innate bias is to be defined as a bias towards "fairness", or rather, a bias towards "unfairness", is also a matter of contention. Further, what consequence, if any, this insight should bear upon the legal discipline in general, and the matter of unfair pricing, is another matter entirely.

---

[110] Wintein and Heilmann (2018), pp. 51–74.

[111] For a detailed account of the different approaches to solving such puzzles see: Broome (1990), pp. 87–101; Kirkpatrick and Eastwood (2015), pp. 82–91; Piller (2017), pp. 214–38; Lazenby (2014), pp. 331–45; Vong (2015), pp. 470–86; Saunders (2010), pp. 41–55; Tomlin (2012), pp. 200–213; Curtis (2014), pp. 47–57.

[112] Chartier and Fox (2019), pp. 253–66.

[113] Mendez (2009), pp. 608–20; Schmidt and Sommerville (2011).

Better explained, if the disclosed manifest human biases would rather expose humans as unfair, would this mean that the legal discipline and its rules should also reflect this human innate trait of "unfairness", and thus, laws should be unfair to reflect human nature, if contrarily the laws should be fair and just to reflect the disclosed human bias towards "fairness" or the aversion towards "unfairness"? And again, is the outcome, or the process, that should be fair and just?

But, a certain progressive coherence in the conceptual framing of fairness and justice seems nonetheless evident, why Aristotle, Thomas Aquinas and Immanuel Kant still can be widely read and re-discovered in an age of algorithms-based economy having nothing in common with the features of their time, but for the eternal human ponderings on the matters of justice and fairness. Although, as mankind develop, so do the concepts of fairness and justice it seems, but certain connectivity is indeed discernible. Why is this the case?

One answer could be that the reason must be sought in an innate, deep-structure of fairness in humans, holding constant over time and pace, however manifested in a myriad of variations, and even, in counterfactuals such as "unfairness" norms and rules.[114] Another answer could be the social element of humans and human society, with a high degree of "acquired" sense of fairness reflecting the traditions, culture, religion and so on.[115]

The Kidney-example can thus serve to illustrate the tension between "efficiency"-oriented Economic Analysis of Law approaches on the one hand, against Law and Economics approaches on the other hand, when facing excessive pricing which is also "unfair" according to the chosen anchorage points, in that the price has no "reasonable" relation to its "economic value", which in turn builds the "unfairness" element of the analysis.

Thus, one must first uncover what is meant by "fairness", and alternatively, "justice", in general, when discussing a general theory of law, or economics. In the words of Alf Ross:

> Like a harlot, natural law is at the disposal of everyone. There is no ideology that cannot be defended by invoking the law of nature. And indeed, how could it be otherwise when the ultimate basis for every natural law is to be found in a private (intra-subjective), direct insight, a self-evident contemplation, an intuition. Cannot my intuition be just as good as yours? Self-evidence as a criterion of truth explains the utterly arbitrary character of metaphysical assertions. It raises them above any form of inter-subjective control and opens the door wide to unbridled fantasy and dogmatism.[116]

Alf Ross defines Justice ultimately as a claim for equality, and moves on to characterising the different approaches to equality, these defined in turn as (i) To each according to his merit; (ii) To each according to his contribution; (iii) To each according to his needs; (iv) From each according to his ability; and finally (v) To each according to rank and station. He then concludes that the formal demand for equality:

---

[114] Taylor (2011).

[115] Williams (1999), pp. 201–16.

[116] Ross (2019a, b), p. 350.

By no means precludes making a difference between persons who are situated in different circumstances. The only requirement is that this difference be motivated by the individuals in question being placed in different classes, according to certain relevant criteria.[117]

Hence, not all should receive equal pay, but only those who do the same kind of work, and not all should receive the same social benefits, but each according to his need, and so on depending on the type of equality notions. Having defined justice as such, Ross concludes that "the ideal of equality, as such, refers only to the correct application of a general rule", since "In the very principle of equality, however, there is nothing that would tell us what criteria are the relevant criteria".[118]

This approach to justice stands in direct opposition to the definition of justice and fairness by Kant, Rawls et alia, who indeed set up various relevant criteria for the general rule and its application, such as the Kantian Categorical Imperative, or the Rawlsian Veil of Ignorance and Original Position. Nonetheless, Ross admits the generality and universality of fairness and justice notions, noting "Even small children appeal to justice if one child gets a thicker apple slice than the other. It has even been claimed that animals possess an incipient sense of justice. The power of justice is enormous."[119]

But this begs the answer of how a universal notion, found even in small children not having any exposure to social context can display such a consistent and "general" notion of justice, which seems to denote "to each its own fair share", which by Ross is translated to equal application of the general rule, even if the general rule does not lead to "to each its own fair share"?

Against this positivist/realist account of justice, disconnecting law from morality, one can invoke the natural law tradition which rejects such an approach and firmly connects law with morality, beyond matters of design of laws and rule of law. This is the inherent content in the Latin legal maxim of *"lex iniusta non est lex"*, re-connecting to the body of Aristotelian thought, which was built upon by Thomas Aquinas, in that:

> Nothing other than an ordinance of reason for the common good, made by the person who has care of the community, and promulgated… it can be taken to assert that law that is not in the service of the common good is defective as law.[120]

The above division is also relevant when discussing the obligation on the part of the citizens to obey the valid law, and what deviations alongside moral norms can be allowed and accepted in the normative against valid law adopted in a procedurally correct fashion by the competent Sovereign. What of unjust laws, laws which run counter to human rights and the universality of moral concepts? The legal positivist "pure" answer is simple, in that:

---

[117] Ross (2019a, b) p. 361.

[118] Ross (2019a, b), pp. 361–362.

[119] Ross (2019a, b), p. 348.

[120] Duke (2017), p. 375.

> If the expression 'human rights' is meant to designate rights that human beings would possess and exercise independently of the state, or even against it, then from a strictly positivist point of view the question is easily resolved: there are no human rights[121]

The positivist position can be contrasted to the concept phrased by Augustine of Hippo, known as St. Augustine, some 1500 years ago, noting that unjust laws are not laws at all.[122] In his approach to legal philosophy by way of semantic deduction of the Latin terms Legere (to read) and Elegere (to select), he concludes that "lex" constitutes a selection of "the just", where he distinguishes between the law of Man, which is temporal and might be just or unjust, and the eternal (natural) law which is inherently just in and of itself.[123]

This view is further endorsed in the legal philosophy of Immanuel Kant as well as John Rawls,[124] and partly characterized in the debate between Ronald Dworkin and H.L.A Hart, with the former offering a scathing criticism of the latter´s positivist approach to law.[125]

Immanuel Kant can be said to have formulated the greatest treatise on the matter, complete with his formulation of the Categorical Imperative, a "moral law" to be determined by reasoned experience, denoting that all actions should be such that they could be elevated to a universal law.[126]

The categorical imperative is the fundamental principle of ethical action in the philosophy of Immanuel Kant, where the criterion of whether an action is morally good, the question is whether it follows a maxim whose validity would be acceptable to everyone, at any time and without exception, and whether all agents concerned are treated not as a mere means to an end, but as "End in itself"—Zweck an Sich.

The Kantian ethics further elevated the autonomy of will, moral duties and inherent human dignity, which would require ethical beings at times to act against their own preferences, in order to satisfy the moral principles adhered to, in direct opposition to the totality of the utilitarian approaches. Regarding the connection between Kantian ethics and legal philosophy and matters related to economics, As noted by Spector, quoting Valcke:

> Under the influence of natural lawyers, the law of contracts in civil law was shaped around the value of individual autonomy, which makes it recalcitrant to welfare maximization accounts. As Professor Catherine Valcke observes, '[t]he three foundational principles of civilian contract law-freedom of contract, binding force of contract, and consensualism - were directly derived from Kant's postulate of the autonomous will.[127]

---

[121] Invernizzi-Accetti (2018), p. 216.

[122] Stephens (2021), p. 1.

[123] Chroust (1950), p. 292 ff.

[124] Kant (1797), trans. Hastie (1887, 2010); Taylor (2011).

[125] Patterson (2019).

[126] Kant (1785, 2016).

[127] Spector (2004), p. 525.

The Kantian approach to the philosophy of science has been described as a Copernican turn in philosophy, with the major work being the Critique of Pure Reason.[128] The subjective manifestations of the objective, or "the original position" in Rawlsian discourse, do not negate the universality of the innate bias towards fairness, nor its capability to be approached from a law and economics perspective. Nevertheless, the Kantian ethics relied on judgement, experience and to balance obligations in a senseful way. As noted by White:

> This strong role for judgment in balancing duties, applying them to real-world circumstances with context, and choosing actions within the constraints of duty, makes his ethics far less demanding than perfectionist versions of utilitarianism, and closer to classical virtue ethics, with its emphasis on judgment and character.[129]

John Rawls on his part developed the concept of "Original Position", denoting a situation where the actors were to choose between different theories of justice and fairness regarding the distribution of outcomes. However, the actors were to be curtailed by a "veil of ignorance", deprived of all knowledge of their own personal characteristics and thus not aware in what position socially and politically they would end up after making the selection.

This would induce the actors towards the most "rational" choice which would be a society providing all actors regardless of their "original position" with the same set of basic freedoms and liberties to be able to pursue the maximum good however conceived by the actors, and equality in education and employment opportunities.[130]

Virtue ethics on the other hand denote the discourse on the virtues of the agents, instead of the consequences of the action, or the volition and intent and duties regarding those actions, re-connecting the theory with Aristotelian ethics as briefly sketched above. As such, and in contrast with the previous approaches, virtue ethics have been described as:

> Whereas consequentialists will define virtues as traits that yield good consequences and deontologists will define them as traits possessed by those who reliably fulfil their duties, virtue ethicists will resist the attempt to define virtues in terms of some other concept that is taken to be more fundamental. Rather, virtues and vices will be foundational for virtue ethical theories and other normative notions will be grounded in them.[131]

---

[128] Kant (1787), § 14; German Original of the entire passage "Es sind nur zwei Fälle möglich, unter denen synthetische Vorstellung und ihre Gegenstände zusammentreffen, sich aufeinander notwendigerweise beziehen, und gleichsam einander begegnen können. Entweder wenn der Gegenstand die Vorstellung, oder diese den Gegenstand allein möglich macht. Ist das erstere, so ist diese Beziehung nur empirisch, und die Vorstellung ist niemals a priori möglich. Und dies ist der Fall mit Erscheinung, in Ansehung dessen, was an ihnen zur Empfindung gehört. Ist aber das zweite, weil Vorstellung an sich selbst (denn von dessen Kausalität, vermittelst des Willens, ist hier gar nicht die Rede,) ihren Gegenstand dem Dasein nach nicht hervorbringt, so ist doch die Vorstellung in Ansehung des Gegenstandes alsdann a priori bestimmend, wenn durch sie allein es möglich ist, etwas als einen Gegenstand zu erkennen.".

[129] White (2019).

[130] Rawls (1999).

[131] Pettigrove and Zalta (2018).

Morality can thus be approached via both normative and descriptive routes, which in turn can be divided into group and individual levels, in defining the harm and good. As noted by Ernst-Joachim Mestmäcker in regard to the divide between Kantian[132] and Kelsenian[133] approach to the philosophy of laws:

> Positive law, according to Kant, is a matter of experience and is not necessarily in harmony with the principles of justice. But there are, according to Kant and contrary to Kelsen, principles of justice that are to guide legislation and adjudication. These principles follow from the inalienable rights of citizens against their sovereign to be respected in their dignity and liberty as self-governing individuals. The sovereign may not impose duties upon its subjects which the subjects would not impose upon themselves. This position is explicitly contrary to Hobbes, Bentham and their positivist followers, who find rights against the sovereign self-contradictory. In this respect, Kelsen is not a Kantian. Law, in his theory, is a normative system backed by credible threats of using physical force against the violator of the norm. The norm is a legal norm not because of its content, but because it is created in a certain way, ultimately in a way determined by a presupposed basic norm.[134]

As also noted by Spector regarding the Kantian element of European legal tradition:

> One cannot understand German legal science, for example, without taking into consideration the influence of rationalist natural lawyers like Pufendorf and Kant. In fact, the most abstract part of Savigny's legal theorizing can be regarded as a philosophical theory of civil law. Though all this fascinating intellectual process was over-shadowed by codification, there is no doubt that the philosophical paradigm can be brought to bear on the explanation of civil law. In fact, the philosophical paradigm is inspired in the rationalistic natural law school, which was historically associated with civil law.[135]

This legal-historical positioning by the Sovereign on "fair pricing" is by some accounts mirrored in the articulation of Article 102a TFEU, so Barry Hawk:

> The emphasis on fairness in pricing is directly mirrored in European notions of competition law, as seen in Article 102a of the Treaty on the Functioning of the European Union's statutory ban on unfair trading conditions (including excessive prices) by dominant firms.[136]

The emphasis on "fairness" can also partly be found in US Law, namely in the Federal Trade Commission Act, 15 U.S. Code § 45, which prohibits "unfair" methods of competition. Neither statues do define "fairness", the reason for which is the fact that fairness is an evolving concept and an operational part of all aspects of law.

The Kantian philosophy of law departs from the proposition that the abstract concept (in this case fairness and justice) can and should be made "real" by way of rational experience and by deference to the universality of the concepts, beyond individual tastes, cultures and so on.[137]

---

[132] Kant (1797).

[133] Kelsen (2009, originally printed 1934).).

[134] Mestmäcker (2007).

[135] Spector (2004).

[136] Hawk (2018), pp. 275–82; See also Gal (2013); and Watkins (1922).

[137] Watkins (2017), pp. 9–27; For a practical application of this "Kantian" approach in legal science, see Kianzad (2020), p. 6.

Nevertheless, as noted by Saad in reviewing Finn's take on Aquinas "the natural law does not entail drawing moral conclusions from facts about human nature. Rather, it means basing moral conclusions on the requirements of practical reason, which process can yield facts about human nature."[138]

This firmly connects the natural law tradition of St. Augustine and Thomas Aquinas to the Kantian approach (and criticism) of practical reason, deflecting the positivist and realist criticism against natural law as not being able to be approached objectively by way of a scientific falsification process.

The positivist criticism points to the fact that accepting the Natural Law approach would rule out all other approaches as standing against "human nature" and "divinity" or some other abstract deities such as "morality" and "universality", thus detracting from the "rational", "objective" and "scientific" element of the theory. The Kantian approach rebuts this criticism, as the "abstract" is being made "real" by way of practical reason and universal experience, thus no longer in the realm of "divinity".

Thus, the positivist criticism is not as strong when abstract matters such as fairness are made "real" by way of practical reason and rational experience in the Kantian sense, making it able to be criticised and analysed in a rational way, where each concept invariably must rely on a validating and "enabling" normative underpinning beyond the object of the study at hand.

Beyond the legal-philosophical perspective, there is support for this Kantian approach in the black letter law of "unfair pricing", not being defined further, and in the jurisprudence attempting to make the abstract "real", by way of the United Brands test targeting "unfair in itself" and "unfair when compared", offering some anchorage points for the fairness analysis to be undertaken, to remove it from the subjective realm and make it approachable, comparable and criticisable, by way of legal-dogmatic and teleological methods.

Hence in the Kantian discourse, it is the structured reasoning acting as a producer of experience, rather than merely a passive recipient of perception, which invariably must be organized. In so doing, Kant uses the legal discipline as an analogy, as one account of his analogy explains "Judges or legislators can be models for the critique because they can evaluate conflicting arguments or rulings and try to solve the dispute without being forced to choose between the claims of the parties."[139]

This point re-connects also to the matter of vagueness in law as opposed to legal certainty, where a great body of thought in both philosophies of law and language has been devoted to the subjects, with some thinkers elevating the need, value and importance of "vagueness in law", while others have castigated vagueness as being in direct conflict with the inherent value of legal certainty.

The division between Hart and Dworkin is apparent once more, in that the former elevated the importance of language philosophy in order to solve the problems created by "vagueness" in law, while the latter forwards a theory of concepts and conceptions, where concepts denote the general terms of the debate, while conceptions translate to a competing understanding of the concepts. According to this view by Dworkin,

---

[138] Saad (2017), p. 264.

[139] Møller (2013), p. 319.

judges would need to unlock the conception behind the concept which best explains it, while Hart disagrees and forwards discretion into the hand of judges.[140]

Fairness and justice may not be universally defined., nor so applied, but the notion of fairness and justice nevertheless forms the existential basis of all human societies throughout recorded history, if one approaches the legal science from a Kantian legal philosophy perspective. As noted by Baumard and Sperber:

> At first sight, moral judgments greatly differ across cultures, suggesting that human morality may be based on radically different systems of values. Evolutionary considerations on the bases of human cooperation suggest, however, that there must be evolved dispositions that make this cooperation sustainable. There are competing views regarding what these dispositions might be, an altruistic disposition to act for the benefit of the group even at an irredeemable cost to oneself, a mutualistic disposition to act and to expect others to act fairly, or some combination of both.[141]

Some may invoke on the other hand that the human nature and the innate nature of human societies is one of self-interest, focus on the immediate group one belongs to, and one of cruelty and injustices to the "other", however defined. Much of this line of argument is construed, supposedly, on a "Darwinian" notion of human evolution, where the process moves alongside "value-free" and "inexorable", almost automated meta-development, conditioned towards "survival of the fittest".

Indeed, the notion of Homo Oeconomicus, its implications for law and economics and the invocation of Darwin have been a matter of much heated debate, regarding individuals, "markets" and political economy at large.[142] However, Darwin himself did not ascribe to such notions, and indeed supported "objective morality" alongside evolutionary ethics, and included in his theory of evolution the evolution of "values" as such. Hence, Darwin noted that:

> There can be no doubt that a tribe including many members who, from possessing in a high degree the spirit of patriotism, fidelity, obedience, courage, and sympathy, were always ready to give aid to each other and to sacrifice themselves for the common good, would be victorious over most other tribes; and this would be natural selection.[143]

Adam Smith, being a moral philosopher, on his part did devote attention to moral philosophy in general, and the philosophy of laws, in particular, as developed in his Theory of Moral Sentiments.[144] For Smith, the basis of rights is a counterfactual account of injury, with Smith juxtaposing this against positive virtues, nevertheless adhering to the "innate" and universal nature of justice, stating:

> The rules of justice are accurate in the highest degree, and admit of no exceptions or modifications but such as may be ascertained as accurately as the rules themselves, and which generally, indeed, flow from the very same principles with them.[145]

---

[140] Endicott (2011), pp. 182 et seqq.

[141] Baumard and Sperber (2012), pp. 611–27.

[142] Fortsont (2001); Dworkin (1998), p. 1718; Hodgson (2002), pp. 259–81; Beck (2017), pp. 58–71.

[143] Darwin (1847); Ruse (2017), pp. 89–100; FitzPatrick (2017), pp. 188–201.

[144] Smith (1767).

[145] Smith, "Theory of Moral Sentiments", III, 6, § 10; cited in Haakonssen (1981).

Adam Smith worked partly in line with the virtue ethics of Plato and Aristotle but showed highly "Kantian" tendencies in connecting the reason-experience-induction dots which were later completed by Kant. As Smith explains:

> It is by reason that we discover those general rules of justice by which we ought to regulate our actions: and it is by the same faculty that we form those more vague and indeterminate ideas of what is prudent, of what is decent, of what is generous or noble, which we carry constantly about with us, and according to which we endeavour, as well as we can, to model the tenor of our conduct. The general maxims of morality are formed, like all other general maxims, from experience and induction.[146]

Thus, the grandfather of political economy seems to realize the inherent importance of fairness in relation to efficiency and its universal implication.[147] As such, both Smith and Darwin recognized not only the existence, but also the importance, of moral bonds and virtues in regard to human society. Nevertheless, Bentham broke with this tradition in forwarding utility as the only relevant and rational yardstick, dismissing philosophical notions of fairness and justice as superfluous. This utilitarian normative approach also dominates the Economic Analysis of Law in the tradition of Posner et alia.[148] As noted by Joe Sery in regard to Posner:

> Posner situates his project as the most reasonable, the most useful, and the most efficient approach to law. In order to do so, Posner articulates a connection between economics and common sense, suggesting the former is simply a codified version of the latter. Good judgment requires common sense, which is economic judgment by his definition.[149]

One could here invoke the criticism mounted by Immanuel Kant in his seminal work Kritik der reinen Vernunft,[150] where he methodically dismantled the rationalist and positivist argument in regard to what can be known to man and how, exposing the biases and conditions for arguments in regard to rationality. Indeed, as noted by Kant regarding the legal principle and maxim of pacta sunt servanda:

> From what has been said, it is evident that all Duties, merely because they are duties, belong to Ethic; and yet the Legislation upon which they are founded is not on that account in all cases contained in Ethics. On the contrary, the Law of many of them lies outside of Ethics. Thus Ethics commands that I must fulfil a promise entered into by Contract, although the other party might not be able to compel me to do so. It adopts the Law 'pacta sunt servanda,' and the Duty corresponding to it, from Jurisprudence or the Science of Right, by which they are established. It is not in Ethics, therefore, but in Jurisprudence, that the principle of the Legislation lies, that 'promises made and accepted must be kept[151]

---

[146] Smith (1861).

[147] Holler and Leroch (2010), pp. 311–19.

[148] Posner (1979b).

[149] Sery (2017).

[150] Kant (1781).

[151] Kant (1797); German Original reads "Hieraus ist zu ersehen, daß alle Pflichten bloß darum weil sie Pflichten sind, mit zur Ethik gehören; aber ihre Gesetzgebung ist darum nicht allemal in der Ethik enthalten, sondern von vielen derselben außerhalb derselben. So gebietet die Ethik, dass ich eine in einem Vertrage getane Anheischigmachung, wenn mich der andere Teil gleich nicht dazu zwingen könnte doch erfüllen müsse: sie nimmt das Gesetz (pacta sunt servanda) und die diesem

The fundamental difference in the normative approach to political economy between a utilitarian view and a Kantian view is thus equally manifest as irreconcilable. The Kantian approach is found essential for the purposes of the present inquiry on "unfair pricing in European competition law", when determining the conditions for knowledge and the boundaries between what can objectively be known about things and concepts in and of themselves regardless of subjective conceptions of those matters and things (das Ding an sich v. das Ding als es erscheint).[152]

This fundamental separation of things as they "appear" to us, on the one hand, and how things "are in themselves", materially a distinction between "sensibility" and "understanding", differ not only in form, but in kind. The concept of "thing in itself", or in the present inquiry, "unfair in itself", amounts to something imaginable and researchable.[153] It is an "abstract" made "real".

The reality of the concept nevertheless need not be theoretically demonstrable - what belongs to it can also be laid bare in practical sources of knowledge[154] and by way of accumulated experience along universal lines.[155] This also re-connects to the philosophy of Dworkin and the criticism of legal positivism of Hart et alia,[156] distinguishing between legal rules and legal principles. As noted by Bellamy:

> Unlike rules, principles—such as "no person may profit from his or her wrong"—do not simply apply or not apply. Rather, they operate as reasons that can be accorded different degrees of "weight" according to both the case at hand and interplay with other principles.[157]

The (in)congruence of abstract and real and their interdependent possibility conditions lies at the heart of the analysis when approaching the law and economics theories. Thus, the wording of "unfair in itself" regarding pricing by a dominant undertaking in United Brands has confounded those departing from the neoclassical-welfarist Economic Analysis of Law. Nevertheless, the legal discipline is both capable of and obliged to work in line with such abstractions as a matter of tradition and principle, with Kant laying some of the foundations of the European philosophy of law, which came to exert an enduring influence on many European legal scholars and constitutions.[158]

The influence of Kantian and Natural Law tradition on European legal development and scholarship diminished due to the emergence of Legal Positivist and

---

korrespondierende Pflicht aus der Rechtslehre als gegeben an. Also nicht in der Ethik, sondern im Jus liegt die Gesetzgebung, das angenommene Versprechen gehalten werden müssen"; Translation from: The Philosophy of Law, an exposition of the Fundamental Principles of Jurisprudence as the Science of Right; Immanuel Kant, translation from German by W.Hastie, B.D. Edinburgh; T & T Clark, 1887; available at: /https://socialsciences.mcmaster.ca/econ/ugcm/3ll3/kant/sciencelaw.pdf, accessed 2020-02-01.

[152] Kant (1781); see also Eisler (2020).

[153] Kianzad (2020), p. 6.

[154] The paragraph is partly an excerpt from Kianzad (2021), pp. 159–163.

[155] Watkins (2017).

[156] Kramer (2019).

[157] Bellamy (2015).

[158] Dietze (1956), pp. 73–91; The paragraph is an excerpt from Kianzad (2020).

Legal Realist schools, but Natural Law had a tremendous impact on the ethical and philosophical roots of European codification of ancient legal and moral norms.[159]

The ratio legis of pacta sunt servanda is thus a moral one, not an economic one, although the concept entails immense relevance regarding economic efficiency.[160] That being said, the question remains how to integrate fairness considerations in pricing and constraints on profit making as evidenced by behavioural economics in competition law assessment when applied to the present context of "unfair prices" as an exploitative abuse under Article 102a TFEU.

In so doing, one need not to endorse the totality of the Natural Law approach to legal philosophy, morality and jurisprudence in order to recognize the limits of legal positivism concerning the relevancy of moral principles and collective preferences related to incommensurable goods (also called public goods, merit goods etc.), beyond a "mechanical jurisprudence". Nonetheless, e.g. the Scandinavian Legal Realism tradition has consistently resisted approaches by other social sciences, including economics, to form a more central role in the jurisprudence.[161]

Hence, granting a free pass to e.g. unfair pricing of e.g. incommensurable goods would contradict the totality of the philosophy of Thomas Aquinas and Scholastic thought which was consequential in its pre-Kantian form, which by Kant came to be categorized as "Metaphysik der Sitten"[162] and also formed the basis of the Kantian Legal Philosophy.[163]

Writings which equate the Scholastic Just Price theory with marginalist and neoclassical "price obtainable in a free market" are a misreading of the Just Price tradition, and more espousing a Roman notion of the going market price under normal conditions.

Whether the only "scientific" way to analyse the competitive process is neoclassical, marginalist and welfarist economics, or if there are other "scientific" ways in economics to analyse the competitive process, or if the economic discipline can be said to adhere to "scientific" principles in the same vein as physics or biology or even other social sciences[164] ties into the grand debate on the claims and assumptions of the said schools, which have garnered much criticism ever since the inception of the disciplines,[165] but is partly outside of the focus of the current inquiry.

Looking at experimental and behavioural economics science, there is ample evidence that both firms and people take fairness seriously also regarding economic decisions. The implication of Fairness concerns for Game Theory and Equilibrium was already high-lighted by Rabin in 1993, noting "People like to help those who are helping them, and to hurt those who are hurting them...one should care not solely

---

[159] Tuck (1987), pp. 99–120; Padoa-Schioppa (2017); Ibbetson (2018).

[160] Mestmäcker (2007).

[161] Skogh (1991), pp. 319–24.

[162] Kant, Metaphysische Anfangsgründe der Rechtslehre, as first part of Metaphysik der Sitten (1797); this article has used Kant (1887, 2010).

[163] Kant (1887, 2010).

[164] Mäki (2002), pp. 3–32.

[165] Sery (2017).

about how concerns for fairness support or interfere with material efficiency, but also about how these concerns affect people's overall welfare."[166]

Earlier still, the seminal work by Kahneman, Knetsch and Thaler in 1986,[167] which is of great importance in the context of the present article on unfair pricing and fairness in economics, demonstrated that people are wary of pricing unfairness, where prior prices of the undertaking served as one benchmark for such fairness considerations. Just a year earlier in 1985, the non-maximising tendencies (framed around non-rationality) and their implications for rationality and overall Economic Equilibrium were also investigated by Akerlof and Yellen.[168]

Building on prior work by Artur Okun in 1981,[169] who had also observed that firms do not maximise prices despite facing excess demand (such as new models of auto-mobiles or tickets for events which ex-ante are known to generate excess demand), Kahneman et alia. investigated the fairness perceptions regarding (unfair)pricing.

The observed behaviour in the experimental games and the asserted human bias towards fairness and equity was by some labelled as altruism, however, the work by Fehr and Schmidt showed that this was not the case, as noted "Altruism is consistent with voluntary giving in dictator and public good games. It is, however, inconsistent with the rejection of offers in the ultimatum game, and it cannot explain the huge behavioural differences between public good games with and without punishment. It also seems difficult to reconcile the extreme outcomes in market games with altruism."[170]

They further showed that the selfish behaviour could also be observed, alongside the fairness considerations, and it was the setting of the game or market overall which also exercised a considerable impact, concluding "For example, in a market game with proposer or responder competition, it is very difficult, if not impossible, for fair players to achieve a "fair" outcome. Likewise, in a simultaneous public good game with punishment, even a small minority of selfish players can trigger the unravelling of cooperation. Yet, we have also shown that a minority of fair-minded players can force a big majority of selfish players to cooperate fully in the public good game with punishment."[171]

In summary, as noted by Maurice Stucke, forwarding a behavioural approach to competition law and policy "… antitrust policy is not divorced from subjective well-being. First, competition does not exist independently of legal and informal norms. Competition is defined in part by the prevailing legal and informal social, ethical, and moral norms",[172] thus underscoring the Kantian argument made in this paper that competition law must invariably rely on a ratio legis, preventing of undue wealth transfer, with fairness being a building block in both law and policy.

[166] Rabin (1993), pp. 1281–1302.
[167] Kahneman, Knetsch, and Thaler (1986a, b).
[168] Akerlof and Yellen (1985), pp. 708–20.
[169] Okun (1981).
[170] Fehr and Schmidt (1999), pp. 817–68.
[171] Fehr and Schmidt (1999).
[172] Stucke (2012).

6.5 Conclusions

As demonstrated, the deontological ethics of Kant stand in opposition to consequentialist and utilitarian approaches, as noted by White "The Kantian sense of autonomy implies that we can recognize reasons for action other than our own preferences and act on them when morality demands it".[173]

The inherent dilemma of using neoclassical economics or Economic Analysis of Law, which does not recognise a concept such as "fairness" and even less so "fairness in pricing", for the purposes of analysis of e.g., antitrust law on the same matters, seems to translate to an intellectual dead-end, not able to advance our knowledge when approaching e.g. the European legal prohibition of unfair and excessive pricing, entailed in e.g. Article 102a TFEU.

The main reason for a Kantian, rights-based approach to Law and Economics is as aforementioned to be found in the internal fallacy of the mainstream strand of Law and Economics school, conflating positive with normative analysis, and thus unable or unwilling to properly account for social preferences and social institutions, such as legal rules, and thus equating the sole object of competition law to promoting efficiency.

Even though the concepts are in and of themselves prone to subjective interpretation, the Kantian experimental thought-scheme discussed above aids the legal system in arriving at a more 'objective' and 'a priori' point in regard to these abstract notions. This process is not always a conscious, philosophical exercise in the minds of judges and lawyers, many of whom might not even be aware of the Kantian tradition influencing their reasoning, but even where it is tacit, the influence is observable.[174]

Engaging with the "mainstream" arguments against the inclusion of "fairness" in a coherent legal-economic discourse on competition law is thus not only warranted by the compounding weight of behavioural, experimental and neuro-economic evidence—It is mainly motivated by the true nature of competition law and economics, if one is to take the "law" as seriously as the latter part of "economics". As rightly pointed out by Mestmäcker, there is a manifest risk that without taking inherent legal values, informed by ethics, into account, the law and economics movement risk to translate to a "legal theory without law".[175]

The criticism is also found in bodies such as the OECD, which in a report in 2019 presented various strands of new economic thinking summarized under the New Approaches to Economic Challenges (NAEC) initiative. The report, titled "Beyond Growth: Towards a New Economic Approach", focused on the short-comings of neo-classical economics and the need to replace the dominant narrative of the past 40 years with a more coherent approach, incorporating the many novel insights available through recent research and experiments. The report focused on the need

---

[173] White (2019).

[174] This brief section on Kantian legal-philosophy is an excerpt from Kianzad (2020), p. 6.

[175] Mestmäcker (2007).

for economic thinking to incorporate more than the overarching goals of neo-classical economics, and the need to give more prominence to questions of "equity."[176]

Naturally, models will become inherently more complex if one is to relax the rationality assumption, but it does not mean that any modelling or prediction would be impossible altogether.[177]

The volition inherent in legal rules matter, not only their fair or unfair consequence, and Pareto efficiency or Pareto Optimality does not mean that a society would be organized "justly", however justice may be defined, why the matter of initial endowments relating to production and property is known.[178]

Recognizing the concept and collective preferences in regard to fairness is nevertheless only the first step in complementing the theories of harm and models used, as the fairness-concept need to be integrated as well. As noted by Schwartz "The difficult question is not whether non-economic considerations are a proper, indeed conventional, component of the antitrust calculus, but how to take them into account."[179]

A considerable body of economics has been devoted to the question of fairness and economics,[180] fairness in law and economics,[181] and related matters of "fair pricing" and "fairness in pricing". The challenge is thus less one of finding alternative approaches, but rather to recognize and integrate such approaches in the "mainstream" neoclassical discourse.

Indeed, the aversion of some strands of law and economics disciplines towards issues of fairness, and their overt focus on over-formalism and parochialism as noted by Mattei have "…consumed much of its early capital of prestige, and that the decline phase of the economic approach in legal reasoning is well on its way"[182]. The neoclassical economists nevertheless continue to predict and profess the "inevitable fall" of what they somewhat derogatory label as "Hipster Antitrust."[183]

As money, markets, government, and property are ipso facto ontologically subjective matters, can they ever be epistemically objectively studied? The answer lies in the affirmative, as the disciplines of economics, political science and the law of property demonstrate, each having its own internal order. Thus, the position by Alf Ross et alia that "fairness" is subjective and prone to be captured by whims and whisks of Zeitgeist to represent all and nothing is itself prone to the same criticism as the totality of law is an observer dependent study, no matter if is framed by way of Kantian or Kelsenian approach.

---

[176] General Secretariat OECD, "BEYOND GROWTH: TOWARDS A NEW ECONOMIC APPROACH—Report of the Secretary General's Advisory Group on a New Growth Narrative," September 12, 2019, p. 5.

[177] Korobokin and Ulen (2000), pp. 1051–1144.

[178] Mathis (2009), p. 35.

[179] Schwartz (1979).

[180] For a major collective works see: Cappelen and Tungodden (2019).

[181] See also Fennell and McAdams (2013).

[182] Mattei (2005).

[183] Wright et al. (2018).

But it is also correct that procedural fairness is more apt to be framed in rational and practical terms, than the general concept of "fairness" without being defined closer, spurring questions such as "fairness to whom". Fairness in this context is thus defined as denoting equitable exchange, in the Aristotelian tradition, where Aristotle defined it as:

> But the justice in transactions between man and man is a sort of equality need, and the injustice a sort of inequality…according to arithmetical proportion…Therefore, this kind of injustice being an inequality, the judge tries to equalize it…therefore the equal is the intermediate between the greater and the less…therefore the corrective justice is the intermediate between loss and gain.[184]

It is further a misunderstanding of the Kantian rights- and duty-based approach of function and nature of laws to equate this line of legitimacy for competition law and consumer welfare standard to include fairness preferences to "distributive justice",[185] since the Kantian discourse targets the corrective and commutative justice function of the laws as normatively relevant.

This further testaments to the universal character of the concept and social preferences, that evolved during the human evolution. This view of fairness, as being both universal as well as evolutionary, is in line with the reasoning of Darwin, Smith, Kant, Rawls, Binmore et alia, and further reinforced by neuro-economic and neuro-psychological research.[186]

Even the claim that fairness is not able to be aggregative and as such is not able to function in commonly used models has been refuted, as noted "We observe that there are theories of fairness, particularly those that are based on cooperative game theory, that do not face the problem of non-aggregativity. We use this observation to argue that the universal claim that no non-trivial theory of fairness can guarantee aggregativity is false."[187]

A Neo-Kantian approach to Competition Law and Economics is long-overdue, where fairness should and could be a vital tenet of competition law, due to historical, legal and economic reasons; and due to the legitimacy of competition law in being capable of fulfilling the most basic legal criterion, that is administering fairness and justice, but also to prevent undue wealth transfer.[188]

Although Competition law might not be intended, nor capable and suitable for solving all the Grand Problems of inequality if approached by way of re-distribution, Competition Law remains the most important tool in regards to the prevention of undue wealth transfer, reversal and correction of initial endowment and thus the main checks-and-balances system in place regarding abuse of market power, which further contributes to in-equality.

---

[184] Aristotle, translated by Ross (1999).

[185] Nance and von Platz (2018), pp. 250–68.

[186] Cappelen et al. (2014).

[187] Wintein and Heilmann (2020), pp. 715–38.

[188] Lande (1982).

As aptly summarized by Klaus Mathis "In people's minds, justice—however it is defined—has an immanent value, which is very difficult to weigh up against an increase in economic efficiency."[189]

Bibliography

Akerlof GA, Yellen JL (1985) Can small deviations from rationality make significant differences to economic equilibria? Am Econ Rev 75(4):708–720

Aristotle (1999) Nicomachean ethics. Translated by W.D Ross. Kitchener

Bartalevich D (2016) The influence of the chicago school on the commission's guidelines, notices and block exemption regulations in EU competition policy: the influence of the Chicago School. JCMS: J Common Market Stud 54(2):267–83

Bashar M (1997) Price control in an Islamic economy. J King Abdulaziz Univ-Islamic Econ 9:29–52

Baumard N, Sperber D (2012) Evolutionary and Cognitive Anthropology. In: Fassin D (ed) A Companion to Moral Anthropology. J. Chichester, pp. 611–627

Beck N (2017) Social darwinism and market morality a modern-day view. In: Ruse M, Richards RJ (eds) The cambridge handbook of evolutionary ethics. Cambridge, pp. 58–71

Bellamy R (2015) Ronald Dworkin, taking rights seriously. In: Levy JT (ed), The Oxford Handbook of Classics in Contemporary Political Theory, Oxford

Berns et al (2012) The price of your soul: neural evidence for the non-utilitarian representation of sacred values. Philos Trans: Biol Sci 367(1589):754–762

Binmore K (2005) Natural justice. Oxford

Bix B H (2017) Moral philosophy and law and economics. The Oxford handbook of law and economics: volume 1: methodology and concepts, Parisi F (ed), vol. 1. Oxford

Blaug M (2001) Is competition such a good thing? Static efficiency versus dynamic efficiency. Rev Indus Organ 19

Bork RH (1978) The antitrust paradox: a policy at war with itself. New York

Broome J (1990) Fairness. Proc Aristot Soc 91:87–101

Calabresi G (2019) Of law and economics and economic analysis of law: the role of the lawyer. Global Jurist 19(3)

Cappelen AW, Eichele T, Hugdahl K, Specht K, Sorensen EO, Tungodden B (2014) Equity theory and fair inequality: a neuroeconomic study. Proc Natl Acad Sci 111(43):15368–15372

Cappelen AW, Tungodden B (eds) (2019) The economics of fairness. International library of critical writings in economics series. Cheltenham

Chartier G, Fox JL (2019) Incommensurable goods. In: Crowe J, Lee C (eds), Research handbook on natural law theory. Cheltenham, pp. 253–66

Chroust AH, Osborn DL (1942) Aristotle's conception of justice. Notre Dame Law Review 17(2)

Chroust A H (1950) St. Augustine's philosophical theory of law. Notre Dame Law Review 5(2)

Curtis BL (2014) To be fair. Analysis 74(1):47–57

Darwin C (1847) The Descent of Man and Selection in Relation to Sex

Dietze G (1956) Natural Law in the Modern European Constitutions. Am J Jurisprud 1(1):73–91

Driesen D, Malloy RP (2017) Critiques of law and economics. In: Parisi F (ed), The Oxford Handbook of Law and Economics, Vol. 1: Methodology and Concepts. Oxford

Duke G (2017) The Common Good. The Cambridge Companion to Natural Law Jurisprudence. In: Duke G and George RP (eds.), 1st ed., Cambridge. pp. 369–96

Dworkin RM (1977) Taking rights seriously. Cambridge MA

Dworkin RM (1980) Is wealth a value? J Leg Stud 9(2):191–226

Dworkin RM (1998) Darwin's new bulldog. Harv Law Rev 111(7):1718

---

[189] Mathis (2009), p. 48.

Eisler R, Das Ding an Sich, in: Kant-Lexikon, available at: https://www.textlog.de/32917.html, accessed 22 October 2020

Endicott T (2011) Vagueness and law. Vagueness: a guide, Ronzitti G (ed). Dordrecht, pp. 182 ff.

Eyster E, Madarasz K, Michaillat P (2020) Pricing under fairness concerns. J Euro Econ Assoc

Fehr E, Schmidt KM (2006) Chapter 8, The economics of fairness, reciprocity and altruism—experimental evidence and new theories. In: Handbook of the Economics of Giving, Altruism and Reciprocity, 1:615–91. Amsterdam

Fehr E, Schmidt KM (1999) A theory of fairness, competition, and cooperation. Q J Econ 114(3):817–868

Fennell LA, McAdams RH (eds) (2013) Fairness in law and economics. Economic approaches to law series. Cheltenham

FitzPatrick WJ (2017) Why darwinism does not debunk objective morality. In: Ruse M, Richards RJ (eds), The Cambridge handbook of evolutionary ethics. Cambridge, pp. 188–201

Fleurbaey M, Tungodden B, Chang HF (2003) Any non-Welfarist method of policy assessment violates the Pareto principle: a comment. J Polit Econ 111(6):1382–1385

Flynn JJ (1988) Legal reasoning, antitrust policy and the social 'science' of economics. Antitrust Bull 33(4):713–743

Fortsont R (2001) Problems with Richard Posner's the problematics of moral and legal theory. William Mitchell Law Rev 27(4):2345–2373

Frédéric J (2018) Abuse of Dominance by firms charging excessive or unfair prices: an assessment. In: Katsoulacos Y, Jenny F (eds), Excessive pricing and competition law enforcement. Cham, pp. 5–70

Garrath W (1999) Nietzsche's Response to Kant's Morality. The Philosophical Forum 30(3):201–216

Glick M, Lozada GA (2021) The erroneous foundations of law and economics. Institute for New Economic Thinking Working Paper Series, February

Greene JD, Nystrom LE, Engell AE, John DD, Cohen JD (2004) The neural bases of cognitive conflict and control in moral judgment. Neuron 44(2):389–400

Haakonssen K (1981) The science of a legislator: the natural jurisprudence of David Hume and Adam Smith. 1st ed. Cambridge

Hart HLA (2012) The concept of law, Raz J (ed). Oxford

Hausman DM, McPherson MS (eds) (2006) Ethics and economics? Economic analysis, moral philosophy and public policy, 2nd ed. Cambridge, pp. 3–11

Hawk B (2018) Antitrust in history. Antitrust Bull 63(3):275–282

Herz H, Taubinsky D (2018) What makes a price fair? an experimental study of transaction experience and endogenous fairness views. J Eur Econ Assoc 16(2):316–352

Hodgson GM (2002) Darwinism in economics: from analogy to ontology. J Evol Econ 12(3):259–281

Holler MJ, Leroch M (2010) Efficiency and justice revisited. Eur J Polit Econ 26(3):311–319

Hovenkamp H (2020) FRAND and antitrust. Cornell Law Rev 105:1683–1744

Hsu M, Anen C, Quartz SR (2008) The right and the good: distributive justice and neural encoding of equity and efficiency. Science 320(5879):1092–1095

Ibbetson D (2018) Natural law in early modern legal thought. In: Pihlajamäki H, Dubber MD, Godfrey M (eds), The Oxford Handbook of European Legal History, vol. 1. Oxford

Invernizzi-Accetti C (2018) Reconciling Legal Positivism and Human Rights: Hans Kelsen's Argument from Relativism, Journal of Human Rights 17, no. 2, pp. 215–28

Jenny F (2018), Abuse of Dominance by Firms Charging Excessive or Unfair Prices: An Assessment, in: Katsoulacos Y, Jenny F (eds), Excessive Pricing and Competition Law Enforcement, Cham, pp. 5–70

Johnson HG (1973), Some Micro-Economic Reflections on Income and Wealth Inequalities, The Annals of the American Academy of Political and Social Science, Vol. 409, pp. 53–60

Kahneman D, Knetsch JL, Thaler RH (1986a) Fairness and the assumptions of economics. J Bus 59(S4):285–300

Kahneman D, Knetsch JL, Thaler RH (1986b) Fairness as a Constraint on Profit Seeking: Entitlements in the Market. Am Econ Rev 76(4):728–774

Kaius T and Björklund H (2019) Roman Law and the Idea of Europe. Europe's Legacy in the Modern World. London

Kant I (1785) Grundlegung zur Metaphysik der Sitten. 2., Durchgesehene Auflage mit aktualisierter Einleitung und Bibliographie. Philosophische Bibliothek, Band 519. Hamburg 2016

Kant I (1797) The philosophy of law. An exposition of the fundamental principles of jurisprudence as the science of right. Translated by W. Hastie. The Lawbook Exchange - Re-printed from Original by T & T Clark, Edingburgh, 1887, 2010

Kant I (1781), Critik der reinen Vernunft, Riga

Kant I (1787), Kritik der reinen Vernunft, Riga

Kaplow L, Shavell S (2001) Fairness versus welfare. Harv Law Rev 114(4):961–1388

Kaplow L, Shavell S (2003) Fairness versus welfare: notes on the pareto principle, preferences, and distributive justice. J Legal Stud 32(1):331–362

Kelsen H (2009) Pure theory of law. Translation from the Second German Edition by Max Knight. Originally published: Berkeley, 1967. Reprinted 2002, 2009 by The Lawbook Exchange, Ltd.

Kianzad B, Minssen T (2018) How much is too much? defining the metes and bounds of excessive pricing in the pharmaceutical sector. Euro Pharm Law Rev 2(3):133–148

Kianzad B (2020) Did the Danish supreme court give the fashion industry the Kantian boot? GRUR International, 6

Kianzad B (2022) The giant awakens: law and economics of excessive pricingduring the COVID-19 crisis. In: Mathis K, Tor A (eds), Law and economics of the coronavirus crisis, vol 13. Economic analysis of law in European legal scholarship. Cham, pp. 123–76

Kirkpatrick JR, Eastwood N (2015) Broome's Theory of Fairness and the Problem of Quantifying the Strengths of Claims. Utilitas 27(1):82–91

Kleinman E (1987) 'Just Price' in Talmudic Literature. History of Political Economy 19, no. 1. Durham

Koehn D, Wilbratte B (2012) A Defense of a Thomistic Concept of the Just Price. Bus Ethics Q 22(3):501–526

Koenigs M, Young L, Adolphs R, Tranel D, Cushman F, Hauser M, Damasio A (2007) Damage to the Prefrontal Cortex Increases Utilitarian Moral Judgements. Nature 446(7138):908–911

Korobokin RB, Ulen TS (2000) Law and Behavioral Science: Removing the Rationality Assumption from Law and Economics. Calif Law Rev 88(4):1051–1144

Kramer M H (2019) The Legal Positivism of H.L.A. Hart. University of Cambridge, Faculty of Law, Research Paper No. 11

Kronman AT (1980) Wealth Maximization as a Normative Principle. J Leg Stud 9(2):227–242

Lande R H (1982) Wealth Transfers as the Original and Primary Concern of Antitrust: The Efficiency Interpretation Challenged. Hastings Law Journal 34, no. 1

Lazenby H (2014) Broome on Fairness and Lotteries. Utilitas 26(4):331–345

Lianos I (2020) Competition Law as a Form of Social Regulation. The Antitrust Bulletin 65(1):3–86

Mäki U (2002) The Dismal Queen of the Social Sciences. In: Mäki U (ed), Fact and Fiction in Economics, 1st ed. Cambridge. pp. 3–32

Makovi M (2016) Price Controls in Jewish Law. Munich Personal RePEc Archive MPRA Paper No. 72821

Malc D, Damijan M, Pisnik A (2016) Exploring Price Fairness Perceptions and Their Influence on Consumer Behavior. J Bus Res 69(9):3693–3697

Marciano A, Ramello GB (2014) Law and Economics: The Legacy of Guido Calabresi. Law Contemp Probl 77(2):8

Mathis K (2009), Efficiency Instead of Justice? Searching for the Philosophical Foundations of the Economic Analysis of Law. Translated by Deborah Shannon. Law and Philosophy Library. New York

Mattei U (2005) The Rise and Fall of Law and Economics: An Essay for Judge Guido Calabresi. Maryland Law Review 64, no. 1.

McAuliffe K, Blake P R and Warneken F (2017) Do Kids Have a Fundamental Sense of Fairness? Scientific American. https://blogs.scientificamerican.com/observations/do-kids-have-a-fundam ental-sense-of-fairness/. Last access 29 November 2023

Mendez MF (2009) The Neurobiology of Moral Behavior: Review and Neuropsychiatric Implications. CNS Spectr 14(11):608–620

Mestmäcker E J A (2007) Legal Theory without Law. Tübingen

Miller J (2011) Aristotle's Nicomachean Ethics a Critical Guide, Cambridge

Møller S C (2013) The Court of Reason in Kant's Critique of Pure Reason. Kant-Studien 104, no. 3

Mousourakis G (2015) Roman Law and the Origins of the Civil Law Tradition. Cham

Nance M and von Platz J (2018) From Justice to Fairness Does Kant's Doctrine of Right Imply a Theory of Distributive Justice. In: Moran KA (ed), Kant on Freedom and Spontaneity. Cambridge, pp. 250–268

Isaac N (1920) The revival of the Justum Pretium. Cornell L. Q 6, no. 381

OECD, General Secretariat. Beyond Growth: Towards a New Economic Approach - Report of the Secretary General's Advisory Group on a New Growth Narrative, September 12, 2019

Okun A (1975), Equality and Efficiency - The Big Tradeoff, New York

Okun A (1981) Prices and Quantities: A Macroeconomic Analysis. Washington, D.C.

Oswald von NB (1950) The concept of just price. Rev Soc Econ 8(2):111–22

Padoa-Schioppa A (2017) A History of Law in Europe: From the Early Middle Ages to the Twentieth Century. Translated by Caterina Fitzgerald. 1st ed. Cambridge

Patterson D (2019) Dworkin's Criticisms of Hart's Positivism. In: In Mindus P and Spaak T (eds.), The Cambridge Companion to Legal Positivism draft of 1 March 2019. Rutgers Law School Research Paper

Pettigrove G and Zalta E N (2018) Virtue Ethics. The Stanford Encyclopedia of Philosophy, Winter Edition

Piller C (2017) Treating Broome Fairly. Utilitas 29(2):214–238

Piron R, Fernandez L (1995) Are Fairness Constraints on Profit-Seeking Important? J Econ Psychol 16(1):73–96

Posner RA (1979a) Some Uses and Abuses of Economics in Law. The University of Chicago Law Review 46(2):281–306

Posner RA (1979b) Utilitarianism, Economics, and Legal Theory. The Journal of Legal Studies 8, no. 1.

Posner RA (1980) The Ethical and Political Basis of the Efficiency Norm in Common Law Adjudication. Hofstra Law Review 8.

Posner A (1986) Economic Analysis of Law. Boston

Posner RA (2014) Economic Analysis of Law. Ninth edition. New York

Rabin M (1993) Incorporating Fairness into Game Theory and Economics. Am Econ Rev 83(5):1281–1302

Radbruch G (1973) Rechtsphilosophie, 8th edn. Wolf E and Schneider HP (eds.), Stuttgart

Rawls JA (1985) Justice as Fairness: Political Not Metaphysical. Philos Public Aff 14(3):223–251

Rawls JA (1999) Theory of Justice, Revised Edition. Cambridge MA

Raz J (1990) The Politics of the Rule of Law. RATIO JURIS 3:331–339

Ross A (2019) [347] Analysis and Critique of the Philosophy of Natural Law. In: On Law and Justice. pp. 335–46. Oxford

Ross A (2019) On Law and Justice. Holtermann H and Bindreiter U (eds.) Oxford

Rotemberg J (2011) Fair Pricing. J Eur Econ Assoc 9(5):952–981

Ruse M (2017) Darwinian Evolutionary Ethics. In: Ruse M, Richards RJ (eds) The Cambridge Handbook of Evolutionary Ethics. Cambridge, pp. 89–100

Saad TC (2017) The Cambridge Companion to Natural Law Jurisprudence. The New Bioethics 23(3):263–265

Salzberger E M (2007) The Economic Analysis of Law - The Dominant Methodology for Legal Research?! University of Haifa Faculty of Law Legal Studies Research Paper No. 1044382

Salzberger E (2013) Law and Economics - Limits of Analysis: The Case of Intellectual Property. In: Metelska-Szaniawska K (ed), Polish Yearbook of Law & Economics, Vol. 2. Wydawnictwo

Saunders B (2010) Fairness Between Competing Claims. Res Publica 16(1):41–55

Schmidt MFH, Sommerville JA (2011) Fairness Expectations and Altruistic Sharing in 15-Month-Old Human Infants. Edited by Matjaz Perc. Plos ONE 6(10):e23223

Schwartz LB (1979) Justice and Other Non-Economic Goals of Antitrust. University of Pennsylvania Law Review 127:1076–1081

Screpanti E and Zamagni S (2005), An Outline of the History of Economic Thought, Oxford.

Sen AK (1984) Resources, values, and development, Cambridge MA

Sery J (2017) Richard Posner and the Rhetoric of (Economic) Common Sense. Common Law Review 16, no. 1

Smith A (1767), The theory of moral sentiments. To which is added a dissertation on the origin of languages, printed for A. Millar, A. Kincaid and J. Bell in Edinburgh; and sold by T. Cadell in the Strand, London, p. 148

Skogh G (1991) Law and Economics in Sweden, International Review of Law and Economics 11, no. 3, pp. 319–24

Smith A (1861) Part VII. Of Systems of Moral Philosophy. In The Theory of Moral Sentiments; or, an Essay towards an Analysis of the Principles by Which Men Naturally Judge Concerning the Conduct and Character, First of Their Neighbors, and Afterwards of Themselves, to Which Is Added a Dissertation on the Origin of Languages (New Ed.)., by Adam Smith, London. pp. 389–538

Spector H (2004) Fairness and Welfare from a Comparative Law Perspective. Chicago-Kent Law Review 79, no. 2 Symposium: Law and Economics and Legal Scholarship, pp. 521–39

Stephens J (2021) Universal Human Rights and Their Justifiability. Academia Letters, 1

Stiglitz J (2017) Towards a Broader View of Competition Policy. In: Bonakele T, Fox EM, and Mncube L (eds), Competition Policy for the New Era: Insights from the BRICS Countries, Oxford

Stiglitz J (2019) Competition policy, the need for a more nuanced view, interview, concurrences, pp. 16–17, n.d

Stucke M E (2012) OECD Hearing on Competition and Behavioural Economics - The Implications of Behavioral Antitrust - DAF/COMP/WD(2012)12

Sunstein CR, Thaler RH, Jolls CM (1998) A Behavioral Approach to Law and Economics. Stanford Law Review 50(5):1471–1550

Taylor RS (2011) Reconstructing Rawls: The Kantian Foundations of Justice as Fairness. University Park

Tocqueville A (1835) Democracy in America, Chapter XV: Unlimited Power Of Majority, And Its Consequences - Part II, 1835, translation by Henry Reeve, A Penn State Electronic Classics Series Publication, 2002 edition, University Park

Tomlin P (2012) On Fairness and Claims. Utilitas 24(2):200–213

Tuck R (1987) The 'Modern' Theory of Natural Law. In: Pagde A (ed), The Languages of Political Theory in Early-Modern Europe, 1st ed., Cambridge. pp. 99–120

Ulen T S (2015) Law and Economics, the Moral Limits of the Market, and Threshold Deontology. In: Hatzis AN and Mercuro N (eds), Law and Economics: Philosophical Issues and Fundamental Questions, 1st ed. Milton Park

Veljanovski CG (1981) Wealth Maximization, Law and Ethics—On the Limits of Economic Efficiency. Int Rev Law Econ 1(1):5–28

von Nell-Breuning O (1950), The Concept of Just Price, Review of Social Economy 8, no. 2, pp. 111–22

Vong G (2015) Fairness, Benefiting by Lottery and the Chancy Satisfaction of Moral Claims. Utilitas 27(4):470–486

Watkins E (1922) The Law and the Profits. Yale Law J 32(1):29–36

Watkins E (2017) Kant on the Distinction between Sensibility and Understanding. In: OShea JR (ed), Kant's Critique of Pure Reason, Cambridge. pp. 9–27.

Werden GJ (2021) Exploitative Abuse of a Dominant Position: A Bad Idea That Now Should Be Abandoned. European Competition Journal 17(3):682–713

White M D (2019) With All Due Respect: A Kantian Approach to Economics. In: Whie MD (ed), The Oxford Handbook of Ethics and Economics. Oxford. pp. 54–76

Williams G (1999) Nietzsche's Response to Kant's Morality, The Philosophical Forum 30, no. 3, pp. 201–16

Wintein S, Heilmann C (2018) Dividing the Indivisible: Apportionment and Philosophical Theories of Fairness. Politics, Philosophy & Economics 17(1):51–74

Wintein S, Heilmann C (2020) Theories of fairness and aggregation. Erkenntnis 85(3):715–738

Wright J D, Dorsey E, Rybnicek J, Klick J (2018) Requiem for a paradox: the dubious rise and inevitable fall of hipster antitrust. George Mason Law and Economics Research Paper No. 18–29, Arizona State Law Journal 2019

Chapter 7
The Relevance of Law and Economics for Practical Reasoning

Régis Lanneau

Abstract In this paper, I will show that most of the debates regarding the relevance of law and economics for practical decision-making (law and economics is then used to make a choice in the real world) are based on the idea that there would exist a scientific "right" way to approach legal issues and decision making. According to this perspective, all issues (legal, political or scientific) should be addressed using the same method and the same scientific rationality. If we deviate from this very modern (and utopic) conceptualization to stress an inherent difference between practical reasoning and scientific reasoning, it is impossible to deny the relevance of law and economics for practical decision-making in the realm of law. This approach will also force us to reconsider the relevance and practice of law and economics.

7.1 Introduction

Law and economics is often considered, by its opponents, as providing an impoverished view of the range of human actions and interactions (since it overemphasizes rationality[1] and the logic of exchange[2]), of law (missing some of its important characteristics[3]) and of morality (focusing exclusively on efficiency[4] and disregarding

---

[1] See for example, Archer and Trittner (2000). Social conditioning, emotions and cultures are difficult to grasp with the idea of rationality.

[2] Any interaction is conceptualized as an exchange which is not necessarily how people conceptualize this.

[3] The question of validity is impossible to understand from the economic logic. Moreover, law and economics does not really define what law is or what are the characteristics that makes a norm a law.

[4] For example, Dworkin (1980).

R. Lanneau (✉)
Institut de Préparation à l'Administration Générale, Université Paris Nanterre, Paris, France
e-mail: rlanneau@parisnanterre.fr

social justice[5]). "Can anyone seriously argue that rape is criminal because otherwise, individuals have the option of changing property rules into liability rules?"[6] Can anyone advocate for a free market for babies?[7] Can we seriously consider that the wealthy should be able to "buy justice"?[8] Can we really argue that efficiency should be the only concerns of judges in a democratic society? Can we seriously consider that evacuating a city would be more efficient through a market system than through command and control?[9] Can we seriously argue that efficiency requires that rich countries should export their trash to poor countries[10]? Is it really sensible to argue that the liberty to procreate should be abandoned[11]? It is certainly possible to do so to be provocative or simply to be read... and it is undeniable that such reads could be quite pleasant. Nevertheless, it is sometimes difficult to know whether (or sometimes to believe that) the authors of these papers really "believe" what they wrote and would be ready to implement the solutions they advocate for. They merely could have tried to "explore" an issue or "explain" a phenomenon using the tools of economics without endorsing the results. However, in that latter case, how could we assess the relevance of these explorations or explanations for practical decision-making[12]?

The normative relevance of law and economics was certainly addressed in some papers and books. For example, Posner tried to justify the ethics of efficiency in his book The Economics of Justice.[13] Russel Hardin also tried to justify the "morality" of law and economics.[14] Not surprisingly, critics of these justifications were numerous stressing the theoretical limits of efficiency[15] or the ideology hidden behind what could have appeared to a non-expert eye as value-neutral.[16] After all, dealing with what ought to be cannot find a scientific answer since any theory of justice relies on certain value judgments which, by definition, cannot be "true" or "false". Does that mean that only those who believe in efficiency as a criterion of justice could become law and economics scholars? And if we do not believe in certain value judgments made by law and economics scholars, does that mean that we could disregard the discipline or consider that it is irrelevant for decision-making or addressing ethical questions?

---

[5] For example, Ackerman and Heinzerling (2004).

[6] Colman (2003 [1998]), p. 162. The discussion on rape appears in the 3rd edition of Richard Posner's Economic analysis of law.

[7] Landes and Posner (1978). If this article is often portrayed as advocating for a free market in babies, a careful reading of the paper imposes more nuance. It is probably required to read the clarification offered by Richard Posner (1987a, 1987b).

[8] Lott (1987).

[9] This point appears in George Stigler autobiography. Stigler (1988).

[10] This proposition was made by Lawrence Summers; See Swaney (1994).

[11] Hardin (1968).

[12] Some academics do not consider that the frontier between positive and normative economics is largely blurred.

[13] Posner (1981). See also Posner (1980).

[14] Hardin (1992).

[15] For example, Dworkin (1980). Zamir and Medina (2010), Mercuro and Ryan (1984).

[16] See for example, Teles (2008), Baker (1975).

It is of course possible, at this stage, to try to dissolve the question (which means that this question did not find an adequate answer) or to find a way to provide a form of an answer. Kaplow and Shavell[17], for example, considered that welfare should be the only relevant basis for social policies. Corrective and redistributive justice and, more largely, fairness would then be irrelevant considerations (they nevertheless defined these notions in a very particular way[18]). This result is largely based on the fact that "tastes for fairness" are included in the preference of individuals. Maximizing welfare thus includes considerations for fairness; focusing solely on fairness would be disregarding individuals' preferences in this matter. If this result is theoretically consistent (considering the definitions of the authors), it is practically difficult to use it for decision-making. Indeed, the aggregation of individuals' well-being is far from being an easy task (there are many arbitrary ways to create a social welfare function[19]) and two or more coherent aggregations of individuals' well-being might lead to different collective decisions (assuming that the decision maker is benevolent which is a strong assumption).

Another strategy would be to "enrich" law and economics such that its results might appear more "relevant" or "compatible" with our moral intuitions. For example, Calabresi recently tried to promote the concept of moral externalities and to reintroduce the concept of merit goods.[20] If these concepts are certainly attractive, it is unclear if their integration within the traditional law and economics framework would really "improve" law and economics.[21]

Disregarding attacks stressing the ideology of the movement (it is supposed to inherently be "conservative" or "libertarian"[22]) to discredit its practical relevance, few are the scholars who consider that law and economics (whatever its methodology) should be the alpha and the omega of all legal issues.[23] Nevertheless, they rarely tried to explain why it is the case and what is then the value of law and economics for practical reasoning and decision-making.

In this paper, I will show that most of the debates regarding the relevance of law and economics for practical decision-making (law and economics is then used to make a choice in the real world) are based on the idea that there would exist a scientific "right" way to approach legal issues and decision making. According to

---

[17] Kaplow and Shavell (2006). The argument was first presented by Kaplow and Shavell (1994).

[18] Kornhauser (2003).

[19] See Arrow (1951). Samuelson also recognized that the social welfare function is arbitrary. See also Kaplow and Shavell (2006).

[20] Calabresi (2016).

[21] See Stojanovic and Silvestri (2019).

[22] See for example, Teles (2008), Baker (1975).

[23] As Frank Knight said: "It is somewhat unusual to begin the treatment of a subject with a warning against attaching too much importance to it; but in the case of economics, such an injunction is quite as much needed as explanation and emphasis of the importance it really has. It is characteristic of the age in which we live to think too much in terms of economics, to see things too predominantly in their economic aspect; and this is especially true of the American people. There is no more important prerequisite to clear thinking in regard to economics itself than is recognition of its limited place among human interests at large" Knight, (2013 [1951]), p. 3.

this perspective, all issues (legal, political or scientific) should be addressed using the same method and the same scientific rationality. If we deviate from this very modern (and utopic) and praxisconceptualization[24] to stress an inherent difference between practical reasoning and scientific reasoning, it is impossible to deny the relevance of law and economics for practical decision-making in the realm of law. This relevance is of course not binary (relevant or not relevant) but should be considered as a continuum (it is always relevant but up to some point). Here is precisely the point which will be made in this paper.

The paper will proceed as follow. First, it will inquire into the notion of practical reasoning (Sect. 7.2). It will appear that practical reasoning and scientific reasoning do not target the same type of phenomenon; thus, for this reason, the type of rationality (and methodology) required to solve scientific issues and political/legal issues cannot be the same. I will then show that, from the perspective of practical reasoning, it is impossible to deny that law and economics (as long as internally consistent) could be relevant for practical decision-making for both theoretical and ethical reasons (Sect. 7.3) whatever the shortcomings we could identify. The question should not thus be whether law and economics is relevant for practical decision-making but how to make the most of it when a practical decision has to be made (Sect. 7.4).

7.2 What is Practical Reasoning?

Oliver Wendell Holmes was invited at the Lowell Institute in Boston to deliver a lecture on the Common law. During this lecture, he declared: "The life of the law has not been logic: it has been experience. The felt necessities of the time, the prevalent moral and political theories, intuitions of public policy, avowed or unconscious, even the prejudices which judges share with their fellow-men, have had a good deal more to do than the syllogism in determining the rules by which men should be governed. The law embodies the story of a nation's development through many centuries, and it cannot be dealt with as if it contained only the axioms and corollaries of a book of mathematics. In order to know what it is, we must know what it has been, and what it tends to become. We must alternately consult history and existing theories of legislation. But the most difficult labor will be to understand the combination of the two into new products at every stage. The substance of the law at any given time pretty nearly corresponds, so far as it goes, with what is then understood to be convenient; but its form and machinery, and the degree to which it is able to work out desired results, depend very much upon its past[25]". If the first sentence of this quote is well known, the justification he gave for his initial statement is quite

---

[24] As Strauss brilliantly said: "the root of all modern darkness from the seventeenth century on is the obscuring of the difference between theory , an obscuring that first leads to a reduction of praxis to theory (this is the meaning of so-called [modern] rationalism) and then, in retaliation, to the rejection of theory in the name of praxis that is no longer intelligible as praxis" Strauss (2002), p. 66. See also Toulmin (2001).

[25] Wendell Holmes (1991 [1881]).

interesting for the purpose of this paper. Indeed, he denied that logic and scientific rationality are sufficient to solve legal or political issues: mathematical problems and legal problems are simply not of the same genre.

What Holmes stated might sound refreshing (or even provocative) for the modern man used to believe that logic and mathematics are the language of science; his analysis would, nevertheless, have appeared quite trivial for Plato and Aristotle. Indeed, they distinguished between three different types of rationality: the scientific rationality (episteme), the practical rationality (phronesis) and a form of poetic or artistic rationality (techne).[26] For them, it was quite obvious that the type of reasoning (and thus of rationality and methodology) required to solve a mathematical problem is clearly different from the type of reasoning required to judge a case or to choose a policy.

In this section, and following the Greek tradition, I will first emphasize the differences between practical reasoning and scientific reasoning (A) and the logic for distinguishing between them. This will also make clear that, indeed, from this perspective, experience is required when addressing legal or political issues. I will then elaborate on the idea that practical reasoning is certainly better understood as a dialogical process (B).

7.2.1 Practical Reasoning and Scientific Reasoning

According to Popper, a theory, to be "scientific", should be falsifiable (or lead to falsifiable predictions); if it is not, it is simply "un-scientific". A scientific theory should then be predictive and testable (otherwise, it could not be falsifiable). This implies that the phenomenon that the scientific theory tries to predict could not be different from what it is (if it were so, nothing would be falsifiable); that the same causes should lead to the same effects. Following this approach, it was possible to study the movement of the planets, to develop the GPS or to understand under what condition an object can fly; it was also possible to predict with accuracy the consequences of a reaction between two or more chemical compounds and to develop nuclear power; it was similarly possible to study the evolution of a human fetus.

Because "the object of scientific knowledge is of necessity",[27] no law could "forbid" the planet to move in such and such way, could ban an eclipse or a particular chemical reaction. The object at stake or the system considered cannot be shaped by

---

[26] On this distinction, see Marshall (2009). See also Toulmin (2001).

[27] Aristotle (1999), 1139b, especially 18–36: "What pure science or scientific knowledge is— in the precise sense of the word and not in any of its wider uses based on mere similarity—will become clear in the following. We are all convinced that what we know scientifically cannot be otherwise than it is; but of facts which can possibly be other than they are we do not know whether or not they continue to be true when removed from our observation. Therefore, an object of scientific knowledge exists of necessity, and is, consequently, eternal. For everything that exists of necessity in an unqualified sense is eternal, and what is eternal is ungenerated and imperishable (and hence cannot be otherwise)."

humans; they constitute natural constraints to human's action. Because the object of scientific knowledge is of necessity, what was true in the past (e.g. a probability distribution) must be true for the future; the future is predetermined and can be predictable (at least statistically). The specificity of the object of science (the phenomenon or the system that it inquires) allows us to make universal statements about it. Following necessity, the object is invariable and context-independent (physics does not work differently in two different communities). Naturally, for this type of object, it is possible to use logic and mathematics to "model" and to predict; this process being informed by empirical work.

If a discipline would like to be considered as "scientific", it should posit or assume that the phenomena it tries to study could not have been different from what they are, that a stable underlying structure of the world (the discipline inquires into) exists. In economics, it is possible to find this type of assumption. For example, Solow declared "My impression is that the best and the brightest in the profession proceed as if economics is the physics of society. There is a single universally valid model of the world. It only needs to be applied".[28] Samuelson went even further considering that the ergodic hypothesis[29] is crucial for scientific economics.[30] Samuelson and Solow do not say that the economic world is "ergodic", simply that it is possible to treat it "as if" it was (and it is possible that some aspects of economics are ergodic). Econometrics often rely on the fact that the economic world (or parts of it) could be understood simply by looking at what people do (since we could not trust what people say and that there is no "right" way to interpret their interpretation of their actions) and, sometimes, assumes that what was statistically significant in the past must still be today and that it is not context-dependent.

If the phenomena or systems explored through economics are not exhibiting this nature, economic models and theory would necessarily be historical and contextual and not as "scientific" as physics. It would of course be possible, in that case, to save the scientific appearance by adding the "ceteris paribus" assumption. This would nevertheless lead to two difficulties. First, in such a case, the model and its prediction are true since it is merely internally consistent: the results derive from the axiomatic system that we call a "model"; the model only produces analytical truth (or tautologies). From this point of view, mathematics is merely a way to ensure internal consistency. Second, it is impossible to know if the model will allow us to predict what will happen in the real world (or we could predict and if we do not observe the result the model was predicting, it is still possible to consider that the model is still valid and that other things were not being equal) or up to what point it could perform the function of anticipating the future. It is required to "assess" the value of the model in a specific historical context... and such an assessment is naturally out of the reach of economic theory or economic models. Moreover, there is no scientific way to determine the scientific value of a model (when this assessment is required).

[28] Solow (1985), p. 330.

[29] See especially Carrion Alvarez and Ehnts (2016). In one of its meaning, ergodicity means that the position of a system can be predicted without having an idea of the full history of the system.

[30] Samuelson (1969), p. 184.

I can certainly say that if there is something like a labour market (in the neoclassical sense), involuntary unemployment could be cured by lowering the minimum wage or facilitating flexibility of wages. Nevertheless, implementing this conceptualization in the real world is at risk of missing the fundamental point: do we indeed have a labour market? Or, up to what point can we consider that we do or do not have a labour market? Answering these questions required more than pure logic and mathematics… and it certainly requires experience.

If it is possible to posit or assume a stable underlying structure of human interactions, such an assumption rapidly seems inadequate with everyday experience (at least if we would like to predict beyond a very short time horizon). Indeed, in such a world, a human would never truly learn, would never truly innovate, or show creativity; they would not be more than predictable (or programmable) robots that we would approach without considering them as "human" but as pawns (and indeed the humanity of economic agents is not something economists are concerned about). Societies would organize in the same way and evolve in the same predictable way; their history would be irrelevant to understand why they evolved and the direction of this evolution[31]; path-dependency would not exist.[32] Time would be purely mechanical and would not bring new information.[33] It seems highly unlikely that the human environment is like the physical environment, it is often non-ergodic in nature. In other words, things could be different from what they were or are, precisely because humans can shape them.

This does not mean that the theory derived from experience (or the past) or a "scientific" approach has no relevance for understanding the present, or for predicting the future. It simply means that the future could be different from the past and that we have to assess or to deliberate about the relevance of any theory or model provided by social sciences if we would like to understand the world we live in and act. Naturally, the type of reasoning required to "assess", "deliberate", or "judge" the relevance of a model or a theory for practical purposes is of a different genre than scientific reasoning. Logic and mathematics are only relevant to inquire into the internal validity (or consistency) of a model. They are not sufficient to appreciate the credibility or plausibility of certain of its hypothesis. They are not sufficient to determine which model or combination of models is more likely to work in the real world (given a certain objective). They are also incapable of determining if the considered change—even if it could make sense according to certain models or theories—is "desirable". It is thus required to use another type of reasoning, a practical reasoning. Context-dependent, it recognizes the variability of the human environment and of human action. The specific nature of practical reasoning is explained by Aristotle: "We may approach the subject of practical wisdom by studying the persons to whom we attribute it. Now, the capacity of deliberating well about what is good and advantageous for oneself is regarded as typical of a man of practical wisdom […] Now no one deliberates about things that cannot be other than they are or about

---

[31] A bit like what can be found in Fukuyama (1992).

[32] On the concept of path dependency, see Arthur (1994).

[33] See especially O'Driscoll and Rizzo (1996 [1985]).

actions that he cannot possibly perform. Since, as we saw, pure science involves demonstration, while things whose starting points or first causes can be other than they are do not admit of demonstration—for such things too (and not merely their first causes) can all be other than they are—and since it is impossible to deliberate about what exists by necessity, we may conclude that practical wisdom is neither a pure science nor an art. It is not a pure science, because matters of action admit of being other than they are".[34]

Scientific reasoning and practical reasoning are thus of a different nature because they do not focus on the same type of phenomenon. Because of this different nature, the "language" of practical reasoning cannot be pure logic and mathematics; a deliberation is quite different from solving a mathematical exercise. It is probably better conceptualized as a dialectical/dialogical process which characteristics will be presented in the next paragraph. Of course, if this distinction is taken seriously, it will naturally transform our understanding of social sciences and of the results of social science... including law and economics.

7.2.2 Practical Reasoning as a Dialogical Process

For Aristotle, practical reasoning is characterized by the idea of "good" deliberation.[35] Nevertheless, he does not then try to define what a good deliberation precisely means. Indeed, for him, a good deliberation does not follow an algorithm or a recipe; it simply cannot be formalized. It would, of course, be possible to try to describe a process (identifying the right goal, the right knowledge, the right means, etc....[36]), but such a description will necessarily be imperfect and incomplete. Because of that, practical reasoning is not something that can fully be taught in theory and applied in practice, it has to be experienced, and experience is required to improve practical reasoning.[37]

Aristotle gave us few intuitions about what practical reasoning might require but most of the statements will appear quite frustrating to the modern ears.

[34] Aristotle (1999), 1140a 24–1140b 12.

[35] Aristotle (1999), 1140a25 and 1141b10.

[36] Phronesis works through deliberation, which gathers and processes the relevant data e.g. the right time, the right way, for the right reasons (Aristotle (1999), 1106b 21–23: "But to experience all this at the right time, toward the right objects, toward the right people, for the right reason, and in the right manner—that is the median and the best course, the course that is a mark of virtue.").

[37] Aristotle (1999), 1142a 11–15: "An indication that what we have said is correct is the following common observation. While young men do indeed become good geometricians and mathematicians and attain theoretical wisdom in such matters, they apparently do not attain practical wisdom. The reason is that practical wisdom is concerned with particulars as well (as with universals), and knowledge of particulars comes from experience.". Aristotle also indicates: "For experience has given such men an eye with which they can see correctly" (1143b 14).

Saying, for example, that deliberating well is being able to "see" what should be done in a particular case[38] does not sound particularly useful and somewhat confusing if we do believe that a sound reasoning is based on logic and proof. Indeed, practical reasoning is a form of intuitive reasoning or integrates an intuitive dimension that cannot be captured "scientifically". For this reason, it is impossible to prove (by arguments) that this or that action is the best possible; it is only possible to try to convince. It is unclear if, for Aristotle, a good deliberation could lead to different actions but there are reasons to believe that it could be the case (since, at least, Aristotle is not even sure that the perfect virtuous man exists).

Likewise, saying that only the virtuous man will be able to deliberate properly cannot fully inform us about how to deliberate.[39] It is certainly evident that some moral qualities and some educations are required to rightly deliberate. An agent only governed by his or her emotions or ideology cannot rightly deliberate and is more prone to mistakes. Moreover, there is the idea that rightly deliberating means not merely trying to promote his or her interest but also the interest of the society. This is the reason why Aristotle distinguishes between the clever man and the wise man. Practical decision-making requires us to be wise; being clever is not sufficient to deliberate adequately[40]. Indeed, the problem is not only to choose what to do but also to choose what is the "right" thing to do.

The same frustration is inevitable when it is stated that the virtuous action should be intermediate (since moderation is a virtue).[41] It seems obvious that the right action is neither an over-reaction, nor an under-reaction. It is equally obvious that the threshold between over and under-reacting will depend on the particulars of the case. It is also probable that different "virtuous" people might strike the balance very differently.

It is also possible to consider that practical reasoning and deliberation is first and foremost a process and that the insights given by Aristotle constitute points of attention inviting us to reflect on our decision-making processes… and that, maybe, the best we could do in the realm of practical decision making is to critically reflect on our own intuitions and decisions. The quality of a decision will thus not depend on the quality of the action chosen but on the process that led to this choice.

---

[38] Aristotle (1999), 1144a 27–35: "That is why men of practical wisdom are often described as "clever" and "knavish." But in fact this capacity (alone) is not practical wisdom, although practical wisdom does not exist without it. Without virtue or excellence, this eye of the soul, (intelligence,) does not acquire the characteristic (of practical wisdom) […] But whatever the true end may be, only a good man can judge it correctly."

[39] Aristotle (1999), 1144a 35–37: "For wickedness distorts and causes us to be completely mistaken about the fundamental principles of action. Hence it is clear that a man cannot have practical wisdom unless he is good".

[40] Aristotle (1999), 1144a 29–30.

[41] Transalation could vary and moderation, temperance and self-control are often used. See, Aristotle (1999), note 12, p. 178: "A sophron is well-balanced through-and through; he gives the impression of 'self-control' without effort or strain". Moderation is thus not the result of a computation, it is also intuitive.

When he mentioned the need to be virtuous, he forces decision-makers or judges to inquire into their motives. Do they choose this or that policy (or solution) because they truly believe it is the best one for the society or do they choose this policy (or solution) because it will promote their private interest? Do they choose this policy (or solution) while adequately considering the critics formulated against it? Do they just follow their emotions and ideology? Do they adequately consider the particulars? Of course, it will be difficult for an outsider to know if it were the case and even the decision maker or the judge might have difficulties to answer these questions. But by considering that the perfectly virtuous man does not probably exist,[42] he invites decision-makers to always doubt about their own motivations.

When he said that decision-makers should be able to see what should be done, Aristotle does not consider that intuition could shortcut deliberation. First, intuition is already the result of some form of deliberation informed by experience or what they learnt. Second, intuition is merely the starting point for a deliberation. Is my intuition sufficiently and properly informed to act on it? Did I consider the particulars of the case or the situation at stake (is my interpretation of the situation adequate)? Did I consider all the relevant options to address the case or the situation? Did I properly assess each of these options? Did I choose the option which is the "best" considering the knowledge I have? Am I not neglecting the long-term consequences of my actions? This does not mean that practical decision-making should consistently gather all possible information in order to decide. It also involves the recognition of the limits of action and the limits of the knowledge on which it rests. As Hayek said: "If man is not to do more harm than good in his efforts to improve the social order, he will have to learn that in this, as in all other fields where essential complexity of an organized kind prevails, he cannot acquire the full knowledge which would make mastery of the events possible"[43]. Moreover, the decision maker should also reflect on the morality of the decision he or she consider. I should not only look for a solution to problems, but I should also look for "right" solutions.

When he considers that moderation is required, he invites policymakers or judges to inquire into the means chosen for their actions. Am I not going too far or am I underreacting, considering the problem I would like to solve? Is the quantum of a sanction appropriate?

Practical decision-making (or practical reasoning) requires a critical dialogue between intuitions and reason but also between different agents. It is thus possible to consider that it is in essence dialectical and dialogical. Dialectical because the decision is the result of an internal deliberation potentially informed by experience or by what others might have said or written. Dialogical because the deliberation is the result of a dialogue in which opinions are shared and considered as a potential source to improve decision-making (and our own ideas)—it requires intercommunication. The ideal of the dialogical reasoning (and practical reasoning) was brilliantly

---

[42] It is possible to consider that Aristotle presents what would be "ideal" even if it is unclear if a man can reach this level.

[43] Hayek (1974).

expressed by John Stuart Mill in On Liberty. Why would we consider that the judgement of a person really deserves confidence? "Because he has kept his mind open to criticism of his opinions and conduct. Because it has been his practice to listen to all that could be said against him; to profit by as much of it as was just, and expound to himself, and upon occasion to others, the fallacy of what was fallacious. Because he has felt, that the only way in which a human being can make some approach to knowing the whole of a subject, is by hearing what can be said about it by persons of every variety of opinion, and studying all modes in which it can be looked at by every character of mind. No wise man ever acquired his wisdom in any mode but this; nor is it in the nature of human intellect to become wise in any other manner".[44]

7.3 Why Law and Economics Could be Relevant for Practical Reasoning?

The reason why we might feel some frustration regarding the idea of practical reasoning is that the purpose of knowledge and sciences, for the modern man, is to know what to do, to reduce mistakes (or, for some, to reach certainty). Science and knowledge should help us to distinguish between right and wrong answers to problems we face. And indeed, some might stress that the "scientific" revolution in economics was to escape from the ambiguity of the institutionalists and political economists to reach a degree of precision that the mathematization of the field allowed. In the domain of law, it is also not infrequent to believe that there is (or must be) a "right" answer to legal problems or a subset of right answers which are not too different from each other. When discretion is recognized to the judge, lawyers are often not trying to understand how this discretion is used and they might simply try to criticize it: the judge is doing politics, not law (and thus, the law should be made clearer).

If we embrace practical reasoning as understood by the Greeks, there is no doubt that law and economics (and social sciences) could contribute to improve decision-making. First, law and economics can participate in the dialectical/dialogical process (A): it offers perspective and arguments which can naturally be discussed. Moreover, most of the time, it specifies the conditions under which its conclusion rests which often facilitates the appreciation of the practical relevance of law and economics statements. Law and economics also has an ethical relevance (B). Indeed, it forces decision-makers to consider tradeoffs and consequences.

---

[44] Stuart Mill (2001 [1859]), pp. 21–22. The paragraph ends like this: "The steady habit of correcting and completing his own opinion by collating it with those of others, so far from causing doubt and hesitation in carrying it into practice, is the only stable foundation for a just reliance on it: for, being cognisant of all that can, at least obviously, be said against him, and having taken up his position against all gainsayers—knowing that he has sought for objections and difficulties, instead of avoiding them, and has shut out no light which can be thrown upon the subject from any quarter— he has a right to think his judgment better than that of any person, or any multitude, who have not gone through a similar process".

7.3.1 The Dialectical/Dialogical Relevance of Law and Economics

As Landes and Posner explained, "One of the major contributions of economic analysis to law has been simplification, enabling enhanced understanding. Economics is complex and difficult but it is less complicated than legal doctrine and it can serve to unify different areas of law [...] By cutting away the dense underbrush of legal technicalities, economic analysis can also bring into sharp definition issues of policy that technicalities may conceal".[45] The purpose of law and economics is thus not to describe legal technicalities or explain how to make the most of these technicalities in a specific legal case, it is to offer an explanation for these legal technicalities by stressing policy issues (and unavoidable tradeoffs). It is primarily a discourse about the law (the law and its concepts are thus considered as an object of inquiry). For the authors, in doing so, law and economics contributes to a better understanding of law, legal doctrines or legal concepts and might even contribute to improve decision-making (since it offers a new way to frame issues).

Following this line of argument, law and economics contributes to improve our practical reasoning for at least two reasons. First, contrary to the traditional legal understanding of law, legal doctrines and legal concepts, law and economics offers a systematic way to inquire into law and legal doctrines. In doing so, it facilitates the appreciation of the potential correspondence between the theory and the world we live in. Second, because the understanding offered by law and economics often differs from a traditional understanding of law, legal doctrines and legal concepts, it allows to "reflect" on these traditional understandings but also on the understanding offered by law and economics. In doing so, it obviously contributes to the dialectical/dialogical process that characterizes practical reasoning.

Most of the time, law students and, sometimes, law professors focus on the content of the law: what is contract law? What is constitutional law? What is the separation of powers? What is a public service? What is the content of this or that legal case? What does "free movement of goods", as understood by the European Court of Justice, entail? And it is undeniable that a large part of the job of a lawyer is to describe the legal environment. It is also to make sense of the diversity of rules and cases, to "define" legal concepts which are used by courts and, sometimes, to advocate for legal improvement(s). When they engage in these latter activities, they rarely explain their methodology or their theoretical assumptions. They will merely try to convince their readers that what they say makes sense. And of course, the idea offered could be debated. In a way, at many levels, law is still practised in the same way today as it was 200 years ago. From the practical reasoning point of view, this situation is not problematic, after all, law is mostly rhetoric. However, since the roots of the reasoning are not explained, it is sometimes difficult to assess the relevance of an explanation, a proposed definition or a recommendation.

---

[45] Landes and Posner (2003a, b), p. 10.

It is at this level that law and economics brings something. Indeed, it is way more systematic than traditional legal reasoning which not only facilitates our inquiry, and our understanding of what is presented but also critical reflection. Typically, regarding agents, law and economics assumes that (1) people do not behave randomly, that (2) they do what they consider to be the best for them,[46] considering their preferences, the information they have, their cognitive capacities and the constraints they face, that (3) they, thus, respond to incentives. Regarding social outcomes, law and economics assumes that (4) they are the results of individual interactions, and that (5) resources should be allocated efficiently or should not be wasted since they are scarce. A value judgment is also often added: (6) the welfare of the society depends on the welfare of all individuals in this society (and that more welfare is better than less welfare). Because they are assumptions, law and economics cannot pretend that explanations derived from these assumptions represent the "truth" about legal phenomena, it is merely a way to look at legal phenomena.

From these assumptions (which will have to be specified, for example, the type of rationality) and value judgment, it is possible to inquire into a body of law,[47] a legal doctrine or a legal concept. Why do we have contracts and contract law?[48] How to make sense of the conditions of validity of a contract?[49] Why do we distinguish between public and private contracts?[50] Between public and private property?[51] How to make sense of the concept of the separation of powers[52] or public service?[53] Why do we have different types of rules and different procedures?[54] If people are rational, is mandated disclosure relevant[55]? If people are rational, can we expect rules and regulations to favour the general interest?[56] If people are rational and if we want to incentivize them to innovate, is it better to use command and control or economic

---

[46] This could be the result of a conscious optimizing behavior or simply the result of an unconscious behavior.

[47] Law and economics does not describe, it offers a way to formulate hypothesis about how the world might be working.

[48] See Posner (2016).

[49] See Posner (2016).

[50] See Lanneau (2023).

[51] See for example Shavell (2004).

[52] Cooter (2000).

[53] See Lanneau (2021).

[54] See indirectly Buchanan and Tullock (1962). The model they use for determining the optimal majority could be use to explain why different rules could be modify using different procedures.

[55] Ben-Shahar and Sneider (2014).

[56] And Public choice tells us that we should not be too hopeful. See Stigler (1971).

incentives to address environmental issues?[57] What are the likely consequences of rent ceiling[58] or our adoption mechanisms?[59] Etc...

The answers/explanations to these questions will derive from assumptions and specifications made by academics in order to provide these answers/explanations. It will naturally be possible to test their robustness by modifying certain specifications (ex: the type of rationality, the type of information, etc....) or to question their external validity (a task which is made easier since the model is fully specified). But law and economics is not only relevant because it offers certain answers and explanations, but it is also relevant at the level of the inquiry process. If economics will not dictate what to include in a model and how to specify it, it will have an influence on what we will look for in order to model (or to explain) using the tools of economics. Assume you would like to inquire into the likely consequences of rent ceiling in a particular city. Economics will not tell you what to include in the model, but since it considers that a social outcome is the result of individual behaviours, you will search for individuals which could be influenced by this rent ceiling (and of course, you will start with tenants, you will also have to introduce homeowners and, why not, real estate promoters). You will then have to specify their rationality (in general, you start with perfect rationality before considering bound rationality), their preferences (homeowners and tenants will prefer having more money to less money), the options they face (buying a house, living in the city, living in the suburbs for the tenant; renting to a tenant, renting to tourists, selling and, in each case, the level of maintenance of the house, for homeowners). Once this is done, you will use economic logic to derive logical consequences to the specifications of your model; you might even attempt to qualify the efficiency of the outcome. You might even compare theoretical consequences to real-world consequences to verify that your model does not provide absurd results.

Naturally, law and economics' explanations and results will then have to be assessed since they are the product of assumptions. But because assumptions are clear, it is possible to inquire into the relevance of each of them (which facilitates the critical assessment task); testing the robustness of an explanation offered is precisely identifying what is the core hypothesis on which it rests and then trying to imagine a "believable" alternative hypothesis.

It is also possible to consider that, since law and economics models are formulated as context-independent (individuals, state, and firms are supposed to work in the same way across time and culture), it forces us to reflect on the particulars of a real-world situation to assess their relevance as an explanation or as a guide for decision making in a particular case. Coase famously criticized blackboard economics (context-independent theorizing) and stressed the need to focus on the particulars!

---

[57] Any environmental economics textbook will show that incentives are higher with economic incentives than with command and control.

[58] Traditional microeconomics textbook will point towards higher demand and lower supply. This is what can indeed be observed in Mumbai (India), in Ireland, and almost everywhere this strategy has been used. See for example Bourne (2014).

[59] See Landes and Posner (1978).

"All solutions have costs and there is no reason to suppose that government regulation is called for simply because the problem is not well handled by the market or the firm. Satisfactory views on policy can only come from a patient study of how, in practice, the market, firms and governments handle the problem of harmful effects".[60] Similarly, Hayek said that "As we advance we find more and more frequently that we can in fact ascertain only some but not all the particular circumstances which determine the outcome of a given process; and in consequence we are able to predict only some but not all the properties of the result we have to expect".[61]

Law and economics also contributes to the dialectical/dialogical process of practical reasoning since it offers an alternative interpretation of legal phenomena and, sometimes, provocative results which will force the reader to find reasons why a certain explanation is not entirely relevant (or satisfactory) or why a certain result cannot be endorsed (dialectical dimension).

Referring to The Economics of Baby Shortage,[62] Margaret Brining noted that "Baby selling became code for the foolish extreme to which its proponents would carry law and economics"[63]. It is certain that the idea of selling babies is shocking at many levels,[64] especially for non-economists. Nevertheless, it is hard to deny that, in their paper, Landes and Posner follow traditional economic theory and that the paper is largely internally consistent (considering their hypotheses). If there is an excess in the demand for something, the way to equilibrate things is indeed to increase the price; if there is an excess in the offer, the logical economic solution is to lower the price. It is also true that prospective parents do pay a price because it will take time before a baby will be allocated to them and because of adoption agency fees. The question is thus much more about the external validity of the reasoning, and it is then possible to stress problems with commodification[65] but also problems with the absence of commodification.[66] It is undeniable that such a paper will trigger critical reflection. For those convinced it is "wrong", they naturally search for reasons to disagree with the conclusions or with the premises of the reasoning; thus convinced with the reasoning might still wonder about the extent of the regulation. It will then be possible to engage in a dialogical process to critically reflect on counterarguments, improve economic arguments and policy recommendations. At an individual level,

---

[60] Coase (1960), p. 18.

[61] Hayek (1974).

[62] Landes and Posner (1978).

[63] Brinig (2000), p. 233.

[64] Even if, the purpose of the paper is probably more to explore ways to "improve" the "market for babies". As Posner said, "the question of public policy is not whether baby selling should be forbidden or allowed but how extensively it should be regulated. I simply think it should be regulated less stringently than is done today" Posner (1987a, 1987b), p. 72.

[65] Radin (1987), p. 1905: "Universal commodification undermines personal identity by conceiving of personal attributes, relationships, and philosophical and moral commitments as monetizable and alienable from self".

[66] Ibid, p. 1917: "if we choose market-inalienability, we might deprive a class of poor and oppressed people of the opportunity to have more money with which to buy adequate food, shelter, and health care in the market, and hence deprive them of a better chance to lead a humane life".

this process will naturally influence the colours of our own ideas. At the intellectual community level, this process is what drives research.

What is true for "selling babies" is also true regarding surrogacy contracts,[67] and selling organs[68] or blood.[69] Law and economics is likely to expose us to a new way to approach the issues and this new way will naturally have an incidence on how we think about this idea (we cannot unlearn an argument). We merely have to recognize that economics is only one way to approach an issue and certainly not the only one. As James Tobin mentioned, "Any good second year graduate student in economics could write a short examination paper proving that voluntary transactions in votes would increase the welfare of the sellers as well as the buyers. But the legitimacy of the political process rests on the prohibition of such transactions. A vote market would concentrate political power in the rich, and especially in those who owe their wealth to government privilege".[70]

To conclude about the dialectical/dialogical relevance of law and economics, it is difficult not to quote Donohue and Ayres commenting on the 3rd edition of Richard Posner's Economic Analysis of Law. "To the extent that Posner alerts readers to view or arguments that they have not considered, his book will continue to be of immense value. But it must always be recognized that the strength of Posner's clear assumptions and clear results is in initiating legal discussions, not in resolving them".[71] It is thus the dialectical/dialogical function performed by law and economics that is fundamental, and it is not because it might appear as too crude that it should be rejected without attention. Ronald Coase does not say otherwise: "But it is, of course, desirable that the choice between different social arrangements for the solution of economic problems should be carried out in broader terms than this [economics] and that the total effect of these arrangements in all spheres of life should be taken into account. As Frank H. Knight has so often emphasized, problems of welfare economics must ultimately dissolve into a study of aesthetics and morals".[72]

7.3.2 The Ethical Relevance of Law and Economics

Law and economics also has an ethical relevance and thus also contributes to identifying what is the "right" decision to take in a particular situation. This might seem obvious for individuals who believe that in order to judge an action, we need to consider the consequences of that action (strict consequentialism); after all economic reasoning focus on consequences. It might seem odd for people who believe that in order to judge an action we need to consider whether this action follows certain duties

---

[67] Posner (1989b).

[68] Hylton (1990).

[69] See for example Titmuss (1997).

[70] Tobin (1970).

[71] Donohue III and Ayres (1987), p. 812.

[72] Coase (1960), p. 43.

or moral rules (deontological ethics). If these duties or moral rules are considered as not defeasible, it might be difficult to understand why consequences should matter. It is also possible to consider that an action will be considered as "just" or "ethical" if it is a result of a proper deliberation; they thus emphasize the process that led to the action rather than the "quality" of the action itself. Whatever our stands on the proper type of ethics, law and economics will always have an ethical relevance. Indeed, deontological ethics cannot escape the argument from responsibility and will thus benefit from being informed about consequences and tradeoffs. Consequentialist ethics will naturally benefit from any technics (including economics) which will help to identify the consequences of an action. Virtue ethics will naturally accept the argument from responsibility, will require to deliberate about tradeoffs and identified consequences. In this section, I will thus develop (1) the argument from responsibility, (2) the relevance of law and economics for thinking about consequences, and (3) for the importance of identifying tradeoffs.

1. The argument from responsibility is relatively easy to understand. The decision maker cannot disregard the consequences of his or her own decision, even if this decision maker believes that he or she has "duties" or should abide by a "moral code" and thus that these consequences will not (or should not) influence his or her decision. Indeed, the decision-maker must take responsibility for the expected consequences of his or her decision.

A decision maker can consider that abortion should be banned, but this decision maker will then have to recognize and accept the consequences of banning abortion on pregnant women who would have chosen abortion (some will still choose abortion but abroad or without the hygiene that a clinic or a hospital would offer), on women in general (since abortion is not an option, their behaviour is expected to change), and on the society as a consequence. A decision maker can consider that the death penalty should be implemented for child rapists, but he or she cannot ignore the consequences of this sanction on the behaviour of potential child rapists. A decision maker can forbid all or some surrogacy contracts (or refuse to enforce them) for ethical reasons, but, once again, he or she cannot disregard de consequences of his or her decision on potential parents, potential surrogate mothers and on children born abroad using this technique. A decision maker can follow his or her moral intuitions about the relevance of rent ceiling, the necessity to act against price gouging or to engage in a war, but he or she cannot disregard the adverse consequences of introducing rent ceiling or rules against price gouging on the market, or the consequences of a war.

Posner uses this argument from responsibility when he urged feminists to consider economic consequences: "Feminists who are not libertarians may not like the vocabulary, methods, and assumptions of economics, but if they refuse to consider the economic consequences of policies affecting women they may end up hurting rather than helping women".[73] In doing so, he does not judge the aims of feminists, he merely stresses the need to consider the consequences of their proposals to see if their proposals are likely to achieve their aims.

---

[73] Posner (1989a), p. 194.

2. Since practical decision-making requires not to ignore consequences, law and economics could be relevant for identifying these consequences. Indeed, most of its program is precisely to approach law, regulation, and legal doctrines through their consequences. Any law and economics textbook will, for example, explain the consequences of property rights, the consequence of their divisibility and the reach of their divisibility, they will explore the consequences of contract law and legal doctrines like duress, they will provide insights into the difference between negligence and strict liability. Specific books and articles will explore, in detail, the consequences of intellectual property law,[74] competition law,[75] common property,[76] constitutional law,[77] environmental law or international law,[78] and their doctrines. When they will advocate for a change in regulation or legal doctrines, it will be based on expected consequences (e.g. radical free movement of persons[79], drastic reduction of mandated disclosure,[80] the relevance of predatory pricing,[81] etc.).

Once again, these explanations and recommendations will derive from economic assumptions and only "economic" consequences will be considered.[82] Nevertheless, even if law and economics only reveals a subset of consequences, knowing about these potential consequences is certainly a plus for practical reasoning and decision-making. Indeed, these potential consequences cannot be ignored and the likelihood they will happen in the real world will have to be assessed. For example, the rent ceiling is considered to increase the demand for rental and to decrease the supply and its quality both directly (homeowners will not rent their place or will lower quality) and indirectly (less houses will be built since the return to investment will be lower). Ignoring these consequences would not be compatible with the argument from responsibility. It might be the case that some positive consequences could counter-balance these adverse consequences and, in that case, they will have to be considered for decision making.

Sometimes, law and economics attempts to put a money figure on these consequences. Doing so is indeed expected to facilitate the choice between different options. For example, it is possible to attempt to put a money figure on the value of a statistical life when decisions regarding safety are considered; it is also possible to assess the costs and benefits of an environmental regulation. It is certainly true that everything will depend on the valuation technique used (e.g. WTP or WTA, contingent valuation, etc.) and that we should thus interpret these values carefully since they derive from many choices made in the model from which they derive.

---

[74] For example, Landes and Posner (2003a, b).

[75] For example, Posner (2001).

[76] For example, Stevenson (2008).

[77] For example, Cooter (2000).

[78] For example, Trachtman (2008).

[79] For example, Somin (2020).

[80] For example, Ben-Shahar and Sneider (2014).

[81] For example, Hovemkampf (2006).

[82] See for example the last section of Coase (1960).

Nevertheless, trying to put a money figure is also inquiring into consequences (e.g. what are the consequences of air pollution on humans?) and asking ethical questions (e.g. should we only consider direct human costs? How should we value the future? What should enter in the cost of a fever?).

3. Even more fundamentally, law and economics is ethically relevant because it identifies tradeoffs. As Arrow said, economists "have to point out the limits of our opportunities",[83] tradeoffs are inescapable.

Any regulation will create winners and losers; this situation will force decision-makers to inquire into the legitimacy of the redistribution it entails (e.g. Regarding agricultural subsidies or protectionism). This regulation might them be supplemented by another form of redistribution to curb the asymmetric distributional effects of the first regulation (e.g. an ecotaxation could lead to direct redistribution in favour of the poorest of the poor). The legitimacy of this second action could also be inquired into. Grandfathering regarding the allocation of pollution permits will clearly favour established industries to the detriment of new competitors which might have to "buy" permits in order to enter the industry. It could be possible to "reserve" part of the pollution permits to new entrants, but this solution is of course not perfect. Allocating pollution permits through an auction system might be considered as favouring new plans (less polluting) compare to old plants (more polluting). Identifying who will win or lose as a result of a regulation is fundamental to ethical reasoning.

Any legal regulation will require the use of public resources, and since public resources are scarce, it is natural to wonder if these public resources could have been spent in a better way. This is especially true in developing countries. For example, the reason why traffic regulation is often enforced very leniently could be that state resources concentrate on more "important" tasks. This consideration for public resources also explains general exemptions of certain anticompetitive practices, per se rules in competition law, the different level of control regarding mergers and seems to indicate that competitive authority should only consider oligopolistic markets when they try to fight collusion. Of course, these regulations will then produce what might appear as imperfect results (certain practices which should have been sanctioned are not sanctioned or certain practices which should not have been sanctioned are sanctioned) but these imperfect results are only imperfect at the level of the norm, not at the level of the system. These tradeoffs will necessarily require some ethical considerations. Moreover, if the question of increasing public resources to "pay" for the costs of a regulation, it will lead to the question regarding the distribution of the extra tax burden.

Any considered regulation will require a comparison between market failures and government failures. Indeed, it is not because there are market failures that the state should regulate a domain (but without market failures, the legitimacy of its intervention can be questioned). And it is not because of government failures (e.g., corruption, rent-seeking, etc....) exist that a domain should be free from government

---

[83] Arrow (1974).

regulation. We have to choose between imperfect alternatives.[84] Recognizing this might have an influence on how the infrastructure of collective decision-making will be structured. Assuming that collective decision-making cannot be perfect, it might try to lower the risks of bad outcomes (which is probably the best we could achieve, even if certain regulations which will derive from this system might be judged as suboptimal). This could explain why certain procedures have to be followed regarding public procurement[85] or why liberal democracy could be considered as the worst regime except all the others.

There is no need to multiply examples. It is difficult (if not impossible) to consider that economics is not irrelevant to practical reasoning and decision-making for both dialectical, dialogical and ethical reasons. However, a question remains: if law and economics is relevant for practical decision-making, how is it possible to make the most of it in practical decision-making?

7.4 Conclusion: From Law and Economics to Practical Decision Making

We probably expect (or fear) too much from law and economics. It is not here to tell us what to do in general or in a specific case. It is not revealing the truth about legal phenomena or describing the real world (this would assume that things could not be different from what they are). It is not even in capacity to predict the behaviour of our fellow humans. Indeed, natural phenomena and human phenomena are different in nature. The human world does not follow necessity and prediction in the human world is of a different nature (and hopefully!). Because it is a social science, relying blindly on economic theory, without paying attention to the particulars of the case (the social, cultural and historical context) and the creativity of humans would be mindless.

Law and economics merely offers a perspective on law, legal concepts and legal doctrines which stresses consequences, and which assumes that people respond to incentives (and experience teaches us that they do up to some point). From this, it is of course possible to derive certain expectations about the behaviour of our fellow humans but not what they will do. The most we could hope to achieve is the type of pattern prediction mentioned by Hayek.[86]

---

[84] For example, Komesar (1997).

[85] For the European Union, see Directive 2014/24/EU on public procurement.

[86] Hayek (1974): "Organized complexity here means that the character of the structures showing it depends not only on the properties of the individual elements of which they are composed, and the relative frequency with which they occur, but also on the manner in which the individual elements are connected with each other. In the explanation of the working of such structures we can for this reason not replace the information about the individual elements by statistical information, but require full information about each element if from our theory we are to derive specific predictions about individual events. Without such specific information about the individual elements we shall be confined to what on another occasion I have called mere pattern predictions – predictions of some

Despite these inherent limitations, law and economics remains a fantastic tool in the hands of a decision-maker who embraces practical reasoning. Indeed, there is no doubt that law and economics contributes to improve deliberation: it highlights incentives, informational needs, and tradeoffs; it offers alternative explanations for certain legal doctrines and concepts; it raises new questions and helps to critically reflect on them. But law and economics is not sufficient for deliberation. It cannot identify the particulars of the situation, it is ill-equipped to understand the social, cultural and historical context, it cannot assess the ethical dimensions of decisions, or fully consider the resourcefulness of humans.

The best we could do, when a practical decision has to be taken, is being ready to doubt. "When the dreams of theory no longer cloud our expectation, we are back in a world of practical hopes and fears".[87]

Bibliography

Ackerman F, Heinzerling L (2004) Priceless: on knowing the price of everything and the value of nothing, New York

Archer M, Trittner J (2000) Rational choice theory, London

Aristotle (1999) Nicomachean ethics, translated by Martin Oswald, Upper Saddle River

Arrow K (1951) Social choice and individual values, New Haven

Arrow K (1974) The limits of organization, New York

Arthur B (1994) Increasing returns and path dependence in the economy. Michigan, Ann Arbor

Baker CE (1975) The ideology of the economic analysis of law. Philos Public Aff 5:3–48

Ben-Shahar O, Sneider C (2014) More than you wanted to know, Princeton

Bourne R (2014) The flaws in rent ceilings, IEA Discussion Paper n°55

Brinig M (2000) Parent and Child. Gerrit de Geest and Boudewijn Bouckaert. Encyclopedia of Law and Economics, Cheltenham, pp 230–273

Buchanan J, Tullock G (1962) The calculus of consent, Ann Arbor

Calabresi G (2016) The future of law and economics, essays in reform and recollection, New Haven

Carrion Alvarez M, Ehnts D (2016) Samuelson and Davidson on ergodicity: a reformulation. Journal of Post Keynesian Economics 39(1):1–16

Coase R (1960) The problem of social cost. J Law Econ 3:1–44

Colman J (2003 [1998]) Markets, morals and the law, Oxford

Cooter R (2000) The strategic constitution, Princeton

Donohue J III, Ayres I (1987) Posner's synphony no. 3: thinking about the unthinkable. Stanford Law Rev 39:791–812

Dworkin R (1980) Why efficiency? a response to professors Calabresi and Posner. Hofstra Law Rev 8(3):563–590

Fukuyama F (1992) The end of history and the last man, New York

Hardin G (1968) The tragedy of the commons. Sciences, New Series 162(3859):1243–1248

Hardin R (1992) The morality of law and economics. Law Philos 11:331–384

Hayek F (1974) The pretence of knowledge, lecture to the memory of Alfred Nobel, December 11

Hovemkampf H (2006) The antitrust enterprise, Cambridge

Hylton KN (1990) The law and economics of organ procurement. Law Policy 12(3):197–224

---

of the general attributes of the structures that will form themselves, but not containing specific statements about the individual elements of which the structures will be made up".

[87] Toulmin (2001), p. 204.

Kaplow L, Shavell S (2006) Fairness versus welfare, Cambridge

Kaplow L, Shavell S (1994) Why the legal system is less efficient than the income tax in redistributing income. Journal of Legal Studies 23(2):667–681

Knight F (2013) The economic organization, London

Komesar N (1997) Imperfect alternatives, Chicago

Kornhauser L (2003) Preferences, well-being and morality in social decisions. J Legal Stud 32(1):303–329

Landes E, Posner R (1978) The economics of baby shortage?, J Legal Stud 7(2):323–348.

Landes W, Posner R (2003) The economic structure of intellectual property law, Cambridge (MA)

Landes W, Posner R (2003) The economic structure of intellectual property law, Cambridge

Lanneau R (2021) Public services as a regulatory strategy. In: Mathis K (ed) Law and economics of regulation, Berlin

Lanneau R (2023) Le risque de gaspillage des ressources publiques comme critère du contrat administratif, Revue de la Recherche Juridique

Lott J (1987) Should the wealthy be able to "buy justice"? J Polit Econ 95(6):1307–1316

Marshall T (2009) A la Recherche de l'Humanité, Paris

Mercuro N, Ryan T (1984) Law. Economics and Public Policy, Greenwich

O'Driscoll G, Rizzo M (1996 [1985]) The Economics of Time and Ignorance, London

Posner R (1980) The ethical and political basis of the efficiency norm in common law adjudication. Hofstra Law Rev 8:487–507

Posner R (1987a) The regulation of the market for adoptions. Boston Univ Law Rev 67:59–72

Posner R (1987b) The regulation of the market in adoptions. Boston Univ Law Rev 67:59–72

Posner R (1989b) The ethics and economics of enforcing contracts of surrogate motherhood. J Contemp Health Law Policy 5:21–31

Posner R (1981) The economics of justice, Cambridge

Posner R (1989) Conservative feminism, University of Chicago Legal Forum, pp 191–217

Posner R (2001) Antitrust law, Chicago

Posner E (2016) Contract law and theory, Frederick (MD), Aspen

Radin M (1987) Market-inalienability. Harv Law Rev 100(8):1849–1937

Samuelson P (1969) Classical and neoclassical theory. In: Clower RW (ed) Monetary theory, London

Shavell S (2004) Foundations of economic analysis of law, Cambridge

Solow R (1985) Economic history and economics. Am Econ Rev 75(2):328–331

Somin I (2020) Free to move, New York

Stevenson G (2008) The economics of common property, Cambridge

Stigler G (1971) The theory of economic regulation. Bell J Econ Manage Sci 3–21

Stigler G (1988) Memoirs of an unregulated economist, Chicago

Stojanovic A, Silvestri P (2019) Special issue: on the future of law and economics by Guido Calabresi: an interdisciplinary dialogue. Global Jurist, 19(3)

Strauss L (2002) Faith and political philosophy: the correspondence between Leo Strauss and Eric Voegelin, 1934–1964, University Park

Stuart Mill J (2001 [1859]) On liberty, Kitchener

Swaney J (1994) So what's wrong with dumping on Africa? J Econ Issues 28(2):367–377

Teles S (2008) The rise of the conservative legal movement: the battle for control of the law, Princeton

Titmuss R (1997) The gift relationship. From Human Blood to Social Policy, New York

Tobin J (1970) On limiting the domain of inequality. J Law Econ 13(2):263–277

Toulmin S (2001) Return to reason, Cambridge

Trachtman J (2008) The economic structure of international law, Cambridge

Wendell Holmes O (1991 [1881]) The common law, New York

Zamir E, Medina B (2010) Law, economics, and morality, Oxford

Chapter 8
Efficiency and International Human Rights Law: Some Preliminary Thoughts

Michael K. Addo

Abstract This chapter explores the question of whether and if so how different disciplines may be enriched from the theories and practices of other disciplines. In this instance, the paper explores how lessons may be shared between law and economics on the one hand and international human rights law on the other. The paper addresses the question of the suitability and benefits to international human rights law of the law and economics methodology. This is in response to the emerging narrative that attributes considerable adverse human rights impacts to liberal economic methodology. The lesson from this section is to highlight the tension between the "sacredness of the market" and the "sacredness of humani dignity". From this tension, the paper assesses some of the ways in which economic theory may be employed to enrich international human rights law and vice versa, that is to say, how international human rights principles and lessons may be employed to enrich our understanding and application of economic theory. The chapter then interrogates one of the most recent developments in the international human rights law field, i.e., business and human rights as a reflection of this reconciliation between microeconomic methodology and human rights principles.

8.1 Introduction

The United Nations Charter[1] marked an important turning point in the development of the law concerning human rights. Amongst other things, it affirmed the place of human rights in international law[2] ostensibly using human rights to achieve the

---

[1] Charter of the United Nations (1945) 1 UNTS XVI.

[2] See, De Schutter (2019).

M. K. Addo (✉)
Professor of Law, University of Notre Dame Law School, London, UK
e-mail: maddo@nd.edu

organisation's objectives. Together with domestic processes,[3] international human rights law has contributed to discernible social and political change through the range of international institutions[4] and mechanisms[5] for the promotion and protection of human rights. At the same time, economic theory is similarly key to the objectives of the United Nations vision as reflected in the central importance of the development objective in the Charter.[6] Alongside the Charter provisions are the Bretton Woods institutions[7] whose objectives seek to support the development objectives of the UN specifically and the human rights objectives generally.

The results of the combined effects of the human rights objectives on the one hand and the economic objectives on the other are no doubt impressive[8] and yet there remain lingering concerns,[9] not without basis, that both subjects promise more positive outcomes than they are able to deliver. This sense of disappointment arises from the belief that the communication between the two disciplines is rather poor with each fixated on its own sacred principles and processes, often viewing the other as a barrier or handicap to the effective performance of its objectives. Some may find such critical perspectives harsh and possibly uninformed but both critics and advocates can agree that for continuously evolving subjects, human rights and economic theory always have room for improvement. No doubt, some of the expected improvements will be generated organically within the disciplines themselves, drawing on their principles and lessons. This possibility should however not preclude the value of even greater enrichment by drawing on principles from each other and other disciplines. In this respect, law and economics,[10] with its promise of a deeper understanding and rationality of legal standards, processes and outcomes through its application of

---

[3] Prior to the development of international human rights standards, national law, through constitutional provision, legislation and judicial decisions protected human rights. International law reinforced and complemented this.

[4] Human rights now form a central part of the objectives of every international and regional organisation, ranging from the United Nations, the European Union, the Organization of American States and the African Union.

[5] A variety of mechanisms including judicial, quasi-judicial, independent experts and peer review mechanisms have either emerged or been established to steer the activities of governments and other actors towards achieving the objectives of the organisations of which they are a part.

[6] See Articles 1(3), 55, Chapter XX (Economic and Social Council) of the UN Charter, loc. cit.

[7] See for the IMF (imf.org), the World Bank Group (worldbank.org) and world trade (gatt.org and wto.org).

[8] International human rights law has transformed our understanding of many social and political issues including the conduct of wars, the migration of people, political independence, migration, education, housing, health, artificial intelligence, and more recently, the conduct of business. In the field of economics, see the work of the UN development Program (UNDP) at undp.org; the World Trade Organization (WTO) wto.org, the World Bank Group (worldbank.org) and the International Monetary Fund (IMF.org).

[9] See, Mcguiness (2006), pp. 393–421; Kedzia (2003), pp. 5–34; Broberg/Sano (2018), pp. 664–680; Rose (2016), pp. 405–438. See also, Wahi (2015/6), pp. 331–407; Campbell (2010), pp. 1–14. For a general review of the criticisms of the IMF, see, Economics Help, criticism of the IMF.

[10] See, Cooter and Ulen (1988); Polisky (2018); Calabresi (2017).

microeconomic principles[11] could represent one such opportunity for an improved international human rights law. Similarly, international human rights law with its basis in ethical principles concerning accountability, human dignity, rule of law, welfare and non-discrimination may be employed to enhance the principles and outcomes in the application of economic theory.

This chapter explores in Part II whether international human rights law is a suitable discipline for the law and economics methodology. In addition, the section will also assess the challenges posed by the conventional positioning of economic theory principles. The lesson from this section is to highlight the tension between the "sacredness of the market" and the "sacredness of human dignity that underlies international human rights principles". In Part III, the paper assesses some of the ways in which economic theory may be employed to enrich international human rights law and vice versa, that is to say, how international human rights principles and lessons may be employed to enrich our understanding and application of economic theory. The chapter then (Part IV) interrogates one of the most recent developments in international human rights law, i.e., business and human rights[12] as a reflection of the reconciliation of microeconomic methodology and human rights principles. Part V will draw some tentative conclusions.

8.2 Why International Human Rights Law?

Considerable scholarly attention has already been given to the application of economic theory to many different dimensions of law and legal practice,[13] ostensibly to enhance their effect.[14] In all of the different instances when such an approach has been adopted, the aim has been to identify opportunities for efficiency and rationality. The value of efficiency and rationality should be shared in other areas of law if possible. This is especially true of international human rights law whose impact is potentially far-reaching.

Economic theory and human rights share some common characteristics, including the centrality of the individual and the importance of maximising utility.[15] In effect, human rights law is about making rational choices about competing claims to shared ideals such as dignity, equality and autonomy. Whilst human rights law currently has methods and mechanisms for dealing with such competing claims[16] these are not, by any means, perfect and so any additional refinement that other disciplines,

---

[11] Posner (2014), p. 10; Mathis (2009), p. 3.

[12] Bernaz, (2017); Baumann-Pauly and Nolan (2016).

[13] See, Posner (1975), pp. 757–782 that illustrates the application of economic theory to a range of substantive legal issues as well as to legal processes and procedure.

[14] Posner (2014), (1975), p. 760.

[15] Posner (1975), pp. 762–763.

[16] The primary process of reconciling competing claims in international human rights law is to apply permissible limitations. On this, see, Badar (2003), pp. 63–92; Mavi (1997), pp. 107–114.

including law and economics, may offer can be invaluable. Furthermore, there are many substantive human rights, especially in the field of economic, social and cultural rights that are founded in economic theory. Rights such as work,[17] health,[18] food,[19] social security,[20] housing[21] and a decent standard of living[22] that have become part of the core legal standards are founded and implemented on account of economic principles. The economic premise of these human rights makes it imperative not to overlook the significance of principles and methods from that discipline that may be useful in gaining a deeper and better understanding of human rights that draw on the same normative foundations.

It is true that the case made here for the applicability of microeconomic principles to economic, social and cultural rights will be less credible unless it can be extended to other categories of international human rights law such as civil and political rights. The general premise of the significance of law and economics to the diverse dimensions of the law[23] supports the inclusion of other categories of human rights law, if only to undertake an informed assessment. Secondly, there is evidence from the scholarship that many aspects of what we know to be under the civil and political category of human rights have already been the subject of successful application of microeconomic theory. The right to life,[24] due process,[25] freedom of expression[26] and non-discrimination[27] are part of the civil and political rights category whose efficiency has been assessed using the microeconomic methodology. Other aspects of this category of rights may thus be open to the assessment for efficiency through the application of microeconomic methodology.

In addition, there is an even more compelling reason offered by international human rights law itself for the application of the economic methodology to all human rights. This argument is premised on the priciples of indivisibility and interdependence of human rights.[28] The principle of indivisibility of rights which has been

---

[17] See Article 6 of International Covenant on Economic, Social and Cultural Rights (ICESCR) (1966). Text at https://www.ohchr.org/en/instruments-mechanisms/instruments/international-cov enant-economic-social-and-cultural-rights.

[18] ICESCR, ibid., Article 11.

[19] Ibid.

[20] Ibid., Article 9.

[21] Ibid., Article 11.

[22] Ibid.

[23] See, Posner (1975), pp. 762–763.

[24] Broome (1991), pp. 281–294.

[25] Posner (1973) pp. 399–458; Becker (1971), pp. 306–310; Bork (1985), pp. 21–26.

[26] Posner (1986) pp. 1–54.

[27] Becker (1971); Posner (1989), pp. 1311–1335.

[28] See, Proclamation of Teheran, Final Act of the International Conference on Human Rights (Teheran, 1968). U.N. Doc. A/CONF./32/41 (1968) para. 13; Vienna Declaration and Programme of Action proclaimed that "[a]ll human rights are universal, indivisible and interdependent and interrelated"—World Conference on Human Rights, Vienna Declaration and Programme of Action, A/Conf.157/23, 25 June 1993, Part II, para 5. Also, General Assembly resolution establishing the

affirmed in the doctrine[29] and practice[30] represents all human rights as a single holistic discipline with components that complement each other. This is to say that the rights such as those listed under one category (e.g., economic social and cultural rights) are stronger and perhaps more efficient when they are seen in the light of other rights such as civil and political rights. According to the Teheran Proclamation adopted at the World Conference on Human Rights, "[s]ince human rights and fundamental freedoms are indivisible, the full realisation of civil and political rights without the enjoyment of economic and social rights is impossible".[31] There is therefore no hierarchy between the two categories of rights. In practice, indivisibility has taken the form of similarity of implementation standards, requiring States to respect, protect and fulfil all human rights.[32] Both the United Nations Human Rights Committee of experts elected to supervise the implementation of the treaty devoted to civil and political rights[33] as well as the Committee on Economic, Social and Cultural Rights, the experts elected to supervise the implementation of the treaty on economic rights[34] have reiterated this principle in their practice.[35]

Similarly, the promotion and protection of all forms of discrimination that has been seen as a foundational norm of international human rights law applies to all rights regardless of category.[36] This affirmation of indivisibility is validated in the treaties specifically devoted to the prohibition of discrimination – the International Convention on the Elimination of All Forms of Racial Discrimination (ICERD)[37] and the Convention on the Elimination of All Forms of Discrimination against Women (CEDAW)[38] in their application to both civil and political rights as well as economic, social and cultural rights. In 1989, the UN Convention on the Rights

---

Human Rights Council affirms this principle that "all human rights are universal, indivisible, interrelated, interdependent and mutually reinforcing"—GA, Res 60/251: Human Rights Council, 15 March 2006, A/RES/60/251, Preamble; HRC, Res 5/1: Institution-building of the United Nations Human Rights Council, 18 June 2007, A/HRC/RES/5/1, Preamble.

[29] Whelan, (2010); Zylberman (2017), pp. 389–418; Patersmann (2003), pp. 381–385; Nickel (2008), pp. 984–1001.

[30] See, note 40 below.

[31] Tehran Proclamation, loc. cit. para. 13.

[32] See, EIDE, Asbjorn, The Right To Adequate Food As A Human Right: Final Report, 7 July 1987, E/Cn.4/Sub.2/1987/23; Shue (1996).

[33] International Covenant on Civil and Political Rights 1966, 999 UNTS 171.

[34] International Covenant on Economic, Social and Cultural Rights 1966, 993 UNTS 3.

[35] See, Human Rights Committee, General Comment No 31: Nature of the General Legal Obligation Imposed on States Parties to the Covenant, 26 May 2006, CCPR/C/21/Rev.1/Add.13, para 6. See, Committee on Economic, Social and Cultural Rights, General Comment No 3: The Nature of State Parties Obligations (Art. 2, par. 1), 14 December 1990, E/1991/23, para 9.

[36] See, for example, Article 2(2) of the Covenant on Economic, Social and Cultural Rights (1966), loc. cit; See Articles 2(1), 4(1), 24 and 26 of the International Covenant on Civil and Political Rights (1966), loc. cit.

[37] International Convention on the Elimination of All Forms of Racial Discrimination 1965, 660 UNTS 195.

[38] Convention on the Elimination of All Forms of Discrimination against Women 1979, 1249 UNTS 13.

of the Child[39] became the first international instrument to define obligations for the different categories of human rights.[40]

There is yet another reason to search for human rights efficiency and rationality through the application of economic principles and methodologies and this is with the recent emergence of the field of business and human rights[41] Business and human rights spotlights the different dimensions in which economic policy (both public and private) impacts on effective protection of human rights. Its modern origins may be traced to the claims in the 1970s for a new international economic order[42] that inspired efforts by the United Nations General Assembly to develop a Draft Code of Conduct for Multinational Enterprises[43] as well as the adoption of important instruments such as the OECD Guidelines for Multinational Enterprises[44] and the ILO Tripartite Declaration on Multinational Enterprises and Social Policy[45].

However, the key turning point for this aspect of international human rights law came in 1999 when the late Kofi Annan, when as the Secretary-General of the United Nations addressed the World Economic Forum in Davos, Switzerland[46], where he called on business leaders "to embrace, support and enact a set of core values in the areas of human rights, labour standards, and environmental practices",[47] because these are the areas where businessmen and women, can make a real difference and ones in which universal values have already been defined by international agreements.[48] He warned against a failure to act risking "a threat to the open global market, and especially to the multilateral trade regime".[49] He concluded his address by proposing that:

> The United Nations agencies -- the United Nations High Commissioner for Human Rights, the International Labour Organization (ILO), the United Nations Environment Programme (UNEP) -- all stand ready to assist you, if you need help, in incorporating these agreed values and principles into your mission statements and corporate practices. And we are ready to facilitate a dialogue between you and other social groups, to help find viable solutions to the genuine concerns that they have raised. ... I believe what I am proposing to you is a genuine compact, because neither side of it can succeed without the other. Without your active commitment and support, there is a danger that universal values will remain little more

---

[39] Convention on the Rights of the Child 1989, 1577 UNTS 3.

[40] Rishmawi (2006), p. 16.

[41] See note 12 supra.

[42] See, General Assembly Resolution 3201 (S-VI) – Declaration on the Establishment of a new International Economic Order (1974); Sauvant and Hasenpflug (1977).

[43] United Nations, Draft Code Of Conduct For Transnational Corporations, UN Doc. E/C.10/1983/S/4 (1983); for a discussion, see, Sauvant (1977), pp. 11–87.

[44] See, Oecd, Policy Brief: The Oecd Guidelines On Multinational Enterprises, For a discussion, see, Häag (1984), pp. 71–76.

[45] Ilo, Tripartite Declaration Of Principles Concerning Multinational Enterprises And Social Policy 1977.

[46] See, https://www.un.org/sg/en/content/sg/speeches/1999-02-01/kofi-annans-address-world-economic-forum-davos.

[47] Ibid.

[48] Ibid.

[49] Ibid.

than fine words -- documents whose anniversaries we can celebrate and make speeches about, but with limited impact on the lives of ordinary people. And unless those values are really seen to be taking hold, I fear we may find it increasingly difficult to make a persuasive case for the open global market.[50]

The significance of Kofi Annan's call for the collaboration of the United Nations as a public institution on the one hand with private business actors on the other hand using the premise of shared universal values in human rights underscores the important point that the disciplines of economics and human rights need to draw on each other. His call led to the establishment of the United Nations Global Compact[51] as the "one-stop shop" for corporations interested in seeking the support of the United Nations to embed the shared values including human rights in their activities. The Compact will grow, over the years, to support business policies and activities to respond to their responsibilities to respect human rights, labour rights, the environment and anti-corruption (The Principles).[52]

The Global Compact idea in 1999 was a radical step because around the time of Kofi Annan's address, the United Nations Sub-Commission on Human Rights was struggling (rather unsuccessfully, at this point) with the exact question of how to ensure the respect of human rights in economic activities. Its flagship initiative to propose the UN Norms on the Responsibilities of Transnational Corporations and Other Business Enterprises[53] flopped spectacularly.[54] Thereafter, the Secretary-General responded to a call from the Commission on Human Rights to continue to study the subject by appointing an independent expert as a Special Representative to undertake that task. In that role, the late John Ruggie drew on the important lessons of the Davos address as well as those of the unsuccessful Norms initiative and spent over six years developing the United Nations Guiding Principles on Business and Human Rights (UNGPs).[55] Ever since UNGPs were endorsed by the Human Rights Council[56] (the successor to the Commission on Human Rights), they have become the global authoritative standard for the place of human rights in economic affairs. The UNGPs (see Part IV below), have clarified the significance of aspects of economic methodology for effective respect and protection of human rights.

Nevertheless, there is no consensus among scholars on the value of applying economic principles and methodology to legal disciplines such as human rights. There are those for whom values such as human rights do not lend themselves so

---

[50] Ibid.

[51] See, https://unglobalcompact.org/.

[52] See, https://unglobalcompact.org/what-is-gc/mission/principles.

[53] U.N. Doc. E/CN.4/Sub.2/2003/12/Rev.2 (2003).

[54] In a resolution, the Commission on Human Rights decided that "the Norms, as a draft proposal not requested by the Commission, has no legal standing and that the Sub-Commission should not perform any monitoring function in this regard." See, U.N. Doc. E/CN.4/2004/L.73/Rev.2.

[55] See, https://www.ohchr.org/sites/default/files/documents/publications/guidingprinciplesbusines shr_en.pdf.

[56] Resolution 17/4, Human Rights and Transnational Corporations and Other Business Enterprises (2011). Text at https://www.right-docs.org/doc/a-hrc-res-17-4/.

easily to the principles and methodology of economic theory.[57] The central importance of the cost–benefit methodology[58] in economic theory for the assessment of
efficiency, for example, has been identified as a classic instance of an unsuitable standard for disciplines such as human rights[59]. According to critics of the cost–benefit
methodology, it requires the ascription of monetary value to the relevant subject, in
this instance, human rights. Whilst the costs of human rights may be monetised, even
if only artificially, the benefits cannot be so credibly be monetised. For Ackerman
and Heinzerling, for example, "cost–benefit analysis involves the creation of artificial
markets for things—like good health, long life and clean air—that are not bought and
sold."[60] After all, "money doesn't buy happiness. Most religions tell us that every
human life is sacred; it is obviously illegal, as well as immoral, to buy and sell human
lives. [...] Monetizing human lives and discounting future benefits seem at odds with
these common perspectives."[61]

There may be elements of truth in this critique of the application of economic
theory to human rights, however, the arguments seem exaggerated. It is not entirely
true that human rights may not be monetised because economic, social and cultural
rights may easily lend themselves to the cost–benefit efficiency analysis. Looking
beyond ESCRs, the principles of indivisibility and interdependence of human rights
(discussed above) suggest possible monetisation opportunities for all human rights
including civil and political rights. In any case, the focus on monetisation may very
well be missing the point of the significance of economic theory to the efficiency of
human rights. Beyond or indeed even in the absence of monetary equivalences for
human rights, the search for further improvements and efficiency cannot and should
not be restricted to opportunities within the specific discipline alone. Disciplinary
isolation tends to yield poor results in contrast to an open-minded search for solutions
beyond individual disciplines.

In any case, emerging developments such as business and human rights directly
challenge the unsustainable separation between human rights and economic fields.
Critics may however disagree, pointing out that business and human rights, as a
dimension of international human rights law, is traditionally associated with public
sphere standards. Upon this premise, critics will choose to recall the adverse human
rights impacts that have come to be associated with economic activities and then
argue that the field of business and human rights has emerged to counter, or at best
moderate the adverse human rights effects of the economic sphere and not to adopt
it. In effect, business and human rights should be viewed as the application of public
law standards (human rights) to the private sphere of the economy.

While this critical argument deserves some attention for specific instances of
factual situations concerning the risks to human rights posed by economic activities, it is not entirely convincing. The primary premise of listing human rights as

---

[57] See, Ackerman and Heizerling (2002), p. 1553–1584.

[58] For a review of the scope of the cost–benefit methodology, see, White (2005), pp. 1–72.

[59] Nussbaum (2000), pp. 1005–1036; Richardson (2000), pp. 971–1003.

[60] Ackerman and Heizerling (2002), p. 1562.

[61] Ackerman and Heizerling (2002), pp. 1562–1563.

exclusively norms of the public sphere is exaggerated and, in any case, this approach misses important lessons. The first of these lessons is the value of the interrelationship between the different disciplines. As much as human rights principles may be presented as capable of moderating economic activities, so could economic principles be drawn upon to enhance human rights. This will be illustrated in Part IV below. In any case, as scholars have pointed out, the real dangers lie in the applications of economic standards out of context or in the abstract[62].

That the application of economic theory can oftentimes lead to adverse human rights is not new[63] but often considered unusual[64]. Upon careful reflection on the challenges between theoretical economic ideals and the reality of their application, however, this true but anomalous effect of economic practice may be explained. To the extent that economic theory and human rights ideals seek to attain similar societal objectives of advancement and development, there should, in principle, be no contradiction between them. However, it is the misapplication or even misuse and abuse of economic theory[65] that can lead to adverse human rights impacts. In this respect, the relationship between human rights and economics is not dissimilar to the relationship between human rights and theories of political democracy, the misapplication of which by despotic governments can contribute to adverse human rights impacts. This is also the sense in which miscarriages of justice occur when legal officials misapply the ideals of the rule of law.

The absence of consensus is complicated by the fact that it is not limited to deontological scholars such as human rights only. Indeed, there are traditional liberal economists whose pursuit of economic efficiency is based on the neutrality of the marketplace in which the primacy of the individual, considered a rational economic actor, is presumed to be a better judge of their self-interest. For this reason, a human rights regime that enables the State or other entity to regulate or oversight individual choices is considered an inappropriate interference in the efficiency of the market.[66] This approach diminishes the significance of moral values such as human rights that may be seen as restraining the freedom of the individual to choose. Whilst this school of thought does not represent all economists, it has proved especially influential in national and international policies and practice to be represented as the mainstream approach.[67] The inflexible application of this approach, often by dominant economic

---

[62] See, Ackerman and Heizerling (2002), pp. 1564–1566, in their discussion of the abstract representation of the economic value of life.

[63] See, United Nations, Corporations And Human Rights: A Survey Of The Scope And Patterns Of Alleged Corporate-Related Human Rights Abuse, Report of the Special Representative of the Secretary-General on the issue of human rights and transnational corporations and other business enterprises. UN Doc. A/HRC/8/5/Add.2 (2008).

[64] See, Zerk (2014).

[65] Posner (1979), pp. 281–306.

[66] Freeman (2015), pp. 150 et seqq.;. Manuel Couret Branco, Economics Against Human Rights,

[67] Dommen (2022), p. 5.

actors, such as transnational corporations has contributed directly to adverse human rights impacts in national and international environments.[68]

The unfortunate disparity of approaches between the disciplines of economics on the one hand and human rights on the other, as well as the perspectives of their practitioners, are a direct product of disciplinary silos coupled with depictions and ascriptions of sacredness to their own principles. There is little or no communication between the disciplines and next to no effort to draw on the lessons from the other discipline. In fact, each discipline seems to represent the other as problematic enough to avoid the opportunities of drawing on each other. The implication for both disciplines is to limit intellectual and practical growth to its narrow scope and thus an avoidable loss to the wider society.

8.3 Economic Theory and Human Rights Law

The important question, therefore, is to assess how the cross-disciplinary application of economic theory and human rights principles may enrich and enhance each other. An effective assessment of this subject however requires further reflection on some well-established ideas, some of which could well be misconceptions. The unnecessary separation of disciplines into the private and public spheres is typical of conventional ideas that are not particularly helpful in the present context. Similarly, the belief that has informed certain sectors of human rights advocacy that free market economic philosophy and practice is, in principle, necessarily detrimental to human rights. In the same vein, the generalization that social norms such as human rights undermine the efficiency of the market should be challenged.

These are unfortunate mischaracterisations and generalisations of the relationship between ideals that are important to our society, but not perfect in practice. As social norms, human rights and economic theory are meant to complement each other with no general principle of hierarchy between them. Inevitably, there would be occasions when their approaches and methodologies may differ and so leading to practical tensions. In such specific instances of unavoidable tension of methodology, however, and depending on the social priorities defined in advance, it is arguable that choices may be made that favour one or the other social ideal. Such choices are determined by favouring the approach that offers the higher value to the community. There is not, necessarily, an automatic superiority of one normative approach over the other.

Both ideals are therefore legitimate and considered valuable in the complex interaction of social values aimed at creating and sustaining a better society. To the extent that each discipline carries the potential to be more efficient in the search for its ideals, it is useful to consider the significance of lessons shared across disciplines as an opportunity to attain qualitatively and quantitatively better outcomes that may not

---

[68] See, United Nations, Corporations And Human Rights: A Survey Of The Scope And Patterns Of Alleged Corporate-Related Human Rights Abuse, Loc. Cit. Un Doc. A/Hrc/8/5/Add.2 (2008).

be evident through the internal processes of a single discipline. This is the context in which economic theory or human rights principles and methodologies, where they have already been demonstrated to heighten social value, may be drawn upon in the search for better outcomes. This may often require the use of analogies, occasional characterisation of standards or indeed the adoption of new vocabulary. This is the nature of dynamic disciplines such as human rights in their search for better outcomes.

8.4 Preferences and Constraints

In this regard, the economic principles for the management of scarcity and making rational choices may have some valuable lessons to share with the efficient management of human rights. Law and economics scholars are right to suggest that, "in principle, all human activity – even in the sphere of inter-personal relationships – is subject to the law of scarcity and so potentially benefit from economic theory".[69] For this reason, according to Mathis, "human action is a rational choice between different alternatives"[70] and such choices "need not always be of material goods but could be of intangibles as well."[71] Economic theory supposes that when an individual makes choices, they do so to maximise their own utility based on their personal and internal motivations but subject to external constraints.[72] This suggests the equal importance, in principle, of both individual preferences on the one hand and constraints on the other with the former defining the ideal and the latter governing the reality of efficient behaviour.[73]

Similar contrasts exist in human rights law between entitlements and permissible limitations for which the jurisprudence and scholarship suggest the marginalisation of permissible limitations.[74] In human rights law, permissible limitations which, as the equivalents of external constraints in economic theory, are not on the same level as the claims and entitlements. Rather they are seen as exceptions to be interpreted strictly and narrowly with a heavy burden of proof on who wishes to rely on them.[75] Whilst there may be instances, often involving actors of unequal power standing (e.g. individuals against oppressive government regimes) where this model may be useful, it may not be so relevant for horizontal inter-individual human rights claims. Such inter-individual cases, which incidentally constitute the vast majority of human rights

---

[69] Mathis (2009), p. 8.

[70] Mathis (2009), p. 7.

[71] Mathis (2009), p. 8.

[72] Mathis (2009), p. 12.

[73] Ibid.

[74] Greer (1997); Gunn (2011), p. 254; Klein (2021), p. 10.

[75] Ibid.

disputes are adjudicated on account of a pressing social need,[76] a formula that favours the majority, the vocal and the visible. The 'pressing social need' in international human rights law is therefore not a neutral standard. If anything, it is likely to favour the status quo which is likely to be unjust and the reason for the initial disaffection in the first place. By diminishing the legitimacy of permissible limitations, the value of human rights entitlements is also lessened because the true balance between the competing claims is not necessarily struck. This is clearly nothing like an efficient or rational outcome.

In addition, the prioritisation of the ideal (the claims and entitlement) over the contextual reality creates false expectations and ultimately disappointments. The current representation of competing human rights claims encourages the making of claims without a detailed consideration of the implications of the constraints of the reality. This leads to the making of uninformed (not so rational) choices in human rights claims. Traditional human rights advocacy, often led by non-governmental organisations, rarely reflects on the permissible limitations until the claims are contested usually through litigation. At this point, the determination of the scope of human rights claims is so late in the process as to be inefficient at best and wasteful at worse. Rather than enabling the individual to make a rational choice of human rights claims based on their own assessment of their personal reality, the decision is deferred to an artificial abstraction based on the aggregation of the 'pressing social need'.

Furthermore, the managers of the determination of the scope of human rights in litigation, the attorneys and judges, are one or even many more steps removed from the reality of the context of the competing claimants. The position of the individual in economic theory to make rational choices based on the level playing field of competing claims offers invaluable lessons to enhance international human rights law.

8.5   Looking Backwards or Forwards

Another characteristic of the economic methodology that may be of value to international human rights is its forward-looking approach to costs. The costs that are important in economic theory for gaining maximum utility are those that lie in the future.[77] Predictably, "the economists normally act *ex ante* rather than an *ex post* perspective" for the very good reason that it makes good business sense.[78] Past and usually lost costs are best recovered either by ensuring that lessons are learned and so not repeated or, if possible, moderated by future plans.

---

[76] See, *The Sunday Times v United Kingdom* (1979) 2 EHRR 245; *Handyside v United Kingdom* (1976) 1 EHRR 737.

[77] Mathis (2009), p. 17.

[78] Ibid.

To the extent that costs may be seen as risk in economics, they bear resemblance to human rights risks. Past human rights violations are not insignificant and should be redressed, but a more efficient regime for the protection of human rights should consider focusing on the future threats rather than those of the past. Whilst the importance of responding to the two dimensions of human rights promotion (redress and prevention) are recognised in international human rights law, the practice has largely been on redressing past violations and less so on their prevention. One of the most important provisions of international human rights treaties is the general obligation clause that sets out the overarching duties of States and it usually seeks to capture both *ex ante and ex post* instances. The text of the International Covenant on Civil and Political Rights (ICCPR), which is not untypical of other human rights treaties, provides in Article 2 that:

1. Each State Party to the present Covenant undertakes to respect and to ensure to all individuals within its territory and subject to its jurisdiction the rights recognised in the present Covenant, without distinction of any kind, such as race, colour, sex, language, religion, political or other opinion, national or social origin, property, birth or other status.
2. Where not already provided for by existing legislative or other measures, each State Party to the present Covenant undertakes to take the necessary steps, in accordance with its constitutional processes and with the provisions of the present Covenant, to adopt such laws or other measures as may be necessary to give effect to the rights recognised in the present Covenant.
3. Each State Party to the Present Covenant Undertakes:

   (a) To ensure that any person whose rights or freedoms as herein recognised are violated shall have an effective remedy, notwithstanding that the violation has been committed by persons acting in an official capacity;
   (b) To ensure that any person claiming such a remedy shall have his right thereto determined by competent judicial, administrative or legislative author-ities, or by any other competent authority provided for by the legal system of the State, and to develop the possibilities of judicial remedy;
   (c) To ensure that the competent authorities shall enforce such remedies when granted.[79]

In practice, however, the supervision of States' implementation of these obliga-tions is assigned to a committee of experts[80], whose mandate is to review periodic reports submitted by States[81] as well as to receive and consider communications

---

[79] International Covenant on Civil and Political Rights (ICCPR) GA Resolution 2200 (XXI) (1966).

[80] The Human Rights Committee oversees States' implementation of obligations under the ICCPR (see, Part IV—Articles 28–45). For the Committee on the Discrimination Against Women see Convention on Discrimination Against Women (CEDAW Convention (1979) Part V—Articles 17–22. The Committee Against Torture under the Convention Against Torture (CAT 1984) Part II—Articles 17–24.

[81] See Article 40, ICCPR, lo. cit.

(complaints) from victims of human rights violations.[82] Inevitably, the bulk of their attention has been focused on seeking redress for past violations. The treaty bodies[83], the groups of experts elected under the treaties to supervise States' implementation of their obligations, are not alone or unusual in this focus on *ex post* review of human rights violations. Other important international human rights mechanisms, including the Special Procedure Mandate system[84] and the Universal Periodic Review[85], tend to lean more towards responding to past violations than setting out ways to prevent violations in the future.

No doubt, there are benefits to giving attention to past risks, including human rights risks, particularly because of the lessons they teach us for future planning, but the benefits of devoting primary attention to the past can be limited, and the reasons why economic investors consider this as "irrational behaviour"[86] could be relevant in international human rights practice.

8.6   Efficiency

Law and economics in its application of economic theory and methodology to the law seeks to achieve efficient outcomes. This is often defined in terms of Pareto Efficiency[87] as making changes that put one member of society in a better position without making another person worse off.[88] This subject has been discussed and critiqued in considerable detail by scholars.[89] One of the primary criticisms of this

---

[82] See Optional Protocol to the International Covenant on Civil and Political Rights, GA Resolution 2200 (XXI (1966). See, also, International Convention for the Elimination of all Forms of Racial Discrimination (ICERD). GA Resolution 2106 (1965); Convention for the Elimination of all Forms of Discrimination Against Women (CEDAW) (979); Convention for the Protection of Human Rights and Fundamental Freedoms (ECHR) 1950 and the African Charter on Human and Peoples' Rights (1981).

[83] See note 80 supra.

[84] The special procedures of the Human Rights Council are independent human rights experts with mandates to report and advise on human rights from a thematic or country-specific perspective. They are non-paid and elected for 3-year mandates that can be reconducted for another three years. As of October 2022, there are 45 thematic and 14 country mandates. See, https://www.ohchr.org/en/special-procedures-human-rights-council.

[85] The Universal Periodic Review (UPR) is a unique process which involves a review of the human rights records of all UN Member States. The UPR is a State-driven process, under the auspices of the Human Rights Council, which provides the opportunity for each State to declare what actions they have taken to improve the human rights situations in their countries and to fulfil their human rights obligations. See, https://www.ohchr.org/en/hr-bodies/upr/upr-main.

[86] Mathis (2009), p. 17.

[87] Mathis (2009), p. 23. For A Review Of This Concept, See, White (2005), pp. 27–28.

[88] Mathis (2009), p. 23.

[89] Calabresi (1990/1), pp. 1211–1237; Sanders (2013).

concept is its separation from moral standards of say, fairness or justice[90] and in this respect, it is seen as upholding the status quo[91] or leading to absurd proposals.[92] Despite these critical perspectives, there are some useful lessons to be shared with international human rights law from the emerging discussions. The most evident lesson here on which most scholars agree is that there is not a single Pareto optimal. Rather, contexts and circumstances mean that there can be multiple optimals.[93]

International human rights law seeks to uphold a universal standard that is applied to everyone everywhere. This is its equivalent of a 'Pareto' maximum, the achievement of which is expected to define the ultimate realisation of the ideals of that discipline. The universality standard is premised on the universality of rights and therefore a common approach to their promotion and protection. The efficiency of this 'one-size-fits-all' approach has not been sufficiently challenged, but lessons from economics may support a reconsideration. The idea of giving attention to the specific human rights needs of the individual is likely to be onerous, but more effective and efficient than the application of a single formula. That outcomes should vary according to the position of the individual is not unreasonable, and it is arguable that courts and tribunals should seek to provide such remedies. However, the traditional approach of the law, with its reliance on precedent, does not lend itself effectively to individualised justice.

Furthermore, the approach to the law founded on defined standards and set procedures is unable and therefore unlikely to consider the needs of the individual. Would the legal process, for example, support the negotiation and tradability of human rights outcomes? In the economy guided by the market, the autonomy of the individual is rated highly enough to foresee the possibility of dialogue, negotiation and trading of rights and resources. Outcomes from such a process would be more likely to satisfy the stakeholders who will respect the outcome and therefore efficient. In the field of law, such a process is likely to reduce the burden on the supervisory agencies and unlikely to create dissatisfied stakeholders. It is an important question to explore in the field of human rights.

Negotiating and trading human rights expectations would not be simple and straightforward and nothing valuable ever is. There are risks of uneven playing fields on account of different knowledge and awareness positions of the negotiators, or indeed the disparities in economic and social standing. None of these are unforeseeable or precarious enough to make the regime of inter-individual human rights dialogue unviable. In any case, the supervisory agencies may continue to have oversight of the process to ensure that the outcomes suit the expectations of the actors. The paternalism of international human rights may not only undermine the autonomy of the individual, but it could also be inefficient.

---

[90] White (2005), pp. 1–6; Mathis (2009), p. 36. See Ackerman and Heizerling (2002), pp. 1553–1555.

[91] Mathis (2009), p. 36.

[92] Ackerman and Heizerling (2002), p. 1553–1556.

[93] White (2005), pp. 6 and 27; Mathis (2009), p. 36.

In as much as international human rights law may benefit from the economic approaches to efficiency, economic methodology can be enhanced by human rights principles. In an environment of multiple Paretos[94], according to Barbara Ann White, "[T]there is no unambiguous way of choosing which among these Pareto Optimal allocations is the 'best one', at least not by the Paretian criteria"[95]. Accordingly, "moving from one Pareto Optimal income distribution to another Pareto Optimal income distribution means that someone would be made worse off while someone else will be made better off. […] What this implies then is that an unfettered marketplace merely leads society to one Pareto Optimal distribution out of many, with no guarantee that it is the socially preferred one."[96] For this, Barbara Ann White concludes on this basis that the only justification for choosing a particular Pareto Optimal has to be on account of ethical (deontological) considerations such as fairness[97]. The value of her conclusion is that there need not be the usual trade-off between economic efficiency and deontological standards like human rights. In fact, human rights can complement and strengthen economic efficiency.

There are many ways in which international human rights ideals may contribute to the determination of a socially appropriate Pareto Optimal. In their report on The Rights-Based Economy[98], Christian Aid and the Centre for Economic and Social Rights argued inter alia that human rights provide a normative value-based framework for analysing the economic system[99]. In the search for deontological values that can help in the determination of the Pareto Optimal that will be socially acceptable, human rights offers standards of accountability, human dignity, non-discrimination, participation, fairness and equity.[100]

8.7   Reconciliation – Business and Human Rights

In this section, the chapter will assess the reality of some of the ideas canvassed in the previous sections by exploring the emerging evidence of the growing reconciliation between economics and human rights law. The evidence is drawn largely from the field of business and human rights, which covers a range of initiatives

---

[94] Ibid.

[95] White (2005), pp. 28–29.

[96] Ibid., p. 29.

[97] Ibid., p. 29 and pp. 42–55.

[98] Christian Aid And The Centre For Economic And Social Rights, The Rights-Based Economy And Social Contract: Natural Allies? (2022).

[99] Ibid.

[100] On this See Dommen (2022), Loc.Cit.; Centre For Economic And Social Rights And Christian Aid, A Right-Based Economy: Putting People And Planet First (2020).

including the United Nations Global Compact,[101] the OECD Guidelines on Multi-national Enterprises,[102] the ILO Tripartite Declaration on Multinational Enterprises and Social Policy[103] and the United National Guiding Principles on Business and Human Rights (UNGPs).[104] This section will draw primarily on the UNGPs as the most authoritative standard for reconciling of business activities and human rights.

As a fairly new field in international human rights law, business and human rights devotes attention (albeit not exclusively) to the management of inter-individual claims of human rights and, in this respect, its attention has focused on the human rights impacts of private business enterprises. For this reason, its underlying principles appreciate the significance of economic theory and methodology more than the traditional mainstream international human rights processes.

The UNGPs were endorsed by the UN Human Rights Council in 2006,[105] described by its author, the late Professor John Ruggie as a policy framework to guide governments, business enterprises and civil society about the place of human rights in the conduct of business. This policy framework is based on three structural pillars: firstly, the State duty to protect against human rights abuses by third parties, including business enterprises; secondly, the responsibility of business enterprises to respect human rights, which entails business taking steps to avoid infringing on the human rights of others, and thirdly, access to an effective remedy for anyone whose rights are violated or adversely affected.[106] The three pillars are at once independent and complementary and according to Ruggie, "[E]ach principle is an essential component of the framework: the State duty to protect because it lies at the core of the international human rights regime; the corporate responsibility to respect because it is the basic expectation society has of business; and access to remedy, because even the most concerted efforts cannot prevent all abuse."[107]

8.8 Dialogue and Negotiations

John Ruggie was at pains to assure all stakeholders that the policy framework and the Guiding Principles do not create new normative standards but rather that they elaborate "the implications of existing standards and practices that are integrated within a single, logically coherent and comprehensive template; and identifying where the current regime falls short and how it should be improved".[108] Secondly, the Guiding Principles propose a cooperative and integrative approach to the reconciliation of

---

[101] Global Compact, loc. cit.

[102] OECD Guidelines on MNEs, loc. cit.

[103] ILO Tripartite Declaration, loc. cit.

[104] UNGPs, loc. cit.

[105] See HRC Resolution 17/4 (2011).

[106] Ibid., UN Doc. A/HRC/8/5, loc. cit.

[107] Ibid., para. 9.

[108] United Nations, Guiding Principles On Business And Human Rights, loc. cit., para. 14.

competing stakeholder claims. In this respect, the Guiding Principles recognise the contribution of every stakeholder to the effective avoidance and remediation of adverse human rights impacts. In the preparation of the UNGPs, this collaborative approach was achieved through a strategy he termed principled pragmatism and defined as:

> [A]n unflinching commitment to the principle of strengthening the promotion and protection of human rights as it relates to business, coupled with a pragmatic attachment to what works best in creating change where it matters most - in the daily lives of people.[109]

Ruggie's early reflections on his mandate as "evidence-based"[110] and, in this context, his emphasis on the importance of mapping corporate policies[111], reviewing the significance of existing standards[112] and survey of government policies[113] did not immediately reveal the full scope of the principled pragmatism strategy, especially the relationship between its two dimensions of principle and pragmatism. This became a lot evident as the UNGPs began to be applied.From the very beginning, the UNGPs had focused on dialogue and negotiations to propose a common understanding amongst the stakeholders founded on the legitimacy of both the preferences of the market on the one hand and the protection of individual rights on the other. This affirms the autonomy and perspectives of the various actors as would be the case in economic theory.

8.9 Prevention—Human Rights Due Diligence

According to the Guiding Principles, the pivot of the corporate responsibility to respect human rights rests on the concept of 'know and show' as set out in Principle 15 of the Guiding Principles, which states that:

> In order to meet their responsibility to respect human rights, business enterprises should have in place policies and processes appropriate to their size and circumstances, including:

o (b) A human rights due diligence process to identify, prevent, mitigate and account for how they address their impacts on human rights.

Effective human rights due diligence involves the assessment of actual and potential human rights impacts, that the business may cause or contribute to, directly or through links with its operations, products or services[114] and undertaken both before the commencement of as well as during the currency of the business.

---

[109] United Nations, Interim Report loc. cit. para. 81.

[110] Ibid.

[111] Ibid., paras. 74 and 75.

[112] Ibid., para. 73.

[113] Ibid., paras. 79 and 80.

[114] See, UNGPs, loc. cit., Principle 17.

A sustainable human rights due diligence assessment will entail a rigorous mapping of a set of procedural and substantive indicators. Guiding Principles 17–21 identify some of these to include mapping (assessing) the actual or potential human rights impact, consultation with potentially affected groups, review and communication of outcomes. This has led some scholars to draw parallels with current human rights impact assessment regimes[115] and essenctially affirming the point laid clearly in the UNGPs that a company's established risk management strategies for its environmental and social impact assessment, as well as its health and safety strategy and also its anti-corruption policy, may reveal the significance of human rights including any potential gaps in its activities.

Knowing and showing that an enterprise respects human rights starts with a rigorous and comprehensive mapping of the human rights landscape, from which evidence of gaps and weaknesses may define the direction that the due diligence should take. It is the mapping exercise that will inform the question of whether the human rights due diligence strategy should be a stand-alone policy or one that can be incorporated into existing mechanisms within the company.

Human rights due diligence is both empowering and challenging at the same time. The principle empowers the business with the appropriate knowledge to meet its strategy to be compliant with its responsibility to respect human rights. In other words, to the extent that the responsibility to respect human rights entails the management of risk, the conduct of due diligence enables the company to take control of how the entire business value and supply chain responds to their human rights responsibilities, and thus avoid the risk of being named and shamed or potentially sued if adverse effects occur.

Human rights due diligence is also a challenge because there is, as yet, no prescribed manner for undertaking this task, primarily because it is an emerging scheme, but also because its very nature in the field of business and human rights depends on the particular contexts and the available knowledge at a certain time.[116] Furthermore, human rights due diligence is not a prescriptive solution or an outcome, that is to say, a one-off undertaking. Rather, it is a set of broad guidelines, including processes that continue to evolve throughout the business undertaking and thus imposing a continuing responsibility for which the enterprise must be at the cutting edge of the due diligence process and the identification of risks. This character of human rights due diligence therefore raises the compelling question of whether human rights due diligence undertaken in good faith and using the most up to date knowledge and expertise available at a point in time may be pleaded in defence to subsequent revelation of risks or indeed adverse impacts that were not revealed at the time of the due diligence search. It must be strongly argued that this cannot be a sustainable defence of adverse risks and impacts. It is incumbent upon the business as part of its continuing review of the risks to appreciate and avoid or mitigate new risks or adverse impacts. Effective due diligence is therefore a long-term undertaking based on a shared understanding of its contents, developed over time through

---

[115] Harrison (2013), pp. 107-117; Deva (2012), pp. 101-109.

[116] UNGP 17, see, especially accompanying commentary.

a process of shared learning by the community of human rights impact assessment practitioners, scholars, corporate executives and civil society representatives.[117]

The significance of the combination of preventive and remedial measures under the Guiding Principles as a credible governance regime lies in the opportunity it offers to stakeholders (States and business enterprises) to take appropriate steps as determined on their own, within the individual circumstances, of their situation to prevent adverse human rights impacts. In the context of the Guiding Principles, although prevention and remediation are meant to complement each other, it is important to give priority to the prevention of adverse human rights impacts and to relegate remediation to an exceptional standard. The expectation is that if stakeholders take effective preventive measures, this reduces the likelihood of adverse impacts and therefore the need for remedial action. Businesses enterprises can relate well to the emphasis on prevention because it allows them to be proactive in their human rights strategy rather than reactive to allegations of adverse impacts over which they have little or no control.

8.10 Flexibility

It is important to affirm the nature of the Framework and the UN Guiding Principles as no more than their titles suggest – a Framework and a set of Guiding Principles. They do not enact rules or directives but guidelines that may be adopted to suit different national and business contexts. Their character is in recognition of the dynamic environment of business and also of human rights. Guiding Principle 14 captures this character well when it provides that:

"The responsibility of business enterprises to respect human rights applies to all enterprises regardless of their size, sector, operational context, ownership and structure. Nevertheless, the scale and complexity of the means through which enterprises meet that responsibility may vary according to these factors and with the severity of the enterprise's adverse human rights impacts."

John Ruggie always insisted that, although the Guiding Principles are meant to be applied in any political context by all business enterprises, they are not meant to be a one-size-fits all.[118] In a world of 193 States of different political and economic complexions, 80,000 transnational corporations and 10 times as many subsidiaries, and not to mention national small and medium-sized enterprises (SMEs), to seek to construct guidelines that fit all will be unrealistic if not impossible. The aim of the Guiding principles is to provide universally applicable guiding principles that allow

---

[117] See, Harrison (2013), p. 111.

[118] United Nations, Business And Human Rights: Further Steps Toward The Operationalization Of The "Protect, Respect And Remedy" Framework. Report of the SRSG on the Issue of Human Rights and Transnational Corporations and Other Business Enterprises. UN Doc. A/HRC/14/27 (2010) para. 82.

companies to apply them in different circumstances taking account of the complexity of tools and processes at their disposal.[119]

In this sense, the Guiding Principles are not intended as a toolkit to be taken off the shelf and applied blindly,[120] they do not represent "a silver bullet solution to the institutional misalignments in the business and human rights domain. Instead, all social actors—governments, business enterprises, and civil society—must learn to do many things differently".[121] The inherent invitation to all stakeholders to participate in the practical development of the Guiding Principles, through their open and dynamic character recalibrates the issue of responsibility in a manner that is completely different from other corporate governance regimes.

8.11 Conclusions

Does progress always come from internal or organically crafted perspectives of a single discipline? Many law and economics scholars have long held the view that all fields of law can benefit from the principles and methodology of economic theory[122]. The rationality and efficiency that this can bring to law is indeed valuable. At first glance, international human rights law with its emphasis on moral standards seems an unlikely window through which to achieve further enhancement. Indeed, some scholars have argued that certain economic methodologies, such as the cost–benefit analysis that depend on the monetisation of resources are particularly unsuitable for human rights. Above all, human rights advocates have argued against the application of economic theory to human rights law precisely because of the adverse human rights effects associated with the conduct of activities based on such theory. In reality, the situation would seem to be a lot more complex than often presented. Upon careful reflection, it becomes clear that human rights law is not exempt from the potential value of the law and economics approach to the law.

At the same time, international human rights law has represented itself as the definitive value-based framework that may be used to moderate the potential excesses of other disciplines, including economics. In fact, scholars and human rights activists have blamed the absence of a moral reference point for the application of economic theory as the basis for the adverse human rights impacts in the economic environment.

As a matter of principle, we know that no discipline, especially one that is based on social interaction, that is isolated and siloed can attain its full potential. Both law and economics on the one hand and international human rights law on the other, seem to perceive ways in which the other discipline may benefit from their normative standards. Unfortunately, this opportunity has not been explored in a dedicated way. This raises the question of how human rights law can usefully draw on law and

---

[119] Ibid. [A/HRC/14/27].

[120] United Nations, Guiding Principles On Business And Human Rights, loc. cit. para. 15.

[121] United Nations, Business And Human Rights: Further Steps, loc. cit., para. 5.

[122] See, generally, Posner (2014), Mathis (2009), p. 8.

economics, and vice versa. This is an important question that can be approached from a variety of angles. This chapter has identified a number of methodologies, favoured by both disciplines, including the relationship between individual preferences on the one hand and constraints on the other, the importance of *ex ante* as against *ex post* approaches and the significance of efficiency to elaborate ways in which international human rights law may be enhanced by law and economics.

In these circumstances, a pressing question from the preceding discussion is whether the thoughts and ideas canvassed can be viable. Business and human rights, an in particular the United Nations Guiding Principles on Business and Human Rights, offer an excellent recognition of how economic practice can be enriched by international human rights standards.[123] This much has been acknowledged by some economics scholars.[124]

Bibliography

Books

Baumann-Pauly D, Nolan J (2016) Business and human rights. From Principles To Practice, Abingdon/New York
Becker G (1971) The economics of discrimination, Chicago
Bernaz N (2017) Business and human rights. history, law and policy. bridging the accountability gap, Abingdon/New York
Branco CM (2008) Economics against human rights, London
Calabresi G (2017) The future of law and economics: essays in reform and recollection, New Haven
Cooter R & Ulen T (1988) Law and economics, New York
Greer S (1977) The exceptions to articles 8–11 of the European convention on human rights. Human Rights Files No. 15
Gunn J (2011) Permissible limitations on the freedom of religion or belief. In Witte J, Green C (eds) Religion and human rights: an introduction, Oxford, pp. 254–268
Klein E (2021) On limits and restrictions of human rights. In David J, Ronen Y, Shaney Y, Weiler JHH (eds) Strengthening human rights protections in Geneva, Israel, The West Bank And Beyond, Cambridge, pp. 10–39
Mathis K (2009) Efficiency instead of justice. Searching for the Philosophical Foundations of the Economic Analysis of Law, Dordrecht
Polisky AM (2018) An introduction to law and economics, 5 Ed., New York
Posner RA (2014) Economic analysis of law, New York
Rishmawi M (2006) Convention on the rights of the child, article 4: the nature of states parties' obligations, vol 4. In: Liefaard T, Sloth-Nielsen J (eds) A commentary on the United Nations convention on the rights of the child, Leiden
Sauvant K, Hasenpflug H (1977) The new international economic order: conflict or cooperation between North and South?, New York
De Schutter O (2019) International human rights law, cases, materials, commentary, Cambridge
Shue H (1996) Basic rights: subsistence, affluence and U.S. Foreign Policy, Princeton
Whelan, D. J (2010) indivisibility of human rights: a history, Philadelphia

---

[123] See, Part IV supra.

[124] On this see, White (2005), p. 51 et seq. See also, Dommen (2022), pp. 14–24.

Articles

Ackerman F, Heizerling L (2002) Pricing the priceless: cost-benefit analysis of environmental protection. Univ Pa Law Rev 150:1553–1584

Badar M (2003) Basic principles governing limitations on individual rights and freedoms in human rights instruments. Int J Hum Rights 7:63–92

Becker ER (1985) The uses of "law and economics" by judges. J Legal Educ 33:306–310

Bork RH (1985) The role of the courts in applying economics. Antitrust Law J 54:21–26

Broberg M, Sano HO (2018) Strengths and weaknesses in a human rights-based approach to international development—an analysis of a rights-based approach to development assistance based on practical experiences. Int J Human Rights 664–680

Broome J (1991) The economic value of life. Economica 52:281–294

Calabresi G (1990/91) The pointlessness of Pareto. Yale Law J 100:211–1237

Campbell H (2010) Structural adjustment policies: a feminist critique. Sigma Jourma J Polit Int Stud 27:1–14

Deva S (2012) Guiding principles on business and human rights: implications for companies. Euro Company Law 9:101–109

Freeman M (2015) Neoliberal policies and human rights. Dokuz Eylul University Law Review. 17(2):141–164

Häag C (1984) The oecd guidelines on multinational enterprises: a critical analysis. J Bus Ethics 3:71–76

Harrison J (2013) Establishing a meaningful human rights due diligence process for corporations: learning from experience of human rights impact assessment. Impact Assess Project Appraisal 31:107–117

Kedzia Z (2003) Present day challenges to human rights. Polish Quarterly Int Aff 12:5–34

Mavi V (1997) Limitations of and derogations from human rights in international human rights instruments. Acta Juridica Hungarica 38:107–114

Mcguiness ME (2006) Exploring the limits of international human rights law. Georgia J Int Comparative Law 34:393–421

Nickel J (2008) Rethinking indivisibility: towards a theory of supporting relations between human rights human rights quarterly 30:984–1001

Nussbaum MC (2000) The cost of tragedy: some moral limits of cost-benefit analysis. J Legal Stud 29:1005–1036

Patersmann E (2003) On 'indivisibility' of human rights. Euro J Int Law 14:381–385

Posner RA (1973) An economic approach to legal procedure and judicial administration. J Legal Stud 2:399–458

Posner RA (1975) The economic approach to law. Texas Law Rev 53:757–782

Posner RA (1979) Some Uses And Abuses Of Economics In Law. Chicago Law Review 46:281–306

Posner RA (1986) Free speech in an economic perspective. Suffolk Univ Law Rev 20:1–54

Posner RA (1989) An economic analysis of sex discrimination laws. Univ Chicago Law Rev 56:1311–1335

Richardson H (2000) The stupidity of the cost-benefit standard. J Legal Stud 29:971–1003

Rose C (2016) The limitations of a human rights approach to corruption. Int Comparative Law Quarterly 22:405–438

Sanders M (2013) The problem with Pareto

Sauvant K (2015) The negotiations of the united nations code of conduct on transnational corporations: experience and lessons learned. J World Investment Trade 16:11–87

Wahi N (2005/2006) Human rights accountability of the IMF and the world bank: a critique of existing mechanisms and articulation of a theory of horizontal accountability. Univ California Davis J Int Law Policy 12:331–407

White B (2005) Economic efficiency and the parameters of fairness: a marriage of marketplace morals and the ethic of care. Cornell J Law Public Policy 15:1–72

Zylberman A (2017) The indivisibility of human rights. Law Philos 36:389–418

Offical Reports and Documents

Centre For Economic And Social Rights And Christian Aid (2020) A rights-based economy: putting people and planet first. https://www.Cesr.Org/Rights-Based-Economy-Putting-People-And-Planet-First/. Last access 15 November 2023

Christian Aid And The Centre For Economic And Social Rights (2022), The Rights-Based Economy And the Social Contract: Natural Allies? https://www.christianaid.org.uk/news/policy/rights-based-economy-and-social-contract-natural-allies. Last access 15 November 2023

Dommen C (2022) Human rights economics. An enquiry. Friedrich Ebert Stiftung. https://humanrightseconomics.ch/wp-content/uploads/2022/07/Human-Rights-Economics-An-Enquiry-2022.pdf. Last access 15 November 2023

Eide A (1987) The right to adequate food as a human right: final report, UN. https://digitallibrary.un.org/record/139080. Last access 15 November 2023

ILO, Tripartite Declaration Of Principles Concerning Multinational Enterprises And Social Policy (First Edition) (1977)

OECD, Policy Brief: The Oecd guidelines on multinational enterprises, At https://Www.Oecd.Org/Investment/Mne/1903291.Pdf. Last access 15 November 2023

United Nations, Business And Human Rights: Further Steps Toward The Operationalization Of The "Protect, Respect And Remedy" Framework. Report Of The Secretary-General On The Issue Of Human Rights And Transnational Corporations And Other Business Enterprises (2010), Un Doc. A/Hrc/14/27

United Nations, Corporations and Human Rights: A Survey of the Scope And Patterns of Alleged Corporate-Related Human Rights Abuse, Report of the Special Representative of the Secretary-General on the Issue Of Human Rights and Transnational Corporations and Other Business Enterprises (2008), Un Doc. A/Hrc/8/5/Add.2

United Nations, Corporations and Human Rights: A Survey of the Scope And Patterns of Alleged Corporate-Related Human Rights Abuse (2008), Loc. Cit. Un Doc. A/Hrc/8/5/Add.2

United Nations, Draft Code Of Conduct For Transnational Corporations, Un Doc. E/C.10/1983/S/4 (1983), Text At https://investmentpolicy.unctad.org/international-investment-agreements/treaty-files/2891/download. Last access 23 November 2023

United Nations, Global Compact, https://Unglobalcompact.Org/What-Is-Gc/Mission/Principles

United Nations, Guiding Principles On Business And Human Rights (2011), https://Www.Ohchr.Org/Sites/Default/Files/Documents/Publications/Guidingprinciplesbusinesshr_En.Pdf. Last access 15 November 2023

Zerk, J., Corporate Liability For Gross Human Rights Violations (2014), https://Www.Ohchr.Org/Sites/Default/Files/Documents/Issues/Business/Domesticlawremedies/Studydomesticelawremedies.Pdf. Last access 15 November 2023

Chapter 9
Efficiency as a Regulatory Goal in Healthcare Law

How the Swiss Health Insurance Act Strikes a Balance Between Efficiency and Justice

Dario Picecchi

Abstract This chapter analyses the relationship between efficiency and fair access to healthcare. The principle of efficiency is one of the guiding principles in the Swiss Health Insurance Act. However, the regulatory framework around the Swiss mandatory healthcare system is equally concerned with the access of sick persons to needed medical care. The fact that the Health Insurance Act pursues these two regulatory goals raises the question of whether there is a potential goal conflict between efficiency and fair access to healthcare. This chapter therefore examines in depth how the Swiss Health Insurance Act strikes a balance between the two regulatory goals. Finally, it will be shown that the relationship between efficiency and fair access to healthcare is much more complex than a simple trade-off. It is ultimately a matter of balancing interests and giving different weight to different objectives.

9.1 Introduction

One of the fundamental underlying principles of the Swiss Health Insurance Act (HIA)[1] is the principle of efficiency. According to art. 32 HIA, health insurers may only reimburse medical services that are effective, appropriate, and efficient.[2] In light of rising healthcare costs and the considerable amount of money spent on

---

[1] In German: *Krankenversicherungsgesetz (KVG)*; SR 832.10.

[2] German Wording of art. 32 para. 1 HIA: "*Die Leistungen nach den Artikeln 25–31 müssen wirksam, zweckmässig und wirtschaftlich sein. Die Wirksamkeit muss nach wissenschaftlichen Methoden nachgewiesen sein*".

D. Picecchi (✉)
Universities of Lucerne and Fribourg, Lucerne and Fribourg, Switzerland
e-mail: dario.picecchi@gmail.com

medical treatments, the efficient use of medical services—and ultimately financial resources—seems to be a reasonable regulatory goal. When it comes to scarce resources, one might even ask whether anything other than an efficient use of them could be justified.[3]

At the same time, however, healthcare law is equally concerned with the access of sick persons to needed medical care. In fact, individuals are entitled to receive medical treatment to exercise their fundamental freedoms. For example, when a health insurer refuses to reimburse an expensive drug for a metabolic disorder, patients cannot afford the drug themselves, leading to a deterioration of their lung capacity and respiratory performance.[4] As a consequence, the refused reimbursement of the medical service *de facto* limits the fundamental rights of the patient, i.e., patients are dependent on artificial ventilation and are physically incapable of walking long distances,[5] which limits their personal freedom.

It is not an easy task to reconcile the two regulatory goals of Swiss healthcare law—quite the contrary. The primary challenge is the fact that efficiency as a regulatory goal is seen as a counterpart to just access to medical care.[6] In other words, there is a potential goal conflict between the reimbursement of efficient medical services and the rather broad access to and just allocation of medical care.

In the following, this chapter will first present the relationship, or even the potential conflict, between efficiency and access to healthcare in Swiss healthcare law (2). As a second step, this chapter explains how Swiss healthcare law strikes a balance between the two regulatory goals (3). Finally, conclusions are drawn from the insights gained, showing the normative and methodological foundations of and the relationship between efficiency and justice in Swiss healthcare law (4).

9.2 The Potential Conflict Between Efficiency and Fair Access to Healthcare

To explore the relationship between efficiency and equitable access to healthcare, the two regulatory goals must be examined in more detail below. For this purpose, it will be first explained to what extent the Swiss Health Insurance Act pursues the regulatory goal of efficiency (2.1). Next, it is necessary to show how and to what degree Swiss law guarantees fair access to healthcare (2.2). Finally, it is possible to draw conclusions on the compatibility of the two regulatory goals (2.3).

---

[3] Cf. for example, Posner who calls waste in a world of scarce resources "immoral". Posner (2014), p. 35.

[4] Cf. the facts of the case in the Swiss Supreme Court Decision 136 V 395, consideration 6.1, p. 400.

[5] Cf. Swiss Supreme Court Decision 136 V 395, consideration 6.8, pp. 403 et seqq., although in this case, because of missing studies and information in the case at hand, it was unclear whether the drug could actually have significantly improved the patient's health condition.

[6] See in general and with further references Mathis (2019), pp. 240 et seqq.

9.2.1 The Principle of Efficiency in the Swiss Health Insurance Act

In short, efficiency means that there is an optimized relationship between the effort and the result when accomplishing a certain task or producing a certain product. Thus, to be efficient, it is necessary to use minimal resources to get the most benefits and, thereby, achieving the best cost-benefit ratio for a given purpose.[7]

In art. 25–31 HIA, the Health Insurance Act provides a comprehensive list of medical services that health insurers will reimburse. However, reimbursement of medical services is only allowed if the requirements of art. 32–34 HIA are met (art. 24 para. 1 HIA). In particular, the reimbursable services must be efficient (art. 32 para. 1 HIA). The criterion of efficiency is only assessed once the medical service in question is deemed to be effective and appropriate.[8] The legislator has not further defined the criterion of efficiency.

An interpretation of the legal term shows that in Swiss health insurance law, efficiency is not understood in strictly economic terms.[9] Rather, a medical service will be considered efficient if it has an adequate cost-benefit ratio, whereby the ratio must be optimized, if possible. In order to assess the adequacy of a cost-benefit ratio, costs and benefits must be weighed and compared with other medical services.[10]

Literature and case law have further substantiated the efficiency criterion. If several treatment alternatives with comparable medical benefits are available, only the alternative with the best cost-benefit ratio, i.e., the cheapest alternative, is deemed efficient.[11] Consequently, health insurers may not reimburse the other treatment alternatives. In cases where only one treatment option is available, this treatment is considered inefficient only if there is a gross disproportion between the costs and the benefits.[12] Thus, if there is no gross disproportion, the health insurers must reimburse the medical service. In addition to reimbursement decisions in individual cases, the regulatory body has issued a list of services that are excluded from the reimbursement obligation of the mandatory health insurance because these services do not meet the reimbursement criteria, e.g., efficiency (art. 33 para. 1 HIA; see also Annex 1 Healthcare Services Ordinance).[13]

---

[7] Mankiw and Taylor (2020), pp. 151 et seq., Mathis (2019), pp. 55, 64 et seqq., Posner (2014), pp. 14 et seq., Rawls (1999), p. 58.

[8] Instead of many Swiss Supreme Court Decision 137 V 295, consideration 6.2, p. 306, Gächter and Rütsche (2018), para. 1058.

[9] Picecchi (2022), para. 44 et seqq.

[10] For more details, see Swiss Supreme Court Decisions 142 V 26, consideration 5.2.1, pp. 34 et seq., 128 V 66, consideration 6, pp. 69 et seq., Federal Administrative Court Decision 2015/51, consideration 8.2.2, p. 768, Picecchi (2022), para. 45 et seq., 425 et seqq.

[11] Swiss Supreme Court Decisions 145 V 116, consideration 3.2.3, pp. 120 et seq., 142 V 26, consideration 5.2.1, p. 35, 136 V 395, consideration 7.4, p. 407.

[12] Instead of many Swiss Supreme Court Decision 136 V 395, consideration 7.4, pp. 407 et seq.

[13] In more detail, see Picecchi (2022), para. 24 et seqq., 650.

When assessing the efficiency of a service, i.e., its cost-benefit ratio, it is important to know the extent of the costs or benefits that must be compared. In fact, comparing costs and benefits is comparing two different things. To at least somewhat bridge the differences between the two parameters, it is therefore essential to determine in advance which dimensions of the parameters are to be compared with each other.

The Swiss Supreme Court has stated in the past that it is the costs incurred by the health insurer, and not the total costs of a particular measure, that are relevant for assessing efficiency.[14] However, there is some uncertainty about the extent to which costs are considered. In another decision on the cost-effectiveness of smoking cessation drugs, the Swiss Supreme Court stated that "if sufficiently quantifiable, all costs to social health insurance should be taken into account",[15] but it is unclear whether this applies to other public costs beyond those directly incurred by health insurers. Moreover, there may be circumstances in which considering only the costs incurred by insurers does not meet the objective of the efficiency requirement, in particular when a medical treatment generates additional, quantifiable direct costs that must be borne by the public sector.[16] This could include costs borne in part by the cantons for inpatient care or medical treatment that has financial implications and follow-up costs for public health insurance and other social insurance programmes. The Swiss Healthcare Act and related materials provide for a comprehensive cost analysis of a medical treatment, as the efficiency requirement is not limited to the costs incurred by health insurers alone.[17] Art. 43a para. 5 Swiss Constitution (Swiss Const.)[18] also supports this view.[19] Consequently, when assessing the efficiency of a service, other clearly quantifiable public costs must also be taken into account, besides the costs that are borne by the health insurers.[20]

The costs of a health service must be distinguished from its benefits, which are the positive effects of a health service. Benefits can be divided into individual, third-party and societal benefits.[21] The benefits of a medical service can relate to different areas of life, such as social life, health, work, and the economy, and must be assessed according to objective criteria in the specific situation. Three areas of benefit are of particular importance: medical benefits, social benefits, and economic benefits. The medical benefit can be preventive, diagnostic, or therapeutic and can improve the physical and/or mental well-being of the insured person. The social benefit refers to all benefits for the social life of an insured person. Economic benefit refers to

---

[14] Swiss Supreme Court Decision 126 V 334, consideration 2c, p. 340.

[15] Swiss Supreme Court Decision 137 V 295, consideration 6.3.4.2, p. 311.

[16] Picecchi (2022), para. 117.

[17] Cf. Swiss Federal Council (1991), pp. 114, 129, 185.

[18] In German: *Bundesverfassung der Schweizerischen Eidgenossenschaft (BV)*; SR 101.

[19] German Wording of art. 43a para. 5 Swiss Const.: *"Staatliche Aufgaben müssen bedarfsgerecht und wirtschaftlich erfüllt werden"*.

[20] Picecchi (2022), para. 118.

[21] Picecchi (2022), para. 119.

the financial benefits of healthcare, such as increased productivity at work.[22] When assessing the efficiency of a health service, the medical benefit—on an individual and societal level—is the most important factor. An associated economic benefit to society can be taken into account as long as this is possible without discrimination and as the benefit can be quantified.[23] However, the direct inclusion of social benefits for third parties is not permitted, as this could lead to discrimination (art. 8 para. 2 Swiss Const.), depending on the social environment or family situation of the individual.[24]

9.2.2   Fair Access to Healthcare

Justice is the concept of treating individuals equitably and protecting their rights and dignity.[25] An important aspect of justice is the equitable distribution of resources. In this context, the term "distributive justice" refers to the equal allocation of resources within a society and its members based on factors such as need, merit, and effort.[26] According to distributive justice, no one should be worse off than others because of their socioeconomic, financial, or individual factors or abilities.[27] Finally, justice requires that the same rules apply to each person in order to access the resources and opportunities needed.[28]

The right to receive or have fair access to medical treatment derives from several fundamental rights which are stipulated *inter alia* in the Swiss Constitution.[29] Particularly important are the right to assistance when in need (art. 12 Swiss Const.)[30] and the right to life and personal freedom (art. 10 para. 1 and 2 Swiss Const.).[31] In this context, one might also argue for a right to health that derives as a partial content of

---

[22] For a more detailed overview of the different types of benefits, see Picecchi (2022), para. 121 et seqq.

[23] Picecchi (2022), para. 124 et seq.

[24] Picecchi (2022), para. 127.

[25] Instead of many, see Beauchamp and Childress (2019), pp. 267 et seqq.

[26] Beauchamp and Childress (2019), p. 268, Kniess (2019), pp. 400 et seq., Lissowski (2013), pp. 17 et seq., Rawls (1999), p. 54.

[27] Kniess (2019), p. 403, Mathis (2019), pp. 233 et seq., Posner (2014), pp. 644 et seq., cf. Kaplow and Shavell (2003), pp. 351 et seq.

[28] Cf. Kaplow and Shavell (2003), pp. 344 et seq., Mathis (2019), p. 233, Rawls (1999), pp. 444 et seq.

[29] In more detail, see Picecchi (2022), para. 682 et seqq.

[30] In German: *Recht auf Hilfe in Notlagen*. German wording of art. 12 Swiss Const.: "*Wer in Not gerät und nicht in der Lage ist, für sich zu sorgen, hat Anspruch auf Hilfe und Betreuung und auf die Mittel, die für ein menschenwürdiges Dasein unerlässlich sind*".

[31] In German: *Recht auf Leben und auf persönliche Freiheit*. German wording of art. 10 para. 1 and 2 Swiss Const.: "*¹ Jeder Mensch hat das Recht auf Leben. Die Todesstrafe ist verboten.*
  ² Jeder Mensch hat das Recht auf persönliche Freiheit, insbesondere auf körperliche und geistige Unversehrtheit und auf Bewegungsfreiheit".

the aforementioned rights.[32] However, the right to health has no explicit basis in the Swiss Constitution or any cantonal constitution.

The scope of the right to receive or have fair access to medical care is disputed. The specific claims depend, among other things, on whether a person invokes the right to life and personal liberty (art. 10 para. 1 and 2 Swiss Const.) or the right to assistance when in need (art. 12 Swiss Const.). In the case of art. 12 Swiss Const., it is debated whether the right to receive or have fair access to medical care is limited to a minimum survival assistance.[33] However, in the author's view, a dignified medical treatment is not only about survival, but also about averting urgent dangers to health and avoiding unnecessary pain.[34] With regard to art. 10 para. 2 Swiss Const., it is recognised that the right to personal freedom guarantees access to generally available medical services,[35] but a majority of legal scholars take the view that this constitutional provision does not establish any claims to reimbursement of benefits.[36] However, in most cases, the denial of reimbursement of benefits by the mandatory health insurance will make access to medical services enormously difficult or *de facto* impossible. According to the view taken here, the right to life and the right to personal freedom (Art. 10 para. 1 and 2 Swiss Const.) therefore also establish entitlements to reimbursement of benefits.[37] The concrete level of the benefits is based on the recognised state of medical art. Moreover, the scope of benefits in terms of costs is not limited from a constitutional point of view.[38]

With regard to distributive justice, art. 8 para. 1 Swiss Const. (principle of equality before the law)[39] constitutionally guarantees equal access to medical services. According to the principle of equality before the law, reimbursement criteria such as efficiency must apply to circumstances in a differentiated manner according to their degree of similarity or dissimilarity.[40] A special aspect of equality before the law is

---

[32] Picecchi (2022), para. 712 et seq.

[33] Swiss Supreme Court Decision 138 V 310, consideration 2.1, p. 313, Amstutz (2002), pp. 245 et seq., 256, Coullery (2001), p. 633, Waldmann (2006), pp. 356 et seq.

[34] For more details, see Picecchi (2022), para. 695, holding a similar view: Gächter (2006), pp. 485 et seq., Steffen (2018), pp. 10 et seq.

[35] Richli (2002), p. 345, Rütsche and Wildi (2016), p. 208.

[36] Gächter and Rütsche (2018), para. 165, Rütsche (2018), p. 121, Schott (2001), pp. 118 et seq., Richli (2002), pp. 345 et seq.

[37] Picecchi (2022), para. 704; holding a similar view: Tschentscher (2015), art. 10 Swiss Const., para. 17.

[38] Picecchi (2022), para. 705 et seqq.

[39] In German: *Rechtsgleichheit*. German wording of art. 8 para. 1 Swiss Const.: "*Alle Menschen sind vor dem Gesetz gleich*".

[40] For more details on the principle of equality in general, see Kiener et al. (2018), § 35, para. 13 et seqq.

the prohibition of discrimination pursuant to art. 8 para. 2 Swiss Const.[41] Accordingly, the principle of efficiency must be applied in a non-discriminatory manner.[42] Thus, a person may not be treated unequally, for example, because of their age or a disability.

In Switzerland, health insurance is mandatory (art. 3 HIA). The mandatory insurance is currently offered by about 50 companies that reimburse services from the catalogue of covered benefits.[43] The reimbursement of services is financed by premiums, cost-sharing by the insured, and federal and cantonal funding (see art. 49*a*, 61, 64, 65, 66 HIA).[44] The reimbursement of medical services in the mandatory health insurance sector constitutes a public task.[45] Thus, health insurers are assigned a public task and are, pursuant to art. 35 para. 2 Swiss Const., bound by constitutional principles and fundamental rights.

A lack of reimbursement of medical services by a mandatory health insurance *de facto* restricts the constitutional rights to medical treatment.[46] If a person does not receive an insurance reimbursement, the denied reimbursement does not directly prevent a person from exercising their fundamental rights. However, the denial of an insurance reimbursement can at least make the exercise of fundamental rights more difficult or impossible, which indirectly impairs the insured person's freedoms.[47]

In the context at hand, the most important reason for a denial of reimbursement by the mandatory health insurance is the lack of efficiency of a medical service pursuant to art. 32 para. 1 HIA. The consequences of a denied reimbursement because of inefficiency can be drastic: For example, a person's life may depend on treatment with novel CAR-T cell therapies, since such therapies are often indicated as a last treatment option. If reimbursement for a CAR-T cell therapy, which is usually very expensive, is denied, the patient can hardly afford the treatment from their own financial resources and, in the worst case, may die.[48] In such a case, refusing to reimburse the costs of a medical treatment constitutes a serious restriction of fundamental rights, first and foremost of art. 10 Swiss Const.

A restriction of the constitutional rights of access to healthcare is permissible if the restriction meets the requirements of art. 36 Swiss Const. According to art. 36 Swiss Const., a refusal by the mandatory health insurance to cover the costs of medical services requires a sufficient legal basis, must be in the public interest, and be proportionate. The previous remarks have shown that Swiss health insurance law

---

[41] In German: *Diskriminierungsverbot*. German wording of art. 8 para. 2 Swiss Const.: "*Niemand darf diskriminiert werden, namentlich nicht wegen der Herkunft, der Rasse, des Geschlechts, des Alters, der Sprache, der sozialen Stellung, der Lebensform, der religiösen, weltanschaulichen oder politischen Überzeugung oder wegen einer körperlichen, geistigen oder psychischen Behinderung*".

[42] For more details on the prohibition of discrimination in general, see Kiener et al. (2018), § 36, para. 15 et seqq.

[43] Federal Office of Public Health (2022), p. 15.

[44] Federal Office of Public Health (2022), p. 6.

[45] Swiss Supreme Court Decision 140 I 338, consideration 6, p. 343.

[46] In more detail, Picecchi (2022), para. 677 et seqq.

[47] Picecchi (2022), para. 720.

[48] Druey Just (2021), pp. 1470 et seq., Swiss Radio and Television (2019).

does not allow for the reimbursement of inefficient services.[49] As a consequence, denying coverage for inefficient services is stipulated in various legal provisions, first and foremost in art. 32 HIA.[50] The statutory framework is then further specified at the ordinance level.[51] The most important public interest in the implementation of the efficiency principle is the desire for health insurers to use financial resources such as premium revenues reasonably and proportionately. In addition, unnecessary costs should be avoided to maintain the financial sustainability of the healthcare insurance system—under the premise that financial resources are indeed limited.[52] Whether a refusal to reimburse costs is proportionate in individual cases must be assessed on a case-by-case basis.[53]

9.2.3 Efficiency vs. Distributive Justice

In view of the previous remarks on efficiency and fair access to healthcare, the question arises as to how the two regulatory goals in Swiss healthcare law relate to each other. In principle, efficiency and distributive justice can be connected in three possible ways, namely in a harmony of goals, in a neutrality of goals, or in a conflict of goals or trade-offs.[54] In the literature, it is often argued that there is an antagonism between efficiency and distributive justice or at least that an efficient resource allocation inevitably leads to a less equitable result.[55] But is there really a conflict between these two regulatory goals?

Looking at the two perspectives of the regulatory goals, it is apparent that they are to some extent in conflict with each other. For instance, in the case of efficiency, a more general perspective is pursued. At its core, efficiency is about society as a whole being better off since the financial resources for the healthcare system, financed by the public, are used cost-effectively and sparingly. In contrast, distributive justice adopts a much more individualistic perspective. The goal is for the individual to be better off since every individual has equal access to resources maximizing their

---

[49] See Chapter 2.1.

[50] See Chapter 2.1; in more detail, see Picecchi (2022), para. 770.

[51] The two main regulations at ordinance level are the Health Insurance Ordinance (in German: Krankenversicherungsverordnung; SR 832.102) and the Healthcare Services Ordinance (in German: Krankenpflege-Leistungsverordnung; SR 832.112.31).

[52] It could be discussed to what extent financial resources are actually limited or to what extent they are unnecessarily limited. Cf. Daniels and Sabin (2002), pp. 18 et seq.

[53] For a selection of typical case constellations, see Picecchi (2022), para. 779 et seqq.

[54] See Mathis (2019), p. 230.

[55] Baumol (1978), p. 10, Beauchamp and Childress (2009), pp. 271 et seq., Engert (2023), pp. 105 et seqq., Lissowski (2013), p. 163, Okun (1975), p. 2, cf. Fennel and McAdams (2016), p. 1054, Rawls (1999), pp. 62 et seqq., Rempel (1969), p. 152, for a more differentiated approach regarding the relation between efficiency and justice, see Mathis (2019), p. 243, Marckmann and in der Schmitten (2014), p. 408, Picecchi (2022), para. 786 et seq.

medical benefit, regardless of their social status, financial circumstances or other personal characteristics.

If there were a trade-off to a certain degree between efficiency and justice, it would be necessary to ask which goal should be given priority. On the one hand, the legislator may prioritize efficiency with the intention of generating more medical benefits for the patients through more efficient medical care. In fact, prioritizing efficiency could lead to better or broader coverage since more resources are available that are not wasted on inefficient medical measures. However, efficient healthcare coverage alone must not guarantee more medical benefits for all patient groups.[56] Instead, to ensure equal and fair access to healthcare, distributive justice would have to be prioritized. This could safeguard that everyone can receive medical services without their personal financial situation or other subjective factors playing a role. At the same time, it must be guaranteed that the criteria are applied equally to everyone and that the principle of legal equality is complied with in the reimbursement of services.[57]

In general, a comprehensive and mandatory healthcare system always aims to guarantee access for everyone to value-based healthcare at the lowest cost possible.[58] Thus, it could be argued that a certain goal conflict between efficiency and distributive justice is already incorporated in the regulatory framework of a mandatory healthcare system. Strict implementation of one regulatory objective may be at the expense of the other. For instance, ensuring high-quality care for all citizens through generous reimbursement schemes may lead to unnecessary or overly complex medical treatments as providers take advantage of the fact that health insurers will generously reimburse medical services. Overall, too little attention could then be paid to efficiency considerations. On the other hand, strict guidelines regarding the efficiency of benefits can lead to a situation where expensive benefits with a rather low chance of success are no longer offered because they are costly and insurers do not easily reimburse them, which means that service providers can end up being stuck with costs. This can have a negative impact on patients who are socio-economically worse off or who cannot inform themselves about innovative therapies and demand them.

Yet, efficiency and distributive justice are regulatory goals. In any balanced legal system, it is the nature of such goals that they are unlikely to be rigorously implemented without regard to each other. Instead, legislators or government officials make trade-offs and, in some cases, deliberate compromises from regulatory goals. The idea that the two goals are mutually exclusive thus falls short. Rather, it is necessary to ask how efficiency and justice are to be balanced within individual spheres to implement both goals to the desired degree. For this purpose, it is useful to specifically examine the implementation of the two regulatory objectives. Usually, the two

---

[56] Salazar and Gross (2020), pp. 1 et seq., cf. Van der Wees et al. (2013), pp. 677 et seq., Expert Group on Health Systems Performance Assessment (2021), pp. 12 et seq.

[57] Cf. Chapter 3.3.

[58] Cf. Expert Group on Health Systems Performance Assessment (2021), pp. 9, 12.

regulatory objectives serve as a motivation or basis when drafting new regulations, but there is little awareness of the extent to which they are implemented at the expense or to the benefit of each other. Thus, greater sensitivity to the implementation of the two goals is crucial to strike the desired balance between them and to make trade-offs where it is actually intended and necessary.

9.3 Balancing Efficiency and Access to Healthcare

The previous remarks have shown that the relationship between efficiency and equity is more complex than a mere antagonism. The two regulatory goals are not mutually exclusive but can be implemented jointly if the goals are balanced against one another. In the following, it will be explained whether one of the two goals—efficiency or distributive justice—has priority under current law (3.1). Afterwards, it is shown how the criterion of efficiency is understood and implemented without massively restricting the goal of fair access to medical services in Swiss healthcare law (3.2). In addition, a uniform application of the efficiency criterion is essential for equal access to healthcare (3.3). Finally, it is argued that efficiency can also promote distributive justice (3.4).

9.3.1 Adequate and Affordable Healthcare for Everyone as a Primary Goal

Assessing the relationship between efficiency and equity or distributive justice to healthcare is implicitly also about eliciting whether and which of the two regulatory goals lawmakers give priority. Such regulatory priority can only be assessed with regard to the specific healthcare system and its regulatory framework. In a mandatory health insurance system that is designed to provide comprehensive healthcare—which is the case in the Swiss system—a certain regulatory focus on fair and easy access to medical services is obvious.

Art. 117a para. 1 of the Swiss Const.[59] expressly states that the federal government and the cantons, within the scope of their powers, must ensure that adequate basic healthcare is accessible to everyone. Although no directly justiciable claims for individuals can be derived from this provision,[60] it is a mandate to the governmental actors.[61] The lawmakers must, for example, provide measures to ensure the

---

[59] German wording of art. 117a para. 1 Swiss Const.: *"Bund und Kantone sorgen im Rahmen ihrer Zuständigkeiten für eine ausreichende, allen zugängliche medizinische Grundversorgung von hoher Qualität. Sie anerkennen und fördern die Hausarztmedizin als einen wesentlichen Bestandteil dieser Grundversorgung"*.

[60] Instead of many Biaggini (2017), art. 117a Swiss Const., para. 2 et seq.

[61] Biaggini (2017), art. 117a Swiss Const., para. 2, Rütsche (2017), para. 58.

availability of basic medical services.[62] In order to fulfil this constitutional mandate, the federal legislator has passed the Health Insurance Act to establish an adequate level of medical care.

The aim of the Health Insurance Act can be described generally as follows: insurers, service providers, and authorities must ensure that high-quality and appropriate healthcare is provided at the lowest possible cost (cf. art. 43 para. 6 HIA).[63,64] The Health Insurance Act guarantees access to medical care primarily with regard to its financing (keyword "financial accessibility"). On the one hand, health insurers are supposed to finance medical services for the entire Swiss population.[65] The mandatory health insurance coverage in art. 3 of the HIA is designed for this purpose. On the other hand, medical services must remain affordable.[66] Accordingly, the Health Insurance Act provides for a moderate use of resources, which is why they must be used efficiently, among other criteria (see art. 32 HIA).

However, the existing efficiency principle does not oppose universally accessible medical care for several reasons: First, the previous remarks have shown that efficiency is not understood in a strictly economic way in the Health Insurance Act.[67] With that rather generous understanding of efficiency, there is no shortfall in the supply of medical services because of the efficiency requirement.[68] Moreover, despite establishing the principle of efficiency in the Health Insurance Act, the legislator explicitly did not want to exclude costly measures from the mandatory health insurance's coverage.[69] Access to healthcare services—even very expensive ones—is thus not dependent on the individual's financial situation or socioeconomic factors.

In summary, the relationship between efficiency and distributive justice in healthcare depends on the regulatory priorities set by the lawmakers for a specific healthcare system. In the case of the Swiss mandatory healthcare system, fair and easy access to medical services is a priority. The Swiss Health Insurance Act is designed accordingly. In particular, the efficiency principle as a guiding principle does not exclude costly measures from mandatory health insurance coverage. Nevertheless, the efficiency criterion prevents services from being reimbursed that do not have an appropriate cost-benefit ratio,[70] thereby striking a balance between efficiency and

---

[62] Cf. Swiss Federal Council (2011), p. 7577, Picecchi (2022), para. 630 et seq., 633.

[63] German wording of art. 43 para. 6 HIA: *"Die Vertragspartner und die zuständigen Behörden achten darauf, dass eine qualitativ hochstehende und zweckmässige gesundheitliche Versorgung zu möglichst günstigen Kosten erreicht wird"*.

[64] Swiss Federal Council (1991), p. 133.

[65] Swiss Supreme Court Decisions 135 V 773, consideration 3.4, p. 454, 132 V 6, consideration 2.4.1. p. 11, Gächter and Rütsche (2018), para. 977, 979, cf. Swiss Supreme Court Decisions 143 V 52, consideration 5.1, p. 54, 125 V 284, consideration 4c, p. 289.

[66] Swiss Federal Council (2011), p. 7577, Picecchi (2022), para. 631.

[67] See Chapter 2.1.

[68] See Picecchi (2022), para. 639 et seqq.

[69] Swiss Federal Council (1991), p. 159.

[70] See Chapter 2.1.

distributive justice. In other words, the goal of comprehensive and affordable health-care does not mean that medical services cannot and must not be efficient at the same time.

9.3.2 A Relative and Individual-Oriented Understanding of Efficiency

The efficiency requirement in the Swiss Health Insurance Act has a comparative character, according to which the costs and benefits of a medical service must be compared with those of similar services.[71] Besides the comparison of treatment alternatives in the treatment of individual patients,[72] comparable medicines or service providers are compared with each other to find out whether they are efficient.[73] These comparisons are based on the assumption that comparable services or service providers also cause comparable costs and that the costs of the comparison group are efficient. The average of the costs of the comparison group is therefore often used as a benchmark.[74] Because of this comparative character of the efficiency principle, legal equality is of great importance, since only services or service providers that are actually comparable can be compared and comparison groups must be representative and homogeneous.[75] In these cost comparisons, however, aspects of benefit analysis are often neglected. Furthermore, the question must be asked whether the costs of the comparison group really are efficient at all.[76]

Moreover, in Swiss health insurance law, there are neither absolute cost ceilings for reimbursement by the mandatory health insurance nor a general global cost limit for medical services.[77] Instead, the cost–benefit assessment must look at the costs incurred in relation to the benefits arising from the treatment of individual patients or, for example in the case of drugs, of the group of patients concerned.[78] The efficiency requirement is thus understood in a highly relative and individual-oriented way. As a result, practitioners and health insurers are primarily concerned with possible treat-ment alternatives for an individual patient and inefficient treatment does not directly

---

[71] Swiss Supreme Court Decision 145 V 116, consideration 3.2.3, p. 120, cf. Chapter 2.1.

[72] Cf. Chapter 2.1.

[73] See for example Swiss Supreme Court Decisions 148 V 348, consideration 4.1, p. 350, 147 V 464, consideration 5.3, p. 468, 144 V 79, consideration 5.3.1, p. 82.

[74] See for example Swiss Supreme Court Decisions 144 V 79, consideration 3, p. 80, considera-tion 6, p. 83, 137 V 43, consideration 2.2, p. 45, Federal Administrative Court Decisions 2014/36, consideration 4.10, p. 592, 2015/8, consideration 4.3.3, p. 115.

[75] Swiss Supreme Court Decision 137 V 43, consideration 2.2, p. 45, Federal Administrative Court Decision 2014/36, consideration 3.8, p. 587, in more detail, see Picecchi (2022), para. 430, 531 et seqq.

[76] Picecchi (2022), para. 453.

[77] Swiss Supreme Court Decision 145 V 116, consideration 5.4, pp. 125 et seq., consideration 6.3, pp. 127 et seq., Rütsche (2018), p. 127, Picecchi (2022), para. 108 et seq.

[78] Instead of many Swiss Supreme Court Decision 136 V 395, consideration 7.4, p. 408.

lead to a shortage of resources for other patients. Consequently, this understanding of efficiency, which is not strictly economic, can prevent stakeholders from asking how money could be spent differently within the system to maximize benefits.

9.3.3 Uniform Application of Efficiency to Ensure Distributive Justice

To ensure equitable access to healthcare, it is essential that the reimbursement criteria in health insurance law are applied in a uniform and consistent manner. Uniform application of the law is particularly important in areas where insurers have considerable discretion in assessing the reimbursement criteria.[79] The equal application of reimbursement criteria ultimately ensures that every person receives benefit payments under the same conditions. In the worst case, inconsistent interpretation and application of reimbursement criteria results in access to individual benefits becoming dependent on the legal application of health insurers—despite comparable circumstances. As a result, the application of reimbursement criteria by health insurers would create differences in the mandatory health insurance benefit catalogue. For instance, the different handling of exceptional reimbursement of drugs has led to discussions in the past, especially because there were concerns about equitable access to drugs.[80] With vague legal terms and discretionary powers, certain differences in the application of the law can hardly be avoided, but it is possible to reduce the differences in application to ensure equal treatment under the law.

A uniform and legally consistent application is also crucial for the criterion of efficiency. Because of the broad scope of the principle of efficiency in healthcare law, a uniform application is important to further shape the contours of the principle. Only if the criterion is repeatedly interpreted and applied in the same way, can it develop and can unresolved questions be answered. As a result, all stakeholders concerned know how to proceed in order to comply with the criterion. In other words, case law is developed that makes it easier to understand and apply the principle of efficiency.

---

[79] An example of an area where there is considerable discretion is the exceptional reimbursement of drugs in individual cases. For more details, see Picecchi et al. (2020), p. 4; on the general relevance of a uniform application of the law concerning the use of discretionary powers, cf. Kiener et al. (2018), § 35, para. 53.

[80] Druey Just (2021), pp. 1475 et seq., Kägi et al. (2020), p. 25, Picecchi et al. (2020), p. 4, Widmer (2013), para. 61 et seqq.

9.3.4   Efficiency as a Means of Improving Access
to Healthcare

In the area of healthcare, efficiency should not be seen as a mere competitor of distributive justice. On the contrary, efficiency can be a factor in increasing equitable access to healthcare. The key is that efficiency leads to better value for money in healthcare. Improving the cost-benefit ratio of medical services simultaneously affects access to healthcare in several ways:

First, more patients can be treated because more time or more medical or human resources are available because of efficient care performance. Furthermore, the improvement of the cost-benefit ratio can lead to a better treatment result, since a qualitatively higher output is generated with the same input. Thus, the treatment benefit and the overall treatment quality is increased. Finally, the resources gained by increasing efficiency can be used to establish a comprehensive catalogue of benefits in the mandatory health insurance system. For example, there is currently a debate in Swiss health insurance law about whether health insurers should reimburse the services of psychotherapists in training who are commissioned and supervised by trained practitioners.[81] If individual health insurers now refuse to reimburse services in these cases, the supply of psychotherapeutic care will become scarcer and, for some patients, access to psychotherapy will depend on their personal finances. Regardless of the legal question of whether Swiss law permits the reimbursement of delegated therapy,[82] authorities could deliberately fund effective, appropriate, and cost-effective delegated psychotherapeutic services by reducing inefficient services elsewhere. This would make access to psychotherapeutic services easier since more practitioners would be available, and therapy would no longer be dependent on the individual patient's financial resources.

Efficiency measures can expand access to healthcare and improve the quality of services.[83] Ultimately, the decisive factor is how the efficiency objectives for healthcare should be achieved. Restrictive cost limits, for example, tend to have a negative impact on access to healthcare,[84] whereas the mandatory use of existing synergies and the increase of treatment quality with the same use of resources will have a completely different effect. In any case, however, it is clear that the often-mentioned antagonism between efficiency and distributive justice is too undifferentiated to describe the relationship between the two regulatory goals in healthcare law.

---

[81] Swiss Radio and Television (2023).

[82] See Kieser (2023), pp. 73 et seqq., Werder and Gächter (2023), para. 34 et seqq.

[83] Service providers also accept this fact in principle. See Marckmann and in der Schmitten (2014), pp. 409 et seq.

[84] Beauchamp and Childress (2019), pp. 255 et seqq., Picecchi (2022), para. 765, cf. Marckmann and in der Schmitten (2014), p. 410, Expert Group on Health Systems Performance Assessment (2021), p. 74.

9.4 Conclusion

In conclusion, efficiency and distributive justice are both important goals of any healthcare system. This chapter has shown that the Swiss healthcare system is leaning towards the goal of equal and fair access to healthcare. Nevertheless, the efficiency principle plays an enormous role in the reimbursement of medical services in the mandatory healthcare insurance system.[85] However, the requirement is not understood in a strictly economic sense, but rather strives to achieve an appropriate—and if possible optimal—cost-benefit ratio.[86] If, however, no treatment alternatives are available, it is essentially a criterion to prevent abusive costs in relation to the expected medical benefit, i.e., inefficient are medical services with a gross disproportion between costs and benefits.[87]

Although some argue that there is an antagonism between efficiency and distributive justice, efficiency can promote distributive justice. For example, through efficiency gains, there are more resources available to increase access to healthcare or to fund new benefits.[88] At the same time, the goal of fair access to healthcare does not prevent the benefits of mandatory health insurance from being efficient.[89] Rather, there is an underlying interest in guaranteeing that the financial resources within the healthcare system are not wasted, but used most beneficially. To ensure that all insured persons have access to the same benefits and are treated equally, the criterion of efficiency must be understood and applied uniformly.[90]

Overall, the relationship between efficiency and justice in healthcare law is much more nuanced than a mere antagonism or conflict of goals. In essence, it is a matter of balancing the two regulatory objectives against each other and enacting rules in awareness of potential trade-offs. The exact design of the relationship between efficiency and access to healthcare is ultimately a policy choice that can turn out differently—to the benefit or detriment of one or the other goal, depending on the specific trade-offs that policymakers make.

Bibliography

Amstutz K (2002) Das Grundrecht auf Existenzsicherung, Bedeutung und inhaltliche Ausgestaltung des Art. 12 der neuen Bundesverfassung, diss. Bern 2001

Baumol WJ (1978) Equity vs. allocative efficiency: toward a theory of distributive justice. Atl Econ J 6:8–16

Beauchamp TL, Childress JF (2009) Principles of biomedical ethics, vol 6. New York/Oxford

---

[85] See Chapter 2.1.

[86] See Chapters 2.1 and 3.2.

[87] See Chapter 2.1.

[88] See Chapter 3.4.

[89] See Chapters 2.3 and 3.1.

[90] See Chapter 3.3.

Biaggini G (2017) Kommentar zur Bundesverfassung der Schweizerischen Eidgenossenschaft, vol 2. Zurich

Coullery P (2001) Der Grundrechtsanspruch auf medizinische Leistungen, Ein verfassungsrechtlicher Diskussionsbeitrag zur Rationierungsdebatte im Gesundheitswesen. AJP 6:632–637

Daniels N, Sabin JE (2002) Setting limits fairly, can we learn to share medical resources?. New York

Druey Just E (2021) Wenn die Behandlung zu teuer ist, Eine Patientengeschichte wirft Fragen auf. AJP 12:1470–1479

Engert A (2023) Equality between efficiency and distribution, a law-and-economics reconceptualization of a principle of justice. In: Grundmann S, Thiessen J (eds) From formal to material equality. Comparative Perspectives from History, Plurality of Disciplines and Theory, Cambridge, pp 91–109

Expert Group on Health Systems Performance Assessment (2021) Improving access to healthcare through more powerful measurement tools. Publications Office of the European Union, Luxembourg, An Overview of Current Approaches and Opportunities for Improvement. https://doi.org/10.2875/776973

Federal Office of Public Health (2022) Top Kennzahlen im Gesundheitswesen, Gesundheitsausgaben Schweiz 2020/2021. https://perma.cc/WU9M-UNQ9

Fennel LA, McAdams RH (2016) The distributive deficit in law and economics. Minnesota Law Rev 100:1051–1127

Gächter T, Rütsche B (2018) Gesundheitsrecht, Ein Grundriss für Studium und Praxis, vol 4. Basel

Gächter T (2006) Grenzen der Solidarität?, Individuelle Ansprüche auf medizinische Leistungen gegenüber der Rechts- und Versichertengemeinschaft. In: Zäch R et al. (eds), Individuum und Verband, Festgabe zum Schweizerischen Juristentag. Zurich/Basel/Genf, pp 473–490

Kägi W, Frey M, Möhr T, Bollag Y, Brugger C (2020) Vergütung von Arzneimitteln im Einzelfall, Schlussbericht im Auftrag des Bundesamtes für Gesundheit (BAG). Basel. https://perma.cc/5LP5-QSLE

Kaplow L, Shavell S (2003) Fairness versus welfare: notes on the pareto principle, preferences, and distributive justice. J Leg Stud 32(1):331–362

Kiener R, Kälin W, Wyttenbach J (2018) Grundrechte, vol 3. Bern

Kieser U (2023) Ärztliche Leistungen in der Krankenversicherung, Wer darf ärztliche Leistungen erbringen und abrechnen?. In: Kieser U et al (eds) Jahrbuch zum Sozialversicherungsrecht. Zurich/St. Gallen, pp 71–80

Kniess J (2019) Justice in the social distribution of health. Soc Theory Pract 45(3):397–425. https://doi.org/10.5840/soctheorpract201992665

Lissowski G (2013) Principles of distributive justice. Leverkusen-Opladen

Mankiw GN, Taylor MP (2020) Economics, vol 5. Hampshire

Marckmann G, in der Schmitten J (2014) Kostenbewusste ärztliche Entscheidungen, Normative Orientierung im Spannungsfeld zwischen Ethik und Ökonomie. Unfallchirurg 117:406–412. https://doi.org/10.1007/s00113-013-2456-4

Mathis K (2019) Effizienz statt Gerechtigkeit?, Auf der Suche nach den philosophischen Grundlagen der Ökonomischen Analyse des Rechts, vol 4. Berlin

Okun AM (1975) Equality and efficiency. The Big Tradeoff, Washington

Picecchi D (2020) Die Zuteilung knapper medizinischer Ressourcen, Rechtliche und medizinethische Grundsätze über COVID-19 hinaus. Sui Generis 2020:297–307. https://doi.org/10.21257/sg.138

Picecchi D, Bertram K, Brücher D, Bauer M (2020) Towards novel reimbursement models for expensive advanced therapy medicinal products (ATMPs). Swiss Med Wkly 150(w20355):1–11. https://doi.org/10.4414/smw.150.20355

Picecchi D (2022) Das Wirtschaftlichkeitsgebot im Krankenversicherungsrecht, diss. 2021 Lucerne. Zurich/St. Gallen

Posner RA (2014) Economic analysis of law, vol 9. New York

Swiss Radio and TV (2019) Profit oder Leben, Wenn das Gesundheitswesen an die Grenze geht. Broadcast from June 27, 2019. https://perma.cc/2A7M-VMV9

Swiss Radio and TV (2023) Patienten ohne Therapeut: Gesetzespfusch bedroht Therapien. Broadcast from February 27, 2023. https://perma.cc/V3FT-C4Z7

Rawls J (1999) A theory of justice, revised edition. Cambridge

Rempel HD (1969) Justice as efficiency. Ethics 79(2):150–155

Richli P (2002) Instrumente des Gesundheits- und Lebensschutzes im neuen Heilmittelgesetz vor dem Hintergrund der Grundrechte. AJP 3:340–355

Rütsche B, Wildi A (2016) Limitierung von Arzneimitteln im Krankenversicherungsrecht, Wo wird die Grenze zur Rationierung überschritten. In: recht 4:199–212

Rütsche B (2017) Zusatzversicherte Leistungen von Spitälern, Zulässigkeit und Grenzen medizinischer Leistungsdifferenzierungen. Zurich/Basel/Geneva

Rütsche B (2018) Rechtsstaatliche Grenzen von Rationierungen im Gesundheitswesen. In: Kieser U, Leu A (eds), 5. St. Galler Gesundheits- und Pflegerechtstagung. Zurich/St. Gallen, pp 109–130

Salazar MC, Gross CP (2020) Improving surgical cancer care: a rising tide may lift all boats, Yet inequity persists. JAMA Netw Open 3(12):1–2. https://doi.org/10.1001/jamanetworkopen.2020.27809

Schott M (2001) Patientenauswahl und Organallokation, diss. Basel. Basel/Geneva/Munich

Steffen G (2018) Soins essentiels, Un droit fondamental qui transcende les frontières?. Basel

Swiss Federal Council (1991) Botschaft über die Revision der Krankenversicherung vom 6. November 1991. BBl 1992 I, pp 93–292. https://perma.cc/QW8C-MMSJ

Swiss Federal Council (2011) Botschaft zur Volksinitiative «Ja zur Hausarztmedizin» vom 16. September 2011. BBl, pp 7553–7590. https://perma.cc/3CCW-BQNG

Tschentscher A (2015) Commentary to art. 10 Swiss Const. In: Waldmann B et al. (eds), Basler Kommentar zur Bundesverfassung der Schweizerischen Eidgenossenschaft. Basel, pp. 232–254

Van der Wees PJ, Zaslavsky AM, Ayanian JZ (2013) Improvements in health status after massachusetts health care reform. Milbank Q 91(4):663–689

Waldmann B (2006) Das Recht auf Nothilfe zwischen Solidarität und Eigenverantwortung. Zbl 107:341–368

Werder G, Gächter T (2023) Delegation an Personen in Weiterbildung, Zum OKP-Pflichtleistungscharakter ärztlicher und psychologisch-psychotherapeutischer Leistungen. Jusletter 02(20):1–26

Widmer S (2013) Off-label-use in der Schweiz. Heilmittelrechtliche Zulässigkeit und Kostenübernahme. Hill 132:1–22

Chapter 10
Accessibility Versus Efficiency in the Judiciary: Evidence from the Polish Court Reforms

Łukasz Dąbroś, Jarosław Bełdowski, and Ido Baum

Abstract This chapter focuses on the 'court reform' in Poland, in particular the restoration of the so-called small courts in 2015. Previously most of such courts were merged into larger entities, but due to the political pressure, they have been restored. The aim of such restoration was to improve access to courts for residents of rural and small-town areas. Using a two-stage test procedure combining non-parametric Data Envelopment Analysis and Tobit regression, we observe that the change was associated with a decrease in the efficiency of those larger courts from which the new courts were separated. It appears that the reintroduction of the small courts was not driven by efficiency but by political considerations.

10.1 Introduction

This chapter focuses on the effects of the court reform in Poland which took place in 2015. Its goal was to improve citizens' access to justice by reconstituting the previously abolished courts of first instance in smaller towns. We examine through quantitative methods how this reform has affected the efficiency of the Polish justice system.

This chapter is divided into six parts. The introduction is followed by the second part, which presents the state of knowledge on the relationship between court size and efficiency. Part three covers a general discussion on the Polish civil justice system and the 2015 court reform. Part four entails the dataset and the empirical strategy that verification of the impact of the reform on the efficiency of the courts. Part five of the study includes a presentation and discussion of the obtained results. The final, sixth part of this chapter concludes and makes an outlook for further research.

Ł. Dąbroś (✉) · J. Bełdowski
Warsaw School of Economics, Warsaw, Poland
e-mail: lukaszdabros@gmail.com

I. Baum
Haim Striks School of Law, Rishon LeZion, Israel

10.2   Relevant Literature

Surprisingly, the importance of the relationship between the size of the court and its efficiency has not received too much scientific attention. In fact, there are only a few studies linking the size of a court to how well it handles incoming cases. Moreover, the results of such studies are often conflicting. For instance, Santos and Amado (2014) using data from Portugal and the Data Envelopment Analysis method showed that smaller Portuguese courts are less effective than their larger counterparts. The authors came to the conclusion that reducing the number of courts by merging them would increase the efficiency of the Portuguese justice system. Contradictory, Peyrache and Zago (2016) came to the opposite conclusions for Italy. They observed that the problem with the Italian judiciary is that the courts are too large. As a way to improve the quality of the justice system in this country, the division into smaller units to deal with the influx of cases more efficiently has been recommended.

In the case of Polish courts, the study by Biga and Możdżeń (2021) is intriguing. The authors demonstrate in their study that larger courts perform significantly poorer when it comes to fulfilling another crucial responsibility: providing access to public information. However, this does not relate directly to the main crust of this chapter.

10.3   Polish Civil Judiciary and the 2015 Reform

The civil judiciary in Poland is structured in a hierarchical tree. For the majority of cases, the first instance courts, in particular district courts (sądy rejonowe), have jurisdiction. As a rule, they deal with civil and commercial cases in which the value of the dispute does not exceed PLN 75.000 (ca. EUR 16.600). For higher-value disputes and certain specific types of cases, the authority is vested in higher courts, namely regional courts (sądy okręgowe). The appeals could be lodged depending on the entry point either to the regional or appeal courts (sądy apelacyjne). Civil courts deal with cases in which at least one of the parties is not an active entrepreneur. Disputes between entrepreneurs are dealt with by commercial courts which are not separate courts, but they are under the umbrella of either district, regional or appeal courts as their divisions. It is worth mentioning that civil divisions of district courts are present by default whereas the commercial ones depend on the decision of the Minister of Justice who takes various conditions into account to maintain the inflow of such disputes.

In our chapter, we deal with four basic types of cases decided by Polish civil courts of the first instance. These are: full trial cases, non-trial cases, writ-of-payment cases and so-called 'other cases'. The former are of contentious character, whereas in the non-trial cases, there are no disputing parties, but the court must, for example, formally recognise a certain state of legal affairs. The writ-of-payment cases cover two non-contentious procedures within which the parties may seek the execution of overdue payments. As they are not separated in the available statistical data we do not make a distinction between them. The last category covers various miscellaneous cases among which the decision to transfer the case into the adequate court in terms of jurisdiction plays an important role.

The number of civil divisions of district courts has fluctuated during the period under our review due to the reform to which we refer here. In 2013–14 (before the 2015 court reform), their number amounted to 242. Following the implementation of the reform, it has been increased to 317–318 covering the period of 2015–2019. It is therefore not difficult to see that the changes introduced have led to a significant (by almost one-third) increase in the number of district civil courts in Poland. The 2015 reform[1] brought an increase in the number of district civil courts by carving out new ones from the territorial jurisdiction of the courts that previously existed. Indeed, one may say that it is simply a reversal of an earlier reform implemented in 2012 which abolished several small civil courts by attaching them to larger units. The courts to be abolished have been identified by the Ministry of Justice.

Nevertheless, the 2012 court reform was criticised as it was argued that it made access to justice more difficult for residents of smaller towns whose courts were merged with larger ones. Three years later, the decision to withdraw from it and restore the previous organisation of the civil courts has been taken. The fact that the year 2015 was an election year was not insignificant as the reinstatement of small courts may have stemmed from a desire to please voters in smaller towns, for whom having a court in their area was not only a matter of convenience but also of prestige.

This structure of the reform means that the district civil courts operating in Poland in 2015 and beyond can be divided into three categories:

- The first category is the courts that were created as a result of the reform—they did not exist in 2013–14, but operated in later years (76 courts).
- The second category consists of large courts in whose territorial jurisdiction new courts were established in 2015. This meant a reduction in the area of operation for them—part of their territorial jurisdiction was taken over by the new courts (71 courts).
- The third group consisted of courts that were not in any way affected by the reform. They operated continuously in 2013–19 and there was no change in their territorial jurisdiction (171 courts).

10.4 Dataset and Empirical Strategy

10.4.1 Dataset

Our study uses data on civil courts made available by the Ministry of Justice of the Republic of Poland for the years 2013–19. The choice of the starting point of the dataset is a direct result of data availability. In the case of the end moment, we decided

---

[1] The reform was ordered by the Minister of Justice in 2014. The changes came into force a year later, which is why we refer to it as the "2015 court reform".

to end the study at the year of 2019 due to the fact that in the following year Poland (like the rest of the world) was struggling with the Covid-19 epidemic, which made a significant impact on the operations of the judiciary everywhere. We have therefore decided not to include data from 2020 and beyond.

For each court surveyed, we have obtained data on the number of cases on the docket and resolved (4 types), and the number of judges and support staff working there. We have included legal clerks *(referendarze)*, court clerks *(urzędnicy)* and judicial assistants *(asystenci)* in the category of support staff.

10.4.2   Methodology

In order to evaluate the effects of the 2015 court reform we used the two-staged approach. In the first step, we used the Data Envelopment Analysis method to calculate efficiency scores for each court in each year of the study. This indicator signifies how well a particular court converts its inputs into outputs. In our study, we consider as inputs the cases on the docket (4 types) and the judges employed in a given court. We consider as output, in turn, the number of cases of each type dealt with by the court. The DEA method has a long tradition of use in judicial research—it was first used by Lewin, Morey and Cook (1982) to investigate courts in the state of North Carolina in the U.S. Kittelsen and Førsund (1992) made the first attempt to use the method to investigate courts in Europe (i.e. in Norway).

As we are unable to assess *ex ante* whether economies of scale exist in the courts, we assume that they are variable (VRS). We use an output-oriented approach—the number of cases reaching the courts is beyond their control (it depends on whether the residents of the area are interested in using justice services). The courts, on the other hand, control their output—their actions influence how many cases on the docket are settled. The use of the non-parametric DEA method in the first stage of the study allows us to avoid problems arising from case heterogeneity. We do not need to examine the relationship between the different types of cases faced by the courts.

In the second stage of the study, we use a parametric Tobit method in which the explanatory variable is a court efficiency score between 0 and 1. Using this method, we explicitly examine how the reform has affected the efficiency of the Polish civil courts. We are not in a position to say directly whether the restoration of small courts has improved their efficiency (as these courts were simply not functioning before the reform). Instead, we can check whether the reconstitution of small courts in 2015 was linked to changes in the effectivity of those large courts from which the new courts were detached. This two-step approach is used in the literature. Deyneli (2012) employed it to investigate the link between judicial efficiency and judges' remuneration in European countries.

For this purpose, we create a dummy variable 'reform' that takes the value of 1 for courts from which small courts were separated in 2015 and later, and 0 for the remaining courts. By plugging this variable into the regression equations, it is therefore possible to see how the reform was related to the efficiency of the courts.

In our study, we use 4 specifications of the regression equation.

1. $$TE_{nt} = \beta_0 + \beta_1 * reform_{nt} + \beta_2 * assistants_{nt} + \beta_3 * court\_clerks_{nt}$$
    $$+ \beta_4 * legal\_clerks_{nt} + \varepsilon_{nt}$$

2. $$TE_{nt} = \beta_0 + \beta_1 * reform_{nt} + \beta_2 * assistants_{nt} + \beta_3 * court\_clerks_{nt}$$
    $$+ \beta_4 * legal\_clerks_{nt} + u_t + \varepsilon_{nt}$$

3. $$TE_{nt} = \beta_0 + \beta_1 * reform_{nt} + \beta_2 * assistants_{nt} + \beta_3 * court\_clerks_{nt}$$
    $$+ \beta_4 * legal\_clerks_{nt} + v_n + \varepsilon_{nt}$$

4. $$TE_{nt} = \beta_0 + \beta_1 * reform_{nt} + \beta_2 * assistants_{nt} + \beta_3 * court\_clerks_{nt}$$
    $$+ \beta_4 * legal\_clerks_{nt} + u_t + v_n + \varepsilon_{nt}$$

The first specification takes into account neither annual effects (approximating other developments in the Polish judiciary) nor individual effects for individual courts (taking into account, for example, the different quality of management of individual courts or their IT equipment). In specification two, we consider only annual effects, and in specification three, only individual court effects. In the fourth and final model specification, we include both types of effects.

The sign of the parameter related to the "reform" variable and its statistical significance will allow us to check how the changes in the organization of courts introduced in 2015 are related to the effectiveness of the affected courts.

10.5   Estimation Results

10.5.1   Data Envelopment Analysis and Efficiency Scores

As described, in the first step of the study, we use the Data Envelopment Analysis method to calculate the performance index for each court and year. In the first stage of the analysis, we visualised the distribution of this efficiency in the consecutive years of our study (Fig. 10.1).

Even a preliminary, graphical analysis shows that there has been a deterioration in the efficiency of the civil courts after 2015. In 2016, the median efficiency and the first and third quartiles worsened relative to the previous year. This suggests that the reform may have had a negative impact on judicial performance.

In the next step of the analysis, we examined changes in this efficiency in specific subgroups of courts: those that were reconstituted; those from which new courts were detached; and those that were not affected by the reform (Fig. 10.2).

An extended graphical analysis of efficiency reveals additional insights. There is a clear breakdown in the efficiency of the large courts from which new units

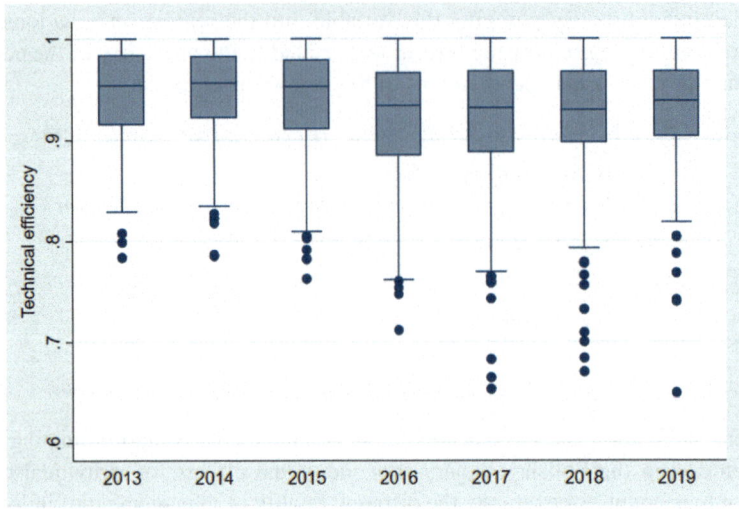

Fig. 10.1 Technical efficiency of Polish first-instance civil courts in the years 2013–2019[2]

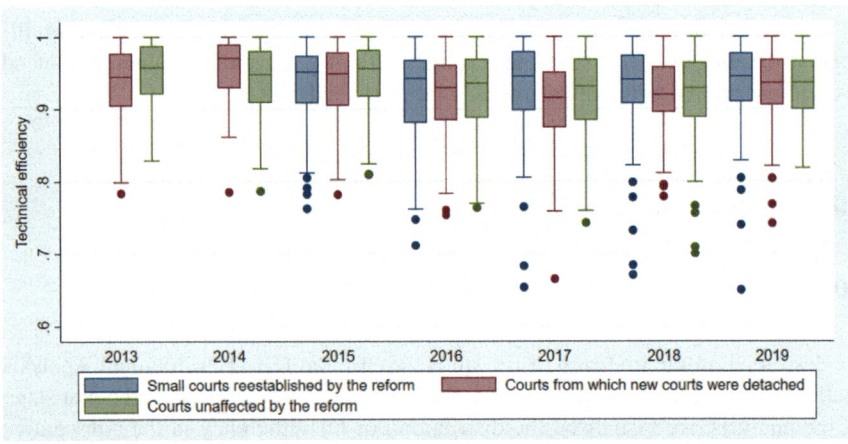

Fig. 10.2 Technical efficiency of Polish district civil courts in the years 2013–2019 by the court category[3]

[2] Source: own calculations based on the data provided by the Ministry of Justice of the Republic of Poland.

[3] Source: own calculations based on the data provided by the Ministry of Justice of the Republic of Poland.

have been reconstituted. The downward trend for these units is evident in 2014–16. However, negative changes can also be seen in the case of courts unaffected by the 2015 reform (i.e., those where no new courts were separated). On the other hand, it should be recognised that the reconstituted small courts were characterised by relatively high efficiency compared to the other units.

In order to address it and to check whether the reform has actually had a negative impact on the efficiency of the courts where it was implemented, we use quantitative methods.

10.5.2 Tobit Regressions

As noted in the methodological section of this text, in the second stage we use parametric methods, namely Tobit regressions in which the explanatory variable is the technical efficiency of the courts as determined by DEA. The choice of the Tobit method is dictated by the fact that, by definition, the technical efficiency of the courts must be between 0 and 1.

On the side of the explanatory variables, however, we include the previously described 'reform' variable measuring the impact of the reform, as well as control variables that can affect court efficiency—support staff (per judge). In the four different model specifications, we also use fixed effects for individual courts, years and for both categories combined (Table 10.1).

The Tobit regressions confirm our earlier suppositions derived from the graphical analysis of the efficiency data. Indeed, courts that have been established by the reform (i.e. new courts have been established in their jurisdiction) were *ceteris paribus* less

Table 10.1 Determinants of technical efficiency of Polish district civil courts in 2013–19

	(1)	(2)	(3)	(4)
Reform	-0.015^{**}	-0.0098	-0.026^{***}	-0.011^*
	(0.01)	(0.01)	(0.01)	(0.01)
Assistants per judge	-0.026^*	-0.016	-0.00068	0.020
	(0.02)	(0.02)	(0.01)	(0.01)
Legal clerks per judge	-0.0049	-0.0011	0.0014	0.0086
	(0.01)	(0.01)	(0.01)	(0.01)
Civil servants per judge	-0.0032	-0.0029	-0.013^{**}	-0.012^{**}
	(0.01)	(0.01)	(0.01)	(0.01)
Court fe	No	No	Yes	Yes
Year fe	No	Yes	No	Yes
N	1688	1688	1688	1688

Note Standard errors are clustered at court level. Statistical significance: * 10%, ** 5%, *** 1%

efficient in the year 2015 and afterwards. This may be due to their overstaffing immediately after the reform.

The variable describing the reform is only statistically insignificant in specification two, where we excluded fixed effects for individual courts, while leaving effects for individual years. This approach could have led to results being distorted by the unobservable heterogeneity of individual courts (e.g. differences in management quality or special local conditions).

10.6   Conclusions

This study focuses on the organisational reform of the Polish civil judiciary in 2015, which consisted of the reconstitution of the so-called small courts that had been abolished several years earlier. Using a two-stage research procedure combining non-parametric Data Envelopment Analysis and parametric Tobit models, we observe that the reform was negatively related to the efficiency of large courts from which smaller units were detached. We have shown that this result also remains stable after including year fixed effects and courts.

The result obtained allows us to make a negative assessment of the 2015 court reform. In our opinion, the emergence of efficient but inherently small courts does not compensate for the decline in the efficiency of the large units from which the small courts were reconstituted. Such an effect and the fact that the change was carried out in the immediate proximity of the elections makes it possible to assume that it was motivated not by improving the performance of the judiciary, but by purely political considerations, primarily satisfying voters' demand for local courts as a method of winning the elections in smaller towns.

Due to data limitations, this chapter does not cover the financial aspects of the 2015 changes. However, in concluding considerations, it is worth emphasising that the restoration of small courts involves additional costs. These are related, for example, to the costs of maintaining the building, employing administrative staff or additional salaries for the court president. Consideration of the financial aspects also suggests that the reform had negative efficiency implications.

The 2015 court reform obviously requires further research. It would be advisable to see how the efficiency of the courts (both the reconstituted small courts and the large courts whose territorial jurisdiction was reduced) developed in the following years which are not covered here. It will be possible as soon as the relevant data is available. We note that the data from the years 2020–21, on the other hand, should be viewed with caution as the Covid-19 pandemic that was ongoing at the time was a phenomenon that also led to major changes in the work of the judiciary. Data from this period may therefore be incomparable with earlier and later years.

References

Biga B, Mozdzen M (2021) Is it Darker in a larger courtroom? On the relationship between the size of regional court and exercising the right to public information in Poland. Euro Res Stud J XXIV(Issue 1):1189–1203

Deyneli F (2012) Analysis of relationship between efficiency of justice services and salaries of judges with two-stage DEA method. Eur J Law Econ 34(3):477–493

Kittelsen SAC, Førsund FR (1992) Efficiency analysis of Norwegian district courts. J Prod Anal 3:277–306

Lewin AY, Morey RC, Cook TJ (1982) Evaluating the administrative efficiency of courts. Omega 10(4):401–411

Peyrache A, Zago A (2016) Large courts, small justice!: the inefficiency and the optimal structure of the Italian justice sector. Omega (united Kingdom) 64:42–56

Santos SP, Amado CAF (2014) On the need for reform of the Portuguese judicial system—does data envelopment analysis assessment support it?. Omega (United Kingdom) 47:1–16

Part III
Reciprocity

Chapter 11
"Shared Joy is Double Joy"

Reciprocal Microfoundations of the Gini Coefficient

Zsófia Hajnal

Abstract One of the most iconic phrases on sharing is the Swedish proverb *"Delad glädje är dubbel glädje; delad sorg är halverad sorg."*—*"Shared joy is a double joy; shared sorrow is half a sorrow."* The focus in this chapter will be on the positive side of this saying, on the value-multiplying effect of sharing, which is a mechanism that connects reciprocity with efficiency. Despite the widely known and accepted general benefits that come from sharing as an ethical deed, attempts at operationalizing, quantifying, and testing–relative to its anticipated potential—are few and far between. This chapter thus contains three parts. First, the theory around sharing, reciprocity and value multiplication, with the review of the literature, as well as proposed systems of equations inclusive. Second, an empirical section, wherein the statements (through the remote connections drawn) will be tested on data. Third and finally, a discussion of the findings ensues, proposing behavioural foundations as reasons for the phenomenon of sharing as value multiplication, including an outlook in the form of further research opportunities.

11.1 Introduction

The legend of St. Martin of Tours (fourth century AD) holds that, when serving as a soldier, and encountering a beggar one night on the road, St. Martin halved his cloak, and gave one-half of it to the beggar. The next day, waking up from a spiritual dream, in which he saw Jesus in the cloak, St. Martin found the garment in a restored state.[1]

The legend points to the rewarding nature of sharing, and is often being taught together with the proverb section *"Shared Joy is Double Joy"*. In this present chapter, I aim to support this saying through existing literature, mathematically, statistically, as well as from a behavioural economic point of view.

Z. Hajnal (✉)
Corvinus University of Budapest, Budapest, Hungary
e-mail: zsofia.hajnal@stud.uni-corvinus.hu

[1] Encyclopaedia Britannica (2023).

By reviewing the literature in a focused manner, I seek out works that reflect on sharing as a value multiplication process, in all of the complexities of the mechanism. The mathematical construct that follows fills the gap in the mathematical description of sharing as a value-multiplying process. I am guiding the reader gradually through the steps of devising, and through the meaning of every equation, from the micro-level of two, scaling it up to an indefinite number of participants. The empirical part, with statistics applied, tests whether the scalability holds in practice, and whether data for multiple indicators can reflect the value-multiplying effects of sharing, measured inversely by looking at the extent of inequality in the given countries. The chapter ends with an interpretation of the results, a discussion of the underlying behavioural factors, and concluding remarks on the findings.

11.2 Theoretical Background to Sharing as a Value Multiplication Process

The idea of value multiplication is core to macroeconomics, and to economic science in general. Value multiplication through mutualities and through the power of community levels can be witnessed early on in economic concepts and models, such as in the Smithian *invisible hand* or in the *Keynesian multiplier*. More recently, there have been a number of attempts to connect value multiplication to the behavioural branch of economics. In order to gain an understanding of the most relevant existing sources, and of the extent to which the phenomenon of sharing and equality as a value multiplication process have been covered in scientific—and in particular: economic—literature, I conduct a focused review of journal articles—the works serving as milestones in the economics scope of the topic. After having identified the gap of the direct mathematical expression of sharing as a value multiplication process, I refer to my first attempts at the equations' construction, and I extend the applicability of the existing equation system, from the micro- to the macro-level.

11.2.1 A Focused Review of the Literature

The search for the relevant literature has been conducted through the Google Scholar engine, as well as the JSTOR digital library, by using the search terms "reciprocity", "sharing", "inequality", and "value creation". A layer of selection has been applied based on titles, keywords, and abstracts, looking for relevance to the current chapter's theme, and—more narrowly—to the equation systems. In particular, I was looking for academic works wherein combinations of the aforementioned search terms appear.

The most common theme of the works selected is reciprocity, often connected to the behavioural concept of altruism (reciprocal altruism). I find the reason for such pieces being more common in the selection than—for instance—the *sharing economy* theme, in that sharing in its "organic" form is linked up closer with reciprocity itself than with the mostly top-down economic facilitations of it. Also, behavioural and ethical elements are represented to a greater extent in the economic literature of reciprocity than in that of the sharing economy.

Chronologically, the review goes back until the year 1996, when Rachel E. Kranton, an economist who studies institutions and networks, wrote about *"Reciprocal Exchange"* as *"A Self-Sustaining System"*.[2] Reciprocal, or gift exchange is described as: *"informally enforced agreements to give goods, services, information, or money in exchange for future compensation in kind"*.[3] It is contrasted with one-time gift-giving, and being considered on-going.[4] The choice, whether one deems sharing as a phenomenon to be closer to reciprocal exchange or gift giving can be telling of the individual's ideological stance, of their approach to the concept of justice. Sharing may stand closer to reciprocal altruism, not in the act of reciprocity, but in the balanced states that it creates.

Kranton was considering the interactions, dynamics, and efficiency of reciprocal and monetary market exchange systems, and how systems converge to one or the other, based on the initial market size. One novelty of her article was thinking about reciprocity in a systems framework.[5] It has also been pointed out how reciprocal exchange has received little attention in the economic literature to that date, with Kranton being able to name only a few fellow authors with related research experience.[6]

Proceeding chronologically and relatedly, the article *"Would you marry your daughter to homo economicus?"*[7] may be brought into this context. The piece is an *"attempt to demonstrate that unselfishness is not necessarily irrational, and that altruism has a* raison d'etre *even in a narrowly defined economy."*[8] The author describes altruism as *"positively internalising the welfare of others (or their consumption ...) into one's utility function"*.[9] Hámori too applies a systems perspective, connecting reciprocal altruism—described as a *"form of altruism that is based upon a mutuality between non-related partners"*—to a *"clearing system of favours"*, also involving a buffer of shared risks.[10] The loose and indirect connection between a good deed and its compensation—which is nevertheless expected—is emphasised, and referred to in a multi-stage context for reciprocal altruism.[11] The article views reciprocal altruism as a cost-efficient (*"cost-cutting"*) phenomenon in general.[12]

---

[2] Kranton (1996).

[3] Kranton (1996), p. 830.

[4] Kranton (1996), p. 832, footnote 5.

[5] Kranton (1996), pp. 830 et seq.

[6] Kranton (1996), p. 832.

[7] Hámori (1999).

[8] Hámori (1999), p. 22.

[9] Rapoport (1995), p. 390, as cited in Hámori (1999), p. 22.

[10] Hámori (1999), pp. 25, 29.

[11] Hámori (1999), pp. 26 et seq.

[12] Hámori (1999), p. 30.

Another substantial contribution to the economic literature of reciprocity and sharing is from around the same time period. The article *"Reciprocity, Self-Interest, and the Welfare State"* by Samuel Bowles and Herbert Gintis opens up to the macroeconomic aspects of strong reciprocity, basic needs generosity (*"a virtually unconditional willingness to share with others to assure them of some minimal standard"*), and reciprocal altruism, along with some direct game-theoretical examples and applications.[13] It is another example of the earlier articles questioning the human model of economics interpreted as selfish. Furthermore, Bowles and Gintis claim that reciprocal altruism in itself is insufficient to explain macro-level phenomena of rather selfless behaviour, such as those manifested in the welfare state, and they assume non-selfish preferences for most of the agents, terming them *homo reciprocans*, whilst still acknowledging the heterogeneity of human motivations.[14] In the article, Bowles and Gintis also embark upon an evolutionary quest of the origins of sharing, and find extensive sharing patterns in the literature on simple societies,[15] which is followed by their review of certain factors that enhance the chances of sharing, such as communication among agents, and that the goods or rewards were acquired by chance rather than by personal effort.[16]

From the perspective of the current chapter, one more article, *"The Structure of Reciprocity"* has been considered.[17] The author of this article can already rely on what evolutionary biologists and experimental economists have proposed: *"that we are hard-wired for reciprocity"*.[18] She distinguishes between negotiated and reciprocal exchange to establish models of reciprocity. Molm's main claims on reciprocity—that it is structured (not just a norm or process), that it has consequences for social relationships (the emergence of trust and solidarity, going as far as social capital production), and that these effects are produced by reciprocal dimensions, through specific mechanisms[19]—are in close connection with the theoretical assumptions of the present chapter. The aforementioned production of social capital, in particular, can be linked to forms of economic and ethical value generation. Many of the positive effects can be just as well described as layers between sharing or reciprocal exchange, and value multiplication. According to Molm, the network structure defines the opportunities for exchange,[20] pathways that I term channels of sharing, and channels of reciprocity. Intriguingly, different experiences of sharing, under different reciprocal structures—diverse structures where even the systems of economic exchange are embedded in—result in various positive effects.[21] Molm even

---

[13] Bowles and Gintis (2000), p. 50.

[14] Bowles and Gintis (2000), pp. 36 et seq.

[15] Bowles and Gintis (2000), pp. 38 et seq.

[16] Bowles and Gintis (2000), pp. 44 et seq.

[17] Molm (2010).

[18] Molm (2010), p. 119.

[19] Molm (2010), p. 120.

[20] Molm (2010), p. 120.

[21] Molm (2010), pp. 124 et seq.

projects relationships between micro- and macro-structures of reciprocity, and that—based on mechanisms that impact power inequality—they are likely to be reciprocal themselves.[22]

This focused review was an attempt to prepare the reader for the micro-level theory, the subsequent macro-level analysis, as well as the behavioural evaluation. The relevant literature covers vast and diverse areas of science, yet neither in the works referred to, nor elsewhere—despite substantial search efforts—have I found the direct mathematical expression (formulae, equations) which would describe sharing as a process of value multiplication. The subsequent subsection will thus look into the origins, the creation, and my extension of such formulae.

11.2.2 Formulae for Sharing as Value Multiplication—The Saint Martin Equations

In the year 2020, an ambitious conference paper titled *Moral Economics—A Theoretical Basis for Building the Next Economic System*, has been published in the collection *Words, Objects and Events in Economics—The Making of Economic Theory*.[23] The piece has briefly touched upon the question of sharing as a value multiplier (subchapter: *The Moral Economic Measurement of Inequalities*), and proposed a short equation system, applicable to two people, resembling the proverb *"Shared joy is double joy"* mathematically. In this subchapter, the equation system—a mathematical argument—will be revisited, transformed and extended to the level of n economic agents, or—more generally—a community of n people.

The concept is as follows. In the context of two people, positive input (denoted with J for joy) is shared. The indices are for person 1 and person 2 respectively. The situation is transparent, and the value arising from sharing may be intrinsic to the value of equality.

The equations are obtained in two steps. First, an inequality indicator (I) is determined by the formula:

$$I = \frac{(|J_1 - J_2|)}{(J_1 + J_2)}$$

I results from taking the absolute value of the difference between the individual joys, and dividing this by the sum of joys. It is a number between 0 and 1, 0 denoting an absolutely equal share, whilst 1 stands for absolute inequality, where one of the two people takes all the available input.

To make this work for the proverb *"Shared joy is double joy"*, I (the inequality indicator) needs to be subtracted from 2 (the number of agents in the present reciprocal system examined), and multiplied by the value of the original input or joy. This way,

---

[22] Molm (2010), p. 129.

[23] Hajnal (2020).

we arrive at the value of shared joy (J_s), a value between ($J_1 + J_2$) and its double, $2*(J_1 + J_2)$:

$$J_s = (J_1 + J_2) * (2 - I)$$

The two formulae expressed as one yield:

$$J_s = (J_1 + J_2) * (2 - \frac{(|J_1 - J_2|)}{(J_1 + J_2)})$$

The first two formulae, or the merged one, for two people, I have also dubbed the "*Saint Martin equations*".

As mentioned before, they can be transformed—from the micro-level of two—to be applicable at macro-levels. In the 2020 book subchapter, the macro-level is approached through drawing vague parallels between the inequality indicator outlined above and the Gini coefficient. This chapter, however, will not make that immediate jump. The macro level is advanced towards by constructing the equation pair for n (n being a positive integer) number of people:

$$I = \frac{\sum_{i=1}^{n} |J_i - - J_n|}{2 * (\sum_{i=1}^{n} J_i)}$$

$$J_s = \sum_{i=1}^{n} J_i * (n - - I)$$

Expressed as one formula:

$$J_s = \sum_{i=1}^{n} J_i * \left(n - - \frac{\sum_{i=1}^{n} |J_i - - J_n|}{2 * (\sum_{i=1}^{n} J_i)} \right)$$

Again, the absolute value of the difference between the individual joys is taken, which must carefully be divided by the number two, for combinatorial reasons (not to count each pair's joy-difference twice), and which is also divided by the sum of joys, to get the inequality indicator. The value of shared joy, in this macro-level case, is determined through multiplying the sum of original joys by the difference between the number of people and the (macro) inequality indicator.

An intriguing finding is that, from the latter equation pair, the one for the inequality indicator (I) closely resembles a common mathematical formula for the Gini coefficient (G):

$$G = \frac{\sum_{i=1}^{n} \sum_{j=1}^{n} |x_i - - x_j|}{2n^2 \mu},$$

where μ is the mean size.[24]

The Gini coefficient is a measure of inequality in a population, ranging from a minimum value of zero, when all individuals are equal (of equal net worth, or wealth, or average income), to a theoretical maximum of one in an infinite population in which every individual except one has a size of zero (net worth, or wealth, or average income).[25]

The above equation coincidence (the fact that the Gini coefficient structure needs to be used to express sharing as value multiplication) is among the relations suggesting that there is a connection between the extent of economic sharing (which reflects the extent of equality, and potentially even that of cooperation) and the benefits that arise through value multiplication (well-being, prosperity).

The following section attempts to find patterns in this context, for the *income inequality—economic prosperity* relationship, on the country level. It asks whether indicators of economic prosperity (traditional, alternative and abstract) correlate negatively with income inequality.

A significant inverse relationship, combined with the equations' coincidence above could strongly support the argument for increasing the opportunities for economic sharing, distribution (through policies, incentives, etc.).

11.3 Testing and Questioning Parallel Patterns on Country Levels

To examine the aforementioned connection between income inequality and economic prosperity, indicators of inequality are paired with those of macroeconomic performance (both conventional and alternative indices of human well-being), searching for correlations. To illustrate the phenomena through the freshest and most reliable macro-indicators possible, data is drawn from OECD, UNDP, the World Bank, and the World Happiness Report databases.

Table 11.1 consists of four variables, the Gini coefficient[26] being the independent one, and GDP per capita[27] the Human Development Index[28], and the Generosity Index[29] being on the dependent side of the relations. The selection of countries reflects the availability of Gini coefficients for the year 2019.

---

[24] Damgaard, n.d.

[25] Damgaard, n.d.

[26] OECD (2023).

[27] World Bank (2023).

[28] UNDP (2023).

[29] The term "Generosity Index" may require further statistical explanation. As it reads in the first report where it emerges in more detail: *"Generosity is the residual of regressing national average of response to the question 'Have you donated money to a charity in the past month?' on GDP per capita."* World Happiness Report (2013), p. 21, (2022).

Table 11.1 Merged data for the independent and dependent variables

Country	Gini 2019	GDP per capita 2019 (current USD, 2022)	HDI 2019	Generosity Index 2019
Austria	0.274	50,070	0.919	0.0577
Belgium	0.262	46,639	0.936	−0.1745
Canada	0.300	46,329	0.937	0.1091
Costa Rica	0.478	12,669	0.819	−0.1523
Czech Republic	0.248	23,665	0.897	NDA
Denmark	0.268	59,593	0.946	0.0176
Estonia	0.305	23,424	0.896	−0.0974
Finland	0.273	48,630	0.939	−0.0541
France	0.292	40.495	0.905	−0.1354
Germany	0.296	46,794	0.948	0.0543
Greece	0.308	19,144	0.889	−0.2893
Hungary	0.286	16,783	0.853	−0.1969
Israel	0.342	44,452	0.921	0.0822
South Korea	0.339	31,902	0.923	−0.0580
Latvia	0.344	17,945	0.871	−0.1965
Lithuania	0.357	19,595	0.884	−0.2542
Luxembourg	0.305	112,622	0.927	−0.0497
Netherlands	0.312	52,476	0.943	0.2103
New Zealand	0.326	42,865	0.937	0.1543
Norway	0.261	75,720	0.961	0.1069
Portugal	0.310	23,331	0.867	−0.2364
Slovak Republic	0.222	19,383	0.862	−0.1293
Slovenia	0.246	26,016	0.921	−0.1045
Spain	0.320	29,582	0.908	−0.0509
Sweden	0.277	51,939	0.947	0.0889
Switzerland	0.316	84,122	0.962	0.0309
Türkiye	0.415	9103	0.842	−0.1377
United Kingdom	0.366	42,747	0.935	0.2670
United States	0.395	65,120	0.930	0.1414
Bulgaria	0.402	9879	0.810	−0.1110
Romania	0.339	12,958	0.832	−0.2234

The year 2019 has been chosen for more data being available than for any more recent year, for the reason that survey fieldwork (data collection) was not affected by the COVID-19 pandemic yet, and because it is nevertheless not too distant a year from the year of writing this chapter. Based on the enlisted characteristics of the data, the preference for the empirical section of the chapter is to make testing cross-sectional. (Using panel data would not change the number of countries significantly, and would thus not eliminate the limitation of their relatively small number.)

From the table, three separate datasets are composed:

1. The Generosity index, paired with the Gini coefficient, for 30 countries (with data missing only for the Czech Republic).
2. The traditional indicator of economic prosperity (the gross domestic product—GDP per capita), paired with the Gini coefficient, for 31 countries.
3. The alternative indicator of economic well-being (the Human Development Index—HDI), paired with the Gini coefficient, for 31 countries.

The three abovementioned datasets are composed from the respective columns of Table 11.1.

11.3.1 Gini and Generosity

The first dataset plotted is linking the Gini coefficient and Generosity index values (Fig. 11.1). Generosity is measured in the *World Happiness Report* along with concepts such as trust, which are expected to be more strongly present in greater equality, and thus to negatively correlate with the Gini coefficient.

After analysing the data, it was found that covariance (≈ -0.00036), which shows the direction of the relationship, was indeed negative, as expected, but the correlation was extremely weak (≈ -0.044). This result, however, is not refuting the suppositions by itself, for the potentially indirect linkages between the indicators.

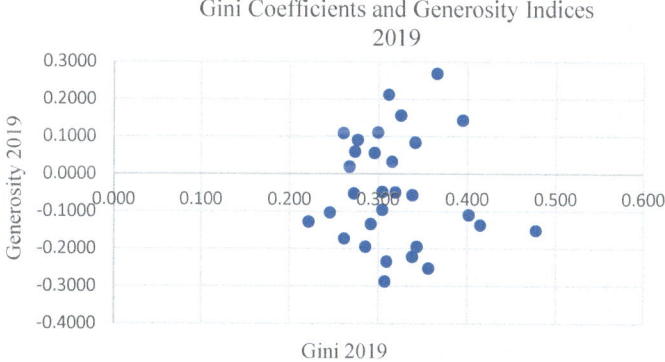

Fig. 11.1 Plot of the Gini Coefficient and Generosity Values

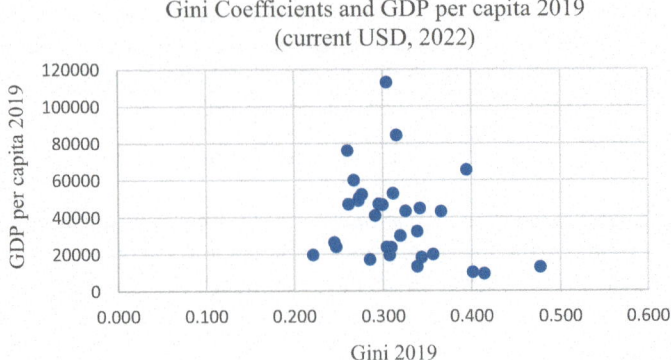

Fig. 11.2 Plot of the Gini Coefficient and GDP per Capita Values

11.3.2   Gini and GDP Per Capita

The second plot links the data of GDP per capita to the Gini coefficient (Fig. 11.2).

In the analysis, covariance was negative again (≈ -352.51), as expected, but the correlation was still weak (≈ -0.2697).

11.3.3   Gini and the HDI

Third, the data of the Gini coefficient and the Human Development Index were connected and plotted (Fig. 11.3).

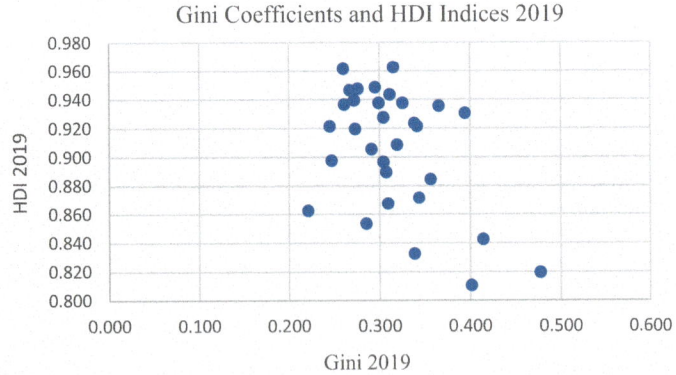

Fig. 11.3 Plot of the gini coefficient and HDI values

Covariance was negative (≈ -0.00113), according to the expectations, and correlation was moderate, stronger than for the Gini coefficient and the GDP per capita or Generosity values, taking a value of roughly -0.484 this time.

11.3.4 An Interpretation of the Patterns Through the Reciprocal Lens

Looking into the consequences of the findings, this part determines whether the equations outlined earlier in this chapter can contribute to the idea of economic sharing being a net value multiplying process.

The original expectations were that, due to the reverse connection between inequality and value multiplication effects in the "Saint Martin equations" (also being extendable to the macro level), the respective macro-level data would display significant negative correlations. I have expected the effects of selfless and reciprocal behaviour patterns to "trickle up" in society. Despite all three of the examined correlations being negative, as expected, their significance level is not strong enough to deduce direct support for the equations.

One potential reason for the lack of correlations can be related to a 2003 article by Nobel Prize-winning economists Esther Duflo and Abhijit V. Banerjee: *"Inequality and Growth: What Can the Data Say?"* Therein, the couple describe the correlations between inequality and the growth rates in cross-country data. Based on previous studies, they caution the reader and the community of fellow economists not to impose a linear structure where theoretical support is not sufficient, in order to avoid misinterpretations.[30] As regards the present chapter, linearity was the bare minimum for the relationships assumed. Nevertheless, and despite an existing theoretical framework, macroeconomic structures and relationships may display a completely new level of complexities, as compared to the micro-level, whilst still containing the mechanism that multiplies value through sharing. The complexities manifest in the Banerjee and Duflo article as follows: *"Even in a world of perfect capital markets, countries can have very different distributions of wealth, because, for example, they have different institutions or distributions of ability."*[31] Further channels, through which inequality could affect growth, such as investment share of GDP, fertility, education, and government spending, are listed.[32] Ultimately, the couple find that *"the growth rate is an inverted U-shaped function of net changes in inequality."*[33]

Through the details of the aforementioned article, the reader could witness the linearity of the relationship between inequality and growth coming into a strong doubt, and so it may be with the relationships between inequality and the previously illustrated measures of economic prosperity. However, even if there had been

---

[30] Banerjee and Duflo (2003), p. 268.

[31] Banerjee and Duflo (2003), p. 280.

[32] Banerjee and Duflo (2003), p. 283.

[33] Banerjee and Duflo (2003), p. 267.

significant correlations, those would have had to be treated with caution, due to the statistical imperative of correlation not implying causation.

Theoretically, the relationships between the variables designated as "dependent" and "independent" may actually be described as interdependent (with each relationship being bidirectional), and as interacting in a continuous manner. This is best understood through the case of the Generosity Index, which—if it takes on greater values– may result in a reduction of inequality, a smaller Gini coefficient, and thus, a potentially stronger negative correlation value.

Moreover, there are other (even measurable) aspects of inequality, outside of that of incomes. One may think of education inequalities, or lifespan inequality too.[34]

Also, between micro and macro-levels, there are several potential layers of other factors (translatable into economic needs and interests), which can make the value-multiplying effects of selflessness, sharing, and reciprocity partially evaporate.

11.4   Behavioural Foundations of Sharing as Value Multiplication

Taking the complexity of the aforementioned layers into account, and keeping the option of sharing being an at least indirect value multiplication process open, this part seeks to dive below the "subatomic" levels of economics, into the very nature of the individual. The goal is to formulate a behavioural explanation for how sharing multiplies value.

To use another metaphor taken from the natural sciences: human needs are economic DNA. Based on the contemporary state of needs theory, however, one may observe that our economic genome-mapping is incomplete. Needs theorists throughout the past century-and-a-half have focused on selfish needs. The theoretical option of incorporating others' well-being into the individuals' own structure of needs, however, remains open, which would imply the possibility of economic, rational selflessness.

Part of selflessness is the trust in positive outcomes beyond the (event) horizon of the self. This trust appears to yield benefits to the individual. The intangible benefits may be formulated as a response to a "need to help others", a notion being neglected in economics and needs theory. If there are types of selflessness existing within human needs, then, economically speaking, a certain amount of moral potential (ethical attitudes convertible into economic well-being) has remained hidden from science.

The broad, general terms of explanations for moral phenomena in economics, such as "humans are social beings", or various economic versions of altruism appear incomplete and insufficient. Selflessness is usually "explained away", either by internalisation, or by outsourcing. Internalisation-based explanations point to

---

[34] Hertog (2013), p. 1.

others' interests as partially being in our interest too, because of interdependence. Another version would be the individual emotionally rewarding themselves for good deeds.[35] Outsourcing concerns nurture, religion and culture as carrying values, and moral codes for society, which the individual follows due to their socialisation, and external pressure. Self-interest, however, is not a one-dimensional driving force in the economy towards progress. Self-interest itself may include selflessness, through the aforementioned "need to help others".

This direction of the interpretation of selflessness towards a rewarding mechanism has further theoretical implications. Through this lens, we may view help as an asymmetrical form of cooperation. There is a giver, and a receiver, but similarly as in cooperation, both sides benefit. Under this scheme, as in the legend of Saint Martin, ending others' suffering opens up new levels of prosperity to individuals.

To end this section with further metaphors: Self-interest may drive members of society, but selflessness is their seatbelt. Self-interest may fuel the economy, but selflessness is its cooling system. Self-interest makes the human "design" genius, but selflessness makes it moral. Ultimately, selflessness is required, sustainable, and— through the mechanism in human needs—it positively blurs the boundaries of the individual.

11.5 Conclusion

This chapter has made a connection between the saying "Shared joy is double joy", and the mathematical formula of the Gini coefficient. The ground was laid by reviewing items of academic literature that combine the notions of reciprocity or sharing, equality or inequality, and value creation or multiplication. After filling the literature gap identified by constructing the mathematical formulae for the macro-level, the presumed relationships have been tested and illustrated for the year 2019, through four macro-indicators for inequality and different approaches to economic prosperity. I have not found significant correlations, yet—it has been reasoned—this may have been due to the complexities of the macro layers, and despite sharing not "trickling up" in the system, neither could one assume the full evaporation of the value multiplying effect. Taking a bigger leap back, to the individual level and beneath, I have utilised needs theory to express a potential explanation for the value multiplying effects of sharing—at least on the micro-level, identifying the "need to help others" as a piece of economic DNA.

The theory presented holds further opportunities for research. Sharing as a value-multiplying process ought to be reviewed and to be tested in micro- and mezo-environments and scales. Prisoner's dilemma styled, and boardgame-framed behavioural experiments could prove key in establishing a more comprehensive theory of the reciprocal microfoundations for the Gini coefficient.

---

[35] See Andreoni (1990).

Acknowledgements I would like to express my gratitude to Dr. Perez Garrido Betsabé (Corvinus University of Budapest), in the frame of whose 2021/22/2 subject the original idea for this chapter has been cultivated, to Dr. David Miller (University of Oxford) for his helpful insights and comments, and to Dr. Balázs Hámori, my PhD supervisor, for his continuous encouragement and support.

References

Andreoni J (1990) Impure altruism and donations to public goods: a theory of warm-glow giving. Econ J 100(401):464–477

Banerjee AV, Duflo E (2003) Inequality and growth: what can the data say? J Econ Growth 8(3):267–299

Bowles S, Gintis H (2000) Reciprocity, self-interest, and the welfare state. Nordic J Polit Econ 26:33–53

Damgaard C (n.d.) Gini Coefficient From MathWorld, A Wolfram Web Resource, created by Eric W. Weisstein. https://mathworld.wolfram.com/GiniCoefficient.html

Hajnal Zs (2020) Moral economics—a theoretical basis for building the next economic system. In: Róna P, Zsolnai L, Wincewicz-Price A (eds), Words, objects and events in economics—the making of economic theory, Cham

Hámori B (1999) Would you marry your daughter to homo economicus? Re-evaluating reciprocal altruism. Soc Econ Central East Euro 21(1)

Hertog S (2013) The association between two measures of inequality in human development: income and life expectancy. United Nations, New York. https://www.un.org/en/development/desa/population/publications/pdf/technical/TP2013-7.pdf

Kranton RE (1996) Reciprocal exchange: a self-sustaining system. Am Econ Rev 86(4):830–851

Molm LD (2010) The structure of reciprocity. Soc Psychol Quarterly 73(2):119–131

OECD (2023) Income distribution, OECD Social and Welfare Statistics (database). https://doi.org/10.1787/data-00654-en

(The Editors of) Encyclopaedia Britannica (2023) St. Martin of Tours, Encyclopedia Britannica, 1 Jan. 2023, https://www.britannica.com/biography/Saint-Martin-of-Tours

UNDP (2023) Human development Index (HDI) https://hdr.undp.org/en/content/download-data

World Bank (2023) GDP per capita (current US$) https://data.worldbank.org/indicator/NY.GDP.PCAP.CD

World Happiness Report (2013) World happiness report https://s3.amazonaws.com/happiness-report/2013/WorldHappinessReport2013_online.pdf

World Happiness Report (2022) World happiness report https://worldhappiness.report/

Chapter 12
The Consumer Welfare Standard, Consumer Sovereignty, and Reciprocity

An Evolutionary Foundation for the Positive Economic Approach to Law that Actually Works

Fabrizio Esposito

Abstract The *Consumer Welfare Hypothesis in Law and Economics* claims that 1) in a partial equilibrium setting, a definition of allocative efficiency with remarkable pedigree uses a consumer welfare maximization standard; 2) this notion of allocative efficiency clearly fits better with EU antitrust and consumer law than the traditional total welfare hypothesis. The second claim is presented as a good reason for taking this notion of allocative efficiency in the economic approach to law seriously. This chapter shows that the consumer welfare hypothesis is supported by an indirect reciprocity mechanism with robust evolutionary credentials. Applied to a market setting, this indirect reciprocity mechanism is supported by the social norm of consumer sovereignty. Among other things, this account straightforwardly connects central themes of Adam Smith's thought: reciprocity, moral equality, division of labour, and consumer sovereignty. Consequently, another advantage of the consumer welfare hypothesis over the total welfare hypothesis is that it can rely on a plausible evolutionary mechanism.

12.1 Overview of the Analysis

In the economic approach to law, all the different notions of efficiency relate to the analysis of allocative problems, namely problems that have to do with the choice of which resources should be used to satisfy which preferences, and under which conditions. A long-lasting critique of this analytical framework is that it fails to give due consideration to distributive concerns. The (perceived) failure to address these critiques has led to the rejection of the economic approach to law in several contexts. Last year, Garoupa and Ulen recognised that the limited success of the economic

F. Esposito (✉)
NOVA School of Law and CEDIS, Universidade Nova de Lisboa, Lisbon, Portugal
e-mail: fabrizio.esposito@novalaw.unl.pt

© The Author(s), under exclusive license to Springer Nature Switzerland AG 2024
K. Mathis and A. Tor (eds.), *Law and Economics of Justice*, Economic Analysis of Law in European Legal Scholarship 17, https://doi.org/10.1007/978-3-031-56822-0_12

approach to comparative legal research is, at least in part, due to this issue.[1] This is just an instance of a broader phenomenon. Legal philosophers and theorists have long lamented the shortcomings of the monistic approach to efficiency.[2] In recent years, the Law and Political Economy movement has arisen with the clear objective of going beyond the use of efficiency as a central analytical and normative concept.[3] In the European Union, the view that markets ought to be efficient and that efficiency disregards distribution is intimately intertwined with the instrumentalization critique of EU consumer law.[4]

For quite some time now, leading scholars in the field have adopted a more pluralist normative approach, where the analysis of legal institutions is performed under a bundle of normative criteria which, typically, include besides efficiency, a concern for the distributive effect of the legal norms for the most disadvantaged members of the community.[5] On the one hand, this approach reduces the attractiveness of the economic approach to law derived from its promised superior analytical transparency, precision, and increased predictability of court decisions. On the other hand, the above-mentioned trends of rejection of the economic approach to law suggest that this compromise solution has failed to soothe the irritation among legal scholars caused by efficiency analysis.[6]

My recent book, *The Consumer Welfare Hypothesis in Law and Economics: Towards a Synthesis for the 21st Century*, offers a different way to address the problem. The solution to the irritation for the lack of distributive consideration in efficiency analysis does not lie in normative pluralism. The solution lies in using a different definition of efficiency. A notion of allocative efficiency which includes distributive effects—at least part of them—in the efficiency calculation: only increases in consumer welfare increase the efficiency of the allocation.

Against this background, this chapter will expand the investigation of the conceptual properties of the consumer welfare conception of allocative efficiency. It will do so by connecting consumer welfare with the literature on reciprocity via the concept of consumer sovereignty. In particular, the connection will focus on indirect reciprocity and its evolutionary or adaptive properties. The claim will be that consumer sovereignty can be seen as the manifestation of the broader cooperative force that sustains the division of labour in a variety of contexts ranging from advanced economies to Australian vampires and even the biology of bacteria.[7] In this way, it will be possible to offer an evolutionary basis for the consumer welfare hypothesis.

---

[1] Garoupa and Ulen (2022).

[2] For example, Dworkin (1980) and Coleman (1988). For a review, see Mathis (2009).

[3] See, for example, Collins et al. (2004) and Britton-Purdy et al. (2020).

[4] Recently, Hesselink (2021), especially pp. 297–9.

[5] See, for example, Bar-Gill and Ben-Shahar (2013); Posner and Sunstein (2022). For a broader analysis of this trend, see Esposito (2017).

[6] I am drawing here a parallel between economic analysis and legal transplants and relying on the famous characterization by Teubner (1998) of legal transplants as legal irritants.

[7] See below, Sect. 3.2.

This is no little finding, considering that for more than half a century, it was unsuccessfully attempted to identify an evolutionary mechanism that would sustain Posner's original efficiency hypothesis of the common law.[8] This finding means there is yet another reason to take the consumer welfare hypothesis seriously.

The chapter contributes to several debates in addition to its main target, namely the notion of efficiency used in the economic approach to law and the methodology to perform positive economic analysis of legal institutions to identify the economic concepts that best fit with the legal ones. First, the chapter shows the need to go deeper than social norms when investigating the social mechanisms that lead to cooperation. In fact, a significant body of literature shows that cooperation is possible even in the absence of social norms, so that social norms must be seen as a complementing mechanism to the more simplistic reciprocity-based ones.[9] Second, the chapter offers another reason to be suspicious of the conceptual separation between efficiency and normative concepts used in moral and political philosophy as well as in law.[10] Third, the chapter suggests that a reciprocity-based mechanism exists for the emergence of consumer sovereignty as a social norm.[11] This account connects several themes in Adam Smith's view of human interactions. Accordingly, the resulting account should be particularly palatable to the advocates of 'humanomics', given their call for the restoration of Adam Smith's approach to economics.[12]

The chapter is structured as follows. Section 12.2 introduces the consumer welfare hypothesis, focusing on the argument supporting it (Sect. 2.1) and the reasons why this hypothesis should be taken seriously (Sect. 2.2). Section 12.3 introduces the notion of reciprocity this chapter relies upon (Sect. 3.1) and then focuses on its adaptive or evolutionary properties (Sect. 3.2). Section 12.4 shows that the concept of consumer sovereignty can be easily qualified as a reciprocity mechanism as well. Section 12.5 concludes by pointing out directions for future research that build specifically on the qualification of consumer sovereignty as a reciprocity mechanism.

12.2   The Consumer Welfare Hypothesis in a Nutshell

The Consumer Welfare Hypothesis proposes a bilateral view of the connection (or nexus) between the law and the economy: "as a matter of economic theory, an allocation of resources in a market can be better or worse based on the benefits it delivers

---

[8] For a discussion of this in particular, see Garoupa and Liguerre (2011), pp. 292–300. For an overall positive overview of the evolutionary economic approach to law, see von Wagenheim (2017); for a more critical analysis, see Deakin and Markou (2021).

[9] See below, Sect. 3.3.

[10] See below, Sect. 12.4.

[11] See below, Sect. 12.5.

[12] See V. Smith and Wilson (2019) and McCloskey (2021).

to consumers; legal structures that are at the centre of the EU market-building project fit with this understanding of allocative efficiency".[13]

The first part of the claim is, in other words, that an allocation A1 is more efficient than an allocation A2 in market M1 when the consumers of the products and services offered in the market M1 are better off in A1 in comparison to A2. The second part of the claim is that the content of legal reasoning in relation to EU antitrust and consumer law has a stronger conceptual fitness with this notion of allocative efficiency rather than with the traditional, total welfare-based one.

Four clarifications are in order. First, M1 is just one of the multiple markets that, together, constitute the relevant market economy. For example, M1 could be the market for pineapples, which would be different from M2 (the market for pizzas), M3 (the market for utility cars), M4 (the market for role-playing video games), etc. This clarification should be enough to dispel any confusion that could derive from Bork's attempt to claim that everyone is a consumer.[14] Second, this definition of allocative efficiency is focused primarily on the inferential component of the analysis, leaving great malleability regarding its referential component. This means that different ways of measuring consumer welfare are compatible with this definition of efficiency, and disagreements about how to best measure consumer welfare remain analytically separate from the claim that—however you measure it—only increments and decrements in consumer welfare determine if an allocation of resources is efficient or not. Third, by design, this definition of allocative efficiency and the hypothesis built upon it is limited to those economic interactions that can be classified as exchanges. This is important because it implies that this hypothesis has very little (but still something)[15] to say about markets for the allocation of factors of production. In particular, this means that the concept of allocative efficiency has little to say regarding how conflicts between capital and labour should be solved.

Fourth, the consumer welfare conception of allocative efficiency is formulated and tested from a merely positive or descriptive perspective. As the next two subsections clarify, the argument supporting it is about how the concept of allocative efficiency is used, and how different uses fit with existing legal reasoning. Nowhere is the argument meant to justify one notion of allocative efficiency as superior to the other for its normative properties. It is for this reason that *The Consumer Welfare Hypothesis* follows a method that can be called Legal-Economic Fitness framework and which builds on the so-called *Samuels-Calabresi Theorem*: identify the concepts that fit with both legal and economic reasoning about the legal–economic nexus.[16]

It is, however, the case that the consumer welfare hypothesis should offer a normatively more attractive efficiency perspective—although not necessarily attractive enough—conception of efficiency because it is not distributive insensitive. Distribution insensitivity is a traditional reason for critique of the total welfare conception

---

[13] Esposito (2022), p. 3.

[14] See Hildebrand (2016), pp. 30 et seq.

[15] Esposito (2022), p. 180 explaining the 'separationist purpose' of the hypothesis for production contracts.

[16] Esposito (2022), pp. 12–6.

of allocative efficiency. At least for those concerned in particular for distribution within the exchange, the consumer welfare hypothesis plays a very different tune: a distributive concern in favour of the consumer is even incorporated in the definition of allocative efficiency.

12.2.1 The Argument in a Nutshell

This section summarises the argumentative structure used in *The Consumer Welfare Hypothesis* in support of the consumer welfare conception of allocative efficiency.

The argument in favour of the consumer welfare conception of allocative efficiency has two main pillars. The first pillar consists of the analysis of the reasons that make the allocation by a first-degree monopoly less efficient than those by a competitive market.[17] Ultimately, the reason for focusing only on the deadweight loss and, by implication, choosing the total welfare standard is a notion of equality that imposes on the decision-maker the duty to treat all market participants equally.[18] The analysis then shows that this equality concern is often ignored in principal-agent models, in particular in corporate governance contexts.[19] At the same time, the concept of consumer sovereignty, once carefully reconstructed, offers a clear equality norm in favour of the consumer welfare standard, namely that we are all treated equally because when we operate as consumers we are suffering, and when we operate as producers we are servants. This passage of the argument will be further developed in this chapter.

For the sake of completeness, it is important to highlight that the first pillar does not end here. In fact, a tailored review of the thought of economists that have fundamentally contributed to the development of the economic approach to law reveals that, in their analyses, it is possible to identify exactly that concern favouring the consumers in a particular market that is at the core of the consumer welfare conception of allocative efficiency. The findings regarding Adam Smith, John Hicks, and Ronald Coase are particularly surprising and consequential.[20] On these grounds, it can be concluded that the consumer welfare conception of allocative efficiency has a notable economic pedigree.

The second pillar of the analysis builds and improves on Richard Posner's path-breaking efficiency hypothesis of the common law. It improves it by avoiding cherry-picking problems, offering a comparative analysis of the relative strength of two competing efficiency hypotheses to—and this is the third improvement—explain the content of legal reasoning, not the effects that the law is expected to be based

---

[17] This means, ultimately, that the book searches for ostensive definitions of "allocative efficiency"; McCloskey (2021), p. 6 does the same for "humanomics".

[18] Esposito (2022), pp. 22–5. For an example of this view, see Cowen and Tabarrok (2011), p. 225.

[19] Esposito (2022), pp. 27–9.

[20] Esposito (2022), pp. 40–56.

on blackboard economic analysis.[21] Four inferential disagreements between a total and a consumer welfare hypothesis were tested for their fitness with a significant portion of legal materials from EU antitrust and EU consumer law. The result is overwhelmingly in favour of the consumer welfare hypothesis.[22]

In a nutshell, the disagreements are:

- Harm: all instrumentally relevant or not?
- Defences and exceptions: internal fuzziness and external clarity or vice versa?
- Sanctions: to deter and redress harm or to internalise social costs?
- Deadweight loss, elasticity, and productive efficiency: quantity-effects over price-effects or vice versa?

The choice of analysing EU antitrust and consumer law is, first, that EU economic law is my primary field of specialization. Second, and most fundamentally, these branches of EU internal market law "are the extreme poles of the axis representing broader [antitrust] and narrower [consumer law] notion of consumers".[23] Hence, if the hypothesis holds here, it is plausible that it will also hold in sectorial contexts.[24]

12.2.2 Reasons to Take the Consumer Welfare Hypothesis Seriously

This subsection articulates four reasons for taking the consumer welfare hypothesis seriously. By "taking it seriously", I mean simply paying attention to it, considering it when studying related topics, testing its epistemic strengths, investigating its normative appeal, and reflecting on its connection with a variety of concepts normally used in the economic approach to law.

The first and overarching reason is that, if the hypothesis is accepted,[25] then a new and rich set of research questions needs to be investigated. The list includes descriptive or positive questions about the law. For example, focusing first on antitrust and consumer law: does the hypothesis work also in the European Union, but at the national level? Does it work in jurisdictions outside the European Union, such as the United States, China, Brazil, Canada, etc.? Moving beyond antitrust and consumer law: does the hypothesis work equally well in the analysis of merger regulations, state aids, sectorial normative frameworks, but also general contract law? Relatedly, how

---

[21] Esposito (2022), pp. 61–66.

[22] Esposito (2022), pp. 175 et seq.

[23] Esposito (2022), p. 86.

[24] Esposito and Grundmann (2017) and Esposito and de Almeida (2018) offer preliminary investigations in the context of EU financial services and energy law, respectively.

[25] I leave undecided, for current purposes, the epistemological question concerning the conditions for accepting a hypothesis. In particular, I wish to take no position, on whether to accept a hypothesis it these sufficient that it is better supported by the evidence than the alternative or one needs to be committed to the truth of the hypothesis.

does the consumer welfare hypothesis require us to reconsider the economic analysis of central contract law doctrines, such as the legal consequences of a contractual breach (so-called efficient breach),[26] or new contractual practices, such as algorithmic price discrimination,[27] and new capital creation and accumulation mechanisms, such as permanent secondary NFT royalties?[28]

This wealth of questions relies also on conceptual guidance derived from the connection between the consumer welfare conception of allocative efficiency and the principal-agent theory.[29] In general terms, the analytical directive is shifting the attention from transaction costs to agency costs. For example, this leads to a reformulation of the *Normative Coase and Hobbes Theorems* formulated by Cooter and Ulen as.[30]

- *Normative Smith-Hutt Theorem*: the law should minimise agency costs by empowering consumers to monitor producers directly.
- *Normative Kaldor-Hicks Theorem*: the law should minimise the agency costs that are not avoided by direct consumer monitoring.

The tailored review of the history of economic thought and the finding of systematic misrepresentation of the thought of central economists, and possibly of the very concept of social welfare, raises questions for the historians of economic thought to investigate. How comes the clear concern for the consumers expressed by those economists has later disappeared? Can it all really be explained only because of the supposed professional need of economists to be scientific, understood as avoiding making value judgments as much as possible? Or are there other forces involved? And if so, do these forces play a significant role in the development of the economic approach to law?

The consumer welfare hypothesis also needs to be investigated for its normative properties. It was noted above that there is an equality norm supporting it. How convincing is this equality norm? Which are the critiques that are normally moved to efficiency-focused analyses that also apply to an analysis meant to maximise consumer welfare in exchange contracts (as defined above)? Ultimately, can we identify a normative synthesis between different theoretical perspectives that would allow us to focus on local disagreements rather than outright rejections?

Besides the wealth of research questions unlocked by the consumer welfare hypothesis, its practical significance cannot be underestimated. Suppose, in fact, that you are an economist acting as an expert testimony in legal proceedings or an advisor to a policymaker or even a private company. The consumer welfare hypothesis requires you to think carefully about the welfare standard that you intend to use when delivering your opinion. Using the wrong welfare standard will greatly reduce

---

[26] See Liao (2017) and Hofmann (2021).

[27] Compare the approach in Esposito (2022b) and Bar-Gill (2018).

[28] See Murray (2022).

[29] Esposito (2022), pp. 27–9.

[30] Cooter and Ulen (2014), pp. 77–9). See also Esposito (2022), pp. 178 et seq.

the usefulness of your analysis and possibly harm your professional reputation.[31] But the opposite is also true: showing that you have understood (or at least care about) the normative foundations of the legal institutions you are analysing will greatly increase the reliability in your intervention.[32]

The rest of this chapter will, in essence, formulate an additional reason for taking the consumer welfare hypothesis seriously. This reason derives from the connection between the hypothesis and the available knowledge on the concept of reciprocity. Indeed, this connection shows that the equality norm (i.e., consumer sovereignty) that underpins the consumer welfare hypothesis can be seen as a manifestation of the more general evolutionary processes behind reciprocal behaviour. This means that the consumer welfare hypothesis can rely on a robust evolutionary explanation, something that Posner's efficiency hypothesis of the common law could never really do.

12.3 Reciprocity as an Evolutionary Mechanism Supported by Norms

This section first provides a taxonomy of the different forms of reciprocity identified by social scientists, and then clarifies that the type of reciprocity on which the argument in this chapter is based is indirect and generalised reciprocity (Sect. 3.1). Next, the chapter reviews the literature attempting to explain the emergence of reciprocal behaviour in an extraordinary variety of contexts, ranging from bacteria to advanced economic systems, via Australian bats (Sect. 3.2). Finally, the chapter focuses on the contribution of norms to support reciprocal behaviour (Sect. 3.3).

12.3.1 Reciprocity: Direct or Indirect, Generalised or Not, Positive or Negative

Reciprocity is one of those terms that has an intuitively clear meaning for ordinary uses, but then receives a very nuanced, and at times conflicting, characterization by academics. Considering that the notion of reciprocity is relied upon by anthropologists, biologists, sociologists, philosophers, zoologists, and more recently economists, this circumstance should not be surprising. In its ordinary meaning, reciprocity refers to "behaviour in which two people or groups of people give each other help and advantages" according to the Cambridge Dictionary.[33] Already in 1998,

---

[31] See Giocoli (2020a, b).

[32] For multiple testimonies from economists working in regulatory agency going in this direction, see Mantzari (2022).

[33] Cambridge Dictionary online (nd); see also Merriam Webster Dictionary online (nd) defines reciprocity as "the quality or state of being reciprocal: mutual dependence, action, or influence".

writing on the *European Economic Review*, Fehr and Gächter declared the existence of the *homo reciprocans* and qualified it as a "key player in the enforcement of social norms".[34]

In the following, I will focus primarily on the distinctions regarding reciprocity that are used in the theoretical and empirical literature that studies how reciprocity can lead to stable patterns of cooperative behaviour in controlled settings.[35] Depending on the research questions, this literature may aim to identify conditions under which reciprocity is sufficient[36] or, on the contrary, to identify additional elements that may sustain cooperation, in particular internalised social norms.[37]

The first distinction to consider is between direct and indirect reciprocity. The second one is between generalised and not generalised reciprocity. Finally, reciprocity can be positive or negative. These three distinctions are complementary, so there are eight possible combinations.

Reciprocity is direct when (as in the definition given by the Cambridge dictionary), agent A performs an action which impacts agent B, and agent B reacts by performing an action which impacts agent A. Instead, reciprocity is indirect when B reacts by performing an action which impacts agent C.[38] Importantly, indirect reciprocity introduces a critical social element in the analytical framework because the relationship between agent A and agent B is fundamentally influenced by the presence of at least one other agent C. One example of direct reciprocity would be to smile back at someone who is smiling at us. An act of indirect reciprocity would be to hold the door to someone after someone has held the door for us.

In parallel, reciprocity can be generalised or not. Here, the critical element is, when reciprocation is expected to take place. If the reciprocal action is expected to happen as an almost immediate reaction, then reciprocity is not generalised. If, instead, a significant amount of time is allowed between the action and its reciprocal reaction, then reciprocity is generalised. This distinction is somewhat vague. However, it will prove rather important for the current analysis. As a case of non-generalised reciprocity, one can think again about the example of someone smiling back. A common case of generalised reciprocity is having a friend or a colleague insist to pay the bill because you paid the bill last time. Additionally, a spot contract is an example of non-generalised reciprocity while a sale with payment in instalments is an example of non generalised reciprocity.

Finally, reciprocity can be positive or negative. We have positive reciprocity when the reaction is beneficial to the recipient and negative reciprocity when the reaction

---

[34] Fehr and Gächter (1998), p. 857.

[35] For overviews, see Nowak and Sigmund (2005) and Okada (2020). The comparison between the two overviews shows that this literature has reached a certain degree of consolidation over the last two decades.

[36] I include in this strand of the literature also the economic studies exploring the economic significance of reciprocal behaviour; for a useful overview, see Fehr and Schmidt (2006).

[37] See below, Sect. 3.3.

[38] Indirect reciprocity is further distinguished between upward and downward indirect reciprocity. See below, Sect. 3.3. Sometimes, following Kolm (1984, 2008) indirect reciprocity is called "reverse reciprocity".

is harmful to the recipient. Normally, positive reciprocity follows beneficial acts, and negative reciprocity follows negative acts, but this is not a conceptual necessity. For example, someone could react to your smile with a disgusted or annoyed face. This would be an example of a negative reaction following a positive action.

12.3.2 Reciprocity: A Formidable Cooperation Mechanism

Reciprocity in its many forms is very common. Reciprocal behaviour has been observed in nature, in cleaning symbioses, communities of Australian vampire bats, dolphins, primates, and other group-living animals, but also bacteria.[39] Moreover, even among economists it is now widely accepted that emotions and feelings support spontaneous cooperation.[40]

This fact has led scholars to investigate the conditions under which reciprocal behaviour becomes stable and the conditions under which this is not the case. For direct reciprocity, it is now widely accepted that tit-for-tat "can guarantee the highest payoff in the long run given certain features of the situations analysed".[41]

The findings in the analysis of indirect and generalised reciprocity are arguably even more surprising. Ohtsuki and Iwasa reached an important milestone in this context by identifying eight patterns of stable indirect and generalised reciprocal behaviour based on reputation ("the leading eight").[42] These patterns share the following properties: being nice, retaliatory, apologetic, and forgiving. The key assumption of the analysis is that the benefit of a good reputation in future inter-actions must be higher than the immediate cost of cooperation. Note also that the setting studied by Ohtsuki and Iwasa allows for cooperation to fail due to error.[43] At the same time, the setting is based on a reputation mechanism based only on the action performed by the agents in the previous interaction. In other words, an agent who cooperated in the previous interaction has a good reputation, and a new agent who did not cooperate in the previous interaction has a bad reputation.

In this setting, being nice means cooperating with agents who have a good reputa-tion and reciprocating positively. Being retaliatory, on the contrary, means refusing to cooperate with agents who have a bad reputation.[44] This behaviour sustains coop-eration in the group by punishing non-cooperators; therefore, retaliation should grant a good reputation to the retaliator.

---

[39] Seminal, in this regard Trivers (1971). See also the discussion in Ridley (1988, pp. 70–2) pointing out that, albeit observed, reciprocal behaviour is rather limited among animals; for a discussion of this point, see Freidin, Carballo, Bentosela (2015). Ridley (1988, p. 14) go as far as extending the insight to bacteria.

[40] See, for example, Gintis (2016) and Bowles (2011, pp. 186–194).

[41] Perugini et al. (2003), p. 252. See also Axelrod (1984) and Axelrod and Dion (1988).

[42] Ohtsuki and Iwasa (2004, 2006).

[43] Ohtsuki and Iwasa (2004, 2006).

[44] See also Fehr et al. (2002) referring to retaliators as 'strong reciprocators'.

At the same time, it is important to allow agents with a bad reputation to restore it. Otherwise, agents with a bad reputation are systematically ostracised by the rest of the players. Systematic exclusion of agents with a bad reputation would be problematic for two reasons. First, as noted above, agents can make mistakes either in assigning reputation to someone else or in their actions. This means that a bad reputation is occasionally not deserved. At the same time, even when it is deserved, it is possible that agents who have deliberately refused to cooperate in the past to have understood that cooperation is in their interest. Agents with a bad reputation can restore it through apology and forgiveness. In the setting of Ohtsuki and Iwasa, an agent with a bad reputation can apologise by playing cooperation; after which, his or her reputation is restored.[45]

In sum, relatively simple conditions must exist for direct or even indirect and generalised reciprocity to sustain cooperative behaviour in the absence of any normative framework.

12.3.3 Norms: A Formidable Complement to Spontaneous Reciprocity

The circumstance that spontaneous reciprocity is a widely observed pattern of behaviour that is capable of sustaining cooperation does not preclude the possibility of improving the performance of the considered group with additional mechanisms. Indeed, social norms and legal institutions can contribute significantly to sustaining cooperative behaviour. In fact, "norms, conventions, and notions of fairness emerge within communities through repeated interactions among constituent members".[46]

The relationship between social norms and legal norms and institutions is now one of the standard areas of research in the economic approach to law. Remarkably, in this literature, some of the mechanisms leading to effective social norms are, ultimately, the same mechanisms that contribute to reciprocal cooperation: "a) coordination in an environment of multiple equilibria; b) fear of non-legal sanctions; c) internalisation".[47]

The idea of coordination in a multiple-equilibriums environment is readily respected in the context of reciprocal cooperation. Agents have a reason to cooperate if they believe the other agent will cooperate, and defect otherwise. The exception is defection as a sanction for previous non-cooperative behaviour (that is, retaliation); as noted above, however, retaliation is a form of cooperation with the rest of the group rather than with the direct counterparty.

What is missing in the properties of the leading eight is internalisation. Internalisation requires the existence of a value or social norm that agents adopt. Once

---

[45] Ohtsuki and Iwasa (2004, 2006).

[46] Salazar et al. (2022), p. 1. See also, Young (1993).

[47] Carbonara (2018), p. 467.

internalised, the value or social norm has a motivating capacity independent of sanctions. At least since Gouldner's seminal paper on the "norm of reciprocity",[48] the status of reciprocity as a social norm has been widely studied and is considered uncontroversial.[49] For example, Jon Elster, writing specifically on the relationship between reciprocity and norms, feels comfortable in simply "assum(ing) that when people reciprocate, return good with good and bad with bad, they do so because they think it is right or morally required".[50] Hence, social norms complement direct and indirect reciprocity in supporting cooperation in the absence of legal norms and institutions.[51]

However, it is uncontroversial that legal norms and institutions may contribute to cooperation. In fact, the legal system is constituted of institutions, tools, and mechanisms that can be used to complement reciprocity and social norms in sustaining cooperation. What actually happens in a context when a legal norm makes cooperation obligatory?

First, cooperation is selected as the desirable equilibrium. Second, detection and retaliation are strengthened by legal enforcement. Third, the phenomenon called the "expressive function of the law" constitutes an additional mechanism for the internalisation of the required behaviour.[52]

Since it is clear that both social and legal norms complement reciprocity in supporting cooperation, it is useful to make explicit some descriptions of the social norms that are associated with indirect (and generalised) reciprocity:

- "I do to you what I think is appropriate based on your reputation from prior interactions with others"[53]
- "help somebody if you receive help from someone"[54]
- "You scratch my back and I'll scratch someone else's" and "I scratch your back and someone else will scratch mine"[55]

In light of this discussion, it is possible to go back to the consumer welfare hypothesis, and in particular to focus on the idea of consumer sovereignty, to show that it constitutes a norm of indirect and generalised reciprocity.

---

[48] Gouldner (1960).

[49] Okada (2020) points out that more than 100'000 papers on indirect reciprocity have been published in the last 30 years; note, however, that the criteria for identifying this number have not been made explicit in the paper, in violation of systematic reviews best practices.

[50] Elster (2011), p. 328.

[51] See Perugini et al. (2003) reviewing the literature on the internalization of the social norm of reciprocity and providing one of the first experimental results showing this norm at work. See also Burger et al. (2009), p. 11 who showed that "individuals return favors even when the initial favor giver will never know of their behavior".

[52] Cooter (1998) offers an interesting analysis of this matter in the economic approach to law. See also, Sunstein (1996); McAdams (2015); Basu (2018) and Sardo and Esposito (2020).

[53] Salazar et al. (2022), p. 2.

[54] Voelkl (2015), p. 17.

[55] Nowak and Sigmund (2005), p. 1291.

12.4 Consumer Sovereignty as a Norm of Indirect and Generalised Reciprocity

In the original, and still unparalleled definition of consumer sovereignty provided by William Hutt,

> The consumer is sovereign when, in his role of citizen, he has not delegated to political institutions for authoritarian use the power which he can exercise socially through his power to demand (or refrain from demanding).[56]

The reciprocity norm, as will be shown, is more easily identified by focusing on this catchphrase: "[a]s consumer the individual is sovereign; as producer he is subject".[57]

Before doing so, it is crucial to point out that Hutt did not claim ownership of the concept of consumer sovereignty. To the contrary, Hutt presented it as "as much a criticism as a vindication of those who have been led to build on the traditions of orthodoxy".[58] This account seems accurate, at least concerning some of his predecessors, namely Adam Smith, Frank Knight, Marshall, and Pigou.[59] In particular, Smith wrote:

> Consumption is the sole end and purpose of all production; and the interest of the producer ought to be attended to, only so far as it may be necessary for promoting that of the consumer. The maxim is so perfectly self-evident, that it would be absurd to attempt to prove it.[60]

Importantly, the concept of consumer sovereignty emerging from this literature is normatively more demanding than the one used in the economic approach to law.[61] According to this literature, it is sufficient that consumer preferences determine what is exchanged. It is however clear that once properly reconstructed, consumer sovereignty incorporates also distributive concerns about the relationship[62]; after all, can consumers who are systematically taken advantage of being meaningfully considered sovereign?

It is also particularly noteworthy that Walraevens points out the centrality of the idea of reciprocity in Adam Smith's system of thought.[63] The idea of consumer sovereignty offers a straightforward connection between this (allegedly) self-evident pro-consumer maxim and Smithian moral egalitarianism via reciprocity. Smith believed that "one of the multitude [is] in no respect better than any other in it" so "we are fundamentally moral equals".[64] Before this consumer-centric account is offered, it is useful to consider an alternative, still egalitarian view, that is arguably

---

[56] Hutt (1936), p. 257.

[57] Hutt (1936), p. 257.

[58] Hutt (1936), p. 34.

[59] See, for more details, Esposito (2022), pp. 42–49 and 53 et seq.

[60] Smith (2007 [1776]), p. 426.

[61] See Schwartz (1988); Sunstein (1999); Liscow and Markovitz (2022).

[62] See Esposito (2022), pp. 31–34.

[63] Walraevens (2020).

[64] Smith (1759) and Anderson (2016), p. 158.

tightly connected to the view that a market is efficient when it maximises total welfare, irrespective of its distribution.

In stark contrast with the widely shared view that efficiency as a normative concept is different and often in conflict with the normative concepts used in moral and political philosophy as well as in legal discourse, it is apparent that an equality-based justification for the total welfare conception of allocative efficiency exists.[65] According to this view, treating with equal respect all market participants does not allow considering monopolistic rents a reason to condemn the monopoly. This position follows from the premise that transfers cancel out each other, so that the benefit of the monopolist is equal to the loss of the consumers caused by rents. Therefore, equal respect implies focusing on another property of monopolies that makes them undesirable; this property is the deadweight loss.

As we have just seen, Smith strongly rejected such a view. Once we look at all agents not only in their capacity as consumers or producers in one single market, but as producers in one market and consumers in all the others, a different equality norm emerges. According to this equality norm, all agents are equal because they are sovereign when they act as consumers, and they are servants when they act as producers. In other words, the proper unit of analysis for applying the notion of equality is not that of a single market but instead that of a market economy. It follows that more complex economies weaken the non-standard reciprocity mechanism (i.e., they make reciprocity more generalised) for several reasons: difficult detection, limited information about reputation and opportunity to punish, etc. Accordingly, stronger social and institutionalised norms are needed to allow agents to reap the benefits of the division of labour.

According to this account, the mechanism of indirect reciprocity at play specifies the norms of indirect reciprocity seen in the previous section as follows (emphasis added to signal the modification):

- I do to you, *consumer,* what I think is appropriate based on your reputation *as producer* from prior interactions with *your consumers.*
- help *a consumer* if you receive help from *a producer.*
- You scratch my back, *producer,* and I'll scratch *a consumer*'s and I scratch your back, *consumer,* and *a producer* will scratch mine.

What is remarkable about this account is that it connects the idea of the division of labour to the idea of reciprocity and, eventually, to consumer sovereignty. Indeed, the evolutionary benefits deriving from reciprocity have been connected both in biological studies and in the analysis of markets to the possibility of specialisation made possible by the division of labour. Most interestingly, for current purposes, in the context of such an analysis, Alexander specifically criticises as narrow the view that indirect reciprocity is irrelevant to market allocation without, however, considering the importance of distinguishing between consumers and producers.[66]

---

[65] See above, Sect. 2.1.

[66] Alexander (1988), p. 159, criticises Titmuss (1971), p. 239. For recent analyses by experts in the importance of reciprocity missing this point, see Gintis (2016), pp. 67–87; Sugden (2018);

At the same time, the present investigation shows the centrality of the different roles of consumers and producers, while recognising the centrality of the broader community in which the exchange takes place.[67] It is true that a competitive market economy achieves an optimum in terms of production. It is also true that consumer sovereignty makes the mechanism of indirect reciprocity, which stimulates producers´ efforts, a social norm. Moreover, as noted in Sect. 12.2, at least in the context of the European Union, such a social norm has been also institutionalised by EU law.

In light of the above, it is clearly possible to complement the consumer welfare hypothesis with a straightforward and robust connection between the institutional role played by consumer welfare, the importance of consumer sovereignty as a social norm, and reciprocity mechanisms. In other words, rational self-interested *hominem reciprocantes* would naturally develop social norms that support the division of labour in a market economy as they are individually advantageous. Consumer sovereignty is a norm that supports such an equilibrium. Not surprisingly, then, consumer sovereignty has been institutionalised through EU law.

12.5 Conclusions

This chapter has used research on reciprocity to offer an evolutionary mechanism that explains why EU law is consistent with the consumer welfare hypothesis—that is, why "legal structures that are at the centre of the EU market-building project fit" with consumer welfare maximization and not total welfare maximization.[68] The argument has essentially three steps.

First, the proposed explanation starts from the features of behavioural regularities that support cooperation under indirect (and generalised) reciprocity. These features are being nice, retaliating, apologising, and forgiving. Second, social and institutionalised norms contribute a great deal to supporting cooperative behaviour. Finally, consumer sovereignty has the features of social norms that support cooperative behaviour. In this context, in line with the recent call for a more humane economics (humanomics), a direct link was identified between different strands of Smithian thought, namely between reciprocity, moral equality, the division of labour, and consumer sovereignty became apparent.

As a semi-final note, it is worth mentioning that the account offered here has similar structural features to the one proposed by Calabresi to overcome the irreconcilable conflict between economic and moral accounts of tort law. The core of his

---

Oliver (2019), pp. 76–92; V. Smith and Wilson (2019), pp. 205–207, and Richter and Siemoneit (2022). The framework by Richter and Siemoneit (2022) is, nevertheless, largely compatible with the one presented in this chapter and in Esposito (2022).

[67] Esposito (2019).

[68] Esposito (2022), p. 3.

argument is that, in torts, "compensation was simply an effective way of charging activities with their costs".[69] However, Calabresi[70] continued,

> if – in order to deter by charging certain activities "their costs" – a society gives people the right to recover, such recoveries will surely affect what people think their rights are. And that in turn will surely affect that society's notions of corrective justice.

Notably, Calabresi did not rely on notions of reciprocity in his analysis. Yet, and ultimately unsurprisingly, his acumen and experience of the relevant social and institutionalised norms let him fill the evolutionary gaps between the economic and moral accounts of tort law and present them as two views of the same cathedral.

The Consumer Welfare Hypothesis offers.

> a novel account of central institutions of the market economy by developing the legal–economics nexus built on the consumer welfare hypothesis and supported by its fitness with EU antitrust and consumer law.[71]

Based on this account, a number of new research questions come to the forefront. This chapter is just an example of the possibilities *The Consumer Welfare Hypothesis* opens up. However, it is an example that strikes a powerful blow at the traditional total-welfare foundations of the economic approach to law: while Posner's efficiency hypothesis fails to rely on a plausible evolutionary mechanism, the consumer welfare hypothesis does. This is what progressive research programs do: they gradually solve the anomalies in incumbent research paradigms.[72] Behavioural science has done this for economics over the last thirty years or so: perhaps it is now time for the Legal-Economic Fitness framework to do the same for the economic approach to law?

Bibliography

Alexander R D (1987) The biology of moral systems, Abingdon
Anderson E (2016) Adam Smith on inequality. In: Hanley RP (ed), Adam Smith (His Life, Thought, and Legacy), pp. 157 et seqq., Princeton
Axelrod R, Dion D (1988) The further evolution of cooperation. Science 242:1385 et seqq.
Axelrod R (1984) The evolution of cooperation, New York
Bar-Gill O, Ben-Shahar O (2013) Regulatory techniques in consumer protection: a critique of European consumer contract law. Common Market Law Rev 50:109 et seqq.
Bar-Gill O (2018) Algorithmic price discrimination when demand is a function of both preferences and (Mis)perceptions. Univ Chicago Law Rev 86(2):217 et seqq.
Basu K (2018) The republic of beliefs: a new approach to law and economics. Princeton
Britton-Purdy J, Grewal D S, Kapczynski A, Rahman K S (2020) Building a Law-and-Political-Economy Framework: Beyond the Twentieth-Century Synthesis, The Yale Law Journal, 129, pp. 1784 et seqq.

---

[69] Calabresi (2007), p. 5.

[70] Calabresi (2007), p. 9.

[71] Esposito (2022), p. 177.

[72] See, Lakatos (1970). For a clear and easily accessible discussion, see Musgrave (2016).

Burger JM, Sanchez J, Imberi JE, Grande LR (2009) The norm of reciprocity as an internalized social norm: returning favors even when no one finds out. Soc Influence 4(1):11 et seqq.

Calabresi G (2007) Towards a unified theory of torts. J Tort Law 1(3):1 et seqq.

Cambridge Dictionary online (nd) Reciprocity, available at https://dictionary.cambridge.org/dictio nary/english/reciprocity

Carbonara E (2017) Law and social norms, in: Parisi F (ed), Oxford Handbook of Law and Economics, vol 1. Oxford. pp. 466 et seqq.

Coleman J (1988) Markets, morals, and the law. New York

Collins H (rapporteur for the Study Group on Social Justice in European Private Law) et al. (2004) Social justice in European contract law: a manifesto. Euro Law J 10(6):653 et seqq.

Cooter R (1998) Expressive law and economics. J Legal Stud 27:58 et seqq.

Cowen T, Tabarrok A (2011) Modern principles of economics. New York

Deakin S, Markou C (2021) Evolutionary law and economics: theory and method. Northern Ireland Legal Quarterly 72(4):682 et seqq.

Dequech D (2006) Institutions and norms in institutional economics and sociology. J Econ Issues 40(2):473 et seqq.

Dworkin R (1980) Is wealth a value? J Legal Stud 9(2):191 et seqq.

Elster J (2011) Reciprocity and norms, in: Fleurbaey M, Salles M, Weymark JA (eds) Social ethics and normative economics: essays in honour of Serge-Christophe Kolm. Berlin and Heidelberg, pp. 327 et seqq.

Esposito F (2022b) The GDPR enshrines the right to the impersonal price. Comput Law Secur Rev 45:105660

Esposito F, de Almeida L (2018) A shocking truth for law and economics: consumer welfare explains the internal market for electricity better than total welfare, in: Mathis K, Huber B (eds). Energy law and economics. Dordrecht. pp. 101 et seqq.

Esposito F, Grundmann SM (2017) Investor-consumer or overall welfare: searching for the paradigm of recent reforms in financial services contracts. EUI Law Department Research Paper Series, 2017/5

Esposito F (2017) How the behavioural turn in law and economics vindicates The New Haven School, Oeconomia, 7(3):375 et seqq.

Esposito F (2019) Carrying the choice theory of contracts further: transfers, welfare, and the size of the community. Euro Rev Contract Law 15(3):297 et seqq.

Esposito F (2022) The consumer welfare hypothesis in law and economics: towards a synthesis for the twenty-first century. Cheltenham

Fehr E, Gächter S (1998) Reciprocity and economics: the economic implications of Homo Reciprocans. Euro Econ Rev 42:845 et seqq.

Fehr E, Fischbacher U, Gächter S (2002) Strong reciprocity, human cooperation, and the enforcement of social norms. Hum Nat 13(1):1 et seqq.

Fehr E, Schmidt KM (2006) The economics of fairness, reciprocity, and altruism—experimental evidence and new theories. In: Kolm S-C, Ythier JM (eds) Handbook of the economics of giving, altruism and reciprocity, vol 1. Amsterdam, pp. 615 et seqq.

Garoupa N, Liguerre CG (2011) The syndrome of the efficiency of the common law. B.U. Int'l L.J., 29:287 et seqq.

Garoupa N, Ulen TS (2021) Comparative law and economics: aspirations and hard realities. Am J Comparative Law 69(4):664 et seqq.

Gintis H (2016) Individuality and entanglement: the moral and material bases of social life. Princeton and Oxford

Giocoli N (2020) Rejected! Antitrust economists as expert witnesses in the post-Daubert world, Journal of the History of Economic Thought, 42(2), pp. 203 et seqq.

Giocoli N (2020b) Why do US judges reject antitrust experts? In: Cserne P, Esposito F (eds) Economics in legal reasoning, London, pp. 101 et seqq.

Gouldner AW (1960) The norm of reciprocity: a preliminary statement. Am Sociol Rev 25(2):161 et seqq.

Hesselink MJ (2021) Justifying contract in Europe. Political Philosophies of European Contract Law, New York

Hildebrand D (2016) The role of economic analysis in EU competition law. The European School, Alphen aan den Rijn

Hofmann O (2021) Breach of contract. An Economic Analysis of the Efficient Breach Scenario, Dordrecht

Hutt WH (1936) Economists and the public interest. A study of competition and opinion, Pretoria

Kolm S-C (1984) La bonne économie: La réciprocité générale, Paris

Kolm S-C (2008) Reciprocity: an economics of social relations, Cambridge

Lakatos I (1970) Falsification and the methodology of scientific research programmes. In: Lakatos I, Musgrave A (eds) Criticism and the Growth of Knowledge, Cambridge, pp. 91et seqq.

Liao W (2017) The application of the theory of efficient breach in contract law. A Comparative Law and Economics Perspective, Cambridge

Liscow Z, Markovitz D, Democratizing behavioural economics. Yale J Regul 39:1217 et seqq.

Mantzari D (2022) Courts, Regulators, and the scrutiny of economic evidence, Oxford

Mathis K (transl S Shannon) (2009) Efficiency instead of justice?: searching for the philosophical foundations of the economic analysis of law. Dordrecht

McAdams R (2015) The expressive powers of law, Harvard

McCloskey DN (2021) Bettering humanomics: a new, and old. Approach to Economic Science, Chicago

Merriam Webster dictionary online (nd), Reciprocity, available at https://www.merriam-webster.com/dictionary/reciprocity

Murray MD (2022) NFTs rescue resale royalties? the wonderfully complicated ability of NFT smart contracts to allow resale royalty rights. available at https://doi.org/10.2139/ssrn.4164029

Musgrave A (2016) Imre Lakatos, Stanford encyclopedia of philosophy, available at https://plato.stanford.edu/entries/lakatos/

Nowak MA, Sigmund K (2005) Evolution of indirect reciprocity. Nature 437(7063):1291 et seqq.

Ohtsuki H and Iwasa Y (2004) How should we define goodness? Reputation dynamics in indirect reciprocity, Journal of Theoretical Biology, 231, pp. 107 et seqq.

Ohtsuki H, Iwasa Y (2006) The leading eight: social norms that can maintain cooperation by indirect reciprocity. J Theor Biol 239:435 et seqq

Okada I (2020) A review of theoretical studies on indirect reciprocity. Games 11(3):27 et seqq.

Oliver A (2019) Reciprocity and the art of behavioural public policy, Cambridge

Perugini M, Gallucci M, Presaghi F, Ercolani AP (2003) The personal norm of reciprocity. Euro J Personal 17(4):251 et seqq

Posner E, Sunstein C (2002) Antitrust and equality. Am J Law Equal 2:190 et seqq

Richters O, Siemoneit A (2022) Making markets just: reciprocity violations as key intervention points. Discussion Paper

Ridley M (1988) The origins of virute. Human Instncts and the Evolution of Cooperation, New York

Salazar M, Joel Shaw D, Czekóová K, Staněk R, Brázdil M (2022) The role of generalised reciprocity and reciprocal tendencies in the emergence of cooperative group norms. J Econ Psychol 90:102520

Sardo A, Esposito F (2020) Homo Ludicus: expected strategies and jurisprudence. TCRS, pp. 95 et seqq.

Schwartz A (1988) Proposals for Products Liability Reform: A Theoretical Synthesis, The Yale Law Journal, 97(3), pp. 353 et seqq.

Smith VL, Wilson BJ (2019) Humanomics: moral sentiments and the wealth of nations for the twenty-first century. New York

Smith A (1759) Theory of moral sentiments

Smith A (2007 [1776]) An inquiry into the nature and causes of the wealth on nations. Petersfield

Sugden R (2018) The community of advantage: a behavioural economist's defence of the market. Oxford

Sunstein C R (1996) On the expressive function of law. Univ Pennsylvania Law Rev 144:2021 et seqq

Sunstein C R (1999) From consumer sovereignty to cost-benefit analysis: an incompletely theorized agreement. Harvard J Law Public Policy 23:203 et seqq

Titmuss RM (1971) The gift relationship. Pantheon Books, New York

Trivers RL (1971) The evolution of reciprocal Altruism. Quarterly Rev Biol 46(1):35 et seqq

Voelkl B (2015) The evolution of generalized reciprocity in social interaction networks. Theor Population Biol 104:17 et seqq

Walraevens B (2020) Reciprocity in Smith. Oeconomia 10(4):657 et seqq

Von Wangenheim G (2017) Evolutionary law and economics, in Parisi F (ed) Oxford handbook of law and economics, vol 1, Oxford, pp. 161 et seqq

Young HP (1993) The evolution of conventions. Econometrica 61:57 et seqq

Part IV
Meritocracy

Chapter 13
Hierarchy, Efficiency, and Merit

Marius Daniel Baumann

Abstract Many people think that structuring at least some of our organizations in a hierarchical way is inevitable, even in modern liberal democracies. When trying to justify this practice, the notions of desert and merit have historically played a major role. However, in recent times, most philosophers have been deeply sceptical about these notions, instead attempting to justify hierarchies by referring to considerations of efficiency. I argue that this comes at a price. More specifically, I argue that although we neither need to nor should refer to merit to justify the mere existence of hierarchies, the notion provides important justificatory resources within hierarchies, i.e., regarding who occupies which position and how the people in a hierarchy should relate to each other. We thus have reason to be hesitant to discard merit altogether when it comes to the of justification of hierarchies.

13.1 Introduction

Hierarchies are a problem for liberal democratic societies. Some people having powers over others potentially affects both our standing as equals and our liberty. If we think that at least some kinds of hierarchies, I'll focus on what I call *functional hierarchies*, are nevertheless necessary, some sort of justification is required. Historically, the notions of merit and desert played a big role in that justification. Some people, the idea goes, deserve higher positions in a society by virtue of being more meritorious, in the sense of having shown superior character, talent and effort. However, most contemporary philosophers, from Rawls (1971) to, more recently, Sandel (2020) are extremely sceptical about the role that notions like merit and desert can play. Not only do they dismiss these notions when it comes to identifying the fundamental principles of justice, but they do so on sceptical grounds that are so deep (regarding both the notion's coherence and its moral desirability) that this precludes us from appealing to these notions in any relevant way at all. The goal of

M. D. Baumann (✉)
Center for Ethics and Philosophy in Practice, Ludwig-Maximilians-Universität Munich, Munich, Germany
e-mail: marius.baumann@lmu.de

this chapter is to show that this comes at a price. Merit, if the notion can be saved from the sceptical attacks, can play an important role in justifying hierarchies in liberal democratic societies. More specifically, even though we neither need to nor should refer to merit to justify the mere existence of hierarchies, the notion provides important justificatory resources within hierarchies, i.e., regarding who occupies which position and how the people in a hierarchy should relate to each other.

Here is how I argue. The first part of the paper dialectically situates the main argument. I cover a lot of ground here, but since it is well-trodden ground and I don't intend to make any original contributions at this point, I will proceed rather quickly. I start by setting up the justification problem that hierarchies pose for liberal societies. Merit might seem to provide a natural solution to this problem, but, as I sketch next, many philosophers are deeply sceptical about the general prospects of this notion. The solution is therefore searched for (and found) in considerations of efficiency. This seems apt since, as I see it, the efficiency argument is sound and it may well suffice to justify the existence of hierarchies in a society.

However, that does not mean that merit has no justificatory role to play. This is what the second part of the paper aims to establish by outlining two important ways in which the notion of merit has to be incorporated *at a later stage*, so to speak. The first way in which merit re-enters the picture is when we try to justify why a particular person should be higher in the hierarchy than another person. Even if both agree that hierarchies are warranted in principle, the subordinate in the hierarchy will still be justified in asking why their superior should be the one on top. Considerations of efficiency alone are not sufficient to answer this question, as I try to show using an example involving nepotism. Second, within functional hierarchies, it matters what kind of relationships typically exist between people. Merit plays an important role insofar as its existence can strengthen and its absence can weaken certain duties on both the superior's and the subordinate's side. Since the former duties are more obvious, I focus on loyalty as one example of the latter type of duty. The upshot, once more, is that considerations of mere efficiency lead us astray when it comes to justification within hierarchies.

In the third part, I briefly outline the implications of this for our general picture of the justification of (functional) hierarchies. What I propose is a two-level model of justification. On the basic level of institutions, which concerns the existence of functional hierarchies themselves, our justification should be one of efficiency alone. On the second level, which concerns relations among citizens within these institutions, merit does play an important role. I argue that rehabilitating merit on the second level does not need to, and indeed should not, lead us to rehabilitate it on the basic level, and thus accept what might be called a *fundamentally merit-based* justification of hierarchies. I finish discussing two objections.

13.2 The Background: Hierarchies, Skepticism about Merit, and Efficiency to the Rescue

13.2.1 The Problem of Hierarchies in Liberal Societies

Even in modern liberal democratic societies, it has seemed plausible to many that some hierarchical structures are inevitable.[1] We need organisations with different roles, where certain people are invested with special responsibilities that come with authority and decision-making power over others. In our everyday lives, we are very familiar with such hierarchies and many of us probably take them for granted. As examples, think of the workplace, schools and universities, political institutions, or even most private clubs. In all of these, we are used to finding organisational structures that invest some members with more authority and power than others, allowing them to command a certain range of actions that affect others in a way that these others can't affect them with their decisions.

What kind of hierarchies are we talking about? A number of useful distinctions have been drawn in the literature that help specify what's at issue (at least for this chapter). First, we are interested in hierarchies between *individuals*, not *group* hierarchies.[2] The issue is not the justification of hierarchies of caste, gender or race, but those between individual adult human beings. Second, and more specifically, we are concerned with *production* hierarchies as distinct from *dominance* hierarchies.[3] Whereas the latter are evolutionarily older and concern the ways in which humans allocate scarce resources and reproductive partners, the former arise only in the organisations that humans set up to facilitate complex common endeavours. Third, the hierarchies we are interested in involve actual differences in social *positions*, not just differences in *esteem*.[4] The question is not simply whether we value one person or one person's qualities more highly. Rather, the issue is that one person, qua their position or office, has the discretionary power to tell the other what (not) to do within a specified realm and, typically, over an extended period of time.

For lack of a better word, I will refer to these as *functional* hierarchies. Of course, the distinctions aren't always as clear-cut in real life as one would want them to be. As many observers have pointed out, a high position in a hierarchy in one realm can lead to spillover effects in others, such as when one deferrs to one's highly qualified doctor in political matters or gives them a better seat at the table at a private event.[5] Still, our acquaintance with functional hierarchies in our everyday life gives us a

---

[1] Compare Scheffler (2005), pp. 17 et seq.; Schuppert (2015), p. 108; Wolff (2019), pp. 5–8 and Kolodny (2022), pp. 261 et. seq.

[2] Compare Wolff (2019) for an argument that we need to take the later hierarchies seriously as well. I don't disagree in principle, but will not consider them in this chapter.

[3] Compare Rubin (2000).

[4] Compare Runciman (1967); Fourie (2015) and Scanlon (2018), pp. 26–39.

[5] The example is from Wolff (2019), p. 10. For a book-length discussion of this problem see also Walzer (1983).

fairly clear intuitive sense of their nature and of where the boundaries should ideally be.

Nevertheless, and despite their ubiquitous nature and the fact that we often take them for granted, functional hierarchies are in need of justification. This is especially poignant from the view of liberal democrats. First, the ability of someone else to require me to do something potentially diminishes my own freedom, impacting the *liberal* side of their commitments. Second, someone else having the discretion to tell me what to do has the potential to call into question our standing as equals, affecting the *democratic* side. How strongly this need for justification is felt does, of course, vary depending on our understanding of the values of equality and liberty. If we think that equality consists not only in the distribution of resources but also concerns our social relations, as so-called *relational* or *social* egalitarians think, hierarchies arguably appear more problematic.[6] If we think that non-domination is an important part of freedom, as *republicans* have forcefully argued, the need to justify hierarchies becomes particularly salient.[7] Yet the need for justification is arguably not limited to these views. Given the broadly shared assumption that we are free and equal, some story has to be told about why we should accept hierarchies in our societies. Hierarchies rub against both the liberal and the egalitarian spirit. Even if people willingly and freely enter hierarchical relations, we should still be concerned about the way that this potentially impacts their status as free and equal, and we should therefore require a good story to be given to justify our practice of having hierarchies.

13.2.2 Skepticism about Merit

What could that story be? At least historically, the notions of *desert* and *merit* have played a major role.[8] If some people are more deserving than others, and if justice requires that we see to it that these people get what they deserve, then we have an outline of a justification for giving these people rewards in the form of income, as well as higher offices and positions. The fact that someone is meritorious, in this view, provides the basis for the desert claim.[9] Of course, what merit consists in is itself a matter of debate. However, as a first approximation, we can follow the popular understanding of merit as a combination of character, talent and effort. Hence, the story goes, a society should ensure that rewards, in the form of income and high positions, go to those who deserve them most, which (usually) are the most meritorious.

---

[6] Compare Miller (1997); Anderson (1999) and Scheffler (2003).

[7] Compare Pettit (1997, 2012).

[8] For an overview of the more recent history of the concept compare Kett (2013) and for a more popular rendering Wooldridge (2021).

[9] Compare Feinberg (1970) for the notion of a *desert base* and Mulligan (2018), pp. 67–71 for this understanding of the relation between merit and desert.

The only problem with this story is that merit and, indeed, desert itself, have not been popular notions in philosophy in recent times, to put it mildly. Instead, the philosophical debate of the last 50 years, at least, has been markedly hostile towards the notions of desert and merit. Most influential in this regard has been John Rawls's treatment of the topic in his 1971 *A Theory of Justice*. As is well known, (one of) the main purpose(s) of that book is to identify the principles of justice that should govern a society. By appealing to the idea of a *veil of ignorance*, Rawls arrives at two main principles. Neither of them makes any reference to desert or merit. This, of course, is no coincidence. As Rawls makes clear in a number of places, he is very sceptical about the idea of desert. Here is perhaps the most famous passage:

> It seems to be one of the fixed points of our considered judgments that no one deserves his place in the distribution of native endowments, any more than one deserves one's initial starting place in society. The assertion that a man deserves the superior character that enables him to make the effort to cultivate his abilities is equally problematic; for his character depends in large part upon fortunate family and social circumstances for which he can claim no credit.[10]

Rawls's argument is quite intuitive. We cannot claim that we deserve our position in a society if that position is itself, to a large degree, determined by factors on which we had no influence and which therefore cannot be said to have been earned. Neither did we choose our parents, nor did we choose the social circumstances in which we were raised. Yet these factor, and this is something that even most defenders of desert and merit would readily accept, have a huge impact on our abilities and character traits, which allow us to achieve high positions in a society in the first place.

Many philosophers have agreed with the broad outlines of Rawls's critique, and not just those who are generally sympathetic towards Rawls's political philosophy. Highly instructive, in this regard, is the fact that even one of Rawls's most important critics, and one of the main proponents of the *communitarian* alternative to Rawls' liberalism, Michael Sandel, shares Rawls' scepticism about desert:

> If our talents are gifts for which we are indebted - whether to the genetic lottery of to God - then it is a mistake and a conceit to assume we deserve the benefits that flow from them.[11]

Indeed, so many philosophers seem to believe similar things that Pojman observes that:

> Merit has been demerited and desert declared undeserving of a serious place in contemporary political theory.[12]

Yet not everyone agrees. Over time, critics of Rawls have offered several responses. Two are especially noteworthy in my opinion. The first one takes issue with the idea that, in order to be deserving, we need to deserve the *desert base* itself. Rawls seems to assume that if our success is based on our upbringing and social circumstances, which

---

[10] Rawls (1971), pp. 103 et seq.

[11] Sandel (2020), p. 123.

[12] Pojman (1997), p. 549. For similar assessments, compare Scheffler (1992), p. 301; Miller (1999) p. 131; Olsaretti (2003), p. 1 and Brouwer and Mulligan (2019) p. 2272.

are a matter of luck, that success itself cannot be earned. However, that claim seems dubious and does not fit the intuitions underlying much of our everyday thinking.[13] Sports provides for good examples. Everyone knows that for being a successful basketball player, a certain physical size is a requirement. No one thinks that people are responsible for their own height. Nevertheless, people are willing to accept that basketball players often deserve their success. The fact that they did not earn one of the key factors of their success does not, in most people's minds, nullify their deservingness.

The second response makes an even stronger point.[14] There is something odd about saying that our natural endowments are a matter of luck and therefore undeserved. Usually, when we make desert claims, we claim that *someone* does or doesn't deserve *some other thing* on the basis of *yet something else*.[15] However, the claim that we don't deserve our natural endowments is different. Our natural endowments (think of our genes, for example) are *constitutive*, or part of the *essence* of who we are. Yet that means that there isn't really a third element on the basis of which we could say that *I* don't deserve something. If that third element were different, I would be different (as in: if my parents weren't my parents, I wouldn't be me).

Whether these responses succeed in countering the sceptical attack on desert is a matter of ongoing debate that is beyond the confines of this chapter. What I want to argue for is the more modest claim that *if* desert and merit can be rescued from the sceptical attacks, we have good reason to give them a place in our theorising about hierarchies. However, before we can turn to this, it is important to be clear about a specific feature of the Rawlsian attack on merit, which is the depth of its scepticism. Rawls's argument is not merely a pragmatic one, i.e., an argument to the effect that organising a society on the basis of desert considerations would be impracticable. Neither is it a political argument, to the effect that a justification based on desert or merit could not be defended in light of the pluralism inherent to liberal societies.[16] Instead, the scepticism underlying the argument is more fundamental. We abandon the notion of desert *for good*.[17] We don't just say that it shouldn't play a role when it comes to identifying the fundamental principles that should govern a society. We discard it *tout court*. As Mulligan describes it:

> [...] Rawls engages in a wholesale, quasi metaphysical rejection of desert [...].[18]

---

[13] Versions of this objection have been put forward by Nozick (1974); Zaitchick (1977) and Sher (1979).

[14] Versions of it can be found in Rescher (1995), pp. 28–31, and Mulligan (2018), pp. 170–75.

[15] Compare Feinberg (1970) and Kleinig (1971).

[16] Rawls does offer an argument of the first kind in *A Theory of Justice* and one can understand his later arguments in *Political Liberalism* as a version of the second argument. However, the argument at stake is independent of these further arguments. I follow Mulligan (2018), pp. 166 et seq. in this assessment.

[17] At least as pertains to the realm of distributive justice. Scheffler (2000) contends that Rawls's sceptical argument does not generalise to the realm of retributive justice. I will gloss over this for the remainder since we are not interested in the later realm.

[18] Mulligan (2018), p. 165. Compare also Miller (1999), p. 131 and Schmidtz (2006), p. 32.

This aspect will become very important in the later part of the paper because it entails that the notion of desert (and merit as its base) has *no* role to play in the justification of hierarchies.

13.2.3 *Efficiency to the Rescue*

What then could a Rawlsian sceptic offer concerning the justification of hierarchies? It seems that the standard move, that is for those critics of desert and merit who accept the necessity of hierarchies, is to bring in considerations of efficiency.[19] The basic reasoning is as follows. Hierarchical organisations sometimes allow for more efficient processes. These efficiency gains could, in principle, benefit everyone. If they do, and if the gains for everyone are large enough to outweigh any disadvantages associated with hierarchical structures, then even those people in the lower ranks of a hierarchy have reason to accept the existence of hierarchies.

Why would one think that hierarchies can lead to such efficiency gains? Looking into this in detail would go beyond the present chapter but, for illustration, let us briefly look at one influential way of arguing for this claim in economics, by means of Ronald Coase's theory of the firm.[20] Kolodny provides a rough outline of the argument:

> The basic idea is that the high costs of market transactions make it inefficient to organize certain processes of production by market transactions among autonomous buyers and sellers of the relevant factors of production, including labor. Organizing those processes instead under the hierarchical direction of a boss – which is what, for Coase at least, defines the firm - lowers those transaction costs. The resulting improvements in efficiency stand to benefit everyone.[21]

Kolodny, of course, is not the first to make this argument. The idea that, whereas some processes in the economy are most effectively coordinated through market transactions, others are more effectively organiszed within the hierarchical set-up of a firm, has wide currency in economics. If something like Coase's model of the role of the firm is correct, firms, constituted in a hierarchical way, play an integral part in a modern economy by reducing transaction costs.

Importantly for our purposes, what needs to be established is not just that there are efficiency gains from having hierarchies. If we want an *all things considered* argument for hierarchies, we also need to show that these gains in efficiency are large enough to outweigh any disadvantages hierarchies may have. This depends, obviously, on the size of the efficiency gains that hierarchies produce. However, as Kolodny (2022, pp. 267–69 and 2023, pp. 97–101) has convincingly argued, it also depends crucially on certain features of the hierarchies at stake, which he calls *tempering* factors. Kolodny identifies several features that contribute to making

---

[19] Indeed, Wolff (2019), pp. 8–10 considers it *the* liberal way of justifying hierarchies.

[20] See Coase (1937). See also Williamson (1973).

[21] Kolodny (2023), p. 150.

specific hierarchies less objectionable or not objectionable at all, such as *context* and *content*, *escapability*, or *higher-level equality*. Thus, whether hierarchies are overall acceptable not only depends on how large the efficiency gains are, but also on factors such as whether they are structured in a way that limits the areas and subjects matters in which we are subordinated to them, whether they leave us a way out, and whether they are situated in a more general (e.g., legal) context in which we still consider each other to be equal.[22]

Taking these factors into consideration complicates the picture. However, I do think that the main line of argument, sufficiently parsed out and generalised beyond the economic realm, is correct. Efficiency considerations can and do provide sufficient justification for the existence of at least some of the functional hierarchies we see in liberal democratic societies. The Rawlsian thus has a way out when it comes to justifying the existence of these hierarchies in a liberal democratic society. Yet, as I will argue in the next section, this is only part of the picture. Efficiency considerations are not always enough when it comes to another level of the justification of hierarchies.

13.3   Merit within Hierarchies

What we have looked at so far, is the justification for the existence of hierarchies. We have searched for (and found) an answer to the question "Why should our societies be hierarchically organised at all?". However, answering this question is not all that the justification of hierarchies requires. Instead, there is a second demand for justification that arises *within* hierarchies. More precisely, there are two questions that follow on the heels of the first: "Why are you on top and not me?" and "What do we owe each other in a hierarchy?". As I will argue below, considerations of efficiency sometimes lead us astray regarding these questions, whereas considerations of merit often offer intuitive and appealing answers.

13.3.1   Why Are You on Top and not Me?

Consider the following scenario:

> Jared: Jared is put into a high government position by his father-in-law, Donald. Jared has no relevant background or expertise in the fields he is supposed to oversee. However, since his job requires extensive coordination with Donald and, as son-in-law, he has more time with, and better access to, Donald than any other person doing the job would have, Jared can do the job in the most efficient way. His subordinates include more able people with far

---

[22] Kolodny (2022), p. 267 and (2023), p. 98 thinks that these tempering factors not only outweigh what might be bad about relations of inferiority but instead can make those relations less of a bad or not a bad at all. I don't take a side on this issue.

more experience in the relevant fields, who have also worked much harder to get to these positions.

The example may seem far-fetched, but the general idea should be clear enough.[23] Because access to his superior is crucial for the position in question, Jared is able to fulfill his duties more efficiently than any other person. Nepotism thus proves to be an effective practice in this instance. Nevertheless, most people would probably agree that Jared's subordinates have strong justification to object to being hierarchically below Jared. Why might this be?[24]

One reason could be that we think that nepotism, as a generally observed practice, is inefficient overall. So even if it were the case that it is sometimes more efficient to put family or close friends in a certain office, we might still object that this practice, when generalised, has overall negative effects. This could be because it establishes an overall harmful precedent, or because it undermines trust in organisations, and so on.

This reasoning, for all I know, may be correct. However, I don't think that efficiency-based objections are the whole, or even the main issue here. We can see this more clearly if we add a further twist to the scenario. Imagine that we, as a society, were presented with good evidence that allocating a very specific set of jobs in a nepotistic way was indeed more efficient than any alternative. Based on that evidence, we would publicly specify which jobs these are, and explicitly allow nepotism in these jobs, while simultaneously upholding bans on nepotism elsewhere. In such a scenario, efficiency considerations would no longer speak against some cases like Jared's. However, it seems clear to me that we would still have reason to object to such cases. Moreover, we could arguably even do so while at the same time acknowledging that, in virtue of how our society allows for certain kinds of nepotism, Jared is *entitled to* and has *legitimate expectations regarding* his job.[25]

What is it then that we object to? The most natural way to understand our objection, I think, is in terms of merit. Jared has none of the qualifications and has put in none of the work that would make him deserve the position, and this speaks against him regardless whether he is capaple of doing the job in the most efficient way. Granted, Donald has some leeway in how he defines the qualifications needed for the position and these need not all to be strictly related to the subject-matter of the fields that Jared is supposed to oversee.[26] However, what makes Jared the most efficient person in this scenario is the fact that Jared is Donald's son-in-law. This is not a qualification of Jared's at all. It is not a fact about Jared's individual merits and thus cannot serve

---

[23] Any similarity to actual persons is purely coincidental. For a more realistic example, compare https://time.com/5766186/jared-kushner-interview.

[24] I am by far not the first person to discuss nepotism in this context. Compare Miller (1999), p. 166 and Kolodny (2023), Chapters 11 and 12.

[25] I discuss the issue of entitlement in the last section.

[26] Indeed, the Jared example is particularily interesting since his position is one, i.e. a high position in government with close access to those in power, where the public is often willing to grant much leeway, in the sense that people like Donald are regarded as justified in filling these positions with people they trust rather than others who have more direct experience in the relevant fields. However, as I am about to argue, there are limits to this.

as a base for deserving the position. Since Jared lacks any other merits with regard to this position, he does not deserve to be put in the position.

This general point is independent of the question of hierarchy, that is, it is independent of whether Jared has any subordinates. One might thus think that it's not really the fact that Jared occupies a certain position *in a hierarchy* that is problematic. However, this is too quick. There is a particular dimension of the problem that has to do with hierarchies and that becomes more salient and more urgent when we put ourselves in the position of the people subordinated to Jared. Consider the long-time, well-experienced public servant who suddenly has to take their orders from Jared. Isn't it clear that this person has an even stronger reason to object? This person is entitled to object by asking "Why are you on top and not me?" And the most natural explanation for why this person has this justification is that this person is more qualified, has put in more effort, has (presumably) achieved their job on the basis of a process that took into account their qualification and effort, and so on. The fact that they have to follow Jared's orders despite being more meritorious and thus more deserving of the job, makes their grievance stronger and more justified. To be clear, offices and jobs aren't allocated as rewards for past performance and thus having proven oneself meritorious in the past doesn't generate a right to a particular position. However, even if the people who have been passed over don't have a right to Jared's position, they do have a legitimate complaint against being subordinated to someone who has failed to show any of the merits they themselves have demonstrated.[27]

The first way in which merit enters the picture *within* hierarchies is therefore in the justification of who occupies which position.

13.3.2 What do we Owe Each Other in a Hierarchy?

The second point where the notion of merit comes back into the picture is with regard to the kinds of relationships that should govern hierarchical organisations. More specifically, I think that merit plays a part in grounding certain obligations that efficiency can't play. This concerns both the way in which superiors should behave towards subordinates and vice versa. Since the duties that superiors have towards their subordinates are well-understood and not very controversial, I won't go into them.[28] The more difficult issue is the reverse relationship.

Might there be duties that subordinates have towards their superiors in a hierarchy? I propose that the answer is yes, and the specific example I will look at is loyalty. The idea, in a nutshell, is that there are certain duties of loyalty towards one's superior, for example, that one objects to them being replaced, which do not arise if one's superior

---

[27] Compare Miller (1999), pp. 166 et seq. for a similar line of reasoning.

[28] For example, the fact that the subordinate person has proven to be especially meritorious might add to the duties a superordinate has, such as when it comes to assisting them in developing special talents.

didn't deserve to be in their position in the first place. What is more, these duties often hold even if the person who is supposed to replace one's superior is more qualified and more efficient. Merit thus helps ground certain duties that wouldn't exist in its absence.

My argument for this claim is an indirect one. I start with a counter-example, that is, a case where most people probably don't think that the person being replaced is owed loyalty, eventhough they have clearly proved their merit. Efficiency considerations, in this example, override considerations of merit. However, I will argue next, the example depends on certain features that are not representative of most of the hierarchical relations we find ourselves in. Seeing how the example differs from ordinary cases thus brings into focus why, usually, merit helps grounding loyalty.

Here is the counter-example:

> Tony: Tony is the well-loved, above-average starting quarterback of a football team. During an injury, his replacement, Dak, plays to great success and when Tony is finally healthy again, the coach decides not to reinstate Tony as the starter. Tony, realising that he will not be able to win back the starting position from Dak, makes the following statement: 'You see football is a meritocracy. You aren't handed anything. You earn everything every single day, over and over again. You have to prove it.[29]

What Tony is doing here, I take it, is acknowledging that he does not deserve loyalty in the sense that he should remain the starter based on his previous effort and success. He thereby makes it clear to both his teammates and his fans that they do not have to stand up for him and oppose the coach's decision.[30] The merits that Tony has acquired over the course of his career don't justify him remaining the starter, because in football the only thing that matters is how one performs in the present.[31]

I think Tony is right, and my guess is that most people (or at least most sports fans) will agree. Some of this probably has to do with the fact that football players make a lot of money, that the active career of a football player is relatively short anyway, and other reasons that speak against us caring too deeply about their (sports) fate. However, the underlying reason why we accept the uncompromising logic that Tony alludes to, I submit, has to do with the nature of sport. In many areas of our lives, we accept competition because we know that it often has positive effects and we also acknowledge, at least grudgingly, that the other person has a right to take a shot at whatever we are trying to achieve. Sport is different. The reason we have sports is not because we value their goals for their own sake (i.e., the goal of winning the Super Bowl). We value sports because we cherish competition. Since this is the case, we also accept a much tougher logic when it comes to who should have the chance to

---

[29] https://www.nfl.com/news/tony-romo-S-complete-statement-to-dallas-media-0ap300000074 0333.

[30] It is doubtful that either Tony's teammates or the fans are ranked lower in a hierarchy than Tony, strictly speaking. Nonetheless, I hope that the reader will see how the message that follows from the example generalizes to actual hierarchies.

[31] This is a bit too quick. One's future potential also factors in. Similarly, one's past record might factor in when it comes to predicting how one will play in the future. The point here is just that one's previous achievements aren't relevant for their own sake.

compete. We accept that Tony is not owed a position as the starter of the team even though he has been an important member of that team in the not-too-distant past. Dak is more effective in playing the position and this reason alone justifies him being the starter.[32]

Here we have an example of a case where we accept the logic of efficiency in its harshest form and to the exclusion of any consideration of merit. However, I also hope that most people will agree that the example is just that, *harsh*. Unlike sports, most of the other things we do in life aren't done for the sake of competition. Instead, we have other goals that we are trying to achieve. Depriving someone of the chance to achieve these goals, even though they have behaved meritoriously in their attempt, betrays a kind of cut-throat logic that most of us don't want to govern our lives outside of sports. That entails that unless the difference between us and someone else is large efficiency-wise, we deserve to continue our efforts.[33]

At this point, some people might be tempted to shoehorn our intuitions into an efficiency argument. Perhaps, from a company's point of view, replacing a well-loved, experienced worker with someone who promises to be more productive is often not the efficient thing to do. The new person is less proven, so there is some uncertainty regarding the potential efficiency gains. In addition, the disruption in the work process might prove too costly. Efficiency considerations, properly understood, don't necessarily lead companies to being overly hasty in replacing people.[34] Yet, once more, these considerations don't seem to capture the full moral force behind our intuitions. Our intuitions tell us that there is something wrong with treating deserving people in a cut-throat way. These intuitions are not about the fact that there are hierarchies in the first place, and they aren't about the efficiency of the decision. Instead, they concern the people being replaced themselves, and what our appropriate feelings and attitudes towards these people should be. If people behave meritoriously, they are owed a certain measure of loyalty.

This seems obvious enough when we consider the way that a company should behave towards its employees. It should honour the talent and the effort its employees have put in. However, there is no reason, in principle, why employees in a company shouldn't adopt the same stance towards each other, including their superiors. There is no reason to think that subordinates should approve of, or shouldn't care about, this cut-throat logic just because it is directed at their superiors or else they would, by the same token, also have to accept the flip side of this, that is, accept that their

---

[32] We might think that Tony is still owed esteem and thus a higher rank in a hierarchy of esteem, but that is not the kind of hierarchy we are interested in here.

[33] This is not contradicting the claim in the last section that jobs aren't allocated as rewards or prices. While I agree with Miller (1999), p. 160 that past performance is not the basis for deserving, but rather a source of evidence for who might be best for, a job the situation changes when we consider people who have already occupied a posion for some time. Meritorious behavior can be the basis for deserving to keep one's job.

[34] On an even more general level, one might also think that having (society- or industry-wide) rules in place that grant people some job security can be overall more efficient for an economy. Thus, what is efficient at the macro level might be different from what is efficient at the micro level.

superiors move on from them at the first hunch that someone else could do a better job. That, I think, would be a morally reprehensible state of affairs.

Of course, and this should go without saying, there are limits to this kind of loyalty. For example, we might not have a duty to object if our own job is at stake. Moreover, loyalty is a particularly tricky value in the context of hierarchies. Hierarchies often come with the power of giving orders, and these orders can often substitute the subordinate's own reasoning. Demanding loyalty might seem to reinforce this and lead to the blind following of orders in a hierarchy. However, this is a misunderstanding of loyalty. Loyalty does not entail blindness, it is not obedience. It is about sticking with someone in the face of adversity, and adversity can consist precisely in a kind of cut-throat efficiency maximisation logic.[35]

But, finally, why think that the duties of loyalty on the side of the subordinate stem from the fact that their superior deserves their position and not just from the fact that the position has been held for some time and that, if a person behaves kindly toward us, we owe them something in return? Even if my superior did not earn their position in the first place, one might think that the fact that they have been kind to me generates some reciprocal duties on my side. I think that this might be right with regard to some duties, such as gratitude, but not with regards to loyalty. This brings us back to Jared. No matter how well Jared behaves towards his subordinates, when the moment comes that he is to be replaced by someone else, his subordinates have no duty of loyalty towards him. Jared's subordinates can still feel grateful for the way they have been treated, but the fact that Jared should never have been in his position in the first place gives them an overriding reason not to object to his replacement. The absence of merit nullifies their duty of loyalty which might have existed had Jared deserved to be in his position.[36]

13.4 A Two-Level Account

If what I have said in the last section is correct, then considerations of merit play an important role in the justification of hierarchical organisations. They do so not at the most fundamental level, the one at which we justify the existence of hierarchies themselves, but at another level, the one that concerns the relationships between actual people within hierarchies. If we can save the notion of merit from the deep sceptical attacks, we thus have good reason to make philosophical use of it. However,

---

[35] Compare Heath (2014), pp. 106 et seq. and Singer (2018), pp. 835 et seq. for the idea that Coase's theory of the firm itself can explain how the obligations in market transactions differ from those within a firm, especially with regard to the prevalence of a competitive logic.

[36] Schmidtz (2006), pp. 40 et seqq. argues that we can sometimes deserve something for what we do after receiving it. However, even if this were true, it would only be so because we have subsequently behaved in a meritorious way, as Schmidtz himself acknowledges. The loyalty we owe our superior might thus stem not (only) from them deserving to be in the job in the first place, but from their later, meritorious, behavior. Thus, the point stands that the loyalty does not stem from the mere fact that the person has behaved kindly towards us, or any such thing.

this raises a new question. Should we rehabilitate merit at both levels, i.e. grant it a role in justifying hierarchies themselves? Or should we try to restrict reliance on the notion to the second level? In the final section, I will argue in favour of the second option and against what could be called *fundamentally merit-based* justifications of hierarchy. I start with an argument against fundamentally merit-based justifications. I'll then defend the two-level account against two objections, which should also help to flesh out the account in some more detail.

13.4.1 Against the Fundamentally Merit-Based Justification

If merit can help us to justify people's positions within hierarchies, why shouldn't we give it a place in justifying those hierarchies themselves?

One reason not to do so is if it turned out that efficiency and merit are deep down incompatible. Hayek (1960) provides a very influential argument to this effect. To arrive at a society in which people get what they deserve, Hayek thinks, we would have to be able to assess and compare their individual talents and efforts. However, as is well-known, Hayek's main argument for liberty precisely assumes that no centralised agency has this kind of information. As he puts it:

> The possibility of a true judgment of merit thus depends on the presence of precisely those conditions whose general absence is the main argument for liberty. It is because we want people to use knowledge which we do not possess that we let them decide for themselves. But insofar as we want them to be free to use capacities and knowledge of facts which we do not have, we are not in a position to judge the merit of their achievements. To decide on merit presupposes that we can judge whether people have made such use of their opportunities as they ought to have made and how much effort of will or self-denial this has cost them; it presupposes also that we can distinguish between that part of their achievement which is due to circumstances within their control and that part which is not.[37]

Hayek's argument here does not pertain to hierarchies per se, but to rewards more generally. However, we can easily see how it can be adapted to (the justification of) hierarchies. If a society justifies the existence of hierarchies on grounds of merit, it has a duty of justice to ensure that the meritorious (and only the meritorious) get high positions. However, Hayek argues, the knowledge we need to ascertain this kind of merit is simply not available in a free society. Since free societies are, very likely, more efficient societies, we would have to jettison efficiency in order to arrive at a more meritorious society.

Some philosophers have tried to assuage these concerns. Miller (1999) and, more recently, Mulligan (2018) have argued that market rewards could at least in theory be much more closely connected to individual merit than Hayek and many others have thought.[38] If true, this would entail that there is no deep tension between efficiency and merit, and merit might no longer be precluded from playing a role in the justification

---

[37] Hayek (1960), p. 95.

[38] Compare also Olsaretti (2004) for a critical assessment of Miller's arguments.

of hierarchies themselves. Whether these arguments are ultimately successful is a question that cannot be answered in this chapter. Fortunately, we may not need to do so. For there is a second reason that speaks against referring to merit in the justification of the existence of hierarchies that is independent of Hayek's argument and, at least with regard to the justification of hierarchies, more powerful.

Indeed, it seems to me that when it comes to justifying the existence of hierarchies, we don't need to consider the relationship of merit and efficiency in the first place because merit, in itself, simply does not provide the relevant kind of justification. To see this, we need to understand how the question of hierarchy differs from that of earnings. When we discuss whether earnings in a society should mirror people's merit, we already take for granted some kind of system that produces those rewards. We assume that someone will get the rewards, and we ask who it should be. The idea that rewards should be allocated by merit is at least a candidate answer to this question.

The justification of hierarchies is different. Here, we are asking how the system itself should be built, and whether there should be any people who have a say over others in the first place. At this level, the fact that some people are more meritorious does not seem to generate the right kind of reasons. Consider, as an analogy, the *epistocratic* idea that knowledgeable people should govern.[39] This idea, I take it, has some initial appeal if we start from the assumption that someone needs to govern. If someone needs to govern, it can be argued, it should be the knowledgeable rather than the ignorant. Yet my hunch is that this tacitly draws on the assumption that knowledgeable people will make better decisions and that society will thus work better for everyone, which is an efficiency argument. In contrast, if someone were to tell us that they think knowledge itself grants people a right to govern, regardless of whether knowledgeable people actually govern better, most of us would arguably not consider this an argument at all.

The case is analogous for merit. The idea that the meritorious should be higher up in a hierarchy is ambiguous. It might just mean that the meritorious should be higher up, in contrast to those of the upper caste, or those who have been put there by their father-in-law. This, I think, is a valuable moral ideal. However, it is not the same as saying that merit itself justifies the existence of hierarchies. The fact that someone is good at a job or meets the requirements of an office is a reason to put them in those jobs or offices. It's not a reason to establish these jobs and offices. Miller makes a similar point about rewards when he claims that:

> Desert does not require that people be paid for productive work, but if people *are* paid for work of this kind, then those whose productivity is higher deserve, *ceteris paribus*, higher pay [...].[40]

Analogously, we can say that desert does not mandate that people be put above each other in hierarchies, but once hierarchies have been established, then those who

---

[39] Compare Brennan (2017) for a recent discussion.

[40] Miller (1999), p. 141.

are more meritorious deserve, *ceteris paribus*, to be in the higher positions.[41] One's personal talents and traits speak in one's favour when it comes to allocating high positions, they don't generate a duty for others to establish these positions.

This last position is what we might call a *fundamentally merit-based* justification of hierarchies. According to it, our institutions should be built in such a way as to best reflect our (moral) merit, with the more meritorious occupying higher places in society's hierarchies. This position, I think, is in tension with the spirit of liberal democracy, which assumes that our institutions should be built in a way to reflect our equality and freedom.[42]

13.4.2 Two Levels

If we want to avoid this tension, we have to dispens with considerations of merit when it comes to justifying the existence of hierarchies in our societies. Merit only enters the picture when it comes to providing justification for who occupies what position in a hierarchy and how we should relate to each other within a hierarchy. We thus arrive at a two-level justification of hierarchies.

Is this a good position to be at? There are at least two reasons why one might think it isn't, and considering them will help us get clearer about both what the position entails and whether it is an overall attractive position.

The first concern is that it is inconsistent to accord such weight to considerations of efficiency at one level but not the other. If efficiency considerations are strong enough to ground the existence of hierarchies in the first place, why aren't they sufficient to decide who occupies what position? The view seems contradictory. First, we acknowledge that the whole purpose of having hierarchies is to organise our societies in a more efficient way. Yet, second, when it comes to choosing the people who fill these hierarchies, we suddenly bring in other considerations that might sometimes even go against efficiency. Isn't that inconsistent? I don't think it is. There are two important points here. First, and most importantly, I do not claim that efficiency considerations play *no* role at the second level. There might well be cases where efficiency considerations are so strong that they outweigh any considerations of merit at the second level as well. Second, even where this isn't the case, it is important to appreciate that considerations of merit are not completely at odds with efficiency. Quite the opposite. In order to merit being in a certain position, one must have the talent and the competence to carry out the responsibilities that come with

---

[41] The 'ceteris paribus' clause is important because nothing in the account requires that there shouldn't be other considerations that come into play when we think about who should occupy which position in a hierarchy. For example, we might well think that considerations of need sometimes outweigh those of desert and the account is also neutral with regard to the idea that when certain historical injustices need to be corrected that can sometimes override considerations of merit.

[42] I am not sure how many people today actually defend this position. Mulligan (2017), p. 77 thinks that he is the only practicing philosopher who is fully committed to meritocracy, but I am not sure even he holds that we need hierarchies in order to give people what they deserve.

that position successfully. In so far as this is the case, merit and efficiency often go hand in hand.[43] However, third, and this is the point that the two examples in the previous section were supposed to drive home, considerations of efficiency and merit do not always lead to the same conclusions. Sometimes, merit goes against efficiency and, if my interpretation of the two examples is correct, we often have good reasons to go with merit in these cases. This is not inconsistent. It just shows that we want our societies to be governed by more than one value. We might value efficiency to the point of embracing hierarchies. However, we do not prefer every gain in efficiency over all other factors. Sometimes, we will prefer a less efficient scenario that is more in line with some of our other values, such as merit.

The second concern is whether we can't have everything we want without bringing in the notion of merit. This worry is particularly poignant since many philosophers, starting with Rawls (1971), have argued that there is a less worrisome notion in the vicinity that can provide what merit can't, namely the notion of *entitlement*. According to Rawls, even though we don't (strictly speaking) deserve the higher positions or wages that our talents secure for us, we can still be entitled to them. This is the case if considerations of justice at the fundamental level require such differences. In Rawls's case, the difference principle stipulates that such differences are justified if and only if they lead to a better overall situation for the worst-off. If certain hierarchical organisations lead to the worst-off in a society being better off and if I am the best person to have one of the high positions in such a hierarchy, then I am entitled to that position. Isn't that all we want to say? I don't think it is, and the reason why should have become clear in the revised version of the Jared example. In that version, a society agrees that nepotism is sometimes more efficient and therefore allows it in certain situations. But, as I have argued, this would not remove the charge against Jared. That charge rests on a notion of merit that is pre-institutional and that the notion of entitlement cannot capture.[44] As Schmidtz (2006, 32) puts it, the kind of critique that Rawls advances has no surgical precision. Instead, it is a wholesale critique that leaves us with only a substitute notion, that of institutional entitlements, which, as I have argued, cannot provide us with all the resources we need when it comes to the second level of justifying hierarchies.[45]

Other worries would have to be tackled in order to make a more decisive case for the two-level account. As this discussion shows, the two-level account is not the simplest or the most elegant. It would be a neater picture if we could generate the

---

[43] Indeed, one might think that the connection between efficiency and merit is even more straightforward. A company is usually more efficient precisely because the people higher-up in the hierarchy are meritorious, in the sense of having the talents required and the willingness to work hard. A hierarchy based on other factors, such as an aristocratic hierarchy, presumably isn't as efficient. This is true. However, one should not lose sight of the fact that Coase's and Williamson's arguments for the efficiency of firms are not in principle wedded to a specific principle of allocating the positions in the firm. Their general point is that organizing certain processes in a hierarchical way within a firm itself sometimes lowers transaction costs.

[44] Compare Feinberg (1970) and Kleinig (1971).

[45] One might still think that Rawls could appeal to some other, justice-based reason(s), besides entitlement to account for the wrongness of the Jared example.

justification for people inhabiting certain positions within a hierarchy on the same grounds as the justification for the existence of the hierarchy itself. However, this neatness does not seem to be available to me. Instead, we should be prepared to accept the fact that grounds for justification can sometimes draw us in different directions. A two-level account may be the best way to capture this. Its main advantage is not its simplicity, but that it allows us to refer to merit when it comes to an important part of the justification of hierarchies that neither considerations of efficiency nor considerations of mere entitlement can deliver. If merit can be saved from the sceptical attacks, we thus have good reason to give it an important place in our justification of hierarchies.

Acknowledgements I want to especially thank Alexander Andersson, Huub Brouwer, Willem van der Deijl-Kloeg, Eran Fish, David Miller and Toby Napoletano for valuable discussions, as well as my colleagues in Monika Betzler's *Bretznrunde* and *Research Colloquium*, students in the *CEPP-Talks* at LMU Munich, the audience at the *10th Law and Economics Conference* in Lucerne, and participants of the *Research Colloquium* at the Center for Ethics in Pardubice.

Bibliography

Anderson ES (1999) What is the point of equality? Ethics 109(2):287–337
Brennan, J (2017) Against democracy. Princeton
Brouwer H, Mulligan T (2019) Why not be a desertist? Three arguments for desert and against luck egalitarianism. Philos Stud 176(9):2271–2288
Coase R (1937) The nature of the firm. Economica 4(16):386–405
Feinberg J (1970) Justice and personal desert. In: Feinberg J (ed) Doing and Deserving. Princeton, pp. 221–250
Fourie C (2015) To praise and to scorn: the problem of inequalities of esteem for social egalitarianism. In: Fourie C, Schuppert F, Wallimann–Helmer I (eds) Social equality: on what it means to be equals. Oxford, pp. 87–106
Hayek FA (1960) The constitution of liberty. Chicago
Heath J (2014) Morality, competition, and the firm. Oxford
Kett JF (2013) Merit: the history of a founding ideal from the American revolution to the twenty-first century. Ithaca
Kleinig J (1971) The concept of desert. Am Philos Q 8(1):71–78
Kolodny N (2022) Towards an analysis of social hierarchy. J Contemp Legal Issues 23(2):261–281
Kolodny N (2023) The pecking order: social hierarchy as a philosophical problem. Cambridge
Miller D (1997) Equality and justice. Ratio 10(3):222–237
Miller D (1999) Principles of social justice. Cambridge
Mulligan T (2017) What's wrong with libertarianism: a meritocratic diagnosis. In: Brennan J, van der Vossen B, Schmidtz D (eds) The routledge handbook of libertarianism. Abingdon, pp. 77–91
Mulligan T (2018) Justice and the meritocratic state. Abingdon
Nozick R (1974) Anarchy, state, and utopia. Oxford
Olsaretti S (2003) Introduction: debating desert and justice. In: Olsaretti S (ed) Desert and justice. Oxford, pp. 1–24
Olsaretti S (2004) Liberty, desert and the market: a philosophical study. Cambridge
Pettit P (1997) Republicanism: a theory of freedom and government. Oxford
Pettit P (2012) On the people's terms: a republican theory and model of democracy. Cambridge
Pojman L (1997) Equality and desert. Philosophy 72(282):549–570

Rawls J (1971) A theory of justice. Cambridge

Rescher N (1995) Luck: the brilliant randomness of everyday life. New York

Rubin PH (2000) Hierarchy. Hum Nat 11(3):259–279

Runciman WG (1967) Social equality. Philos Quarterly 17(68):221–230

Sandel MJ (2020) The tyranny of merit. London

Scanlon TM (2018) Why does inequality matter? Oxford

Scheffler S (2000) Justice and desert in liberal theory. Calif Law Rev 88(3):965–990

Scheffler S (2003) What is egalitarianism? Philos Public Aff 31(1):5–39

Scheffler S (2005) Choice, circumstance, and the value of equality. Politics Philos Econ 4(1):5–28

Scheffler S (1992) Responsibility, reactive attitudes, and liberalism. In: Philosophy and politics. Philosophy and Public Affairs 21(4):299–323

Schmidtz D (2006) Elements of justice. Cambridge

Schuppert F (2015) Being equals: analyzing the nature of social egalitarian relationships. In: Fourie C, Schuppert F, Wallimann-Helmer I (eds) Social equality: on what it means to be equals. Oxford, pp. 107–26

Sher G (1979) Effort, ability, and personal desert. Philos Public Aff 8:361–376

Singer A (2018) The political nature of the firm and the cost of norms. J Polit 80(3):831–844

Walzer M (1983) Spheres of justice: a defense of pluralism and equality. New York

Williamson OE (1973) Markets and hierarchies: some elementary considerations. Am Econ Rev 63(2):316–325

Wolff J (2019) I-the presidential address: equality and hierarchy. Proc Aristot Soc 119(1):1–23

Wooldridge A (2021) The aristocracy of talent: how meritocracy made the modern world. London

Zaitchick A (1977) On deserving to deserve. Philos Public Aff 6(1):370–388

Chapter 14
The Ethics of Meritocratic Competition

Malte Dold and Andrew Gewecke

Abstract In this chapter we examine the preference-shaping power of meritocratic competition. On the centenary of Frank Knight's influential thesis that systems of competitive selection can cause pervasive shifts in our values, we use recent advances in behavioural economics and psychology to develop this philosophical assertion into a more structured critique of meritocratic institutions. Drawing on Knight's insights on the social context-dependence of preferences, we recommend that the use of meritocratic selection be subjected to public, iterative analysis that takes advantage of the norms of deliberative democracy. Meritocracy has notable strengths, including its emphasis on the priority of equality of opportunity and its direction of social activities towards efficiency. But even at its best, it can exercise a subtle and domineering effect on our values and our perceptions if it is applied excessively. In understanding where competitive norms can be deployed to positive effect, and where they might do more harm than good, we better equip ourselves to determine meritocracy's proper boundaries.

14.1 Introduction

The principle of meritocracy—the idea, broadly speaking, that individuals should receive rewards according to their abilities and efforts—has emerged as the main principle used to organise economic and social institutions in modern societies.[1] For instance, it plays a dominant role in our current systems of educational evaluation (e.g., college admission) and professional assessment (e.g., hiring and promotion decisions). Meritocracy is widely considered to be society's main tool for generating wealth and allocating positions, power, and prestige.[2] Because it exercises such a profound influence on the present experiences and future prospects of almost every

---

[1] See Wooldridge (2021).

[2] See Sen (2000).

M. Dold (✉) · A. Gewecke
Pomona College, Claremont, US
e-mail: malte.dold@pomona.edu

263

K. Mathis and A. Tor (eds.), *Law and Economics of Justice*, Economic Analysis of Law
in European Legal Scholarship 17, https://doi.org/10.1007/978-3-031-56822-0_14

member of society, it is crucial that it be subjected to a particularly thorough investigation before it is accepted as a guiding principle of our social, economic, and political systems.

The most common critique of meritocracy is one which we call the *implementation objection*. This strain of criticism identifies meritocratic selection as a noble ideal that has been implemented imperfectly, but which would be laudable if it was put into practice in its purest, uncorrupted form.[3] These arguments suggest that societies that are superficially "meritocratic" are still unfair in the sense that individuals are not given the opportunities to compete on an equal footing. Arbitrary principles of distribution, such as "tradition... sexual and racial prejudice... [and] the natural desire to favour one's friends and relations" pollute the meritocratic allocation process.[4] But, if these confounding variables are eliminated, critics should be satisfied: "there is no reason in principle why an advanced industrial society in which the market plays a central role shouldn't be meritocratic."[5] The central aim of this chapter is to question this conclusion. We argue that even an ideal meritocratic society, in which rewards are consistently allocated according to ability and effort, would come at a social cost that is not to be underestimated. Specifically, it might change the preferences and beliefs of people, "making *emulation* and *rivalry* the outstanding quality in the character[s]" of the actors who routinely engage in meritocratic competition.[6] While "emulation and rivalry" might be productive values in certain areas of social life (e.g., hiring and promotion decisions), they might lead to problematic results in others (e.g., in education and schooling) as we will argue in this chapter.

One of meritocracy's primary strengths is that it disregards baselessly unfair standards of value. It does not recognise the propriety of inheritance, prejudice, aristocracy, or other systems of allocation that arbitrarily and disproportionately favour some individuals over others. It is intensely concerned with the matter of equality of opportunity; all competitors should get the same chance of success, regardless of who they are, and normatively irrelevant factors such as race, sex, or traditional prejudice should have no bearing on whether they succeed or not. Against systems of wealth allocation that do not even support this basic tenet of equality of opportunity, meritocracy is a powerful and welcome advocate. It is also a system that is well-suited to enhance the productivity of our institutions, since, when it works correctly, it allocates positions based on who is most qualified for them. We do not intend to contest these strengths. Nor do we aim to advance a critique of market competition, per se. Rather, we want to highlight a weakness of meritocracy that we believe is not given sufficient weight in current debates, and to explore how we might address this shortcoming. We take our cue here from the work of the famous economist Frank Knight on the preference-shaping power of institutions.

One hundred years ago, Knight published the essay *The Ethics of Competition* (1923) in which he posed a question that targeted the core of our relationship

---

[3] See Wooldridge (2021); Miller (1999) and Marshall and Swift (1993).

[4] See Miller (1999), p. 179.

[5] Ibid.

[6] See Knight (1923), p. 586, emphasis added.

with our economic institutions: how does competition change us? The question is a notable one, especially since in the decades after his work, during which neoclassical economics evolved as an axiomatised, highly abstract theory, the effect of competition on people's values was largely considered to be null. Viewed generally, individuals in neoclassical theory are modelled as agents with stable preferences who choose rationally among options that lie within their budget constraints. In doing so, individuals are assumed to exercise a profound agency: they cannot always control their environment, but their reaction to it is always a rational response to changes in relative prices. The methodological perspective is, accordingly, individualistic.[7] The relationship between the agent and the institution is clearly demarcated: the agent reacts to and engages with but is not shaped by their institutional environment. Thus, Stigler and Becker would respond to Knight's question by maintaining that an agent's preferences are not changed by their environment. Hence, for economic analysis "one may usefully treat tastes as stable over time and similar among people."[8]

In his essay, Knight takes a more radical view. He asserts that our participation in competitive production and consumption can change our character: "[w]hile men are 'playing the game' of business, they are also moulding their own and other personalities."[9] Being repeatedly exposed to competitive situations can change our preferences: "the economic order does far more than select and compare wants for exchangeable goods and services: its activity extends to the formation and radical transformation, if not to the outright creation, of the wants themselves."[10] All told, the individual "is in large measure a product of the economic system, which is a fundamental part of the cultural environment that has formed his desires and needs."[11] Knight does not mean to credit the economic system alone with such a power. The general claim that our social environments have the capacity to influence our character is broadly applicable, and indeed could be applied to "most of education, and of civilisation in general; for most of the desires which distinguish man from the brutes are artificially created."[12] But his argument has particular force when applied to economic institutions that aim to enhance competition precisely because prevailing neoclassical theory has often failed to acknowledge the ways in which competition can shape the preferences and beliefs of individuals.

---

[7] See Dold (forthcoming).

[8] See Stigler and Becker (1977), p. 76.

[9] See Knight (1923), p. 587.

[10] Id., p. 585.

[11] Id., p. 590.

[12] Id., p. 585.

14.2 The Preference-Shaping Power of the Social Environment

Recent research in behavioural economics and psychology has given Knight's arguments new empirical force. In an overview article, Hoff and Stiglitz orient the claim that a person's social and institutional environment can shape their preferences and beliefs within an empirical behavioural economics literature.[13] They class the process of endogenous preference formation as part of *strand II behavioural economics*, a subfield concerned with environmental effects that change the way we reason and perceive the world around us in lasting ways. *Strand I behavioural economics*, conversely, examines more ephemeral situational influences (such as informational framing or the order of items on a menu) that affect individual choices without changing an agent's preferences and beliefs on a deeper level. Both types of effects operate by influencing the formation and selection of our *cultural mental models*.[14] These are the durable sets of preconceptions and value standards that we use when we process information and categorise the world around us. Individuals can subscribe to multiple competing mental models, and environmental cues affect how a person's attention is distributed between these various perspectives. Different contexts make different mental models more salient, affecting which one ultimately influences a person's decision-making. The decisions a person makes at any given moment are thus influenced by both the external cues that emphasise some mental models over others (strand I behavioural economics), and the formation of mental models that can theoretically be cued (strand II behavioural economics). The process of preference formation is best understood in terms of this mental model alteration. For instance, repeated exposure to the competitive logic at play within a meritocratic system activates a mental model that highlights competitive values, such as rivalry and emulation. The activated mental model alters the things that motivate us and the way we see ourselves and others (more on this below). Preference shifts occur when repeated external environmental stimuli change the composition and interplay of our various mental models which then express themselves in altered patterns of behaviour.[15]

Importantly, once our preferences change, they can have a much greater influence on our behaviour than we might at first assume. Bowles argues that "institutions may induce specific behaviours—self-regarding, opportunistic, or cooperative, say— which then become part of the behavioural repertoire of the individual."[16] This means that preferences that are internalised in one environment are often generalised to other unrelated ones. Various programs of empirical research have conceived of different ways of describing this phenomenon, but the basic principle that underlies it can be framed within the theory of cultural mental models outlined above. When

---

[13] See Hoff and Stiglitz (2016).

[14] See Dold (2022).

[15] See Dold and Lewis (2022).

[16] See Bowles (1998), p. 80.

environmental stimuli emphasise one mental model over others, the preferences associated with that mental model become more salient in the individual's mind. When said preferences become susceptible to activation by cues that are distinct from the ones that initially triggered them, we can say that they have been generalised to new situations. This phenomenon is captured by the notion of "behavioral spillover," defined as what occurs when an "attempt to encourage behavior change" has an effect on "subsequent behaviors" that it does not aim to influence.[17] A cascade of preferences in the form of behavioural spillover effects can be socially productive, e.g., in the case of generalised values of reciprocity or solidarity. However, they can also be problematic, e.g., when the values of competitiveness or rivalry that are inherent in meritocratic contests extend beyond our professional identity and affect how we structure our relationships in the private sphere.

The identity that we attribute to ourselves plays a significant role in the process of preference generalisation. As Truelove et al. point out, "when a social identity is salient, individuals report the feeling of an 'inner obligation to act' to uphold the relevant group's goals."[18] Moreover, "perceived norms of what is typical or desirable in a given situation are also known to be powerful motivators of behavior."[19] Our adoption of an identity furnishes us with a set of values which can in turn be activated by environmental cues. By making particular facets of our identities more salient, the environments we encounter can produce far-reaching changes in our preferences and beliefs. Empirical research on the effect of occupation on behavioural spillovers can help make this point more concrete. Different jobs bring with them different norms, and a person's membership in an occupational group can make up a notable part of their self-conception. Cohn et al.'s investigation of the effect of norms maintained by the banking industry bears out this hypothesis.[20] Making banking employees' occupations salient to them before an experimental task, which asks subjects to honestly report the results of coin flips, produces a higher incidence of cheating in those employees. Each employee in the treatment group is asked before the task to answer questions about the details of their employment that are meant to remind them of their occupation. Cohn et al. posit that, in priming this consciousness of occupation in these subjects, they cue whatever set of preferences those subjects usually adopt as employees of their bank. The higher incidence of cheating, conducted during a test that has no bearing whatsoever on the world of banking or the obligations of the subjects' jobs, suggests a consequent spillover effect. A certain facet of the subjects' identities is emphasised, and the subjects, striving to conform to that identity, conjure up the norms that they usually maintain as employees and apply them to a new environment. Of course, studies such as these do not predict in which way meritocratic institutions shape our preferences and beliefs. However, they suggest that the preferences and beliefs we acquire in meritocratic settings (such as schooling or work environments) can have behavioural

---

[17] See Truelove et al. (2014), pp. 127 et seq.; see also Weck-Hannemann and Frey (1995).

[18] See Truelove et al. (2014), p. 131.

[19] Ibid.

[20] See Cohn et al. (2014).

spillover effects into other areas of our lives—in particular, if we are exposed to cues in the decision environment in those other areas that trigger a meritocratic competitive logic (for instance on dating apps or social media).

14.3 Education: A Case Study in Meritocratic Socialisation

Meritocracy is present in many stages and spheres of life, but its ability to change preferences is particularly visible in the realm of education.[21] Meritocratic competition is a pervasive factor in educational institutions, at play in the formal assessments taken by students, the pressure created by constant evaluations, and the performance-based allocation of scarce positions after school, such as in higher education and the job market.[22] Moreover, research suggests that people are most likely to invest time and effort in competitive procedures with extra psychological significance when they are in their formative years, and student's educational experience often provides this formative influence.[23] Thus, education is a stage of life in which meritocratic logic is both especially observable and especially impactful. It provides a jumping-off point from which to describe the norms at play in meritocratic competition more generally, to analyse the process by which those norms might be internalised, and to identify what values might be lost if the preference structure of meritocratic competition is prioritised to the exclusion of other normative considerations.

The example set by the educational institutions and atmosphere encountered by a student can have a profound effect on the preferences and beliefs that a student comes to hold. As Butera et al. point out, "there is a consistent relationship between the goal structure in which the students are embedded and the goals they endorse."[24] These goals, moreover, can lead to behavioural spillovers when they become incorporated into the way students view the world around them, even when they are not in an explicitly competitive educational environment. As Ryan and Reeve note, "people can bring all the external-environmental elements of the competitive situation into themselves, and further, these intrapersonal events have motivational effects that mimic those of their corresponding external events."[25] Indeed, "repeated exposure to a competitive structure may create a self-sufficient competitive ethos that requires little additional input from the teachers."[26] Students who internalise this ethos are liable to deploy it preemptively, "project[ing] competition onto their environment" even when such a projection is unwarranted.[27] Habitual exposure to competitive goals can produce a tendency to reference those goals automatically and excessively.

---

[21] See Markovits (2019).

[22] See Butera et al. (2021).

[23] See Converse et al. (2022).

[24] See Butera et al. (2021), Goal Structure, para. 2.

[25] See Ryan and Reeve (2021), CET Proposition 5, para. 2.

[26] See Butera et al. (2021), Goal Structure, para. 2.

[27] Ibid.

In this way, competition becomes an enduring norm and a default in a student's repertoire of behaviour.

The process we have just described frames the competitive perspective as a psychological response developed by persistent environmental stimuli. The behaviour of multiple competing students should be viewed through the same lens, and it is with this vocabulary that we will characterise the phenomenon Knight called "rivalry." That social comparison is a driving factor of competitive behaviour is a well-established idea.[28] More relevant to our thesis of preference formation is the fact that the details of this social comparison perception can be unique to the competing students. Converse et al. characterise rivalry as "a subjective competitive relationship that an actor has with another actor that entails increased psychological stakes of competition for the focal actor, independent of the objective characteristics of the situation."[29] A student engaged in a rivalry is not concerned only with the material consequences of their actions. Their performance in such a competition has typically psychological weight that is often not justified by the contest's stakes. Rivalries arise over "things about whose significance, beyond furnishing objectives for the competition itself, little question is asked."[30] Accordingly, the behaviour of rival students is often affected by factors that change their subjective experiences of a contest without altering its strategic aspects. The personalities of the competitors, their affective states, the size of a contest, and the degree of publicity it is afforded can all affect competitor behaviour, and often the choices that competing agents make under these pressures, such as overbidding and excess entry, are disproportionate given the stakes involved.[31]

Preferences are further altered by the second process Knight refers to: emulation. By "emulation" we refer to the efforts of imitation that students often undertake when vying for rewards. Meritocratic competition must, in measuring multiple students against a single metric of performance, refer to some external standard of value. Accordingly, it is to this standard of value that hopeful competitors must tailor their activity. Students engaged in the competition, therefore, have the incentive to model their behaviour not only on the theoretical ideal presented by such a standard, but also on the conduct of those competitors that most closely achieve such an ideal. In creating this incentive, competitive selection exerts a homogenising influence on individual students. While such an effect could serve to orient behaviour according to some individually and socially productive goal, it could also impose an external standard of value on students that subtly shapes or undermines their own views. When this standard is over-applied in a meritocracy, the effect is one of value compression. To succeed in a process of meritocratic competition, a student's value system has to be narrow and targeted to the chosen competitive goal. When these priorities become excessively internalised, they effect other values unrelated to the contest being pursued, and it is when this process occurs that what began as an instrumental

---

[28] See Festinger (1954) and Garcia et al. (2013).

[29] See Converse et al (2022), Rivalry in Nature, para. 6.

[30] See Knight (1923), p. 587.

[31] See Haran and Bereby-Meyer (2022).

tool for success in a contest becomes an enduring facet of a student's character. Such a shift is precisely what Knight references when he argues that "success in a contest" is classed, not only as a method of gaining some reward but as a more fundamental "ethical value."[32]

The overemphasis on this particular ethical standard can lead to what Samuel Bowles has termed the "crowding-out" of other priorities.[33] The standard of measurable achievement that often predominates in educational settings, for example, incentivises the adoption of a particular competitive mental model. When values of personal flourishing are overshadowed by values of competitive success, the intrinsic motivation of students can erode. An educational program meant to produce measurable improvement and, eventually, a stable progression into the job market risks ensuring that "the development of knowledge is... subordinated to the criteria of usefulness, scalability, and efficiency."[34] A loss of intrinsically motivated goals can have far-reaching consequences for students' well-being and life choices, especially when it is internalised in the manner discussed above. Research in behavioural economics suggests indeed that a reliance on external rewards to incentivise particular behaviours in an attempt to maximise efficiency can crowd out intrinsic motivations with problematic individual and social consequences.[35]

A hyper-focus on individual achievement can also weaken students' social bonds. The variety of competition that is most germane to meritocratic institutions, particularly those related to education, is the *tournament*, whereby "competition takes the form of an incentive system that links players' rewards to their rank among competitors on a focal dimension, rather than to their absolute performance or result on that dimension."[36] Performance in tournaments is judged according to an external standard, and rewards are allocated solely based on how a student ranks relative to the others in the group. As a result, students exposed to particularly competitive tournament environments are less likely to act on social or other-regarding preferences. For example, "competitive social comparison in classrooms... [elicits] extrinsic and performance-oriented personal goals, which in turn result in a greater propensity to cheat."[37] Such a finding should not be surprising when the importance of a student's results in the classroom is continually highlighted without a corresponding emphasis on the importance of obtaining those results appropriately. More generally, people acting in a competitive frame display a higher predilection towards sabotaging, exploiting, and bullying their rivals.[38] They demonstrate a "reduce[d]... willingness to help their competitors... [and an increased] propensity to inflict punishment

---

[32] See Knight (1923), p. 586.

[33] See Bowles (2016).

[34] See Butera et al. (2021), Productivism, para. 1.

[35] See Wrzesniewski et al. (2014); Gneezy and Rustichini (2000) and White and Sheldon (2014).

[36] See Haran and Bereby-Meyer (2022), Rank-Order Tournaments, para. 1.

[37] See Butera et al. (2021), Cheating, para. 1.

[38] Ibid.

upon each other."[39] They can exhibit a greater degree of aggressive or unsportspersonlike behaviour and a diminished propensity for prosocial collaboration, and they can experience a decline in their personal relationships.[40] Further research identifies similar effects resulting from a pronounced emphasis on external rewards, which is often brought about by an emphasis on tournament competition.[41] An excessive application of competitive values can therefore equip students with preferences that are more individualistic, more self-serving, less invested in social rules, and less concerned with social cohesion or collaboration.

Finally, the internalisation of a competitive ethic influences the way students view themselves in relation to their competitors. Meritocratic competition in education is built on a narrative of desert; rewards are allocated based on performance, and those who receive the most, or least, are classed as the most, or least, deserving. When meritocratic competition in education is implemented poorly, this rationale can malfunction in two ways, either by obscuring systemic inequality with a false promise that a student will in the future be offered an equal chance to advance according to their merits, or by justifying said inequalities with the claim that entrenched hierarchy is the product of fair competition.[42] But even when meritocratic competition in education is implemented well it can be damaging, because the losers of competitive games are faced with the judgment that they have earned their failure. This narrative leaves those who lose competitions with an indigestible sense of themselves: "For those who can't find work or make ends meet, it is hard to escape the demoralizing thought that their failure is their own doing, that they simply lack the talent and drive to succeed."[43] Michael Young, the scholar who first coined the term "meritocracy" in 1958, echoes this sentiment. "It is hard indeed in a society that makes so much of merit," he says, "to be judged as having none. No underclass has ever been left as morally naked as that."[44]

The goal of this critique is not to argue that the losers of meritocratic competition in education are entitled to different institutional arrangements simply because they are unsatisfied with their own position. Rather, criticism should aim at the socialising facets of competitive selection that, even after allocating praise according to performance, establish a narrative surrounding failure that is both unnecessary and damaging. The way in which a student is treated after losing a competition has a significant effect on the way their self-perception changes. Students have a psychological need to feel that they are, to some degree, good at what they do.[45] But, crucially, "it is perceived competence (rather than the objective competitive outcome

[39] See Haran and Bereby-Meyer (2022), When competition becomes counterproductive, para. 1.

[40] See Ryan and Reeve (2021).

[41] See Cardenas et al. (2000) and Kasser et al. (2007).

[42] See Butera et al. (2021).

[43] See Sandel (2020), p. 26.

[44] See Young (2001).

[45] See Ryan and Deci (2017).

per se) that explains variations in intrinsic motivation."[46] Students' perceived competence depends in large part on the feedback they receive after competing. When such feedback acknowledges their strengths and points them towards areas for growth, it is "informational," and such assessment can "communicate or aid one's sense of effectance" instead of "frustrat[ing] a sense of competence."[47] Crucially, a student can enjoy the benefits of this effectance-promoting feedback even after a relatively bad outcome in educational assessments. Indeed, when such feedback is present, the "motivational profile[s]" of the outcompeted student can in some cases become "interchangeable with [those of] competitive winners."[48]

The negative self-perception that Sandel and Young refer to arises when this beneficial assessment is replaced by what Ryan and Reeve call "*ego-involvement*," defined as motivation driven by self-esteem concerns."[49] Ego-involvement occurs when "a competitor has internalised external contingencies such that they now define their own worth in terms of competitive success."[50] Such a mindset is indicative of a domineering overemphasis on the importance of competitive performance; recall Knight's claim that "success in a contest" is often treated as an unduly influential "ethical value." The ethical freight involved in this characterisation, and the influence it has on the self-perceptions of students, is significant, especially because nothing in the definition of meritocracy requires that this influence be negative.

It is important that we duly consider these psychological phenomena because the norms inculcated in students during the educational process are liable to be generalised into society at large when those students graduate. As Butera et al. explain, the interplay between educational institutions and broad social norms creates an ideological feedback loop: "students socialized at school with values derived from the dominant ideologies in society will later contribute to those same ideologies by perpetuating them."[51] The analysis of the effects of competition in education thus motivates a more general examination of the effects of meritocracy on the values and norms of society.

14.4   A Deliberative Examination of Meritocracy

Meritocratic competition has the potential to exercise a domineering effect on its agents. This is true not only because the competitive social games we play with each other on a day-to-day basis change what we value in the abstract, but because many of our current institutions emphasise these competitive games to such an extent that any preference changes they cause will likely be particularly pervasive. People are

---

[46] See Ryan and Reeve (2021), Feedback and Competitive Outcome, para. 3.

[47] Id., CET Proposition 2, para. 1.

[48] Id., Feedback and Competitive Outcome, para. 3.

[49] Id., Ego-involvement, para 1, emphasis in original.

[50] Ibid.

[51] Butera et al. (2021), Conclusions, para. 2.

introduced to meritocracy early when they compete for grades in school. Competition for grades is eventually linked to competition for admission to higher education and, after that, competition for job placement. Those who secure jobs compete in turn to advance their careers. Thus, an individual in a meritocratic system might find that large portions of their professional and social lives, beginning in school and continuing until retirement, are guided by the competitive principle.[52] Moreover, the effects of such immersion may be largely unchosen by agents. By and large, it seems fair to say that we do not take sufficient account of the effect of meritocratic competitionn on our motivational setup and our cultural mental models—on how we perceive ourselves and others. And, regardless, actors have few alternatives to competition if they hope to be financially secure and socially acknowledged. It is easy, in other words, to take meritocracy for granted, even when the consequences of continuous meritocratic competition are problematic for individual well-being and intrinsic motivation as well as social values, such as empathy and solidarity. Thus, following Knight's seminal 1923 article, the central recommendation of this chapter is to call for a critical and inclusive examination of whether the effects that meritocracy has on people's motivations and values are defensible or not.

14.4.1 Public Deliberation

Knight places a high premium on public deliberation, treating "social institutions as a product of social choice based on social knowledge of patterns between which choice is made, and has meaning only insofar as such social choice may be real."[53] Our existing meritocratic institutions fit poorly with this priority. People are exposed to their effects consistently, including during their formative years, are offered few alternatives, and, if anything, are liable to become more automatically and indiscriminately attached to meritocratic norms as they are more firmly internalised. A return to a Knightian scheme of public deliberation is therefore appropriate. Deliberation should be public, inclusive and egalitarian.[54] It then can help make people more aware of the interplay between institutions and preferences and inform their institutional choices.

Deliberative public discourse is well-suited addressing the problems we have examined in this chapter. Our current meritocratic institutions have the potential to change preferences in ways that people have not sufficiently acknowledged or examined. Meritocratic institutions have become reliant on a narrow, rather than a pluralistic, allocative principle of desert (typically measured by simple evaluative variables such as grades, GPAs, or degrees from prestigious institutions). And they are entrenched in almost every aspect of our society when they should instead be subjected to critical reassessment. A deliberative examination of our institutions helps

---

[52] See Markovits (2019).

[53] See Knight (1942), p. 285.

[54] See Sandel (2020) and Bruni and Santori (2022).

ameliorate these concerns. As Habermas has argued, deliberation, carried out in "a public sphere in which the communicative practices of opinion- and will-formation would occur," is meant to promote "autonomy and self-realisation."[55] It is through this manifestation of popular sovereignty that political and institutional authority is legitimated.[56] Accordingly, discourse justifies, among other things, the ways we allocate resources and positions in society. Habermas adds a crucial caveat: these justificatory "normative reasons" keep their integrity "only to the extent that the political system does not, for its part, steer the very production of these reasons."[57] The discourse in question must be personal—to the greatest extent possible, it should not be a product of the institutions that already exist. The socialising power of our current meritocracy cuts against this condition. Its ability to change our preferences and beliefs acts as an institutional force with the potential to unduly influences the reasons we bring to bear in public deliberations. As Habermas points out, a deliberative frame views the current state of a society as "the rationally motivated but *fallible* result of an attempt to determine what is right through a discussion that has been brought to a *provisional* close under the pressure to decide."[58] We have noted above how early, and how extensively, students encounter the forces of meritocratic competition and selection. Habermas suggests that such an overwhelming push in one direction is not in the spirit of deliberative democracy. The institutions we establish discursively should always be open to revision. Especially when our preferences are multifaceted, to begin with and changeable over time, the unitary system of allocation that we have now might not be normatively appropriate.

In processes of public deliberation, Knight did not think that economic reasoning and moral reasoning should occupy the same sphere of discourse: "Rational economic behaviour where individuals use the best available means to realise given ends subject to constraints" formed a distinct brand of reasoning for Knight.[59] "Value deliberation where the 'evaluation of the end is the main deliberative problem'" constituted a wholly separate mode of reasoning.[60] The former instrumental rationality is a means towards preference satisfaction. But the satisfaction of preferences should not automatically be taken as a valid ethical principle. As Knight argues: "we cannot accept want-satisfaction as a final criterion of value because we do not in fact regard our wants as final; instead of resting in the view that there is no disputing about tastes, we dispute about them more than anything else; our most difficult problem in valuation is the evaluation of our wants themselves and our most troublesome want is the desire for wants of the 'right' kind."[61] From a Knightian perspective, therefore, the question of what our wants *ought to be* should be strictly differentiated from the question of how our wants, once we select them, should be fulfilled. A passive acceptance of

---

[55] See Habermas (1997), pp. 52 and 41.

[56] Id., p. 39.

[57] Id., p. 56.

[58] Id., p. 47, emphasis in original.

[59] See Hands (2022), p. 6.

[60] Ibid.

[61] See Knight (1923), p. 580.

the meritocratic logic undermines this project, especially if we acknowledge that the social institutions we endorse passively have the ability to alter our preferences in their favour. Following Knight and Habermas, we ought instead to determine our wants via open, public discourse. In this process, Knight believed that "there were no formulas or rules for success in social science and policy, only the hard work of pursuing the conversation about who we are and want to be."[62]

According to Knight, individuals should discuss different value standards in the public arena based on the 'given' ethical ideals that exist in a society as "relatively absolutes."[63] Knight is optimistic that ethical discussions can contribute to a partial ranking of the "goodness of wants" since moral standards of character or personality are "part of our culture and are sufficiently uniform to form a useful standard of comparison for a given country at a given time."[64] Even if they disagree often, most people base their moral judgments on the same, or similar, broad principles: "No one contends that a bottle of old wine is ethically worth as much as a barrel of flour, or a fantastic evening wrap for some potentate's mistress as much as a substantial dwelling-house."[65] Knight adds: "people do manage to 'understand each other' more or less, in conversation about things which are not matters of scientific fact, but of interpretation, as in discussions of art and of character or personality."[66] People will often disagree in their normative positions, but the discussion of values does not need to result in consensus to be productive. More important is a question which Knight answers in the positive: can interlocutors find enough initial common ground to communicate effectively and agree upon a partial ranking of values?

Knight's argument is a crucial one because it allows for the activity of critical ethical comparison in academic economics that has often been characterised by a bid for strict value neutrality. Convention in economics would normally frown on the categorisation of some goods as intrinsically more valuable than others. Even if Knight is correct in assuming that no one would value *haute couture* over shelter, such a judgment would have weight in the neoclassical sphere only as a guide to what consumers would prefer and, accordingly, to what the market supplies. It would not be taken to reveal anything about the fundamental worth of wraps or homes. We aim to go beyond this variety of minimalist analysis. The type of discussion we recommend in this chapter belongs to the field of normative, rather than positive, economics. It is, in fact, in an important sense political, in that it calls for debate over how our institutions should be structured. Recall the distinction that Knight makes between economic and ethical reasoning. Our institutions are at their weakest when we insist that, because they are ultimately concerned with economic activity, they should only be assessed with the tools of economic reasoning. We should instead maintain that, concerned as they are with the well-being of the people in our society, institutions should be the subject of ethical analysis.

---

[62] See Emmett (1999), p. ix.

[63] See Knight (1923), p. 584.

[64] Id., p. 583.

[65] Id., p. 598.

[66] Id., p. 617.

Knight contends that ethical discussions are necessary for the harmonisation of economic prosperity with individual flourishing. When individuals take part in ethical discourse, "[they] are impelled to look for ends in the economic process itself, other than the mere consumption of the produce, and to give thoughtful consideration to the possibilities of participation in economic activity as a sphere of self-expression and creative achievement."[67] By exposing themselves to a wide range of normative opinions in ethical discussions, individuals become aware of their unexamined convictions, which can in turn spur conscious reflection and active choice of their wants and values. In other words, it makes them take up a more general point of view.[68] Knight's proposal is provocative and many economists might dismiss it at the outset. However, it is close to a modern position advocated by Cowen that "[p]referred policies, including laissez-faire, must ultimately be judged not only on traditional efficiency grounds, but also as a program for favoring one set of preferences over another. While we cannot eliminate the arbitrariness in policy evaluation, we should at least be more explicit about the subjective nature of the underlying values we choose to promote."[69]

14.4.2 An Endorsement of Pluralism

We have so far argued that, when competitive norms are unduly emphasised in agents' psychological landscape, their preferences can change in problematic ways. However, this effect is not a necessary consequence of the logic of meritocratic competition. In fact, competitive logic, applied in the right context in the right way, can actually increase an agent's intrinsic motivation and well-being. As Ryan and Reeve point out: "by decreasing the salience of competition's controlling, pressuring, and needs-frustrating elements and increasing the salience of its informational and needs-satisfying elements, competitors' intrinsic motivation and positive experiences can be enhanced."[70] The problem of competition in general, and of meritocratic competition in particular, is thus one of meaning and degree. Competitive stimuli that are well-crafted, and applied only in particular circumstances, can be welfare-enhancing. If they provide agents with positive feedback, showing where they perform well and how they might improve, they can "strongly satisfy needs for competence, and in doing so enhance intrinsic motivation."[71] Conversely, if they are deployed so frequently that they are internalised by actors, referenced habitually and in inappropriate contexts, and inflated until they begin to crowd out other important goals and norms, they can shift preferences in individually and socially problematic ways.

---

[67] Id., p. 602.

[68] See Lewis and Dold (2020).

[69] See Cowen (1993), p. 267.

[70] Ryan and Reeve (2021), Bright and Dark Sides, para 1.

[71] Id., CET Proposition 2, para. 3.

In light of this analysis, one core question guiding institutional reform should be that of differentiation. The meritocratic principle is a narrow one, appropriate in some contexts but too single-edged for ubiquitous application. There are some situations in which resources should likely not be allocated according to the principle of merit, and where our perceptions of ourselves and others should not be tied to how well we compete against each other. We can currently observe in our society situations in which one's performance in competition begins to have a bearing even on whether one can procure basic needs. The result is a jarring contrast between an apparently defensible principle of meritocracy and a set of outcomes that are at times unconscionable. This shortcoming is the product of an excessive application of a potentially helpful principle—an imbalance caused when we accept meritocratic competition as the only means to allocate resources. But even proponents of meritocracy reject this idea. As Miller argues, "[m]erit of any sort should only be allowed to govern the distribution of a certain range of goods and services, and in particular not those goods and services that people regard as necessities, such as health care."[72] Diverse standards should inform who gets what. Miller insists, for example, that "the meritocratic allocation of jobs and rewards needs to be offset by a robust form of equal citizenship" that is the controlling principle for goods such as health care and education.[73] In this case, one's status as a citizen would provide an entitlement that would exist independently of what one deserved in the competitive system. If this is true, the provision of some goods ought to depend on one's citizenship entitlement, while other goods could be allocated based on meritocratic competition.

A similar measure could address the deficiency of esteem that Sandel and Young describe. Bell has argued, for example, that the only type of justifiable meritocracy is one in which "one can still observe the equality of respect due to all and the differential degree of praise owed to some."[74] Here we have another entitlement that could be conceived of as existing independently of the meritocratic standard: that of equal respect. One could attach tangible goods to this type of entitlement, possibly returning to the topic of basic needs. Thus, an entitlement to sufficient housing could, for example, be justified by one's status as a citizen and a claimant of universal respect, instead of as the victor of a competitive social game.[75] When we adopt this type of value pluralism, the challenge becomes identifying which spheres of life demand an increased emphasis on which allocative principles. The process by which we draw these conclusions should be public and collaborative, guided by the standards of public, normative deliberation outlined above.

It could also be the case that, while value pluralism might be an appropriate goal, a neat differentiation between those spheres of life where merit should be

---

[72] See Miller (1999), p. 200.

[73] Ibid.

[74] See Bell (1972), p. 68.

[75] A helpful blueprint for this type of theoretical work might be the capabilities approach developed by Amartya Sen (1999) and, later, Martha Nussbaum (2011). Such a project asserts that there exist some human capacities that a society should empower its citizens to cultivate if it is to be considered "minimally just" (Nussbaum 2011, 28). Within this paradigm, the resources allocated to each agent depend not only on conditions of merit, but also on conditions of justice.

the sole principle of allocation and those where it should not be applied might be illusory. Scott et al., for instance, argue that such rigid reasoning does not come naturally to people.[76] The current preeminence of the meritocratic principle does not correspond to the views people generally hold about how resources should be allocated. A meritocratic system relies on a single principle (desert/merit) to decide who should get what. But Scott et al. find that agents do not only consider questions of merit when asked to rank different distributions of hypothetical resources from "very bad" to "very good." They also value principles of need, equality, and efficiency. And, crucially, these different standards interact with each other: "most individuals use all or most of these principles simultaneously in making judgments rather than applying different norms in separate 'spheres.'"[77] The majority of the subjects in Scott et al.'s study, for example, used "both equality and efficiency as allocation principles and [made] tradeoffs between them."[78] In the light of these results, it may be the wrong question to identify a discrete sphere within which meritocratic logic can be applied. Going forward, the task for our deliberative populace may be to make our institutions reflect our pluralistic allocative values, and to decide where particular values should have the most weight.

These results help ground Knight's conceptualisation of institutions in general and the economic sphere in particular, as places that are not dominated solely by the singular values of competition and comparison. The idea that the social realm of "economic activity" could be seen as "a sphere of self-expression and creative achievement" makes more sense when it is oriented within Scott et al.'s project. It should not be taken as a given that the allocation of positions and resources within modern institutions must be as relentlessly meritocratic as it currently tends to be. If humans are disposed to simultaneously apply multiple standards of value to particular types of institutions, it may be possible to recast those institutions as places to cultivate multiple types of value. Nor should an excessive use of meritocratic competition and selection be justified by the fear that the only other alternative is an abandonment of the principle of equality of opportunity and an endorsement of aristocratic prejudice. Revising a system that is currently over-applied is not equivalent to nullifying its positive effects. And the principles that, for example, Scott et al. identify as potential competitors with that of merit (i.e., need, equality, and efficiency) are diverse and often egalitarian in their content, not narrowly hierarchical or oppressive.

---

[76] See Scott et al. (2001).

[77] Id., p. 762.

[78] Id., p. 756.

14.5   Conclusion

When Knight published *The Ethics of Competition* in 1923, he advanced a philosophical critique that challenged its readers to question the ways in which their economic lives affected their personal values, their social relationships, and their political systems. He adopted "a wider frame of reference than do most contemporary economists," unabashedly investigating the ethical significance of our economic systems using both an individual and an institutional frame.[79] In doing so, Knight set a powerful precedent, providing a framework within which to embed a critical, empirical analysis of the competitive, meritocratic "games" we play today. As the scope of experimental analysis of the effect of competition on value formation has expanded in recent decades, behavioral economics and psychology have provided a nuanced criticism of how our institutional environment changes the way we think in a manner we might neither expect nor desire. This chapter has attempted to trace the provenance of this critique back to Frank Knight, one of the founding fathers of modern economics, to expand its scope by infusing it with current insights, and to apply its force to the current discussion surrounding the positive and negative effects of meritocracy.

Knight's arguments lend themselves especially well to an examination of meritocracy. Meritocratic competition and selection functions by using competitive games (tournaments) to determine what agents deserve and then allocating resources, prestige, and positions according to those judgments. But every aspect of this process— the process of habitual comparison, the establishment of the external rewards used in competition, and judgments of desert that underlie the entire process—affects the way agents view themselves and others. The "career meritocrat" runs the risk of becoming less intrinsically motivated and more individualistic, of internalising a damaging, merit-centric self-perception, of summarily losing their self-esteem when they are outcompeted, and of forming harsh judgments of their peers whether they are outcompeted or not. And all of these effects can become durable parts of an individual's cultural mental model and identity, ensuring that the influence of meritocracy is as persistent as it is pervasive.

We argued that the best response to this set of challenges is public deliberation that assesses the values underlying the institutions we usually take for granted. This assessment should be pluralistic, leveraging the manifold value judgments that characterise a complex society instead of the singular metric of merit. Against this background, our judgments can become expansive instead of myopic. Meritocratic competition can be treated like the tool it is instead of the overarching principle of social order which it really should not be; it can be applied where it is appropriate and revised where it is not. Such a strategy might allow us to fully endorse meritocracy's benefits—and, indeed, to enhance its strengths by applying it where it is most warranted—without downplaying the crucial role of other standards of value. In doing so, we would be doing justice to Frank Knight's incisive analysis. Whether meritocratic competition enhances or warps our well-being today will largely be a

---

[79] See Emmett (2006), p. 102.

question of how well we understand its effect on our processes of value formation. If we take an active role in this process of inquiry, we may yet thrive.

Bibliography

Bell D (1972) On meritocracy and equality. Public Interest 29:29–68

Bowles S (1998) Endogenous preferences: the cultural consequences of markets and other economic institutions. J Econ Literature 36:75–111

Bowles S (2016) The moral economy: why good incentives are no substitute for good citizens. New Haven

Bruni L, Santori P (2022) The illusion of merit and the demons of economic meritocracy: which are the legitimate expectations of the market? J Bus Ethics 176:415–427

Butera F, Świątkowski W, Dompnier B (2021) Competition in education. In: Garcia, SM, Tor A, Elliot AJ (eds) The Oxford handbook of the psychology of competition, online edn, 13 Oct 2021. https://doi.org/10.1093/oxfordhb/9780190060800.013.24

Cardenas JC, Stranlund J, Willis C (2000) Local environmental control and institutional crowding out. World Dev 28:1719–1733

Cohn A, Fehr E, Maréchal MA (2014) Business culture and dishonesty in the banking industry. Nature 516:86–89

Converse BA, Reinhard, DA, Austin, MMK (2022) Psychology of rivalry: a social-cognitive approach to competitive relationships. In: Garcia, SM, Tor A and Elliot AJ (eds) The Oxford handbook of the psychology of competition, online edn, 13 Oct 2021. https://doi.org/10.1093/oxfordhb/9780190060800.013.18

Cowen T (1993) The scope and limits of preference sovereignty. Econ Philos 9:253–269

Dold M (forthcoming) Methodological individualism in behavioural economics. In: Bulle N, Di Iorio F (eds) The Palgrave handbook of methodological individualism. London

Dold M, Lewis P (2022) FA Hayek on the political economy of endogenous preferences: an historical overview and contemporary assessment. J Econ Behav Organ 196:104–119

Dold M (2022) Endogenous preferences: a challenge to ordoliberalism's normative foundations? RG Working Paper. https://doi.org/10.13140/RG.2.2.36182.93761/1

Emmett RB (1999) Selected essays by Frank H. Knight, Chicago

Festinger L (1954) A theory of social comparison processes. Hum Relations 7:117–140

Garcia SM, Tor A, Schiff TM (2013) The psychology of competition: a social comparison perspective. Perspect Psychol Sci 8:634–650

Gneezy U, Rustichini A (2000) Pay enough or don't pay at all. Q J Econ 115:791–810

Habermas J (1997) Popular sovereignty as procedure. In: Bohman J, Rehg, W (eds) Deliberative democracy: essays on reason and politics. Cambridge

Hands DW (2022) Frank Knight and behavioural economics. Working Paper.

Haran U, Bereby-Meyer, Y (2022) Competition in psychology and experimental economics. In: Garcia, SM, Tor A, Elliot AJ (eds), The Oxford handbook of the psychology of competition, online edn, 13 Oct 2021. https://doi.org/10.1093/oxfordhb/9780190060800.013.2

Hoff K, Stiglitz JE (2016) Striving for balance in economics: towards a theory of the social determination of behaviour. J Econ Behav Organ 126:25–57

Kasser T, Cohn S, Kanner AD, Ryan RM (2007) Some costs of American corporate capitalism: a psychological exploration of value and goal conflicts. Psychol Inq 18:1–22

Knight FH (1923) The ethics of competition. Q J Econ 37:579–624

Lewis P, Dold M (2020) James Buchanan on the nature of choice: ontology, artifactual man and the constitutional moment in political economy. Camb J Econ 44:1159–1179

Markovits D (2019) The meritocracy trap: how America's foundational myth feeds inequality, dismantles the middle class, and devours the elite. New York

Marshall G, Swift A (1993) Social class and social justice. Br J Sociol 44:187–211

Miller D (1999) Principles of Social justice. Cambridge

Nussbaum MC (2011) Creating capabilities: the human development approach. Cambridge

Ryan RM, Deci EL (2017) Self-determination theory: basic psychological needs in motivation, development, and wellness. New York

Ryan RM, Reeve J (2021) Intrinsic motivation, psychological needs, and competition: a self-determination theory analysis. In: Garcia, SM, Tor A, Elliot AJ (eds) The Oxford handbook of the psychology of competition, online edn, 13 Oct 2021. https://doi.org/10.1093/oxfordhb/9780190060800.013.10

Sandel MJ (2020) The Tyranny of merit: what's become of the common good? New York

Scott JT, Matland RE, Michelbach PA, Bornstein BH (2001) Just deserts: an experimental study of distributive justice norms. Am J Polit Sci 45:749–767

Sen A (1999) Development as freedom. Oxford

Sen AK (2000) Merit and justice. In: Arrow KJ, Bowles S, Durlauf S (eds) Meritocracy and economic inequality. Princeton, pp. 5–16

Stigler GJ, Becker GS (1977) De gustibus non est disputandum. Am Econ Rev 67:76–90

Truelove HB, Carrico AR, Weber EU, Raimi KT, Vandenbergh MP (2014) Positive and negative spillover of pro-environmental behaviour: an integrative review and theoretical framework. Glob Environ Chang 29:127–138

Weck-Hannemann H, Frey BS (1995) Are incentive instruments as good as economists believe? Some new considerations. In: Bovenberg L, Cnossen S (eds) Public economics and the environment in an imperfect world. New York, pp. 172–186

White MH, Sheldon KM (2014) The contract year syndrome in the NBA and MLB: a classic undermining pattern. Motiv Emot 38:196–205

Wooldridge A (2021) The aristocracy of talent: how meritocracy made the modern world. London

Wrzesniewski A, Schwartz B, Cong X, Kane M, Omar A, Kolditz T (2014) Multiple types of motives don't multiply the motivation of West Point cadets. Proc Natl Acad Sci 111:10990–10995

Young M (2001) Down with meritocracy. The Guardian

Chapter 15
Equal Opportunity in an Unequal Society

Eran Fish

Abstract Many share the view that even though gross inequalities of wealth are something to worry about, it makes a difference whether or not they are accompanied by substantive equality of opportunity. If people or their children are able to climb up and down the economic hierarchy, inequality is no longer deemed so objectionable. In this chapter I examine the soundness of this common view. I argue that against the backdrop of acute economic inequality, equal opportunity and mobility might be less morally significant than we often assume.

15.1 Introduction

Suppose that a certain cohort consists of two persons, A and B. Assume, further, that one of these persons will end up working as an average corporate employee, while the other will pursue a more lucrative career as a highly paid executive. The pay disparity between the two careers, assume, is about as vast as it is in many firms today—1 to 600.

Person A was born into a wealthier family. Even if formal equality of opportunity is secured, and hiring is done according to merit alone, A is all but guaranteed to acquire better qualifications, and to consequently win the better job. By

I am grateful to the participants at the 10th Law and Economics Conference at the University of Lucerne for their helpful comments.

E. Fish (✉)
Max Planck Institute for the Study of Crime, Security and Law, Freiburg I. Br., Germany
e-mail: e.fish@csl.mpg.de

Table 15.1 The distribution of payoffs under each policy

	State 1 (0.5)	State 2 (0.5)
Formal opportunity	(600, 1)	(600, 1)
Substantive opportunity	(600, 1)	(1, 600)

contrast, under a policy of substantive equal opportunity,[1] imagine, public education is provided in such a way that differences are entirely compensated: at birth, it is entirely unpredictable which of the two children will grow up to acquire the better skills and become an executive, and who will be an average employee.

Table 15.1 illustrates the distribution of payoffs under each policy given two equiprobable states of the world. In each pair of payoffs (n, m), the number on the left represents person A's payoff and the number on the right represents B's. The two states are the possibilities at the time of A and B's birth. Under a policy of formal opportunity, A will have the better qualifications and therefore the distribution is bound to be (600, 1) no matter what happens. Under a policy of substantive opportunity, however, it remains open whether A or B will end up better off: it is possible that person A will prove more talented or skilful, in which case the distribution will be as in State 1. But it is equally possible that B will become the better qualified and have the better job, as in State 2.

Based on much of the literature, as well as some strong intuitions many of us share, the following claims seem natural to hold:

1. The income disparity between the two jobs is excessive and prima facie objectionable.
2. A policy of merely formal equality of opportunity does not make this income disparity any less objectionable.
3. However, the income disparity is less objectionable if a policy of substantive equality of opportunity is adopted.

The first claim could draw support from several moral theories. Rawlsians may argue that, compared to various other possible ways of distributing income, a disparity of 1:600 does not work to the benefit of the worst-off.[2] Contractualists could say that a system that generates so deep a disparity cannot be justified in the right way to those who are affected by this inequality.[3] Relational egalitarians would argue, perhaps, that the life experience of people earning $12,000,000 is so far removed from that of people living on $20,000, that a society in which they can relate as one another's

---

[1] By 'substantive equality of opportunity' I mean a standard similar to Rawls' 'fair equality of opportunity'. According to Rawls, what this principle requires is that "...those who are at the same level of talent and ability, and have the same willingness to use them, should have the same prospects of success regardless of their initial place in the social system." (1971), p. 73. This is to be contrasted with a policy of merely formal equality of opportunity, which enables everyone to compete for education and jobs on the basis of merit but takes no positive measures to equalize access to gaining the requisite merit.

[2] Rawls (1971), p. 75.

[3] Scanlon (2018), Ch. 9.

equals is unthinkable.[4] Even desert-theorists, who believe that differences in merit *require* unequal rewards, might consider a disparity of that magnitude dispropor-tionate. After all, even when some people are more meritorious than others, the difference in levels of desert is unlikely to be as great as 1:600. Even desert theories often prefer an equal distribution over one that rewards desert disproportionately.[5]

The second claim has been recently highlighted by critics of meritocracy. Famously, Daniel Markovits (2019) argued that meritocracy has not lived up to its promise of equality. On the one hand, universities and employers *do* open their doors to all those who excel. And those who make it into lucrative paths to wealth *are* indeed qualified. But on the other hand, children coming from rich households are disproportionately more likely than poor and middle-class children to become qualified in the first place, thanks to the vastly superior investment that richer families can afford. This fact, according to the critique, means that a mere formal equality of opportunity fails to mitigate social inequality.

The third claim enjoys very wide resonance as well. It is often argued that meaningful, substantive equality of opportunity, which brings about effective social mobility, can mitigate whatever it is that is objectionable about income inequality.[6] According to a common thought, even when the disparity between the richest and the poorest is acute, this effect may be balanced over time by enabling people to move up and down the economic ladder. Whether mobility occurs intra- or intergen-erationally, it can equalize people's expected life experience, even if some fare much better than others at any particular time.[7] Thus, it is believed, while inequality might matter, it makes a difference whether it is accompanied by substantive equality of opportunity or not.

In what follows I will subject these intuitions to some scrutiny. I will consider different ways in which substantive opportunity is thought to mitigate inequality: by rendering the distribution more justifiable, by equalizing expected utility, and by matching rewards to desert. Given plausible assumptions, as I will show, there is reason to doubt that substantive opportunity does better than mere formal opportunity on any of these criteria. This should give us a reason to rethink at least one of the claims above. Either the great disparity of income in this case is unobjectionable to begin with, or, if it *is* objectionable, it remains so with or without substantive equality of opportunity.

---

[4] Anderson (1999), Scheffler (2003).

[5] There is another important argument to that effect. According to Miller (1996), p. 299, merit is manifest in more ways, and more people are in fact meritorious, than the market economy recognizes. This speaks for a more equal distribution of rewards according to a theory of desert as properly understood.

[6] Friedman (1962), Horwitz (2015), Persad (2015), Carroll and Chen (2016).

[7] Persad (2015), p. 167.

15.2 Opportunity and Mobility

The intuitive force of the idea that opportunity compensates for inequality is well captured in the following metaphor, as proposed by the Economic Mobility Project[8]:

> Think of a hotel in which some of the rooms are luxurious executive suites while others are small and modest. The executive suites may be getting fancier over time and the modest rooms ever more modest. But if a different group of people occupies the executive suites each year, and everyone has a decent shot at staying in these fancier rooms, people have less reason to complain. Relative mobility is similar to this kind of room-changing. In particular, if relative mobility had increased at the same time that income inequality has risen, then there would be less reason for concern about rising inequality.

The fact that some people stay in luxurious suites and others in a small budget room is prima facie objectionable, even on this view. However, it is claimed, this concern is considerably diminished once it is known that the allocation of good and bad rooms is a dynamic one. As this short quote suggests, one reason for this has to do with justification. The idea is that if one has been given the opportunity to occupy a better position, or a prospect of occupying a better position in the future—whether for oneself or for one's children—then one's current lot becomes more *acceptable*. Being destined to be worse off than others often raises a legitimate moral complaint, at least pro tanto. But if positions are not fixed, the arrangement is potentially justifiable to all.

Another compelling thought is that substantive equality of opportunity may give people an equal *expectation* of being better off. Instead of equality ex post, it makes everyone equal ex ante. In this regard, it contrasts sharply with mere formal equality of opportunity, which gives every prospect of success exclusively to the rich and none to the poor.[9] To some, equality ex ante might seem as desirable as, if not more than, equality of outcomes. An equal chance at success might be ex ante Pareto superior to a certain but modest equal share.

Along these lines, it has been argued that even though the gap between the rich and the poor is constantly on the rise, this fact should be weighed against possible improvements in income mobility during that period. According to Steven Horwitz, "[a]ny analysis of income inequality must consider that *who constitutes* the rich and the poor changes from year to year."[10] It may be true that the 'rich' as a category are richer at time t_2 than they were at time t_1, but the particular people who happen to be rich at t_1 might not be the same as the people who are rich at t_2. That, it is claimed, makes inequality less worrying than it is thought to be.[11]

There is no denying the strong appeal of this idea. And yet, closer inspection may raise questions. Important as it is to level the playing field in general, how important is this sort of fairness when the race itself is objectionable or cruel? Is there no legitimate complaint to be made even when substantive opportunity is given? And

---

[8] Isaacs et al. (2008), p. 29.

[9] This concern is at the heart of Markovits' critique of present-day meritocracy (2019).

[10] Horwitz (2015), p. 73.

[11] Carroll and Chen (2016).

would equality ex ante still seem compelling if the pay gap were to grow further still, to 1:6,000 or 1:6,000,000? If not, why?

What is more, one may question the presumed difference between the two policies in Table 15.1: as it is, substantive opportunity does not seem to rank above the alternative either on a scale of either utility or equality. As we will see later on, from the standpoint of decision theory it is not quite obvious that the two policies differ at all. This raises a question as to the coherence of believing that inequality is justified under one of these policies but unjustified under the other.

To evaluate the basic intuition—that substantive opportunity may compensate for otherwise objectionable economic disparities—it is therefore worthwhile to consider the main arguments in its support, one at a time.

15.3 Fairness and Justifiability

As mentioned earlier, one promising way of spelling out the normative importance of substantive opportunity is in terms of justifiability. An inequality that is accompanied by substantive equality of opportunity appears more likely to be justifiable to those who end up being worse off. Under merely formal opportunity, the person with the worse career has a strong complaint, namely that she never had a fair opportunity to do better, no matter how much she would have tried. Substantive opportunity seems to correct this moral flaw. It offers at least part of a satisfactory response to the person who objects to her unfavourable relative position.[12] A contractualist approach along these lines can explain, first, what it is that is wrong about unequal chances.[13] And second, it makes sense of the idea that two states of affairs can differ morally despite being otherwise alike. Even if two policies lead to the exact same result, it may still be the case that this result is either justified or unjustified, depending on how it had been achieved.

Indeed, justifiability may explain why dividing chances equally is the right thing to do in some of the most paradigmatic cases. For example, if there is one kidney available and two patients need a transplant, then giving each patient a chance to be helped seems like what we should do, other things being the same.[14] That is not because the chance to be helped somehow substitutes the actual receiving of help—it clearly doesn't. Rather, it is because it makes the outcome justifiable to both patients.

There is, however, something that is important to notice here. The kidney case, like many others that call for drawing lots, is one in which equalizing chances is the only acceptable way of treating people fairly. An equal *outcome* can only be achieved by denying help to both patients, and that is an unacceptable alternative. Giving one patient a life-saving treatment is an optimal option by all accounts. The most acceptable thing to do is *that*, despite the unequal outcome.

---

[12] Scanlon (2018), Ch. 5.

[13] Saunders (2008).

[14] Broome (1990).

But the case at hand is importantly different. Unlike the unequal but optimal life-saving treatment, a pay disparity of 1:600 strikes many of us as far from optimal, morally speaking. There are countless other realistic ways to distribute income more equally which would seem at least as acceptable, if not preferable. In contrast to the kidney example, in which outcome inequality is in a sense *desirable*, the radical disparity between executive and workers' pay is something we may well have a valid reason to object to. There is at least some good reason to want a more equal outcome in this case, rather than merely an equal *chance* for an unequal share.

The importance of this distinction is as follows. Equal chances and opportunities can only serve as *part* of a justification: equal opportunity offers an adequate response to the question 'why am *I* the worse off and not someone else'. But the fact that *anyone* should be worse off than someone else requires a justification too. As Scanlon argues, both conceptions of equal opportunity—the formal and the substantive—serve as a necessary but insufficient justification for those affected by inequality.[15] A full response to a complaint by those who are worse off would require, in addition, a justification at the level of institutions: why a scheme that generates inequality is justified at all, and, importantly, why a disparity of that magnitude is justified. If that institutional justification is missing, inequality remains unjustifiable whether with or without substantive opportunity.

In the transplant case, it is in fact misleading to say that having had an equal chance is what makes the outcome justifiable to the patients. It can only do so in combination with the fact that the unequal outcome is already independently justified (in that case, it is justified because it would be unacceptable to let both patients die in the name of equality). By the same token, substantive opportunity cannot justify *everything* about the fact that one person earns 600 times less than another. It can only serve as a supplementary justification if this pay gap—if the fact that anyone should earn so much less than another—can be justified independently.

The problem is that a pay disparity of this proportion seems objectionable precisely on contractualist grounds. The present inequality of income between top executives and their employees is one for which there might not be an obvious justification.[16] There are serious doubts that it can be supported by considerations of efficiency, for example. For one thing, there is not enough evidence to show that excessive executive pay correlates with better performance. Higher compensation for CEOs seems, rather, to correspond to trends in the industry in which a firm operates, not to the performance of the firm itself.[17] The belief that such a vast income gap serves as an effective incentive, and may therefore be justified on grounds of productivity, is something that remains to be substantiated. Secondly, even if this level of inequality

---

[15] Scanlon (2018), p. 41.

[16] Scanlon (2018), pp. 138 et seq.

[17] According to Mishel and Davis (2015), p. 11: "CEO pay reflects rents, concessions CEOs can draw from the economy not by virtue of their contribution to economic output but by virtue of their position. Consequently, CEO pay could be reduced and the economy would not suffer any loss of output. Another implication of rising executive pay is that it reflects income that otherwise would have accrued to others".
See also discussion in Scanlon (2018), pp. 143 et seq.

could be shown to be efficient, a question remains as to whether it benefits, or at least tends to benefit, more than a small group of highly paid individuals. If a system or an institution are to be justifiable to everyone, its profitability alone is not enough. Maximized profits would not render a policy any more justifiable if—to take an extreme example—CEOs were the only ones to benefit.[18] They could not serve as a response to a legitimate complaint by those who are not among the happy few.

If that is true, the normative difference between the two policies in Table 15.1 seems considerably less significant. If a 1:600 pay disparity is hard to justify in principle, then it would seem to *remain* unjustifiable whether the people affected have a fair chance or not. The fact that one had a fair shot at success might justify one dimension of the unequal outcome: it might justify the fact that this person is worse off and not her competitor. But that is not enough to justify the inequality itself. It offers no obvious justification for the fact that one person should be worse off than another in the first place—still less that one person should fare as much as 600 times worse.

To some, this result may sound counterintuitive. Giving people a fair opportunity in life is among our most noble and widely cherished moral ideals. How can it fail to make a moral difference whether people have it or not?

The answer to that, I think, is that it is conceptually possible even for unquestionably cherished moral ideals to fail to bear on a normative choice in a particular case. Consider due process, for instance. No one would doubt the gravity of this requirement or the wrongness of denying a defendant a fair trial. And yet if a defendant is convicted and sentenced for what is clearly an unjustifiable punishment based on an unjustifiable law—say, corporal punishment for dressing immodestly—it is no more than a pedantic matter whether due process had been observed or not. The defendant has every right to complain even if all procedural rules were kept to the letter. Due process is a necessary but by no means a sufficient requirement for a sentence to be just. And in this case, there is no meaningful sense in which respecting her procedural rights renders the punishment justifiable to her. It is thus perfectly consistent to say that due process is vastly important *and* that it makes no difference whether or not it has been observed in a particular context.

Something similar can be said concerning the fair distribution of life chances within an unjustifiable distribution of benefits. If it turned out that there is no good enough a reason why one person should be paid 600 times less than someone else, substantive equality of opportunity is unlikely to supply that missing justifying reason.

---

[18] Scanlon (2018), p. 141.

15.4   Equality ex ante

If that is correct, then the justifiability explanation is unconvincing. A fair opportunity is not enough to render inequality justifiable. If the pattern of distribution itself is unjust, then all that a fair opportunity can do is to reallocate people into their respective unjust positions. The person who ends up poorer would still have a valid complaint, with or without substantive opportunity.

But other arguments may be offered in support of the idea that substantive equal opportunity compensates for economic inequality. These other arguments appeal to the thought that even if income inequality is not made *justifiable*, in the contractualist sense, it might be made *less important* given equality of opportunity.

For instance, one argument is that the pain of economic inequality could be lessened by social mobility. Substantive opportunity can alleviate the plight of the poor by making it less permanent. In the case of intragenerational mobility, those who are currently poor can look forward to a prospect of improving their position within their lifetime. And even if mobility is only intergenerational, those at the bottom are given the no less important hope that their children will one day climb higher up than they had. In that sense, it is said, "[i]f rich households are richer in relative terms, but poor households are still reasonably able to eventually reach the top quintile or two, then the observed growth in inequality might be less troubling."[19]

The prospect of escaping the bottom of the economic hierarchy is tremendously important and should not be underestimated. But this line of argument has an obvious problem too. Assuming that social mobility is not entirely painless—that is, that upward mobility correlates with at least some degree of mobility *downwards*—the positive and negative effects of equal opportunity could cancel each other out.[20] Insofar as equal opportunity does not mean 'more opportunity', but rather a greater number of smaller opportunities, then upward mobility for some can only be achieved at the expense of some others who are left behind. The promise that social mobility offers the poor is mirrored by the danger it poses to those who are not currently poor. When the risk of falling down concerns the very richest, this might not sound particularly worrying. But downward mobility may affect the middle class as well, or those that are barely above the poverty line. From the point of view of society, mobility can be a mixed blessing. It is good for some as it is bad for others.

There is, however, another way of making this basic intuition plausible—the intuition, that is, that there is something less important about economic inequality once equal opportunities are offered. It may be argued that substantive opportunity equalizes something that is no less important from the standpoint of justice, namely people's life *prospects*. When viewed ex ante, substantive opportunity appears more attractive in comparison to both formal opportunity and other possible distributions. First, substantive opportunity seems preferable to merely formal opportunity in that

---

[19] Horwitz (2015), p. 73.

[20] According to Brian Barry (2005), pp. 60 et seqq. with the decline of a middle class that can absorb the upward mobility of the working class, mobility is becoming zero-sum, such that moving on to an upper position requires that somebody else move downwards.

it offers each person an equal expected payoff. Second, substantive opportunity is as good, ex ante speaking, as a policy that divides the same overall payoff equally, and better than any equal distribution of a smaller overall sum. For example, a policy that offers both A and B an equal chance of having either 600 or 1, is *ex ante* Pareto superior to a policy that guarantees a payoff of 250 for each. In this respect, some could argue, under substantive equal opportunity the objection to income inequality itself may become weaker. Ex ante, it may well be better to choose an *unequal* distribution of income with a higher expected utility for everyone, or so some are inclined to argue.

Now, there is much to be said for looking at choices of public policy from an ex ante perspective. It should be noted, however, that the theoretical implications of taking such a perspective may be far-reaching. As we shift to explicating our notions of fairness and equality in ex ante terms, the distinction between these ideals and full-blown utilitarianism—which assigns no importance to equality as such— risks collapsing. Firstly, viewed ex ante, inequalities might seem justified even when opportunities are *not* equal. As utilitarians are wont to argue, any distribution that brings about greater aggregate utility, however unequally, can in principle be justified ex ante—be it earlier in time or conceptually prior, as it were behind a veil of ignorance.[21] Therefore, if ex ante is the perspective to take, then perhaps inequality is not *mitigated* by equality of opportunity after all: as a utilitarian might say, income inequality was already unobjectionable to begin with.

Secondly, in terms of expected utility, formal equality of opportunity might not only be good enough. It may in fact be indistinguishable from substantive opportunity. This second point has long been identified by Peter Diamond[22]: from the standpoint of expected utility, it is difficult to see the difference between two policies such as those in Table 15.1. Our intuitive notion of fairness would seem to favour substantive opportunity. But favouring any of the policies, in this case, conflicts with a fundamental axiom of rational choice, namely the sure-thing principle. According to this principle, if two policies produce equally good outcomes in any state of the world, then these two policies are equally good. In Table 15.1, the two policies result in exactly the same outcome in State 1, and equally good outcomes in State 2. Despite what fairness would seem to recommend, rational choice demands that we remain indifferent between the two alternatives.

Some theorists have proposed a seemingly easy fix to this problem. According to this solution, the distribution of payoffs as it appears in Table 15.1 is under-described, and fails to include all the information which an informed choice requires. They argue that if there is indeed something that makes substantive opportunity better—say, the fact that it is *fair*—then this feature should be incorporated into the description of this policy's prospective outcomes.[23] Thus, the suggestion is that Diamond's problem may be avoided if the choice is described more fully, as in Table 15.2:

---

[21] Harsanyi (1955).

[22] Diamond (1967).

[23] Broome (1991), Fleurbaey (2010), Risse (2002).

Table 15.2 The distribution of payoffs: redescribed

	State 1 (0.5)	State 2 (0.5)
Formal opportunity	(600, 1) and the policy is unfair	(600, 1) and the policy is unfair
Substantive opportunity	(600, 1) and the policy is fair	(1, 600) and the policy is fair

Re-described in this way, the sure-thing principle does not stand in the way of preferring substantive opportunity. It is no longer the case that the policies result in equally good outcomes in every possible world. Instead, the second policy results in a better outcome in every state.

However, while that may seem like an elegant technical solution to a technical problem, there are reasons to think that Diamond's argument cuts deeper, and that the problem it captures might not be solved so easily. One worry has to do with the structure of rational decision theory. Clearly, in order to rank policies meaningfully we need to describe their prospective outcomes in a way that would include all relevant information. But there is an important conceptual constraint on what this description may include. As decision theorists observe, the normative concepts in light of which choice is supposed to be made—normative concepts such as 'good' or 'choice-worthy'—cannot themselves be part of the object of choice.[24] The point of decision theory is to provide the chooser with a set of options that she herself can rank in some order of goodness or choice-worthiness. Normative principles are therefore meant to be external to the act of choosing. The options themselves should be described in terms of their relevant *non*-normative features, leaving it to the chooser to evaluate them against her relevant normative principle.[25]

Thus, insofar as we understand the description 'fair' as we normally do—i.e. as a normative concept according to which policies should be ranked—it cannot be part of the description of the two policies' outcomes. The purpose of describing the options, to repeat, is to allow the decisionmaker to decide what is best (or fairest), rather than to decide it for her in advance.

The only coherent way of describing outcomes as 'fair' is by using fairness in some non-normative sense. Indeed, those who appeal to the re-describing solution understand 'fairness' in precisely this unconventional way: i.e., as a kind of personal payoff, similar to well-being or income. 'Unfairness' is used as a sort of harm, and fairness as a benefit.[26] But while this makes the re-describing tactic coherent, some philosophers find this use of the term 'fair' implausibly artificial.[27] Notice that the claim made is not that unfairness is bad for a person because of some further harm, emotional or otherwise, that it might cause, but rather that unfairness itself constitutes harm. It is not immediately clear, however, what such harm might consist in. From the point of view of prudential value, the difference between ending up being poor

---

[24] Neumann (2007). However, some theorists support de-dicto descriptions that are not explicitly normative. Sen (2002).

[25] Rulli and Worsnip (2016).

[26] Broome (1991).

[27] Hooker (2005), pp. 335 et seq.

fairly and ending equally poor but unfairly appears negligible. Nor does fairness seem to contribute to overall social utility in the same way that payoffs usually do. Unlike happiness or income, fairness is not typically thought of as a good to be aggregated at all. For instance, a utilitarian would think it better if there are four happy people rather than just two, other things being equal. But surely there is no more total value in distributing chances fairly among four people rather than just among two. Generally speaking, unfairness seems to be qualitatively different from more commonly recognized components of personal good.

In any case, these remarks merely concern the mechanics of rational decision theory. Maybe there *is* some technical way of accommodating the intuition that substantive opportunity is better. But Diamond's point may be thought of in less technical terms too. The fact that expected utility doesn't immediately capture the difference between the two policies raises a normative question: there is obviously *some* difference—in that one policy offers equal chances and the other does not. The question is, however, whether this particular probabilistic difference truely makes one of the policies better than the other. Re-describing these outcomes as 'fair' and 'unfair' merely begs the question: if the pay disparity is known to be 1:600 either way, and the only difference is one of probability, is one policy really better or fairer?

There are good reasons to doubt that it is. Equalizing chances is often important, but, as argued in the previous section, only when it is part of a scheme that can be justified as a whole. Many lotteries do not seem to play any justificatory role at all. To take a familiar example, we do not think that the badness of economic inequality would be mitigated by a baby-swapping scheme—in which newborns are distributed at random among rich and poor families.[28] Nor do we consider the so-called 'lottery of nature' as a fair mechanism that could justify inequalities. If inequality itself cannot be justified, all that a brute randomized process can do is shift this injustice from one person to another, not mitigate it.

15.5   Desert

Indeed, theories of substantive equality of opportunity often view this ideal as more than just a mechanism for equalizing the mere *probability* of winning the race. Arguably, that objective could have been achieved by a fair lottery, which would be a cheaper, more direct means. A central motivation behind merit-based equality of opportunity is the idea that it is intrinsically good for benefits to go to those who deserve them most. In addition to eliminating discrimination, it is committed to the principle that merit ought to be rewarded, and that more merit ought to be rewarded more. Merit-based theories hold that in a choice between two otherwise equal alternatives, one in which the more deserving do better than the less deserving is pro tanto better.

---

[28] Harsanyi (1975), pp. 316 et seq.

Accordingly, some might argue that what substantive opportunity can do—or what non-substantive opportunity fails to do—is to make inequality more just by better matching merit with reward. One motivation for this view might rest on a certain reading of Rawls.[29] On this reading, it is wrong for a distribution of rewards to be determined by facts that are arbitrary from a moral point of view: it is wrong, that is, to reward advantages such as inherited wealth, good upbringing, and talent, for which a person cannot claim credit. Since one does not deserve to enjoy these gifts of good fortune, one does not deserve the fruits of these gifts either. This may invite the following thought: substantive opportunity is better than mere formal opportunity because it reduces the impact of morally arbitrary factors. The winner under substantive opportunity is *more deserving*—the thought goes—than the winner under merely formal opportunity. Even if substantive opportunity does not neutralize *all* morally arbitrary factors (e.g., talent), the winner under such a policy has at least won the race on a more level playing field. She can claim more credit for her win than a winner with a better start in life might.

However, as several writers have pointed out, this conclusion is at least partly unwarranted.[30] The fact that one does not deserve one's better starting point does not imply that one shouldn't be rewarded. It only means that the better starting point itself does not justify a reward, and another justification is required.[31] Even if the best qualified people cannot claim credit for being better skilled, there are clearly some good reasons to select and hire them over less qualified candidates. Not only is it in the interest of an institution, efficiency-wise, to be staffed with better candidates. Merit-based selection is also supported by certain considerations of justice. There is, prima facie, a valid moral complaint to be made when the best qualified candidate is rejected and someone less qualified is hired instead. What this complaint consists in is partly the fact that the person who got the job does not *deserve* it. The concept of desert need not presuppose that the basis for desert should itself be deserved. We do not think, for example, that the winner of a race is less deserving of her medal because her athleticism is inborn and effortless. Not only is she formally *entitled* to her win, she also has a more substantive, *merit*-based claim to it.

If that is true, then the difference between the two policies is no longer so clear. Inasmuch as qualifications are a basis for desert, selecting the most skilful person meets the requirements of desert even when those lucky candidates do not deserve their skills. *Both* policies award the greater benefit to the more qualified person, and therefore both are equally good, desert-wise.[32]

It might be objected, perhaps, that merely formal equality of opportunity doesn't *really* pick out the most qualified person: if only a subset of society ever gets to have the necessary skills to even enter the contest, the winners of the race need only be

---

[29] Rawls (1971).

[30] Sher (1979), Miller (1996).

[31] Scanlon (2018), Cohen (2008), pp. 158 et seq.

[32] It might be objected that had the athlete been somewhat less gifted—if her win were somewhat more down to effort—the medal would have been more deserved still. But that case is not easy to make. For one thing, the propensity to make effort is often an undeserved gift in and of itself.

good enough to prevail over that small group. But if everyone could be candidates—so the argument—it would take better skills to win the race, and the winners would be in this sense more deserving of their rewards—that is, more deserving than the winners of the formal opportunity race would be.

This conjecture is not implausible. There is reason to believe that substantive equality of opportunity, by expanding the pool of skilled candidates, would result in more qualified winners. This may be desirable from a utilitarian point of view, at least so long as the marginal benefit from selecting more qualified people is greater than the marginal cost of training the population to develop better skills. However, that doesn't yet mean that the ideal of *desert* would be in some sense more fully satisfied. Meritocracy does not require advantageous positions to go to those who are best qualified *out of all possible worlds*. After all, substantive opportunity does not meet that standard either. It merely demands that among those who actually compete for a benefit, selection should be merit-based. This requirement can be met equally by both conceptions of equal opportunity. Formal equality of opportunity may fail to do enough to help more people become deserving, but it doesn't discriminate against candidates who are actually deserving.

Thus, the two policies seem to be equivalent from the standpoint of desert, too. To the extent that any one of them can justify inequality, by matching differing levels of reward to differing levels of merit, so can the other policy. Conversely, if one of the policies (formal opportunity) fails to make the inequality just, there is no merit-based reason to think that the other would succeed.

15.6 Conclusion

There may well be additional arguments to consider. The discussion in this chapter was limited only to the most prominent and common among them. Nevertheless, the foregoing discussion puts pressure on some of our widely shared intuitions. We often think that certain disparities of income *are* wrong, but that their wrongfulness varies depending on the level of opportunity and mobility that is available to people. However, when it comes to those inequalities that we find prima facie objectionable, the difference between enabling and not enabling mobility has turned out difficult to maintain.

That is not to say that it is *unimportant* to provide everyone with a real chance in life. Still less does it show that denying substantive opportunity to parts of the population is not wrong. The discussion in this chapter merely cautions against making a further common but unwarranted leap of reasoning: namely to believe that merely by providing opportunity and mobility, our concerns regarding inequality are dealt with. In the same way that a criminal sentence can remain equally unjust with and without due process, extreme inequalities of wealth can remain objectionable both with and without substantive equal opportunity.

References

Anderson E (1999) What is the point of equality? Ethics 109:287–337

Barry B (2005) Why social justice matters. Polity, Cambridge

Broome J (1990) Fairness. Proc Aristot Soc 91:87–101

Broome J (1991) Weighing goods. Blackwell

Carroll D, Chen A (2016) Income inequality matters, but mobility is just as important. Economic Commentary

Diamond P (1967) Cardinal welfare, individualistic ethics, and interpersonal comparisons of utility: a comment. J Polit Econ 75:765–766

Fleurbaey M (2010) Assessing risky social situations. J Polit Econ 118:649–680

Friedman M (1962) Capitalism and freedom. Chicago

Harsanyi J (1955) Cardinal welfare, individualistic ethics, and interpersonal comparisons of utility. J Polit Econ 63:309–321

Harsanyi J (1975) Nonlinear social welfare functions. Theor Decis 6(1/4):311–332

Hooker B (2005) Fairness. Ethical Theory Moral Pract 8:329–352

Horwitz S (2015) Inequality, mobility, and being poor in America. Soc Philos Policy, 70–91

Isaacs JB, Isabel VS, Ron H (2008) Getting ahead or losing ground: economic mobility in America. Washington, DC, Economic Mobility Project. https://www.brookings.edu/research/getting-ahead-or-losing-ground-economic-mobility-in-america/

Markovits D (2019) The meritocracy trap. New York

Miller D (1996) Two cheers for meritocracy. J Polit Philos 4:277–301

Mishel L, Davis A (2015) Top CEOs make 300 times more than typical workers. Report. Economic Policy Institute Issue Brief #399

Neumann M (2007) Choosing and Describing: Sen and the independence of irrelevant alternatives. Theor Decis 63(1):79–94

Persad G (2015) Equality via mobility: why socioeconomic mobility matters for relational equality, distributive equality, and equality of opportunity. Soc Philos Policy, pp 158–179

Rawls J (1971) A theory of justice. Cambridge

Risse M (2002) Harsanyi's 'utilitarian theorem' and utilitarianism. Nous 36(40):550–577

Rulli T, Worsnip A (2016) IIA, rationality, and individuation. Philos Stud 173:205–221

Saunders B (2008) The equality of lotteries. Philosophy 83:359–372

Scanlon TM (2018) Why does inequality matter? Oxford

Scheffler S (2003) What is equality? Philos Public Aff 31(1):5–38

Sen A (2002) Internal consistency of choice. In: Rationality and freedom. Cambridge and London, pp. 121–157

Sher G (1979) Effort, ability, and personal desert. Philos Public Aff 8:361–376

Chapter 16
Redefining a Normative Framework for Meritocracy in the Era of Generative AI: An Inter-Disciplinary Perspective

Kalpana Tyagi

Abstract Meritocracy is the hallmark of our modern day societies. It is widely believed, and also empirically established, that meritocratic systems outshine non-meritocratic ones. Meritocratic individuals, on average, tend to perform better. Meritocracy takes subjective elements, such as chance, and luck out of the equation, and seeks to reward those with intelligence, and fortitude. From the Silicon Valley in the US, Singapore's political and economic growth, to the rise, and the sustenance of the big pharma in Switzerland, meritocracy has consistently nourished these economies to catapult them to the world's leading economies, and innovation systems. The meteoric rise of Singapore from a resource-deprived and newly independent country (in 1959) to the world's fifth richest Nation State (in 2022) may be attributed in part to its unique, meritocratic political system. What then is this meritocracy? Is there one standard understanding of meritocracy, or does it vary by the State, the context, or is it simply a narrative of the times that we live in? Is there a correlation between meritocracy and inequality? This research article discusses the nature of meritocracy, and how the fallacies of meritocratic societies be remedied to ensure a balance between meritocracy, egalitarianism, and justice. The article discusses the foregoing issues against the backdrop of the fast-rising Generative Artificial Intelligence, that just like meritocracy, contributes to growth, while simultaneously exacerbating the societal inequalities (and its accompanying discontent). From a normative perspective, this research suggests a Scandinavian approach to balancing wealth creation with a more positive and detailed welfare-state institution that will not only foster increased social trust; it will also ensure that those with "merit" are able to exercise it with "empathy" in the age of Generative AI.

K. Tyagi (✉)
Maastricht University, Maastricht, The Netherlands
e-mail: k.tyagi@maastrichtuniversity.nl

16.1 Introduction

In his classic and highly entertaining work, Michael Young fast forwards his alter ego to 2034 and imagines a merit-based world, where the subjects are constantly required to either get high scores in different IQ tests for promotion, or else face the threat of demotion as scores decline.[1] In the book, Young imagines a world where entry and sustenance in the job market is based on one's education, intellect and merit. At the time, Young had a difficult time to get his work published, as many had failed to understand the forward-looking nature of his work and how he sarcastically highlighted the fallacies of the incumbent system. Young challenged the systematic and the corrupt trap that the hyper competition-driven system had created. About 60 + years later, Yale Professor Markovits" book, "The Meritocracy Trap" was published.[2] This coupled with the College Admissions" scandal in the US[3] once again put the meritocracy debate center-stage. Markovits' key concern with the system is that the current social set up creates a hyperloop that "engineers and reproduces inequalities".[4] An evaluation of people on the merits, such as through entrance exams, repeatedly gets those with superior financial background and educated parents to better colleges and higher paying jobs. Further, the biggest irony of all this is that even the winners are not happy with their social and financial achievements. In other words, a meritocratic system - driven by merit and strength – that has significantly contributed to higher GDP, more innovation and growth from the US to Singapore, from the UK to Switzerland, is being questioned for its efficiency, effectiveness and the ensuing outcome.

The current debate on meritocracy cannot and should not be seen in isolation. The rise of big data and the fast-approaching Generative AI has offered a significant impetus to this debate. In the fourth industrial revolution, devices will be able to talk to each other and work with more efficiency. This is the result of a number of technologies, including but not limited to the internet of things, the Artificial Intelligence (AI) and the Blockchain technology.[5] Improved efficiency also means redundancy for many of the current jobs. In addition, this will also call for an even more, then the currently available, highly skilled workforce. A skilled workforce comprises of meritocratic employees, in other words, those who are hardworking and highly intelligent. In this respect, the big data-driven economy, and the forthcoming Industry 4.0 not only benefits from a meritocratic system, it also offers an impetus to further strengthen the current approach. A call against meritocracy will be a call to retard the current pace of growth, tread backwards and slow down our march towards Industry 4.0, and reap the benefits of Generative AI. Likewise, if we do not address the inefficiencies in the current approach to achieve meritocracy, it carries an inbuilt danger of creating social unrest and a dystopian society. How does one

---

[1] Young (1958).

[2] Markovits (2020).

[3] Nelson (2019).

[4] Markovits (2020).

[5] Tyagi (2023).

then balance these competing interests? This article contemplates on the foregoing issues. Section 16.2 seeks to define meritocracy, and in the process, tries to segregate the distinct elements that make up a meritocratic system. The section also seeks to establish a link between meritocracy, and whether it leads to content and happy subjects in the society. Section 16.3 looks at the organization, and the management of the following meritocratic societies - the US' high-tech sector, Singapore's political system, and the Swiss pharmaceuticals sector – to identify the common elements that define a meritocratic system. Section 16.4 looks at the platform economy, and the fast emerging AI technology, and how this may add to the disillusion with the current societal set-up. Particularly the section deep dives into the rise and uptake of Generative AI, and how it may affect the demand for labour. Section 16.5 concludes, with some thoughts on how the discontents of the current meritocratic systems be addressed effectively. This section then tries to look at how the fallacies in these systems can be addressed in a timely manner to ensure egalitarianism, and opportunities for the system as a whole, as distinct for benefits that remain available to only a select few in the society.

16.2   Meritocracy and its Contribution to Innovation

In his classic work, "The Rise of Meritocracy", Michael Young first used the term "meritocracy". A meritocrat was one who was identified early on for his talent, and abilities, and was nurtured to be an achiever. A meritocrat was rewarded for his intelligence, and hard work, as distinct from some co-incidental factors, such as being born into a royal or an aristocratic family. Young's definition of meritocracy made its way into the English dictionary, as a word that can be mathematically defined thus, IQ + Effort = Merit.[6] As chance, and coincidence were relegated to the background, meritocracy introduced a quantifiable element in our social set-up, and professional selection system. An individual's success could now be reasonably predicted on the basis of his intelligence (measured in terms of IQ, Intelligence Quotient), and his hard-work, in other words, his effort. This created a "merit-based system. Many economies recognized the prowess of this meritocratic system and developed entire innovation ecosystems around this robust and reasonable meritocratic order. The following Sect. 16.3 discusses three such meritocratic systems, namely the US' Silicon Valley, the Swiss Pharma sector, and Singapore's political system, and how they have contributed to the growth of these economies. It was the positive and directly co-relatable effects of a meritocratic approach that led to a widespread belief and acceptance, that the most efficient way to manage companies, or run a country should be rooted in the principles of meritocracy. These positive effects clearly reflected in higher gross domestic product (GDP) for nation states, and greater profitability and robust balance sheets for the industries.

---

[6] Young (1958).

16.2.1   Meritocracy and the Hyper-Competition Loop

Promising as the foregoing may sound, not all is perfect in even the most meritocratic societies. Meritocracy had a role to play at each stage of innovation. This meritocratic content, though, was soon accompanied by despondency, as the hyper-competition loop in meritocratic societies, gave way to a systematic and corrupt trap. This is not to say that the counter-factual, meaning an aristocratic society, or meritocracy (-less) society (such as a reservation driven system, whether community, gender or race-based) works any better or generates a more efficient outcome. However, within the scope of this research, the observations in this article are limited to the discontents of a meritocratic society. A meritocracy (-less) society has far greater discontents, which may in turn get reflected in lower GDP and less innovation. Less innovation may, in turn, lead to economic stagnation. But here in this article, and within the scope of this research, observations are limited only to a meritocracy-driven society and the meritocratic discontent therein.

How can an efficiency-driven meritocratic system generate an inefficient outcome? In other words, how did the meritocratic loop gave way to a hyper-competition and corrupt trap? These are the unintended results of meritocracy. Success in the meritocratic race is time bound. It is not a one-time, hard-work, and intelligence-driven lottery that generates a positive outcome for its winners. It is a constant race, an everyday competition. Simply put, in order to succeed in a meritocratic set-up, one is not only required to perform well; one must continuously perform well. This test for performance commences early on in one's life. From the high school grades, to university grades, to constant evaluation at the workplace, one must perform, and perform well to progress. At each stage of the academic and professional growth, there is a hurdle. This hurdle, in a meritocratic race, takes the shape of competition. When one successfully, and with better results clears one hurdle, there is another higher, and more competitive hurdle waiting to traverse. Further, the meritocratic wins cannot be inherited, unlike the aristocratic advantages that effortlessly flow from one generation to the next. What then is the meaning and advantage of the wealth that follows from one successful meritocratic generation to the next? Surprising as it may sound, the accumulated meritocratic wealth of one generation forms the springboard for the next generation. This accumulated meritocratic wealth of one generation, firstly, offers the next generation a possibility to remain in the race, and secondly, it also determines the probability of success in this meritocratic race. Here, an earlier accumulated wealth can go a long way in sustaining a lead. This means, that in order to discern the grain from the chaff, there are two elements of a meritocratic system: first, a "merit-based system", and second, "uneven opportunities to grow, and develop.[7] While a merit-based system adds a metric to measure one's ability, uneven opportunities create imbalances. In the field of copyright (a type of intellectual property right), one uses the expression "inter-generational equity" to explain how works are not created in solitude. Each successive generation of new works, and creations, are based on, and are inspired

---

[7] Markovits (2020).

from earlier pre-existing works. As Bloom argues, "all poetry involves a misreading of one's predecessors [such that each piece of work] be read as rewritings of other poems".[8] This is referred to as "inter-generational equity", and it draws an interesting paradox with what I call, the concept of "intergenerational transmission of economic advantage". Whereas the former works for the benefit of a society, a civilization as a whole; the latter works to the advantage of those in the immediate family tree. I define "Intergenerational transmission of economic advantage" as an advantage that those with more wealthy, and prosperous families have in the form of access to better opportunities to compete in the meritocratic race (and potentially succeed therein). Competing with this additional access to resources (such as more extra-curricular activities, and private classes to learn a complex subject) puts a select few in a position of advantage. A superior training offers an edge in the meritocratic race. This, I define as the "intergenerational transmission of economic advantage" in its simplest form. However, the system can get worse, as the parasite of corruption debases the foundations of a performance-driven meritocratic system. Consider for instance, the recent "college admissions scandal" in the US, whereby over 750 families were found to have participated in the scheme to pay additional fee for admission in top universities.[9] This means that admission to these top universities was not the result of the efforts of participating students; it was instead the result of accumulated wealth of these 750 + participating families. This almost seems like an aristocracy's problem, albeit with another and more well-demeanoured name, namely meritocracy. When one explores further, it emerges that this apparently upright concept, may in some cases be even more problematic than aristocracy. This can be articulated on the basis that even though the results of the system prima facie seem meritocratic, they are, in fact, aristocratic. In short, the meritocratic system looks like a dressed-up and camouflaged version of an aristocratic system, the very system that it was meant to supersede. So, a new nomenclature replaces the old system, whereby effects and phenomenon essentially remain the same. This in turn creates a false belief amongst those privileged that a jump in the meritocratic race may improve their conditions and chances of success in life. Morris et al. undertake a Household Longitudinal Study in the United States and the UK and find that notwithstanding the wealth concentration in the hands of a select few, meaning those at the top of the pyramid, "meritocracy [is] an important tool of psychological resilience for low-income individuals".[10]

Above-referred is but, one problematic aspect of meritocracy. Worse still, is another accompanying aspect that is even the winners of the meritocratic system are not content. As discussed above, one-time success in the meritocratic race is inadequate to sustain a comfortable life. This race, and the hurdles therein are repetitive and continuous. Success in one meritocratic loop puts an individual in another higher level, endless meritocratic loop. Success at school helps gain admission in a good university. Admission at a good university means a good job. A good job means more hard work to get promotions. The loop is endless. There is not a moment to

---

[8] Gordon (1993), p. 1558.

[9] Nelson (2019).

[10] Morriw, Bühlmann, Sommet, Vendecasteele (2022).

pause and reflect whether the results may lead to a final satisfactory outcome. To illustrate with an example, some of the most ethically questionable industries may also be some of the most profitable industries to work for. If the results are driven by and measured in terms of monetary compensation, then it automatically tips, even the most passionate, sustainable and ethical to choose a field, an industry that is most profitable. As Prof. Markovits eloquently puts it, "Meritocratic inequality might free the rich in consumption, but it enslaves them in production".[11] In this age and race of hypercompetition, one's passion or interests no longer drive their actions. Instead, the race is to fit into the society, and to succeed. The results of success are then proportionately (sometimes, even disproportionately, such as is the case with executive compensation and golden parachutes in corporate pay) remunerated through monetary compensation that in turn offers the possibility to have a luxurious and comfortable existence. The role for passion and interests are limited if any.

It must however, also be added that here meritocracy alone is not at fault. There is another additional element of the modern day society that though contributes to efficiency (at the production, and societal level), it creates disgruntlement for the meritocrat. This is specialisation, and the division of labour. The societal drive for division of labour, and specialisation are correlated positively. At the onset of the industrial revolution, it was identified that breaking a complex task into manageable tasks leads to outcomes that are more efficient. When a complex, and large task can be broken down into smaller assignments, then individuals can, based on their specialisation, and the level of knowledge, take particular tasks in this value chain. As early as 1776, Adam Smith envisioned the potential efficiencies resulting from the "division of labour". In his classic work, "An Inquiry into the Nature and Cause of the Wealth of Nations", Smith dedicated an entire chapter to the "Division of Labour". Notably, Smith was of the opinion that,

> The greatest improvement in the productive powers of labour, and the greatest part of the skill, dexterity, and judgment with which it is any where directed, or applied, seem to have been the effects of the division of labour.[12]

While on a positive note, this "division of labour" leads to higher output, and more productivity; it also chimes in a tone of monotony in work. The repetitive nature of one's tasks, and the need to work for long hours, irrespective of one's job description, creates limited possibilities to think creatively, or to think out of the box. This then, may also adversely affect the "creative quotient" of the society as a whole. While creativity may be a gift of nature and genes; it also needs to be nurtured to develop and blossom in its full potential.

Ludwig von Mises further develops this thought in his work, "Human Action", when he suggests thus:

> The total complex of the mutual relations created by concerted actions is called society. It substitutes collaboration for the – at least conceivable – isolated life of individuals. Society is the division of labour, and combination of labour. In his capacity as an acting animal man becomes a social animal.

---

[11] Markovits (2020), p. 40.

[12] Smith (1776) Book 1, Chapter 1.

To summarize, there are three aspects to this debate – first, a meritocracy-based selection system, second, and as I define, "an Intergenerational transmission of economic advantage", and third, the "division and specialisation of labour". To understand, and address the discontent with the current meritocratic set-up, this distinction needs to be kept under consideration. Before, we look for remedies, such as how "economic disadvantage" amongst those from distinct financial backgrounds be addressed, let us first look at three meritocracy-driven systems, namely, Singapore, Silicon Valley and the Swiss life sciences sector.

16.3   Meritocratic Order in the Silicon Valley, Singapore, the Swiss Life Sciences Sector

Taking the definition of meritocracy, as a system wherein diligent individuals with higher intelligence lead the system, this section elaborates on the US' high-tech sector, Singapore's political system and the Swiss pharmaceuticals sector – wherein meritocracy has contributed to efficiency, competition on the merits and in turn, higher GDP for the economy. The US has for long been known as the land of dreams. This promise (and the perils therein) is rooted in the promise of meritocracy. The ideals of the meritocratic society ensured that the society was driven by, and "ruled by knowledge and intelligence".[13] This meritocracy-driven culture is also the hallmark of the Silicon Valley, home to the world's most highly valued digital firms, the GAFAM (Google, Apple, Facebook (since Meta), Amazon and Microsoft).[14] Even though the Silicon Valley boasts of some of the world's most profitable companies, it is not without its discontent. Overtime, discontent emerged as certain sections of the society came to be over-represented in the name of "culture fit", and this fit became the basis for operalization of bias in the Silicon Valley.[15] The concern that emerges (and remains unaddressed) is that "[as] the Silicon Valley profits from [the fallacies of the current approach it] actually obfuscates them".[16] However, as discussed in Sect. 16.4 *infra*, as Generative AI, once again a product of the digital revolution, and the Silicon Valley in particular, becomes mainstream; we may need to seriously re-think our currently convenient meritocratic approach. Before we explore the rise of the Generative AI (and the discontents therein), it may be vital to elaborate on the meritocratic approach in the Singapore's Political System and the Swiss pharma. In 1959, Singapore was a poor, resource-deprived, newly independent nation that had just emerged from the World War II and the long rule of the British crown. The socio-economic set-up was not in favour of Singapore, as different communities, cultures, and religions clashed to establish their primacy in the region. However, Lee Kuan Yun, independent Singapore's first prime minister, and a revered leader,

---

[13] Petersen (2020).

[14] Lee (2012).

[15] Noble, Roberts (2019), p. 6.

[16] Noble, Roberts (2019), p. 15.

had a vision for the country. With his People's Action Party (PAP), he represented a unique set-up wherein selection into the political system was merit-based, whereby the new elite were to be those with "an innate and demonstrated talent".[17] In the political context, the concept of meritocracy was further fine-tuned as the "utilitarian formula that asserts those who purposefully contribute to a system's 'well-being'".[18] Considering the small size, and the globalized nature of the city-state, Singapore must identify and swiftly respond to both - the challenges as well as opportunities. This calls for swiftness and outstanding high flyers with innate talent, qualities and merit, that can proactively and effectively manage the political affairs of the country. This awareness and search for competition is pervasive across the political and social level, as Singaporeans realise that "staying ahead is the only way Singapore can survive and prosper".[19] Pay for those in government jobs, and ministers matches earnings in top private sector jobs.[20] These salaries are positively correlated with the economic performance of the country, meaning that the minister's salary and bonus increase or decrease, as the economy fares well, or performs poorly.[21] This merit-driven policy is reflected in Singapore's economic performance, as it compares to the world's leading economic indicators, such as its Gross Domestic Product (GDP) per capita and the purchasing power parity (PPP).[22]

Another interesting example of where meritocracy has generated economic dividends for the society is the Swiss Life Sciences industry. In the year 2021, Switzerland had a trade surplus of CHF 100 billion. Out of this 100 billion-trade surplus, the pharmaceuticals sector contributed CHF 54 billion (comprising of CHF 33 billion from immunological products, and CHF 21 million from the export of medicines).[23] This lion's share of the pharma sector [approximately 50 per cent of total exports] to the Swiss economy can be attributed to the knowledge-based and innovation-driven, Swiss pharma clusters, whereby there is a regular flow of knowledge between firms, and employees and "from the larger supply of skilled labour".[24] Remarkably this innovation-driven sector whose exports surpass the "combined exports of Swiss chocolate, cheese and watches", employees only 74,000 people in Switzerland.[25] On average, the labour productivity and the level of territory education in the sector is much higher compared to the other sectors of the economy. Over 28,500 of these

---

[17] Bellows (2009) pp. 24–25.

[18] See reference to Krauze and Slomczynski, Green and Pojman in Thomas J. Bellows (2009), p. 26.

[19] Bellows (2009) p. 32.

[20] Bellows (2009, p. 37.

[21] Bellows (2009), pp. 37–38.

[22] International Monetary Fund (2023).

[23] KOF Swiss Economic Institute (2 December 2022).

[24] KOF Swiss Economic Institute (2 December 2022).

[25] Chemical and pharmaceutical industry (2023); Flow Bank Insight on LinkedIn (6 November 2023).

Please note that the number of people employed varies as some sources count only those employed in the pharmaceuticals sector (47,010 people); whereas others count chemicals and pharmaceuticals industry collectively (74,000 people). The expressions pharmaceuticals, and life sciences, for the purposes of this research, shall, accordingly be used interchangeably.

employees have a tertiary education with over 9,800 amongst them being scientists.[26] The value added in the year 2020, for example, was "820,000 Swiss francs of value added per full-time equivalent [FTE] or 459 Swiss francs per hour worked", which is over "five times higher […] than [average] in the Swiss economy".[27] It is this high labour productivity that despite Switzerland being a resource poor country, and with high labour costs of labour, makes it one of the world's most attractive destination for investment.[28] The Swiss sector is one of the most competitive and productive in the industry worldwide. This is reflected in the R&D output, whereby, the country boats of 48 patents per million inhabitants.[29] However, vital to recall is the fact that sector employs a very small part of the Swiss population that also then reaps in a large share of the profit in the form of high employee compensation, and remuneration. This generates inequalities in income across the sectors. To add to the comprehensiveness of the discussion, it may also be important to add that even though the sector employs only a handful highly qualified and limited population of the 9 million plus Swiss, it has a high multiplier and spillover effect across the other sectors of the economy. The spillover or multiplier effect of the sector is up to 5.4 times, and it generates an additional 210,000 jobs across the economy.[30] Even though the sector overall contributes substantially to the Swiss economy, it is not without its discontents. This discontent can be attributed to the fact that benefits of these high income percolate only to a select few in the economy (around 70,000 for a population of 9 million plus). Further, even those in the contest for the profits are under the constant pressure to perform to strengthen the bottom line, the revenue growth of the company. The life sciences sector is largely innovation-driven. Patents, a form of intellectual property, are a key indicator of this innovation. As a large number of these protected drugs go off patent, the sector has been under constant pressure since the start of the decade. This trend started in early 2010, when over $255 billion (worldwide) worth of drugs went off-patent, and is further expected to accelerate in the coming decade.[31] It is anticipated that between 2023 and 2030, approximately $200 + billion revenue (worldwide) of the sector may affected as many blockbuster molecules that drive the profitability of the sector go off-patent.[32] Thus, the sector not only benefits a select few; the pie also seems to shrinking, or at least stabilizing, with fewer new and disruptive innovations coming to the market. The Swiss life sciences sector is not alone to address the meritocratic debate and the interlude to innovation. The Silicon Valley, that epitomizes the race to innovation via the meritocratic channel, encounters a similar stumbling block. The big disruption in the digital economy emerged

---

[26] BAK Economics (2020), p. 8.

[27] BAK Economics (2020), p. 43.

[28] Blok (28 October 2022).

[29] An average of 48 patents (per million inhabitants) were registered in Switzerland between 2014–2018. Source: Blok (28 October 2022).

[30] BAK Economics (2020), pp. 9–10.

[31] Fischer (2011).

[32] Gardner (2023).

as markets came to tip to a handful of global players.[33] Moreover, considering the substantial sunk costs, and long gestation periods before these digital start-ups and platforms can first see some profit, funding becomes an important barrier to market entry. To get this funding, start-ups normally look to the venture capitalists. Venture capitalists are a key catalyst to sustenance in markets with long gestation periods. In other words, in markets with substantial sunk costs, it takes a significant time-period before the firm commences operations, and its business becomes profitable. Consider the case of Amazon. The world's leading e-retailer was in the red zone for close to two decades before its balance sheet exhibited signs of breakeven profits.[34] What sustains an unprofitable business for so long? Here, the role of venture capitalists (VC) gains center-stage. In the digital markets with substantial sunk costs, it is the constant pumping in of the funds by these VCs that sustains and facilitates the development of these markets before they see profits coming in. Considering that some of the segments of these digital markets display signs of maturity, it emerges that one cannot rely on Schumpeter's wave of creative destruction[35] for self-correction by these market players. In fact, the venture capitalists frequently refer to these markets as "kill zones", meaning that any investment by them therein is unlikely, if ever, to turn profitable.[36] In recent years, the venture capitalists have successfully limited their investment in the sector. From the year 2018 to 2019 alone, the venture capital investment in the ad-tech and the mar-tech startups dried down from $7.2 billion (in 2018) to $ 1.8 billion (in 2019).[37] Key reasons for these VC's pessimism include Google and Facebook's position of supra-dominance in the sector; regulatory interventions, such as the EU General Data Protection Regulation (GDPR) that further help the incumbent big tech refuse access to data on regulatory grounds and the rapid rise of Generative AI. To put it succinctly, the meritocracy and capitalist divided (of profits) that first led to the rise and the sustenance of the world's leading economies, are now creating a meritocratic upheaval as the divide between the haves and have-nots seems to increase at a rapid rate. This, and rightly so, is a cause of concern, because, if not addressed in a timely manner, this may foster and facilitate conditions of social and political mayhem. The rise of the Generative AI has added further complexity to the meritocracy debate. The following section, accordingly, discusses the concept of Generative AI, and how it may further upset our current world order, and selection system (in other words, meritocracy-based selection system).

---

[33] For a detailed discussion on the economics of the digital multi-sided platform economy, and how it has led the global market to concentrate in the hands of a few digital players (and what role therein for merger control), *see* Tyagi (2019).

[34] Molla, Del Rey (2017); Perez JC (28 January 2004).

[35] Schumpeter (1942).

[36] Stigler Committee on Digital Platforms (2019), p. 9.

[37] Shields (2018).

16.4   How Generative AI may Further Add to the Societal Discontent with Meritocracy?

The section focuses on the high-tech sector, particularly in a capitalistic set-up, such as the US, wherein meritocracy that first led to the success of the nation, may also emerge as a reason for discontent amongst those who are successively excluded from this merit-based system.

The rise and uptake of first, the platform economy, and now the Generative AI has offered a renewed tone and tenor to the "meritocracy" debate. Platformisation of the economy means that the market is now increasingly concentrated in the hands of a few corporate oligarchs, as distinct from a normal freely-functioning market, whereby the dividends of a profitable market may be more unevenly spread amongst distinct market players. Consider the case of the Generative AI, that has since 2022, taken the world by storm. Generative AI tools such as ChatGPT, and Bard, may simply put, be defined as programs that generate "content upon prompt".[38] Even though the first AI-generated images date back to Harold Cohen's works in 1970s, it may be no exaggeration to suggest that the Generative AI debate became mainstream in intellectual property law generally, and copyright in particular, starting in 2022.[39] What prompted this turning point was that now AI could generate original output based on prompts, with creative combination of imaginative, and otherwise "unrelated concepts".[40] Whereas Generative AI tools, such as Dall-E 2, Midjourney, Stability AI, Google's Imagen and Meta's Make-a-Scene could generate creative high quality images; tools such as OpenAI's ChatGPT could generate distinctive written output, such as articles, books, and journalistic outputs.[41] Trapova and Mezei, for instance, study the emerging field of robojournalism, whereby AI is used to produce "journalistic outputs". With the uptake of natural language generation (NLG) technology, AI-based reporting is not merely limited to computer-assisted reporting; algorithms are, in fact, used to create full-fledged reports in sports, weather and finance, amongst others.[42] Following the NLG-generated output, editing is used to add the personal touch of a human author.[43] In other words, the rise of Generative AI means that human intervention now comes at a much higher level in the value chain. Likewise, the market for artworks is a case in point, whereby art can now be generated with a mere creative prompt and set of instructions to the Gen AI tools. Not only artworks, but entire books, novels and other works, can now be generated with a mere prompt. These developments have brought many novel legal issues before the courts worldwide. To illustrate and reflect on how GenAI uses copyright protected works, and in the process also replaces the meritocratic human labour, Authors Guild/Open AI

---

[38] Tyagi (2023).

[39] Hervey (2023).

[40] Hervey (2023).

[41] Hervey (2023).

[42] Trapova/Mezei (2022).

[43] Trapova/Mezei (2022).

case, currently pending before the US courts is insightful. The Authors Guild, the Plaintiffs in the Authors Guild/ Open AI case, illustrate how ChatGPT (a technical equivalent of GPT 3.5) could generate accurate and precise summaries of works by the author, Mignon G. Eberhart's copyright protected works such as, "While the Patient Slept' and the 'The Patient in Room 18'".[44] Chat GPT, could, in addition, also generate the next edition in this series using the same characters (as in Eberhart's other works) and it also offered a title to this allegedly infringing and unauthorized derivative as, "Shadows Over Federie House".[45] Likewise, the Complaint illustrates this infringement, with several other examples, such as infringement by GenAI of protected works of renowned authors such as, Connelly, Day, Grisham, Hilderbrand etc.[46] Creatively, the ChatGPT even offered an attractive name to the follow-on version of Grisham's "The King of Torts", as "The Kingdom of Consequences".[47] This follow-on derivative work not only uses the same characters from Grisham's "The King of Torts", it also meaningfully, and constructively develops the storyline, the characters and the theme in the original work.[48] The Complaint alleges direct infringement of copyright-protected works, as OpenAI is "trained" on "caches of pilfered copyrighted works".[49]

The success and performing capabilities of OpenAI's GPT-4 has raised some scholars to consider whether it is "an early (yet still incomplete) version of an AGI", as GPT-4 could "transfer learning between text, speech, image, and video recognition with [varying] degrees of precision".[50]

These developments not only raise concerns about labour market, and fairness, but they also seem problematic that these new GenAI tools now offer a handful of global corporations, clustered in limited geographical spaces greater control of creative output, and future works. In other words, the generation of creative content, may soon be controlled by a few global digital gatekeepers, "who may have no interest in the livelihood of artists and no appetite for risk".[51] The case of the creative industry is only indicative of how the rise of Generative AI may make us re-consider our approach to an innovation-driven society founded on meritocratic ideals.

---

[44] Authors Guild v. Open AI (Complaint filed on 19 September 2023) No. 1:23-cv-8292, at paras 134–143.

[45] Authors Guild v. Open AI (Complaint filed on 19 September 2023) No. 1:23-cv-8292, at paras 134–143.

[46] Authors Guild v. Open AI (Complaint filed on 19 September 2023) No. 1:23-cv-8292, at paras 144–309.

[47] Authors Guild v. Open AI (Complaint filed on 19 September 2023) No. 1:23-cv-8292, at para 199.

[48] Authors Guild v. Open AI (Complaint filed on 19 September 2023) No. 1:23-cv-8292, at para 198–199.

[49] Authors Guild v. Open AI (Complaint filed on 19 September 2023) No. 1:23-cv-8292, at para 339.

[50] OECD Digital Economy Papers (2023) AI Language Models: Technological, Socio-Economic and Policy Considerations, p. 25.

[51] Trendacosta, Doctorow (2023).

16.5 Conclusion and Policy Recommendations

This chapter intricately looked at the rise and widespread acceptance of the notion of meritocracy. It also mapped how the concept has contributed to not only individual success, but also the success of Nation States. However, the rise of two potent forces, firstly, the rising concentration of wealth and opportunities in a meritocratic society, and secondly, the rise of Generative AI have challenged the widespread societal embrace of meritocracy. Interestingly, and paradoxical as it may sound, income inequality tends to create "stronger meritocratic beliefs". This, as the psychologists explain, can be explained with the theory of "systems justification [whereby people] have an inherent need to see the status quo as good and fair" irrespective of whether [or not] they benefit from it.[52] Interestingly, while those who may least benefit from a meritocratic order hardly seem to question its authority, the challenge to the meritocratic order comes from elsewhere. In a recent change of hiring policy, Australia's leading Science and Technology University, the Queensland University of Technology consciously decided to remove all references to "the merit principle" in its hiring policy, and instead replace it with a new and all-encompassing "more inclusive suitability assessment".[53] The new policy, shall, as per the University, factor in hitherto slighted factors such as "gender, ethnicity and departmental balance".[54] While it may be too early to predict how these experimental approaches to the selection system may play out in the long-run, it is incontestable that cracks in the meritocratic wall have begun to surface.

This research contribution takes the position that the challenge is not so much with a meritocratic society; the challenge instead is the inadvertent spill-over effects of a capitalism-driven meritocratic system, whereby the very possibility to participate in the meritocratic race is determined by, what I call the "intergenerational transmission of economic advantage". Hereby, comes a normative recommendation to ensure a fairer and just system wherein all get to compete with an equivalent competitive advantage and create a truly meritocratic order. In other words, the problem comes not so much from the meritocratic system; the issue instead is who are the ones that best profit from this new and emerging re-organization of the factors of production, and what is their relative value in the production value chain. In this respect, lessons can be drawn from a more balanced socialistic-inspired capitalist approach, wherein the less privileged have an equal opportunity to emerge and showcase their merits for the welfare of the society. Reference here must be made to the approach to the creation of social capital in Scandinavia, whereby the system creates conditions conducive for sustaining and developing a civil society infrastructure.[55] This approach may not only be suited to arrest the gaps in the meritocratic order; they may, also, be helpful to address an upcoming challenge, namely the rise of Generative AI. In the world of ChatGPT, Bard, and other Generative AI tools, one will see the rise of

---

[52] Morriw, Bühlmann, Sommet, Vendecasteele (2022).

[53] Sato (2023).

[54] Sato (2023).

[55] Torpe (2003).

more concentrated, and technical jobs, that will require a highly specialized skill set. A Scandinavian approach to balancing wealth creation with a more positive and detailed welfare-state institution will not only foster increased social trust[56]; it will also ensure that those with "merit" are able to exercise it with "empathy" in the age of Generative AI.

Bibliography

About Switzerland, Chemical and pharmaceutical industry (2023). https://www.eda.admin.ch/abo utswitzerland/en/home/wirtschaft/taetigkeitsgebiete/chemie-und-pharma.html. Last access 23 November 2023

Authors Guild v. Open AI (Complaint filed on 19 September 2023), No. 1:23-cv-8292 (S.D.N.Y.)

BAK Economics (2020) The Importance of the Pharmaceutical Industry for Switzerland. https:// www.interpharma.ch/wp-content/uploads/2021/11/BAK_Economics_Interpharma_Volkswirt schaftliche_Bedeutung_Pharmaindustrie_2020_en.pdf. Last access 23 November 2023

Bellows TJ (2009) Meritocracy and the Singapore Political System. Asian Journal of Political Science 17(1): 24–44

Blok D (2022) How did a small country like Switzerland become a pharma giant? PharmaOffer: Market Analysis and Data. https://pharmaoffer.com/blog/how-did-a-small-country-like-switze rland-become-a-pharma-giant/. Last access 23 November 2023

Fischer E (2011) The patent cliff: rise of the generics. Pharmaceutical Technology. https://www. pharmaceutical-technology.com/features/featurethe-patent-cliff-rise-of-the-generics/?cf-view. Last access 23 November 2023

Gardner J (2023) Big pharma's looming threat: a patent cliff of 'tectonic magnitude, BigPharma Dive. https://www.biopharmadive.com/news/pharma-patent-cliff-biologic-drugs-humira-keytruda/642660/. Last access 23 November 2023

Gordon WJ (1993) 'A Property Right in Self-Expression: Equality and Individualism in the Natural Law of Intellectual Property. Yale Law J 102(7): 1535–1609

Hervey M (2023) AI and Copyright in 2022, Kluwer Copyright Blog. https://copyrightblog.kluwer iplaw.com/2023/02/02/ai-and-copyright-in-2022/. Last access 23 November 2023

International Monetary Fund (2023) World Economic Outlook Database. https://www.imf.org/ en/Publications/SPROLLS/world-economic-outlook-databases#sort=%40imfdate%20desc ending. Last access 23 November 2023

KOF Swiss Economic Institute (2nd December 2022) available here: https://kof.ethz.ch/en/news-and-events/kof-bulletin/kof-bulletin/2022/12/The-pharmaceutical-industry-is-Switzerlands-growth-engine.html. Last access 23 November 2023

Kumlin S and Rothstein B (2005) Making and Breaking Social Capital: The Impact of Welfare-State Institutions. Comparative Political Studies 38(4)

Lee TB (2012) The Capital of Meritocracy is Silicon Valley, Not Wall Street. Forbes. https://www. forbes.com/sites/timothylee/2012/06/23/dont-blame-meritocracy-for-wall-street/?sh=2d1a11 a2946e. Last access 23 November 2023

Markovits D (2020) The Meritocracy Trap. London

McLaughlin K, Cohen R, Goodwin G E (12 May 2023) The full list of everyone who's been sentenced in the college admissions scandal so far. Business Insider. https://www.insider.com/ college-admissions-scandal-full-list-people-sentenced-2019-9. Last access 27 November 2023

Molla R and Del Rey J (2027) Amazon's epic 20-year run as a public company, explained in five charts. Vox. available here: https://www.vox.com/2017/5/15/15610786/amazon-jeff-bezos-pub lic-company-profit-revenue-explained-five-charts. Last access 23 November 2023

---

[56] Kumlin/Rothstein (2005).

Morriw K, Bühlmann F, Sommet N and Vendecasteele L (2022) Why do people believe in meritocracy? Understanding Society: The UK Household Longitudinal Study. https://www.understandingsociety.ac.uk/blog/2022/06/08/why-do-people-believe-in-meritocracy

Nelson L (2019) The real college admissions scandal is what's legal, Vox. https://www.vox.com/2019/3/12/18262037/college-admissions-scandal-felicity-huffman. Last access 23 November 2023

Noble S U and Roberts S T (2019) Technological Elites, the Meritocracy, and Postracial Myths in Silicon Valley. UCLA Scholarship. https://escholarship.org/uc/item/7z3629nh. Last access 23 November 2023

OECD Digital Economy Papers (2023) AI Language Models: Technological. Socio-Economic and Policy Considerations. https://doi.org/10.1787/20716826. Last access 27 November 2023

Perez JC (28 January 2004) Amazon records first profitable year in its history. Computerworld. https://www.computerworld.com/article/2575106/amazon-records-first-profitable-year-in-its-history.html. Last access 23 November 2023

Petersen C (2020) Meritocracy in America, 1885–2007 (Doctoral Dissertation) Harvard University Graduate School of Arts and Sciences

Sato K (16 November 2023) Queensland University of Technology defends removing 'merit' from hiring policy. ABC Radio Brisbane: News. https://amp-abc-net-au.cdn.ampproject.org/c/s/amp.abc.net.au/article/103114562. Last access 23 November 2023

Schumpeter JA (2006) Capitalism, Socialism, and Democracy, New Edition of 6 revised Edition, London/New York (first published 1942, New York)

Shields R (7 November 2018) Investment in Ad Tech Grown Increasingly Scarce, with Forrester predicting a 75% drop in venture capital Adweek. https://www.adweek.com/programmatic/investment-in-ad-tech-grows-increasingly-scarce-with-forrester-predicting-a-75-drop-in-venture-capital/ Last access 23 November 2023

Smith A (1776) An inquiry into the nature and causes of the wealth of nations

Stigler Committee on Digital Platforms (2019) Final Report. https://www.chicagobooth.edu/-/media/research/stigler/pdfs/digital-platforms---committee-report---stigler-center.pdf.   Last access 27 November 2023

Torpe L (2003) Social Capital in Denmark: A Deviant Case? Scand Polit Stud 26(1): 27–48

Trapova A, Mezei P (2022) Robojournalism – A Copyright Study on the Use of Artificial Intelligence in the European News Industry. Kluwer Copyright Blog. https://copyrightblog.kluweriplaw.com/2022/03/03/robojournalism-a-copyright-study-on-the-use-of-artificial-intelligence-in-the-european-news-industry/. Last access 27 November 2023

Trendacosta K, Doctorow C (3 April 2023) AI Art Generators and the Online Image Market. EFF. https://www.eff.org/deeplinks/2023/04/ai-art-generators-and-online-image-market. Last access 27 November 2023

Tyagi K (2019) Promoting Competition in Innovation through Merger Control in the ICT Sector: A Comparative and Interdisciplinary Study. Berlin, Heidelberg

Tyagi K (2023) The Copyright, Text & Data Mining and the Innovation Dimension of Generative AI. Journal of Intellectual Property Law & Practice

Von Mises L (1949) Human Action: A Treatise on Economics. Edinburgh, Glasgow, London

Why Pharma is so Big for Switzerland? Flow Bank Insight on LinkedIn (6 November 2023). https://www.linkedin.com/pulse/why-pharma-so-big-switzerland-flowbank-xs9xe/?trk=organization_guest_main-feed-card_feed-article-content. Last access 23 November 2023

Young M (1958) The Rise of Meritocracy, pp. 1870–2033. London

Index

Printed by Printforce, United Kingdom